Aesthetics

Dietrich von Hildebrand

Aesthetics

VOLUME I

Dietrich von Hildebrand

—

Translated by Fr. Brian McNeil

Edited by John F. Crosby

THE HILDEBRAND PROJECT

Originally published in German as *Ästhetik*. 1. Teil. Gesammelte Werke Band V. Stuttgart: Kohlhammer. 1977. 492 S. 1989 übernommen vom Eos Verlag, St. Ottilien

English translation published 2016 by Hildebrand Project
1235 University Blvd, Steubenville, Ohio 43952

Copyright © 2016 Dietrich von Hildebrand Legacy Project
All rights reserved

Cataloguing-in-Publication Information

Von Hildebrand, Dietrich, 1889–1977, author.
[Ästhetik. English]
Aesthetics. Vol. I / translated by Brian McNeil;
edited by John F. Crosby; foreword by Dana Gioia;
preface by Robert E. Wood; introduction by John F. Crosby.
pages cm
Includes index.
ISBN 978-1-939773-04-3

1. Aesthetics. I. Crosby, John F., 1944– editor.
II. McNeil, Brian, translator. III. Translation of: Von
Hildebrand, Dietrich, 1889–1977. Ästhetik. IV. Title.
B3359.V63A8813 2015 193
QBI15-600216

Library of Congress Preassigned Control Number: 20159208544

Book design by Mark McGarry, Texas Type & Book Works
Set in Adobe Caslon

Cover Design by Marylouise McGraw

Cover Image: La Primavera, by Sandro Botticelli, in the Uffizi Gallery, Florence.
Image from Wikimedia Commons.

Front Cover Font: Circular Bold by Laurenz Brunner

www.hildebrandproject.org

SUAVISSIMAE DILECTISSIMAE UXORI

To my most sweet and beloved wife

Contents

Dietrich von Hildebrand

Dietrich von Hildebrand was born in Florence in 1889, and studied philosophy under Adolf Reinach, Max Scheler, and Edmund Husserl. He was received into the Catholic Church in 1914. He distinguished himself with many publications in moral philosophy, in social philosophy, in the philosophy of the interpersonal, and in aesthetics. He taught in Munich, Vienna, and New York. In the 1930s, he was one of the strongest voices in Europe against Nazism. He died in New Rochelle, New York in 1977.

Hildebrand Project

We advance the rich tradition of Christian personalism, especially as developed by Dietrich von Hildebrand and Karol Wojtyla (Pope St. John Paul II), in the service of intellectual and cultural renewal.

Our publications, academic programs, and public events introduce the great personalist thinkers and witnesses of the twentieth century. Animated by a heightened sense of the mystery and dignity of the human person, they developed a personalism that sheds new light on freedom and conscience, the religious transcendence of the person, the relationship between individual and community, the love between man and woman, and the life-giving power of beauty. We connect their vision of the human person with the great traditions of Western and Christian thought, and draw from their personalism in addressing the deepest needs and aspirations of our contemporaries. For more information, please visit: www.hildebrandproject.org

Editorial Board

General Editor: John F. Crosby*
Franciscan University of Steubenville

Dana Gioia
Judge Widney Professor of Poetry and Public Culture
University of Southern California

Fritz Wenisch*
University of Rhode Island

Roger Scruton
Ethics and Public Policy Center

Josef Seifert*
Edith Stein Institute of Philosophy, Granada, Spain

Rocco Buttiglione
Pontifical Lateran University
John Paul II Chair for Philosophy and History of European Institutions

Hanna-Barbara Gerl-Falkovitz
Technische Universität Dresden, Emerita
Hochschule Heiligenkreuz

Antonio Calcagno
King's University College at The University of Western Ontario

Joseph Koterski, SJ
Fordham University

Christoph Cardinal Schönborn
Archbishop of Vienna

Rémi Brague
University of Paris, Sorbonne, Emeritus
Romano Guardini Chair of Philosophy, Ludwig Maximilian
University of Munich, Emeritus

D. C. Schindler
Pontifical John Paul II Institute for Studies on Marriage and Family
Washington, DC

John Haldane
University of St. Andrews
Baylor University

Alice von Hildebrand*
Widow of Dietrich von Hildebrand

Special Thanks

We gratefully acknowledge the vision and generosity of the many friends who have supported our publications and helped bring this particular volume to fruition:

EXTRAORDINARY SUPPORT

Howard and Roberta Ahmanson • Dana Gioia • Robert L. Luddy • James N. Perry, Jr.

PATRONS

The Catholic Association Foundation • Cushman Foundation • Alice von Hildebrand • Patricia C. Lynch • Lee and Margaret Matherne and Family • National Endowment for the Arts

BENEFACTORS

Budnik Family Foundation • Rafael Madan and Lilian Casas Foundation • Daniel and Teresa Cotter • Madeline L. Cottrell • Michael W.

Doherty • Rose-Marie Fox-Shanahan • Mary G. Georgopulos • Julia Harrison • Nicholas and Jane Healy • Barbara B. Henkels • Robert Hurt • Robert Kreppel • Franco Madan • Jeffrey and Mary Petrino • Jules and Katie van Schaijik • Charles Scribner III

FRIENDS

Hedy K. Boelte • Douglas Brown • John F. Cannon • Allison Coates and Joshua Kneubuhl • Edward and Alice Ann Grayson • Patrick Hart • Roy and Elizabeth Heyne • Maestro Manfred Honeck • Thomas Howard • Michael C. Jordan • Alasdair MacIntyre • Gerard and Germana Mitchell • Colin Moran • Kevin and Dawn O'Scannlain • Timothy and Judy Rudderow • Duncan C. Sahner • Daniel and Annie Schreck • Stephen D. Schwarz • Madeleine F. Stebbins

Foreword
By Dana Gioia

OVER THE PAST half century the concept of beauty became disreputable in artistic and intellectual circles. When the word was used at all, it was treated with condescension or irony as the quaint vestige of a simpler age with little relevance to contemporary society. Eventually in postmodern theory, the study of aesthetics came to imply the complete rejection of beauty in any positive sense. Beauty was declared a social fiction or political strategy with no objective connection to nature or reality. The vast damage this glib and hollow conceit did to the arts, education, and intellectual life is now unmistakable to any unbiased observer.

Dietrich von Hildebrand was among the first to recognize the magnitude of the intellectual crisis. He understood the centrality of beauty not merely to art but to philosophy, theology, and ethics. In his ambitious and comprehensive *Aesthetics*, now translated into English for the first

Dana Gioia is an internationally acclaimed and award-winning poet. He was Chairman of the National Endowment for the Arts from 2003-2009, and in 2011 became the Judge Widney Professor of Poetry and Public Culture at the University of Southern California.

time, Hildebrand rehabilitates the concept of beauty as an objective rather than purely subjective phenomenon. His systematic account renews the Classical and Christian vision of beauty as a reliable mode of perception that leads humanity toward the true, the good, and ultimately the divine.

There is no more important issue in our culture—sacred or secular—than the restoration of beauty. And there is no better place to start this urgent enterprise than Dietrich von Hildebrand's *Aesthetics*.

Dana Gioia
Judge Widney Professor of Poetry and Public Culture
University of Southern California

Preface
By Robert E. Wood

DIETRICH VON HILDEBRAND was a philosopher who devoted a great deal of his attention to "matters of the heart." His small book *The Heart* anchors what he is typically after in the region of experience largely bypassed in the philosophic tradition. His lifework highlights the fundamental character of human dispositions—matters of the heart—that make possible the discernment of values in various regions of human experience. His work on *The Nature of Love* carefully distinguishes every aspect of the topic with an unmatched thoroughness. His several works on ethics highlight proper dispositions. One might add his two-volume *Aesthetics* to the areas where the heart is operative and applaud its appearance in English.

Hildebrand's father, Adolf, was a sculptor of some repute who also wrote about the general character of form in art. The house in which his son grew up was an elegant mansion full of notable artworks. Dietrich

Robert E. Wood is Professor of Philosophy in the Institute for Philosophic Studies at the University of Dallas. He is the author of *Placing Aesthetics: Reflections on the Philosophic Tradition* and *The Beautiful, the True & the Good: Studies in the History of Thought*, along with numerous other books and over eighty published articles.

exhibits a keen appreciation for the beauty of the built environment, focusing appreciatively not only on buildings, paintings, and sculpture, but also on items of luxury like furniture, carpets, utensils, and even the color and texture of fabrics. One could be sure that music and literature were an essential part of growing up in such an aesthetically rich environment.

Hildebrand is particularly apt at attending to the kind of dispositions, like humility and reverence, which enkindle love and make possible the deepest access to each of the regions of values. Like Kierkegaard, he is critical of the aesthete who enjoys himself but is unable to open himself in reverence and humility to the transformative possibilities of the depth of aesthetic experience.

In terms of sheer bulk, Hildebrand's two-volume work on *Aesthetics* rivals Hegel's monumental two-volume work. And though, like Hegel's, this work, in its philosophical aspect, makes explicit the essential distinctions operative within each area of aesthetics, the distinguishing characteristic of Hildebrand's work here, in addition to his philosophical analysis, is his role as critic. He exhibits a broad and very finely developed sense of individual items in the regions covered and offers extended critical and comparative remarks about particular works in each region.

His attention to individual works and his critical judgment distinguish his from other comprehensive approaches to aesthetics. Kant, whose 'disinterestedness' he appropriates, pays little attention to the various regions of aesthetics and concentrates on the general characteristics of the aesthetic, while Schopenhauer pays more attention to the various regions. Dewey pays special attention to the rootedness of the aesthetic in the rhythmic relation of the organism to the environment, to the synesthesia this involves, to the way tradition enters into aesthetic perception, and to a background relation to the universe. He would be, in a way, a supplement to Hildebrand's analysis. This allows Dewey to appreciate the more abstract forms of recent art which Hildebrand ignores, perhaps because he does repudiate recent art that deviates from the natural, God-given forms.

While Hegel turned the attention of the philosophic community away from nature—"too indeterminate for a science of aesthetics"—to focus exclusively on art, by contrast, Hildebrand is equally attentive to the beauties of nature, especially as the matrix for architecture. He must have travelled widely and attended carefully to the particular works and regions explored. He is able to speak about the peculiarities of many natural environments and of the interplay between the natural and the built environment in the great cities of Europe, especially in Italy.

Regarding nature, Hildebrand appreciates the various animal forms and what they each contribute to the beauty of their environments; nonetheless, for him lions and horses stand at the top of the hierarchy of beautiful animal types, with hippopotamuses and hyenas at the bottom. In all the aesthetic regions he explores, he is always after evaluation and consequent hierarchical ranking, which most people would not be in a position to dispute. He violates with a vengeance Horace's adage: *de gustibus non est disputandum.*

Properly cultivated taste becomes the measure as it attends to the features of the aesthetic object. Hildebrand's general assessment of critics is not too favorable. According to him, too many follow current fashion and have an insufficiently developed appreciation of the full range of the artform about which they write. What that presupposes in him is a sufficiently developed sensibility capable of discerning those incapacities. This is especially true in music. His appreciation is very broad and tied in with a strong sense of individual works. He exhibits an extraordinary capacity to pay attention to all the aspects of a given work, assess its hills and valleys, and compare it with others. As an example of the author's comparative judgment, he declares Beethoven's *Missa solemnis* "the polyphonic mass *par excellence*," whose *Benedictus* is the highpoint. What would it take to challenge that?

He is able to discern and remember dead spots in classic works. He distinguishes between perfection and depth. He makes claims to the unsuitability of some written works to musical accompaniment that composers have nonetheless undertaken. He crowns Shakespeare king of tragedy, Cervantes king of comedy, and Beethoven king of the symphony.

He contrasts the rootedness of folk music with the ephemeral character of popular hits (a phenomenon of the past hundred years), but locates both of them within the realm of beauty as lesser forms, though not elevated enough to qualify as art. His taste throughout is what one might call *classical.*

And yet, he appreciates what he calls the *poetry* of the pre-technological everyday world, working with one's hands, attending the market, participating in festivals rooted in the love of family and friends and in the love of Christ. He claims that even today, rural Spaniards are happier than people in the United States. Though he does not make it explicit here, for him a crucial part of the transformation of commoners and elites alike is attending with proper disposition a properly performed liturgy. (See his *Liturgy and Personality.*) Masses by Mozart and Beethoven and Bach's oratorios provide unsurpassable depth that can be appreciated in differing degrees by all and enhance their participation in the liturgy.

One has to be impressed by Hildebrand's philosophic ability to anatomize the entire region of matters aesthetic, extending it even to everyday life and interior decoration; but one has to be equally impressed by his role as a critic and his confidence in providing a ranking of artworks. This book will reward careful study and ground the expansion and deepening of one's own aesthetic sensibility.

Robert E. Wood
Institute of Philosophic Studies
University of Dallas

The Aesthetics of Dietrich von Hildebrand
By John F. Crosby

DIETRICH VON HILDEBRAND was born in Florence in 1889, and the circumstances of his birth are significant for his later work in aesthetics. His father was Adolf von Hildebrand, one of the best known German sculptors of the turn-of-the-century period. Young Dietrich von Hildebrand inherited keen sensibilities for art and enjoyed an upbringing that was ideally suited to awakening and developing them. He grew up in his father's villa in Florence, where from his earliest years he lived immersed in the beauties of Renaissance Florence. Great artists from all over Europe visited the Hildebrand villa, including Richard Wagner, Hugo von Hofmannsthal, Rainer Maria Rilke, Richard Strauss (who was visiting the Hildebrands on the day of Dietrich's birth). Thus it was that Dietrich von Hildebrand grew up in the midst of the highest artistic culture. One of his sisters became a distinguished painter, another married the well-known German composer Walter Braunfels. Dietrich was a

John F. Crosby is Professor and Director of the MA Program in Philosophy at Franciscan University of Steubenville. He has published extensively on the philosophy of human person, including *The Selfhood of the Human Person* and *The Personalism of John Henry Newman.* He was a student and friend of Dietrich von Hildebrand, and is Co-Founder of the Hildebrand Project.

childhood friend of Wilhelm Furtwängler, who later became one of Germany's greatest conductors. In 1906 Dietrich was invited by the widow of Richard Wagner to the festival of Wagner's operas in Bayreuth, Germany; it was the beginning of his life-long passion for the music of Wagner. If it is true that a philosopher can do fruitful work in aesthetics only if he or she brings to the issues of aesthetics some real aesthetic sensibility, and some real experience of art, then Dietrich von Hildebrand was uniquely well prepared by his upbringing to do work in aesthetics.

The aesthetician also needs, of course, a phenomenological formation, and this Hildebrand received directly from Edmund Husserl and Max Scheler. He began the study of philosophy at the University of Munich in 1907, where he immediately came in contact with the Munich phenomenologists, who were enthralled by Husserl's *Logical Investigations.* Drawn by this epoch-making work, Hildebrand studied with Husserl in Göttingen for several years, completing his dissertation, *Die Idee der sittlichen Handlung* (*The Idea of Moral Action*), under Husserl's direction in 1912. Husserl esteemed it so highly that he wrote in his evaluation of it: "I almost want to say that the genius of Adolf von Hildebrand has been inherited by his son, the author, as a philosophical genius."[1] He also said that Hildebrand "astonishes the reader by an incomparably intimate knowledge of the various formations of affective consciousness and their objective correlates." Recent research at the Husserl archive in Leuven has shown that Husserl made repeated use of Hildebrand's dissertation in his own research.[2] Husserl published the whole of the dissertation in the first volume of his *Jahrbuch für Philosophie und phänomenologische Forschung.* In later years Hildebrand distanced himself from Husserl because of the master's turn to an idealist phenomenology; Hildebrand remained from beginning to end a philosophical realist. He had received Husserlian phenomenology not only

1. Edmund Husserl, "Urteil über Hildebrands Doktorarbeit," *Aletheia* 5 (1992): 5. This is the first-time publication of Husserl's written evaluation of Hildebrand's doctoral dissertation. English by John F. Crosby in Dietrich von Hildebrand, *The Heart* (South Bend, Ind.: St. Augustine's Press, 2007), xvi.

2. See Karl Schumann, "Husserl und Hildebrand," *Aletheia* 5 (1992): 6–33.

through Husserl himself but also through his revered teacher, Adolf Reinach, who from the beginning had given phenomenology a distinctly realist interpretation.

But much as Hildebrand owed to the early Husserl, he owed far more to Max Scheler, whom he first met in Munich in 1907 and with whom he was bound in a very close friendship for some fifteen years. Hildebrand entirely shared Scheler's interests in an ethical personalism and in the philosophy of religion. His doctoral dissertation, dedicated to Scheler, owes much to Scheler's value-based ethics, even if Hildebrand departs in some important ways from Scheler's concept of value. Scheler was also instrumental in Hildebrand's conversion to Catholicism in 1914. It must be remembered that Hildebrand had received no religious formation at home; everything there had centered around high aesthetic culture. But he had shown from a very early age an unusual religious sensibility. When Scheler spoke to Hildebrand about the phenomenon of personal holiness as lived by the Christian saints, he encountered a great receptivity in the young Hildebrand. But Hildebrand was different from other Catholic converts of the time, like Jacques Maritain, in that he felt no need to remake himself into a Thomist. He remained entirely faithful to his phenomenological roots, and in fact much of his work in ethics is conducted in debate with Thomistic philosophy. Most of the works that Hildebrand published during his lifetime deal with issues of ethics and philosophy of religion (though there are exceptions, such as his *Metaphysik der Gemeinschaft* and his epistemological treatise, *What is Philosophy?*). Among the works that he published, only one deals with aesthetics, a short book entitled *Mozart, Beethoven, Schubert*.[3]

But he had from the beginning been deeply concerned with issues of aesthetics. Indeed, his very first public presentation, given at age seventeen in 1907 to a society formed by the Munich phenomenologists, was devoted to a question of aesthetics: "Stoff und Form in der Kunst" (Mat-

3. Dietrich von Hildebrand, *Mozart, Beethoven, Schubert* (Regensburg: Josef Habbel Verlag, 1962). The chapter on Mozart has been translated by John Henry Crosby in *Logos* 7, no. 2 (Spring 2004): 189–212. The chapter on Schubert has been translated by John Henry Crosby in *Communio* (English-language edition) 33, no. 3 (Fall 2003): 478–501.

ter and Form in Art). He often gave courses on aesthetics throughout his teaching career (which began in Munich in 1918 and ended at Fordham University in New York in 1960). His strong ethical and religious interests and commitments did not in any way weaken his lived relation to beauty and art or his passion for the problems of aesthetics. And so toward the end of his life, when he was eighty, he set out to write the treatise on aesthetics that had been growing in him throughout his life. It came to a work of one thousand pages and was published posthumously in two volumes under the title *Äesthetik*. The first volume offers a philosophy of beauty, the second a philosophy of art and of the arts (this second volume does not seem to be entirely finished). It is surely one of the richest phenomenological achievements in aesthetics, though it is still relatively little known. Let me survey some of the main insights of this work, giving particular attention to what Hildebrand saw as his greatest single contribution to aesthetics.

The first thing to be said about Hildebrand's aesthetics is that it is embedded in his value philosophy. The concept of value that he had developed already in his doctoral dissertation[4] and employed throughout his ethics[5] is taken over in the aesthetics. By value Hildebrand means the intrinsic worthiness or excellence or nobility or splendor or dignity of a being. And according to him values are not scattered and random phenomena, but they are gathered into an ordered whole, a cosmos, which he expresses whenever he speaks of "the world of values." Value for him differs from the traditional *bonum* in that *bonum* expresses the idea of "perfective of" someone, or "beneficial for" someone, whereas value lacks this relation to a perfected or benefitted person; it expresses a non-relational or absolute worthiness. Whenever Hildebrand discusses value he usually inserts it in the larger whole that he called value-response (*Wertantwort*), by which he means a response given to some valuable being in the consciousness that my response is *merited* by it, or is *due* to it. Thus when I express a value-responding admiration for someone, I am not pri-

4. Dietrich von Hildebrand, *Die Idee der sittlichen Handlung*, in *Jahrbuch für Philosophie und phänomenologische Forschung* 3 (1916): 126–251.

5. The fullest statement of his value philosophy is found in his *Ethics*, chapters 1–15.

marily trying to benefit or enhance that person but am rather filled with the consciousness that the person is by his or her value *worthy of my admiration.* Now in the first volume of his aesthetics he speaks of aesthetic values, of their relation to beauty, of their main kinds, of their unity, of their antitheses, of the ways of experiencing them, and of course, of aesthetic value-response.

Hildebrand finds a path from value in general to specifically aesthetic value in the following way. Take moral values, such as generosity, faithfulness, truthfulness; all of these, though not themselves aesthetic values but rather moral values, have a certain radiance or splendor of beauty and thus have aesthetic value. They are not in the first place aesthetic values, but they *also* have aesthetic value. Hildebrand finds that with all values that are not in the first place aesthetic values there is this radiance of beauty, and thus that all these values *also* have aesthetic value. For example, we speak of the dignity of human persons; though this is certainly not what is called an aesthetic value, it "gives off" its own beauty and thus also has its own aesthetic value. He gives a name to this aesthetic value that arises everywhere in the world of value, calling it "metaphysical beauty." This metaphysical beauty played a large role in Hildebrand's conversion; what Scheler disclosed to him in the saints was precisely the beauty of their holiness. His conversion was not just based on the "apologetic" arguments on behalf of Christianity, including various historical arguments; it was also, and perhaps above all, based on this sacred beauty. It was the metaphysical beauty of Christian holiness and of the God-man of Christianity that caught and fired Hildebrand's religious imagination.

It is worth noting that metaphysical beauty also plays a role in Hildebrand's magisterial treatise *The Nature of Love.* He insists at the beginning of that work that love is a value-response, which means that it is awakened by the sight of some personal value in the beloved person. He then develops the idea that this value, though not a value that is in the first place an aesthetic value, is perceived by the one who loves as being radiant with beauty, and that it is only in this aesthetically potent way that it awakens love. In other words, Hildebrand explores the connection, first studied by Plato, between love and beauty, and the beauty at stake in interpersonal love is what in his aesthetics he calls metaphysical beauty.

Now from metaphysical beauty he distinguishes all those values that are in the first place aesthetic values; these arise without the mediation of any other kind of value. For example, a well-formed human face may have a loveliness that is not the radiance of, say, the worthy moral character of the person, or of the dignity that the person has as person, but a loveliness that appears immediately in and on the face; here we have what we commonly call an aesthetic value. A lovely melody gives us another example of an aesthetic value that is nothing but an aesthetic value. Hildebrand tries to capture these aesthetic values with the name "the beauty of visible and audible form." Thus he begins his work in aesthetics by dividing the realm of beauty into metaphysical beauty and the beauty of the visible and the audible.

Hildebrand also engages in debate the claims of aesthetic subjectivism, giving particular attention to the subjectivism of Hume, Santayana, and W. D. Ross. Against all these subjectivisms he argues forcefully for the objectivity of aesthetic value. By objectivity he of course means, for a start, that aesthetic value is given to us not in our experiencing (as if it were a part of our conscious experiencing, or *Erleben*) but is given over against us, as an intentional object, in or on some being. But he also means more than this; he also means that beings having aesthetic value really do have it, so that they show themselves for what they really are when we experience them as beautiful, which means that people who fail to experience them as beautiful also fail to experience what is really there. Thus his philosophical realism shows itself in his account of the ontological status of aesthetic values. He shows himself quite mindful of the special difficulties that one encounters in arguing for such objectivity precisely in the case of aesthetic values. For instance, he is fully aware that the visible and audible bearers of many aesthetic values are things of appearance, existing only in their being seen or being heard by human subjects. He argues that the appearance-character of the bearer does not interfere with the full objectivity of the aesthetic value that is based on the appearances. But Hildebrand does not give attention to the issues of cultural and historical relativity that are often raised by way of challenging the objectivity of all value, including aesthetic value (Scheler was more sensitive to these issues than was Hildebrand).

We now come to what Hildebrand regarded, and rightly regarded, as his greatest single contribution to aesthetics. It is situated within his discussion of the beauty of the visible and audible. Take the beauty of the streaked colors appearing in a clear sky at dawn; Hildebrand is struck by the depth and sublimity that can be found in this beauty *and also struck by the fact that the beauty does not seem to be proper to, or proportioned to, the light and colors and spatial expanse from which it arises.* He means that this sublime beauty surpasses by far the "aesthetic capacity" of light and color and spatial expanse. He even suggests that this sublime beauty is somehow akin to the aesthetic dimension of the greatest moral value. But in the case of moral value we at least understand where it comes from; we understand the value, and the beauty of the value, of a person exercising his freedom and committing himself to the good. But with the comparably sublime beauty appearing in the sky at dawn we cannot achieve the same kind of understanding, for the visible appearance qualities seem to be ontologically too modest to give rise to such beauty. Hildebrand recognizes that visible and audible appearance qualities have some modest aesthetic value that is proper to them; he speaks here of *Sinnenschönheit*, or sense beauty, examples of which would be the beauty of a circle, or the rich mellow sound of a well-tuned cello. But this is for him a more primitive beauty, or what he calls a "beauty of the first power," which he contrasts with a "beauty raised to the second power," which is the beauty that mysteriously exceeds the aesthetic capacity of the visible and audible elements out of which it arises. The first and more primitive kind of beauty is the natural effluence of these elements, the second rests on them as on a pedestal. It is, of course, not only in nature but also in art that this mysterious beauty is found. Thus a haunting melody of Schubert, which moves us deeply and makes us shudder within ourselves, seems not to grow out of its musical elements but, as it were, to descend on them from above.

Hildebrand considers and rejects as un-phenomenological two ways of dealing with this phenomenon. There is first of all the view that all beauty of the visible and audible can only be a thing of sense beauty and that the feeling we have in some cases of an "excess" of beauty must be an illusion. He objects that one is simply not letting this excess come to evidence, that one is suppressing it because one feels that it is so inexplicable that it ought not exist. But Hildebrand also rejects the idea that this excess of beauty is to be explained by associating it with some great reality other than the audible and visible bearer of it. For example, some say that the mysterious beauty of a mountain as seen in a certain light arises only for a viewer who is reminded by the mountain of the immensity of God; one thinks that the sublime beauty of the mountain is now intelligible as being grounded not just in a physical reality but also in a divine reality. Hildebrand objects that there is no phenomenological basis for such a supposition; a viewer of the mountain can fully experience its sublime beauty without any such theological thought in the back of his mind. Hildebrand ends by marveling at the "sacramental" relation that exists between certain visible and audible things, on the one hand, and the sublime, unearthly beauty that is attached to them and exceeds them, on the other. The result he achieves displays a kind of paradox: by staying very close to the experience of this beauty, he discerns in it a mysterious "signal of transcendence," which does not, as one might at first think, come from some un-phenomenological construction, but which on the contrary is blocked by un-phenomenological constructions and is brought to evidence by letting the beauty show itself for what it is.

The account so far given of Hildebrand's aesthetics has neglected one remarkable aspect of it: the concreteness of the aesthetic phenomena analyzed by him. I have so far presented some fundamental divisions that he makes within the realm of beauty, and one particularly significant structure that he tries to understand, but from this presentation of fundamentals the reader would never know that he deals throughout his aesthetics with very concrete aesthetic phenomena such as the poetical, the festive, the elegant, the trivial, the prosaic, the aesthetically boring, and the comical; nor would the reader suspect that he exhibits great phenomenological sensitivity in expressing the aesthetic values that belong to the different times of day, such as morning, evening, and nighttime. Thus Hildebrand's work in aesthetics conveys a much stronger "taste" of the aesthetic world than we find in some of the works in aesthetics by Roman Ingarden, who, in *The Literary Work of Art*, for example, stays for the most part at the level of rather abstract logical theory. Hildebrand puts into practice the phenomenological principle that philosophical insight is not restricted to the most general first principles but extends even to more particular structures, such as the comical or the festive.

We see more of this concreteness of Hildebrand in the second volume of his aesthetics, in which he discusses five different realms of art: architecture, sculpture, painting, literature, and music. In connection with these he tries to characterize particularly significant individual works of art, such as Beethoven's *Fidelio* or Bach's *St. Matthew Passion*, an undertaking that is akin to the project of his earlier work *Mozart, Beethoven, Schubert*, in which he tries to do a phenomenology of the spirit and genius of the music of each of these composers. Of course he knows that he cannot achieve with respect to individual composers the same kind of essential insight which he as phenomenologist tries to achieve throughout the first volume of his aesthetics, but everyone who reads Hildebrand on the composers or on individual works of art will recognize his studies as eminent phenomenological achievements.[6]

John F. Crosby
Co-Founder, Hildebrand Project
Professor of Philosophy, Franciscan University of Steubenville

6. An earlier version of this introductory study appeared in *Handbook of Phenomenological Aesthetics*, ed. Hans Rainer Sepp and Lester Embree (Heidelberg: Springer Verlag, 2010), 145–49, and is used here with the permission of Springer.

A Note on the Text

ALL HIS LIFE LONG my late husband Dietrich von Hildebrand had wanted to write a book on aesthetics. Circumstances, however, always seemed to dictate that his primary mission lay elsewhere. Only in his early eighties did he finally feel free to embrace this great task.

It was February 1970. We had just returned from California where we had been lecturing. Upon entering our apartment in New Rochelle, he said to me suddenly, "The time has come for me to write a work on beauty." He started the very next day. He had a rare power of concentration and could write for hours on end without putting his pen down, sometimes producing thirty pages in a single day. When interrupted by a meal, he could rush back to his manuscript and continue writing without even rereading his last paragraph. By the time we left for Europe at the end of June, volume one was finished.

Though he did not usually write during the summers—being busy giving talks and visiting family and friends—his reflections continued to mature in his mind. I still remember, on a visit to my parents in my native Belgium, the striking remarks he made about the mystical character of Flemish landscapes. We returned to America in late August. As soon as he had overcome the jetlag, he was back at his desk working on volume two (which, by the way, contains an entire chapter on the beauty of landscapes). By the end of January 1971, he had largely finished the manuscript.

Inevitably during the last years of his life, his health gave me grave concerns; not only his heart (he had a heart attack in Mexico City in January 1964), but other problems as well. In the fall of 1970, he had to have a colonoscopy, not a pleasant experience as those who have had one can attest. I recall entering the office in fear and trembling. I was told to wait and that it would take quite a while. There I was, terrified at the thought that he might have intestinal cancer and need an operation. My French imagination ran wild, and I was in a pitiful state. I turned to prayer, with my rosary in my hand, interjecting each decade with ardent supplications. Finally, after waiting what seemed to be an eternity, the doctor opened the door and said to me, "Good news, there is no tumor. He should, however, be careful about his diet." I felt like kissing him as a huge burden fell off my shoulders. I prayed a Magnificat.

Some moments later my husband came out. Looking at me with a radiant smile, and without even alluding to the good news, he said to me, "While the doctor was examining me, I had such deep insights into beauty! Let us rush home so that I can immediately incorporate them into the text!" That was typical of him and of the religious, intellectual, artistic world in which he lived.

My husband did not live to see the publication of his *Aesthetics*; volume one was published in 1977, the year of his death, while volume two only appeared in 1984. The former is far more finished than the latter. Unlike major works like his *Ethics*, which is truly "finished," both volumes of the *Aesthetics*, and especially the second, are best understood as an explosion of insights. He knew he was running out of time, and so he tried to capture the Niagara Falls of ideas that flowed out of him. He was also busy writing his meditation on death and his little booklet on gratitude. He would want readers of his *Aesthetics* to receive and develop his rich insights. I do not recall whether he received the galleys for volume one; of course, he could not have seen those for the second volume which was prepared for publication only after his death by Karla Mertens, founder of the Hildebrand Gesellschaft in Germany. By the way, she is almost certainly the source of the chapter and section subtitles in the German edition of the *Aesthetics* which are preserved in this translation.

My husband would have been immensely happy to see this long-awaited English edition. But nothing would have gladdened him more than to know that his explorations of beauty had awakened in even one reader a portion of his own reverence, joy, and gratitude for all things beautiful.

Alice von Hildebrand
Widow of Dietrich von Hildebrand
Co-Founder, Hildebrand Project

Introduction

> Give me a lover and he feels what I am saying: give me one who yearns, give me one who hungers... give me one like this, and he knows what I am saying. But if I speak to one who is cold, he does not know what I am saying.[1]

SOME THINGS can be approached only with great reverence, for it is only then that they disclose themselves to us as they truly are. One of these is beauty. It is of course true that the philosophical analysis of beauty demands a genuine sobriety and the thirst for truth that is required by philosophical *eros*; but this analysis also requires us to approach beauty with reverence, indeed with love. Beauty kindles love, and only the one who remains captivated by it, only the one who is intoxicated by it, only the one who remains a lover while he is investigating its essence, can hope to penetrate its essence.

Plato, Saints Augustine, Anselm, and Bonaventure have repeatedly insisted on the importance of our inner disposition with regard to something, if we wish to get to know it truly. In chapter 1 of his *Proslogion* Saint Anselm writes that without prayer there is no access to a philosophical knowledge of God. We need not approach beauty on our knees, but we must be reverent and receptive, listening in all humility.

1. "*Da amantem, et sentit quod dico: da desiderantem, da esurientem... da talem, et scit, quid dicam. Si autem frigido loquor, nescit quid loquor.*" Saint Augustine, *In Joannis Evangelium*, treatise 36.4.

The subject of this book is purely philosophical. We ask the ancient Platonic question: *ti esti*, "What is it?", with reference to the essence of beauty, to the basic forms of beauty, and to the whole realm of the beautiful.

This book is neither a history of aesthetics nor a debate with everything that others have said in the past about the sphere of the beautiful. My aim is simply to work out the essence of beauty and of aesthetic values, and I shall refer to earlier insights into the aesthetic sphere and to erroneous theses about it only when we are helped, by the critical assessment of them, to work out the truth of the matter.

Some theses, such as any kind of relativism, get the essence of beauty wrong from the beginning, and interpret beauty as a merely subjective feeling. We need not discuss all of these in detail, but we must thoroughly refute what is common to them all, and we must do this with reference to one or the other author. For it is impossible to separate the formulation of truth from the refutation of error.

Our primary aim is to gain knowledge of genuine essential relations. In the realm of the beautiful, in the aesthetic sphere, there are many matters that are accessible only to philosophical insight and to the philosophical method of investigation, even though they do not possess the character of absolute necessity. This is the necessity found in typical essential laws, such as 2 + 2 = 4; color presupposes extension; moral values cannot belong to impersonal beings; responsibility presupposes freedom. Josef Seifert has written of this distinction between different kinds of essential laws in the introduction to his book *Leib und Seele*.[2]

In this introduction I should like to point out the existential urgency and relevance of an investigation of the true essence of beauty. Beauty is of fundamental importance for the human person, but this is not the primary perspective from which we will look at beauty. Above all, beauty is a reflection of God, a reflection of His own infinite beauty, a genuine value, something that is important-in-itself, something that praises God. This means that the question of the contribution that beauty makes to

2. Josef Seifert, *Leib und Seele* (Salzburg: A. Pustet Verlag, 1973).

human life is secondary. Nevertheless, this question is highly significant, since it is extremely important to understand the central objective good that the existence of beautiful things is for the human person. And from the perspective of the ecology of the spirit, it is necessary for us to grasp that the elimination of poetry from life, the destruction of the beauty of nature and especially of the beauty of architecture, terribly impoverishes human existence, and indeed damages and undermines it. We proceed now to point to the fundamental significance of beauty for the human person for his happiness, his character, his moral growth, and his spiritual development.

Beauty as a central source of human happiness

The role of beauty for human happiness is not restricted to those moments in which one is consciously looking at beautiful things. Beauty is active even at those times when one's attention is directed to completely different things. The beauty of the environment in which one lives—one's house, even if it is very simple, like the farmhouses in Tuscany; the view from one's house, both near and far; the architectural beauty of the neighboring houses; the beauty of the sun that shines into the house, and of the shadow cast by a tree—all this nourishes the soul even of the simplest man or woman, entering into their pores even when they are not concentrating on it. And this applies to every situation in life. In the past when a person worked with his hands, bought and sold in the market, and celebrated feasts, he was surrounded by the poetry of these existential situations. This poetry nourished him. He no doubt lacked the understanding of poetry that a poet has when he observes these situations and consciously enjoys them. The simple person did not look at these situations but took them for granted, living in them unselfconsciously. Their poetry nourished his spirit, irrespective of how far he consciously grasped it.

One should not make the mistake of assuming that because many people today apparently lack any sensitivity to beauty, beauty is not a fundamental source of happiness, even for the simplest people. One should not forget the role that beauty plays for the happiness of people—of all people. The atrophy of this sensitivity is a terrible loss, and this ought not to be interpreted as a progress that modern man has made in the industrialized world. We should instead seek to understand the consequences for man of the withdrawal of this spiritual nourishment. The fact that one does not know the causes of a sickness is no proof that one is not sick.

People have grown accustomed to the elimination of the poetry of the world, to the mechanization of life, to the expulsion of beauty; but this does not make any less real the influence on human happiness of this destruction of the charm of an organic, truly human life. People have grown accustomed today to the din to which they are exposed on the street and at home by the many machines that they use; but this does not mean that our nerves escape unscathed from all this cacophony.

It is easy to see the great decrease in human happiness today,[3] and the great increase in the number of psychopaths, suicides, crimes, disorders, revolutions, protests, etc. Are these not unambiguous symptoms of unhappiness, of an unfulfilled hunger for happiness? Why, for example, are the people in Spain so much happier than the people in the United States, although they are much poorer and their life is much less comfortable? They sing while they work, they adorn their simple houses with flowers, and their faces have a happy expression, especially in Andalusia. They are joyful as they gather on the street in the evening, and one cannot fail to see their delight in life and their vitality. As yet there has been little industrialization in the country in which they live. The organic rhythm of life and the poetry of life still survive there to some extent, and very little of the beauty has been destroyed.

There can be no doubt that beauty is one of the great sources of joy in human life. Naturally, like all the central sources of joy, it has many gradations, in accordance with the receptivity of the individual.

No one with eyes to see will deny that the love between husband and wife is one of the greatest sources of happiness in human life. There can

3. Cf. my book, *The Devastated Vineyard* (Fort Collins, Col.: Roman Catholic Books, 1985), part I, chap. 4.

be no doubt that a great truth finds expression in the words of Schiller in the *Ode to Joy* ("Whoever calls even only *one* soul *his own*, let him join in the exultation! But let anyone who never achieved this, slink away weeping from our brotherhood!") and of Goethe in *Egmont* ("Only the soul that loves is happy"). Naturally, however, the potential for love varies tremendously from one individual to another. One man can love more deeply, more strongly, and more faithfully than another. He can feel more deeply than another the sweet bliss of a love that is requited, the unheard-of gift of gazing into the eyes of a beloved person. But this does not prevent love from being one of the deepest sources of joy for all human persons. This is true not only of the love between husband and wife, but of love as such, be it the love of friends, of parents for their children or of children for their parents, or the other forms of love. And it applies in an incomparably superior manner to the love for God, the love for Christ.

In the same way, the degree and depth of the happiness caused by beauty has many gradations in different persons. But this does not keep beauty from being a great source of happiness for anyone who is not completely obtuse. Even children are delighted by the beauty of nature, by the poetry of the various seasons of the year, by sunrise and sunset.

The significance of beauty for the development of personality

Beauty is not only a central source of joy. It also possesses a great significance for the development of personality, especially in a moral sense. Plato writes: "At the sight of beauty the soul grows wings."[4] Genuine beauty liberates us in many ways from the force of gravity, drawing us out of the dull captivity of daily life. At the sight of the truly beautiful we are freed from the tension that urges us on toward some immediate practical goal. We become contemplative, and this is immensely valuable. We expand, and even our soul itself becomes more beautiful when beauty comes to meet us, takes hold of us, and fires us with enthusiasm. It lifts us up above all that is base and common. It opens our eyes to the baseness, impurity, and wickedness of many things. Ernest Hello makes a

4. Plato, *Phaedrus* 249d.

very profound point when he says: "The mediocre person has only one passion, namely hatred of the beautiful."[5] Beauty is the archenemy of mediocrity.

The appreciation of beauty, the interest in beauty, the longing for beauty, the need of beauty—all this has often been seen as a danger for the full understanding of moral values and their ultimate seriousness, or else as something effeminate, something only for aesthetes.

This is to confuse true sensitivity for beauty, true love for all bearers of genuine beauty, with aestheticism, which is a perversion with dangerous effects on the moral quality of the personality. Aestheticism undermines the personality and robs it of its ultimate seriousness. The aesthete does not in any way do justice to the true mystery of beauty and to the message from God that beauty contains. He does not understand that beauty is a value, and so he treats beautiful things as if they were only subjectively gratifying. Kierkegaard calls the unserious playfulness of the aesthete, his coldness and self-centeredness, the "aesthetic attitude," which he contrasts with the ethical sphere and *a fortiori* with the religious sphere.[6] This attitude has nothing in common with receptivity to beauty, with being affected by beauty, or with the value-response to beautiful things. Both Kant and Schopenhauer, each in his own way, saw the nobility that lies in the contemplation of the beautiful and in the love of beautiful things.[7] And Herbart went so far as to regard ethics as a subdivision of aesthetics.[8]

Without discussing this thesis in detail here, let me affirm unambiguously that beauty does in fact have an ennobling effect. Contact with an environment permeated by beauty not only offers real protection against impurity, baseness, every kind of letting oneself go, brutality, and untruthfulness; it has also the positive effect of raising us up in a moral sense. It does not draw us into a self-centered pleasure where our only

5. Ernest Hello, *L'Homme* (Paris: Perrin, 1936), in the chapter entitled "L'homme mediocre," 59–60.

6. Søren Kierkegaard, *Either/Or*, trans. David F. Swenson (Princeton: Princeton University Press, 1959), part 2.

7. The references to Kant and Schopenhauer are given in chap. 16 below.

8. Johann Herbart, *Lehrbuch zur Einleitung in die Philosophie* (Leipzig: Meiner, 1912), 3rd section.

wish is to indulge ourselves. On the contrary, it opens our hearts, inviting us to transcendence and leading us *in conspectu Dei* ("before the face of God"), before the face of God. Naturally, this last point applies above all to the high, exalted beauty which Kant calls the "sublime" [*das Erhabene*] and which he contrasts with the "beautiful." But even in little things that are charming and graceful, even in the more modest beautiful things, one can find a trace of the pure and the noble. This may perhaps not lead us *in conspectu Dei*, but it does fill us with gratitude to God. It frees us from captivity in our egoistic interests and undoes the fetters of our hearts, releasing us (even if only for a short time) from the wild passions that convulse them.

The distinction between beauty and luxury

There also exists a pseudo-democratic antipathy against beauty, an attitude full of resentment: beauty is regarded as luxury for the elite in society, as an antisocial indulgence that ignores urgent social problems. Luxury, we are told, is morally negative; we must fight against it and abolish it.

A first point: beauty in general, beauty as such, is confused here with refined culture. Obviously, it is ignorant nonsense to regard the beauty of the blue sky in the sunshine, of the mountains, of the sea, of the springtime, summer, fall, and winter, of morning, noon, and evening, or the beauty of architectonic forms (even when these are very simple) as a luxury for the social elite.

Let us think, by contrast, of a really cultivated atmosphere, of the beauty of a noble house with high-quality furniture, curtains, and carpets. This is not in the least "luxurious." It is instead a kind of beauty that presupposes a certain level of culture, a special artistic gift that enables one to create the beauty, and a refined taste in order to appreciate it and enjoy it to the full. The term "elite" may in some sense be appropriate here, but this kind of beauty is no luxury. It therefore retains both its value and its *raison d'être.*

Above all, however, we must explain the true meaning of "luxury."

This term is used with three distinct meanings, each of which denotes something devoid of value, unnecessary, superfluous.

1) The first meaning of the word derives from an incorrect use of the term. Anything that is not useful (in the narrowest sense of this word) is considered superfluous. This is due to an ambiguity in the word "superfluous." On the one hand, it means that from a practical, utilitarian perspective something is not required. In this case, the word does not imply that something is valueless, unserious, or dilettantish. The opposite is true: culture as a whole (in contrast to civilization) is "superfluous" in this sense, as is beauty. Beauty is a pure gift, a superfluity (literally, an "overflowing") in the highest sense of the word. Beauty may well be called unnecessary, if one equates "necessary," "serious," and "entitled to exist" with "indispensable in order to achieve a practical goal." Something that is "superabundant" in this sense clearly possesses a high value and is not in any sense a luxury. It is not at all acceptable to apply the term "luxury" to everything that is superfluous in the sense of superabundant; it reveals a blindness to values, a purely utilitarian attitude, a radical philistinism. To call such things luxury is, as I said, to extend the concept to embrace the totality of culture, the world of beauty, and even moral values, that is, things that are much more important, more necessary, and more serious than all those things that are merely useful. This is a typical instance of an unjustified term which is essentially flawed, indeed based on a contradiction: it takes something that is profoundly meaningful and absolutely necessary, and calls it superfluous and unnecessary.

2) Where, however, the term "luxury" is applied to things that serve only an exaggerated comfort,[9] things that are agreeable but have no inherent value whatever and need not be used from the perspective of usefulness, we are justified in calling them superfluous and in speaking

9. We should note that the superfluity that entitles us to speak of "luxury" does not begin with those things that are given up in a life governed by a vow of poverty (for example, in the case of a hermit who leads a life of penance and who restricts himself to those things necessary for sheer survival). The distinction between a normal life and a life led in holy poverty (or the life of a penitent) is very different from the distinction between the presence and absence of luxury, but we shall not discuss this any further here. Luxury does not refer to this distinction. We are speaking of a normal, comfortable life.

of luxury. Many "beauty products," chairs, carpets, etc. are neither beautiful nor necessary for our daily lives. In other words, they have no inherent aesthetic value and they are superfluous from the practical perspective of achieving goals, that is to say, they are a sheer luxury, especially when they are also expensive. (The concept of luxury includes the idea that something is expensive.)

3) The term "luxury" has a third meaning, this one referring to quantity. Like the second meaning, this third one refers to something real. This sense of luxury does not assume that the object is not a bearer of value; superfluity is present not due to worthlessness, but to the fact that something is present in a quantity wholly disproportionate to its actual use. If someone has fifty neckties instead of ten, this is clearly a luxury; the same is true of one who has a hundred pairs of shoes or two hundred different dresses, irrespective of how aesthetically valuable they all may be. This is luxury, firstly, because someone possesses much more of such things than he can use, no matter how elegant he might wish to appear. A superfluity of this kind is literally meaningless. Secondly, this superfluity is luxury because it is very expensive and entails an irresponsible relationship to money. There is something disgusting about it and extremely antisocial. To squander money in such a meaningless manner is immoral.

This type of luxury does, however, presuppose that these things are in fact destined to be used. The situation is completely different where someone owns a hundred valuable paintings; it would be meaningless to speak here of luxury. Only those who are well-off can afford aesthetically noble, cultivated furnishings, since these cost a great deal of money. But this is no luxury, since such furnishings have a high value of their own. Their legitimacy is therefore unquestionable, even if only a small number of persons can enjoy them.

We are interested primarily in the difference between such special beauty, which we may say is for the social elite (without thereby disputing its legitimacy or classifying it as luxury), and beauty in general, which is accessible to all and is a highly significant objective good for the person.

Aesthetic experience as "distinterested" and anti-pragmatic

Beauty has a special significance for the spiritual development of the person. In the act of looking at the beautiful—I have in mind here the conscious concentration on something that is beautiful—there lies a special form of the act of self-transcendence, a certain contemplative objectivity. I have frequently pointed to the gesture of transcendence that is contained in every value-response. Here I want to point to one special dimension of this transcendence which belongs specifically to the value-response to the beautiful. Kant aims at this in speaking about the "disinterestedness" [*Uninteressiertheit*] of aesthetic experience. I want to refer here to the thing that Kant saw and that he probably intended to describe, although he did not in fact give an unambiguous explanation of the term "disinterestedness," and indeed failed to distinguish it from a false interpretation. More on this subject in chapter 16.

The objectivity that I envisage lies in the fact that our own person is not always included in a special way in the experience, as in the case of moral value-response. This inclusion applies especially to all morally obligatory actions, in which we reflect consciously not only on the value of the good that we are dealing with, but also on its moral significance, that is, on the rightness of my moral conduct. This is not true of the response to beauty. Another pointer to the existence of a special dimension of self-transcendence is the fact that all value-responses to the beautiful are of a purely contemplative nature, whereas in moral value-response the decisive role is mostly played by the will (and in many cases, by action).

Every genuine value-response is disinterested in the sense that the person does not seek his own advantage, but gives himself over to the importance that the good possesses in itself. In one sense this transcendence attains its high point in the value-response to morally relevant goods. I have described in detail the various dimensions of transcendence in my book *The Nature of Love*, especially chapter 4.

The beautiful can attract us and make us happy, but its importance is inherently and specifically anti-pragmatic. It penetrates very little into the realm of our own interests, whether into the practical conduct of our lives, our relationships and conflicts with other people, or the way we earn our daily bread. In this way beauty is a typical representative of the valuable, that is, of that which all genuine values possess, of that which characterizes them as values.

This, however, shows us the seriousness and importance of beauty, and it is for this reason that aesthetics, the exact philosophical analysis of the realm of beauty, is an important part of philosophy. And as we have seen, it takes on a particular relevance today.

In this book, I shall attempt to present an aesthetics that keeps its distance to all constructions, that does justice to the essence of beauty and of all aesthetic values, and seeks to penetrate their essence, without taking for granted unexamined theories.

As I have already mentioned, this book is not a debate with already existing theories about beauty, but an analysis of the essence of the world of the beautiful. I should like to repeat Aristotle's words in the *De Anima* (412a), which I have quoted in my *Ethics*: "Let us now make a completely new beginning and attempt to give an exact answer to the question: 'What is the soul?'" We propose to apply this to beauty.

CHAPTER ONE

The Objectivity of Beauty

"... apart from the fact that it matters very little to me whether I am the first or the last to write the things I write. All that matters is that they be true ..."[1]

I HAVE ALREADY pointed out in the Introduction that beauty is a primordial phenomenon of the utmost importance and one of the greatest sources of profound joy. If we take an unprejudiced look at what we mean when we say that an object is beautiful—whether it be a melody, a tree, or a human face—we see clearly that beauty is a quality of these objects, that it characterizes them in an important manner. We also grasp unambiguously that what we describe by means of the predicate "beautiful" is not some neutral quality, as for example when we say that a melody is long, a face round, or a tree lofty. Rather, we are focusing on a certain value of these objects.

A brief description of the three categories of importance

Unfortunately, the term "value" is frequently employed in an equivocal sense. This obliges us to specify which of the meanings of this term is

1. Descartes, letter to Father Vatier, February 22, 1638, quoted from Jacques Chevalier, *Descartes* (Paris: Plon, 1921), 53.

being used when we describe beauty as a value. In my *Ethics,* I have attempted to investigate the essence of value in general. The first point to be emphasized is the character of importance, which distinguishes what is valuable from all that is merely neutral. However, when we draw the distinction between importance and neutrality, we have not yet described value in the real meaning of the term, since there are other kinds of importance too: first of all, that which is merely subjectively satisfying; secondly, the objective good for the person; and thirdly, that which is important-in-itself.

"Let us suppose that someone pays us a compliment. We are perhaps aware that we do not fully deserve it, but it is nevertheless an agreeable and pleasurable experience. It is not a matter neutral and indifferent to us as in the case where someone tells us that his name begins with a T. We may have been told many things before this compliment, things which had a neutral and indifferent character, but now in the face of all other statements the compliment is thrown into relief. It presents itself as agreeable and as possessing the character of a *bonum*, in short, as something important.

[Now] let us suppose that we witness a generous action, a man's forgiveness of a grave injury. This again strikes us as distinguishable from the neutral activity of a man dressing himself or lighting a cigarette. Indeed, the act of generous forgiveness shines forth with the mark of importance, with the mark of something noble and precious. It moves us and engenders our admiration. We are not only aware that this act occurs, but that it is *better* that it occurs, *better* that the man acted in this way rather than in another. We are conscious that this act is something that *ought to be*, something *important.*

If we compare these types of importance, we will soon discover the essential difference between them. The first, that is, the compliment, is merely *subjectively* important; while the latter, the act of forgiving, is *important-in-itself.* We are fully conscious that the compliment possesses a character of importance only insofar as it gives us pleasure. Its importance is drawn solely from its relation to our pleasure—as soon as the compliment is divorced from our pleasure, it sinks back into the anonymity of the neutral and indifferent.

In contrast, the generous act of forgiveness presents itself as something intrinsically important. We are clearly conscious that its importance in no way depends on any effect which it produces in us. Its particular importance is not drawn from any relation to our pleasure and satisfaction. It stands before us as intrinsically and autonomously important, in no way dependent on any relation to our reaction."[2]

"Value embodies the true, the valid, the objectively important. It has a place in the order of fundamental notions other than the subjectively satisfying. It belongs... to those ultimate data and notions such as being, truth, and knowledge, which can neither be defined nor denied without tacitly re-introducing them. This is the reason why Aristippus' attempt to do away with any objective measure and to admit only a subjective importance, is in fact always unsuccessful. After eliminating with a rare consistency... all other measures except those which apply to the degrees of pleasure, he warns against following our instincts in a brutelike way and advises us to examine a thing before we choose it to see whether it really guarantees the most intense and lasting pleasure: here he tacitly opposes the reasonable pursuit of pleasure to an unreasonable surrender to every attraction or temptation. And he claims that the reasonable pursuit is the wiser attitude, the attitude we *should* have.

But why *should* we be wise? If the merely subjectively satisfying is the norm, why should anyone object to a man who pretends that he prefers to yield to every instinct without bothering about whether something else could give him more pleasure? Obviously Aristippus silently presupposes still another norm besides that of pleasure, an objective norm: the value of wisdom, in the sense of a reasonable, systematic pursuit of pleasure as opposed to the brutelike and unreasonable instinctual pursuit of pleasure. This norm is independent of the question of whether it is more or less subjectively satisfying. Thus, in a completely general and formal way, the notion of value is presupposed. Certainly, there is no question of moral

2. Dietrich von Hildebrand, *Ethics* (Chicago: Franciscan Herald Press, 1972), chap. 3.

value. But in recommending the systematic and rational pursuit of pleasure as an ideal, as something we should aim at, he implicitly claims that it is objectively preferable to do so, that it should be so rather than not: thereby the notion of value of the important-in-itself is tacitly presupposed."[3]

Only that which is important-in-itself is a value in the true sense. When we define this most fundamental datum of the important-in-itself as the true sense of the term "value," we are justified by the fact that this is what people are aiming at (albeit in an unclear manner) in using the term "value." Besides this, when someone says that an action is noble and good, or when he speaks of the dignity of the person, he has in mind this meaning of the term "value." This is true of Nietzsche, who first introduced the term, and above all of Scheler. Although Scheler did not elaborate the differences among the various categories of importance, he is primarily concerned with that which is important-in-itself.

Beauty is an objective value

Our language itself expresses clearly the fact that beauty is a value, not merely something that is satisfying for me. The preposition "for," as linked organically to something that is merely pleasant, would have a wholly different meaning if it were attached to the predicate "beautiful." Normally, we say, "This color is beautiful, this melody is beautiful"—not "beautiful for me." In the exceptional case where we do say this, the word "for" does not mean that the importance of the color or the melody has its origin in the pleasant effect it has on me; rather, we mean, "In my opinion, they are beautiful." In this case, the preposition expresses a relationship to my judgment, which discerns the beauty: "Others may not find them beautiful, but I do." The importance that is expressed in the term "beauty" is not in any way expressed by the phrase "for me," as it is when I say that something is gratifying for me. For example, if someone says, "It is very advantageous for me that this man has resigned as chairman," he clearly means a kind of importance that is constituted by his

3. *Ethics*, chap. 3.

own personal interests: it is gratifying for him. This, however, says nothing about whether this event is important in itself, whether its content elevates it above the realm of things indifferent, or whether it possesses a value (and if so, which value). There can be no doubt about it: when we see a landscape and exclaim, "How beautiful it is!" we are referring primarily to a quality of the landscape, not to an effect it has on us. Above all, however, our use of the word "beautiful" points to a value, to something important-in-itself.

There is unfortunately a widespread prejudice with regard to all values; one says that they are not qualities of an object, but only feelings or effects that an object evokes in us. It is asserted that we cannot examine, observe, and note in an object the values that we ascribe to it, in the same way as we do with neutral qualities.

Like so many other errors, this fateful error of the subjectivization of values has won many adherents thanks to David Hume. In no other philosopher is there such a vast disproportion between the significance that he has as a philosopher and the influence that he has exercised in the history of philosophy.[4]

Hume's theory: beauty is an effect on our mind

In *An Enquiry Concerning the Principles of Morals*, Hume writes that Euclid gave an exhaustive account of all the qualities of the circle but did not speak in any of his propositions about its beauty. The reason is obvious, he says: beauty is not a quality of the circle but only an effect that it exercises upon our mind. We cannot establish the presence of beauty either through our senses or through mathematical reflection.[5]

4. Hume was a superficial philosopher, in many respects a chatterer who made an impression primarily by means of his skepticism and his cynical elegance. Without noticing what he was doing, he continually put forward mutually contradictory assertions and claimed that these were evident. Nevertheless, his influence on a mind of such mighty power and thoroughness as Kant was so great that the latter said he had been awakened from a "dogmatic slumber" by Hume (cf. Introduction to his *Prolegomena to Any Future Metaphyiscs*). Above all, however, Hume's influence is disproportionately great. He is the father of all the variants of positivism, of empiro-criticism, psychologism, and of many other disastrous philosophical aberrations.

5. David Hume, *Enquiry Concerning the Principles of Morals*, appendix I.

This observation by Hume is characteristic of his nonchalant superficiality in three ways. First, if Euclid does not mention the beauty of the circle when he lists all its geometrical qualities, this omission may be for some reason other than that beauty is not a genuine quality of the circle; the reason may well be that beauty is not the topic in a geometrical analysis. This is one of the many instances in which Hume puts forward as evident something that is not in the least evident. Secondly, the fact that beauty is something profoundly different from neutral qualities, that it is a value, does not in the least mean that it is impossible for it to be an objective quality of the object. Thirdly, Hume arbitrarily employs a false alternative to exclude the possibility of the objectivity of values. He argues that every genuine quality belonging to an object, if it is to be recognized when one observes the object in question, must either be a datum of the senses or else be derivable from premises; but this merely begs the question. This assertion is unproven; still less is it at all evident. And it is self-contradictory, because it is itself an assertion that is derived neither from a sense-experience nor from an analytical proposition. This means that it contradicts Hume's own celebrated thesis,[6] which itself fits neither category but is a philosophical assertion of a quite different nature. According to its own verdict, therefore, *An Enquiry Concerning Human Understanding* ought to be committed to the flames.

The widespread claim that we cannot grasp values or know them, since they are properly speaking a "feeling" we have in the presence of something we perceive, is completely unfounded and unproven, and still less is it evident. It appears in various forms, but it always involves the positing of an antithesis between *value* (which is distorted beyond recognition) and *fact.*

Various kinds of perception, corresponding to the variety of objects

Before looking individually at the typical forms of this subjectivization of values in general, and of the aesthetic values in particular, we wish to

6. "If we take in our hand any volume; of divinity or school metaphysics, for example; let us ask, *Does it contain any abstract reasoning concerning quantity or number?* No. *Does it contain any experimental reasoning concerning matter of fact and existence?* No. Commit it then to the flames: for it can contain nothing but sophistry and illusion." David Hume, *An Enquiry Concerning Human Understanding*, final paragraph of the book.

investigate briefly the justification given for the distinction between values and facts. If this is intended to refer to the difference between neutral facts and the mysterious importance that objects can possess—especially the importance-in-itself of value—then there is no reason to object. For there is obviously a great difference between merely noting that something exists and speaking of the value of this thing. The affirmation, "music is playing there," is obviously completely different from the affirmation, "beautiful or ugly music is playing there."

If one mentions the value of something, either in very general terms (for example, "Justice is morally good") or in a concrete instance (for example, "The attitude of this person is noble"), it is clear that one is making an affirmation that points in a wholly different direction from the registering of a neutral fact (for example, "This room is five meters in length"). The affirmation of a value is a completely new dimension, a completely new theme. But this difference does not at all mean that I cease to register something real. When I grasp the moral value of an act of forgiveness or the value of the dignity of the human being as a person, this knowledge is analogous to my knowledge that a tree is green or a syllogism false. No doubt, the act of knowing is radically different. The type of perception with which I grasp values is not the same as that with which I see colors, recognize a voice, or grasp that 7 + 5 = 12. But the difference between the act of knowing values and the act of knowing neutral facts does not disqualify the perception of values from being a genuine act of knowing.

There are very different kinds of immediate apprehension—of perception in the broad sense of the term—and they depend on the kind of object that is known. We need one organ in order to grasp colors, another in order to grasp sounds; we can only see colors, only hear sounds. The knowledge of physical objects is completely different in kind from the knowledge of persons. The perception of a melody is much more demanding than the hearing of sounds. Completely unmusical people do not recognize any melody, although they are not deaf. One of the most interesting and captivating tasks for a philosopher is to investigate the correlation between the act of apprehending and the object apprehended, and also to determine the different kinds of apprehending the various types of object. First of all, what content can be grasped immediately in a given case? What content can be grasped only through deduction? What can be grasped only through hearing it from another, and so on? Within the spectrum of these various "types of perception," one must then investigate the kind of knowledge that, always changing according to the nature of the object in question, alone enables us to grasp this object. However, the fact that the act of apprehending a value is different from the act of knowing a neutral fact does not in any way entitle us to assert that the former does not entail any kind of apprehending at all, in the sense of a perception (in the broad sense of the term), a clear and explicit "consciousness of."

When we hear that someone has been unfaithful to his wife, we immediately realize the moral disvalue of this action. Although we hear about this action only in a mediated manner, through communication, the moral disvalue which unambiguously attaches to this conduct is immediately apprehended by us. The most important point in the present context is that the value or disvalue unambiguously stands on the object side, and that a clear "consciousness of" is present in our perceiving of the value. Less important for us at present is the fact that the moral disvalue of the adultery is given to us with an immediacy that is not found in the givenness of the bearer of the disvalue, that is, the act of adultery (of which we are informed).

"Frontal" consciousness and "lateral" consciousness

The greatest distinction in the realm of experience (in the most general sense of *Erfahren*) is that between the "frontal consciousness" and the "lateral consciousness" of something. Whatever does not belong to my own person is given to me only in a "consciousness of," as an object which discloses itself to my mind, something I perceive on the object side. It may be a color, a material object, the facts of a situation, or another person: in each instance, there is a frontal "consciousness of."

When, however, I am full of joy or enthusiasm, when I weep or grieve, love or hate, there is no "consciousness of," but rather something consciously enacted, something which does not stand over against me frontally. Naturally, joy and enthusiasm always presuppose a "consciousness of" the object which kindles the joy and enthusiasm in me; but the responses, the acts of joy and enthusiasm themselves, are not a "consciousness of," but are beings that exist consciously. All acts of knowing belong to this category. Seeing is not given to me in the same manner as that which I see. I perform the act of seeing and am conscious of seeing—but in a lateral, not in a frontal, consciousness. One can speak of knowledge only in the case of a "consciousness of." Not every "consciousness of" is an act of knowing; it may, for example, be an act of imagining something or of thinking about something. But every act of knowing in the true sense is always a "consciousness of."

In the performance of my own actions, I come to know these acts from within. When someone falls in love, he is indeed totally oriented toward the person with whom he is in love. He has a "consciousness of" this person, but he also learns thereby what being in love means. The consciously lived reality of love discloses itself to him in its own distinct character, although this happens only in a lateral manner. If one wishes to call this too "knowledge," one must always bear in mind that the knowledge is not in any way the theme of the experience. This theme is the joy itself, the rejoicing, the conscious existence of joy, and the experience of joy—not the act by which one comes to know joy. At the same time, however, one learns in a very specific way what joy is. If one wishes to make joy the subject matter of knowledge, for example, as the object of a philosophical analysis, one makes it an object like those objects which are not a part of our conscious existence, and analyzes it in a "consciousness of"; one looks at it in the frontal direction. Naturally, it ceases at that very moment to be something consciously lived. What I learned about it in lateral consciousness is made into an object, and the lateral consciousness is replaced by a "consciousness of." It is of course impossible to have an immediate perception of the joy that has been made the object of our act of knowledge. An intuitive givenness of joy, as in the case of the perception of a color or a tree, is impossible; we can touch joy in reality only in the lateral consciousness of what we are living from within. As soon as I make it the object of my act of knowing, it ceases (at least at the level of "actual" consciousness) to exist in its real form as conscious being, as a part of my conscious being. However, joy is an intelligible essence—and this means that even if I make the datum of joy, which I have come to know through living it, into an object, its essence will nevertheless be immediately present to me in an intellectual intuition. This principle of immediate givenness applies to all genuine essences.

After this brief excursion into the field of epistemology, it has become obvious that there is no reason whatever to assert that because the beauty of a melody is a value and because it cannot be perceived in the same manner as facts, it cannot be known.

The representatives of this theory equate "fact" with "neutral fact." This is why an author such as George Santayana dogmatically asserts that only facts can be perceived and discerned;[7] accordingly, values can be neither known nor described.

We have already seen that values can be grasped in exactly the same manner as any neutral object or any neutral fact. When I hear a melody, its beauty or ugliness is just as immediate and independently present as the melody itself; it belongs on the side of the object just as much as something that is distinct from my own self, and it is different from all experiences of lateral consciousness. I discover the beauty of the melody as something that adheres to the melody. When I come to know the melody, I also come to know and to realize its beauty. This knowing or cognizing of beauty is a completely different way of apprehending, a completely different type of perception which differs much more strongly from the other types of perception than the act of seeing differs from the act of hearing. But this does not alter the fact that this knowledge is a genuine "consciousness of," a genuine perception in the broader sense, which is radically different from all other kinds of lateral consciousness of what one experiences from within.

7. George Santayana, *The Sense of Beauty* (New York: Charles Scribner's Sons, 1896), 20, 49.

Confusing the apprehension of beauty with bodily experiences (the James-Lang theory of emotion)

The assertion that beauty is an emotional experience, in the sense of being something consciously experienced, is clearly a violent distortion of the facts.[8] There is an act of joy, or an affective response of joy which we experience from within, but there is no act of beauty, no beauty as something that exists consciously and is lived by us in the same way as joy, love, hatred, etc. are lived. There is no act of the person that would have beauty as its content in just the way in which joy, love, or faithfulness is the content of a response. When Max Scheler speaks of a "feeling of value" [*Wertfühlen*],[9] he clearly means a special kind of "consciousness of," not a feeling that occurs in me as something which exists as part of my conscious being. He is referring to a special form of the intuitive perception of values that differs from the act of seeing in that it involves a more intimate and less distant contact with the object of perception. Nevertheless, it remains a pure "consciousness of."

One might object at this point that we are not forced to choose between the alternatives of frontal and lateral consciousness, or between the unambiguous "consciousness of" something lying on the side of the object and the experience whereby we consciously experience something from within. There are also phenomena, such as physical pain, which undeniably occur in me and which draw their existence from the fact that they are "felt"; at the same time, however, I "have" this pain, and it does not stand wholly on the side of the subject. This bodily pain is not something I enact laterally—I am not painful; rather, I have this pain—whereas I do not have joy, but am joyful. This kind of experience

8. The most precise formulation of this disastrous subjectivization of beauty can be found in the Italian philosopher Benedetto Croce, especially in his *Estetica in nuce* (Bari: Laterza & Figli, 1946). He applies to value, and in particular to beauty, the aphorism coined by George Berkeley: *esse est percipi*, "to be is to be perceived." In Berkeley, this interpretation of existence concerns the world of physical bodies, but Croce applies it only to values, and especially to beauty. In his eyes, "facts" possess a complete reality in themselves, whereas the existence of beauty consists exclusively in its being perceived by a human being. This is not the same form of subjectivism that we find in Santayana; for Croce, beauty is not a feeling but a merely human aspect.

9. Max Scheler, *Der Formalismus in der Ethik und die materiale Wertethik* (Bern: Francke Verlag, 1954), beginning at 271.

has a semi-objective character. Such experiences take place in me, but they are neither responses nor acts; nor are they profound states of my soul, such as happiness. They resemble the lateral experiences in that when I feel bodily pain, it is not knowledge that is at issue. But unlike all responses, acts, and the acts of knowledge, these bodily pains do not cease to be experienced at the level of actual consciousness when I make them the object of my knowledge. Their semi-objective character makes it possible to look at them in a "consciousness of" and to recognize their specific character, unless other reasons make this impossible, as in the case of severe physical pains, the strength of which limits our ability to look at them in such a way as to be concerned with knowledge of them.

One might perhaps think that the idea of making beauty a mere bodily experience of pleasure is so utterly absurd that no one could ever seriously maintain it. Unfortunately, however, there is no affirmation—no matter how much it may contradict the facts—that has *never* been maintained by a philosopher.

Even a philosopher as important as William James, who had so many sound insights, succumbed to this wretched error for a time. It finds expression in the so-called James-Lange theory of emotion, which defines all affective and meaningful responses such as joy, grief, veneration, contempt, love, and hatred as merely bodily experiences like a stomach ache or a heartbeat: it is only by means of association that such experiences are linked to the idea of an object. This amounts to the denial of all affective mental experiences, from pure states of depression to the intentional affective responses of joy and grief, and this is surely one of the most audacious constructions, indeed one of the most absurd "theories" that flagrantly contradict reality, that has ever been put forward. It simply ignores facts—it is as if a blind person were to talk about colors. The effort involved in refuting this theory is not really worthwhile. It would be more interesting to clear up the psychological problem of how it was possible for such a stimulating and many-sided thinker as William James—to whom we owe the fine aphorism *I see what I see*, whereby he refused to acquiesce in a discussion of *theories* that would eliminate *facts*—to succumb to such a primitive error that so crudely violates the principle *I see what I see.*

Nor is this theory content with subjectivizing beauty: it reduces all affective experience in the human person to specific bodily experiences.

My primary concern here is to show that beauty is not in the least a mental, personal reality. It is not an "emotion" of any kind. It is neither a bodily, semi-objective emotion nor an emotion that belongs wholly to the subject and is experienced in its lateral enactment in the same way as all affective states and responses. Beauty presents itself unambiguously as a property of an object—more specifically, as a value. It does not belong to the ontological domain of that which exists as consciously lived: about this, there can be no doubt.

The erroneous interpretation of all values as mental experiences (Santayana)

Some philosophers assert that all values are mental experiences. Santayana, Dewey, Carnap, and many others portray this completely ungrounded—indeed, evidently false—assertion, made with dogmatic emphasis, as something evidently true. This is one example of a very interesting general phenomenon: it is remarkable how often philosophers take something that is neither evidently true nor in any way proven and portray it as indubitable, as something to be taken for granted. There are innumerable instances of this in David Hume's books. These theses not only lack any evidential character and are unproven; they are downright false. Nevertheless, they possess a pseudo-obviousness which reduces the reader to silence.[10] In my *Ethics* I have presented a detailed refutation of this thesis that reinterprets values as mere mental experiences.[11]

Here I should like to point out that this thesis entails a failure to recognize the ontological character of value, since such philosophers do not see that (like truth) value is not something that exists as consciously lived (for example, as some kind of personal experiencing). This thesis also fails to grasp what distinguishes a value from a neutral being and makes it a

10. Cf. Alice von Hildebrand, "On the Pseudo-Obvious," in *Wahrheit, Wert und Sein, Festgabe für Dietrich von Hildebrand zum 80. Geburtstag*, ed. Balduin Schwarz (Regensburg: Habbel, 1970), 25–32.

11. *Ethics*, chap. 9, 7ff.

value. It also fails to recognize the difference between a value (as something that is important-in-itself) and all that is merely subjectively satisfying for myself.

If one's starting point is the above-mentioned prejudice that values do not exist objectively, like facts, but that all values are merely a reaction on our part to an object, then it is clear that the affirmation that beauty is a value also means that beauty is subjectivized. This is a pure begging of the question. When the subjectivity of all values (*the very thing the objectivist has to prove*) is tacitly presupposed, the correct observation that beauty is a value (and not something neutral) must then lead to the further inference that beauty is a mental reality. But as soon as one has discovered the completely erroneous character of the assertion that values are mental entities, the entire house of cards—and *a fortiori* the merely subjective validity that is alleged for value—collapses. Once the equivocation in the term "value" is discovered—that is to say, that there are two radically different kinds of importance, that which is important-in-itself and that which is only important for me—it becomes clear that, while the observation "beauty is a value" (and not some neutral property) is correct, the inference that we have here something of purely subjective validity is completely wrong.

We find in Santayana the proposition that as soon as we eliminate consciousness, the possibility of value is likewise eliminated.[12] He is clearly failing to make a distinction here between the "consciousness of" something and conscious existence, that is to say, a form of being which is enacted in a personal and conscious manner. As soon as one has understood this central difference, one sees that the term "consciousness" is employed equivocally in Santayana. It is obvious that two distinct theses are entailed here. First, there is the assertion that the existence of values presupposes a "consciousness of," and that if no person could grasp them, values would not exist; and secondly, the assertion that both value and disvalue are themselves things that exist as consciously lived, with the consequence that if no persons existed, neither value nor disvalue would

12. Santayana, *The Sense of Beauty*, 17.

exist—just as the acts of inference, insight, willing, veneration, and love could not exist in an apersonal world.

As we have already seen, this last assertion is clearly erroneous. Neither moral value nor the aesthetic values are personally enacted beings. It would be more correct to say that in a world without persons, it would never be possible for moral values such as justice, purity, or generosity to be realized, since they necessarily presuppose persons as the bearers of these values. This, however, is not true of aesthetic values, since many apersonal forms are bearers of beauty; and besides this, as Max Scheler correctly observed, the moral values exist "on the back of the human act."[13] Since this act is their bearer, they never themselves become something that is consciously experienced from within. We do not come to know them in the enactment of the act, in a lateral consciousness; we do not come to know them in the same way as we come to know joy or love.

This is a very interesting problem, but we need not discuss it here, since it is clearly not an essential trait of values *qua* values that they adhere to persons and presuppose the acts of these persons as their bearers. Rather, this is a specific characteristic of moral values. It is indeed found in other values too, such as "intellectual" values, but certainly not in all values—neither in values belonging to states-of-affairs nor (above all) in aesthetic values. It is clear that when Santayana makes his assertion, he is not thinking of the question of what kind of being is presupposed for the *objective* bearing of values; instead, he attempts to interpret all values as "emotions."[14]

The alleged dependence of all values on personal consciousness

But Santayana is not in the first place concerned with affirming that values are of such a nature that their existence would disintegrate if it were not grasped by a personal spirit. And besides, this affirmation would be incorrect. It is certainly meaningful to say that there would be no illusion,

13. Ibid., 49.
14. Ibid., 17–18.

nor any dream, if there were no persons and no "consciousness of." In an apersonal world, there would be only the distinction between existing and not existing—but never between existing in reality and existing in appearance. In the appearance, there is an essential relationship to a person and this person's "consciousness of"; it is only *for someone* that something can appear. The house in one's hallucination does not really exist; it is only the conscious act of hallucinating that is full reality. The encounter with another person of which one dreamed did not take place in reality; but the "consciousness of," which is represented by the act of dreaming, was completely real. This is the glorious discovery of Saint Augustine in his *si fallor, sum*,[15] and the basic truth justifiably emphasized by Descartes in his *cogito, ergo sum*. Each of these propositions is the fundamental refutation of skepticism, each is the absolutely certain affirmation of authentic objective reality.

The assertion that values would not exist if they were not perceived by a person—implying that it would be meaningless to say, "Justice is a moral value," if there is no one who has a consciousness of it—would either present values as mere illusions, robbing them totally of the autonomy of their being, or else declare that they come into existence only in relation to a personal spirit. An example of the latter: a fact serving as a premise (unlike efficient causes and all essential ontological relationships) essentially includes a relationship to a possible act of knowing. The premise is objectively valid and is not in any way subjective, but it includes an essential "for" some possible knower.

The assertion that values are mere illusions is completely unproven, indeed clearly false. It is obvious that we make a distinction here (as we do everywhere in the knowledge of values) between illusion and reality. We can make a mistake by following an ideal that subsequently turns out to be an idol. We can be mistaken about the concrete value of a person or an action; for example, we can come to see that an apparently selfless action was in reality determined by egotistic motives. There is no basis whatever for the assertion that all values entail the kind of dependence

15. Saint Augustine, *The City of God*, book 11, section 26: "If I err, I am."

on the *person* who is possessed by the hallucinated object (in contradistinction to the real object). In this dependence we see a minimal existence which is derived only from being the content of a "consciousness of." But this is not what Santayana means when he says that with the disappearance of the consciousness all values disappear as well. As for the completely objective, essential relationship to a personal act that exists in a premise, this is also not present in values. It would be entirely false to assert that the genuine values are essentially related to the act of knowledge. The relationship between moral value and justice does not contain any kind of relation to knowledge, as we can see when we compare this with the relationship of guarantee that exists when we say, "I see smoke, so there must be a fire." Rather, this relationship between justice and moral value is objectively based in the essence of justice. However, Santayana has something else in mind.

His subsequent remarks make clear what he means when he asserts that all values stand and fall with the existence of personal consciousness. He not only says that "consciousness" is the indispensable presupposition of values, but he speaks here explicitly of "emotional consciousness." In a world in which there existed only a purely intellectual consciousness—a world in which the object of knowledge evoked no emotion, in which every event was registered and the relationships between events were noted, but without the slightest trace of desire, pleasure, or regret—no event would be repulsive, no situation terrible. He then infers that we can conceive of a world in which there was no will. In that case, all values would disappear, just as in a world devoid of all consciousness.[16]

The sudden transition from emotional experiences to the will, or the equation between desiring (*desiderare*) and the will, is surprising. The will is a spiritual act that presupposes an object endowed with one of the three forms of importance. The only situations we can desire are those that are important in one form or another. If the only situations that existed were neutral and indifferent, there would be no possible motivation for the will. It would then be correct to say that in a completely neutral world, in

16. Santayana, *The Sense of Beauty*, 17–18.

which there was no form of importance—neither that which is important-in-itself (a value), nor an objective good for the person, nor something that was satisfying in a merely subjective manner—the will could not function. It is not the importance that presupposes the will, but *vice versa*: it is the will that presupposes the importance.

In addition, it is very infelicitous to say that the will belongs to the "emotional" consciousness, since this involves a serious confusion. If need be, all emotional experiences can be called "affective." This includes everything from physical pleasure and pain, states such as depression, good and bad moods, up to the spiritual affective responses such as joy, grief, love, and all those experiences where we can make a distinction between negative and positive, in the sense that some of these experiences make us happy and others make us unhappy. The emotional experiences in this broadest sense of the term also include the various forms of being-affected (being touched, being deeply shaken by an event) and entirely different experiences such as enjoying. Similarly, every desire, every yearning, every longing is emotional in this broader sense. But the will cannot be subsumed even under this broadened, imprecise, and infelicitous concept of "the emotional"—infelicitous because its starting point is the lowest forms of "emotion," and because these serve as the paradigm for the entire affective realm. The volitional reactions are clearly distinct from the affective responses, as well as from the purely theoretical responses such as conviction and doubt. Even when we take our starting point in the highest forms of the "emotional" sphere, namely, the spiritual affective responses, the will is clearly distinct from these, since it is completely different from them in a formal sense.[17]

The distortion of values by the appetitus theory

In our present context, however, there is something much more important than these confusions in Santayana's thesis, namely, the affirmation which he presents as an axiom and which is an unambiguous expression

17. Cf. my *Ethics*, chap. 17.

of the value relativism that takes on so many forms. He declares that there is an axiom fundamental to every ethics, an axiom "fatal to certain stubborn patterns of thought," namely, that there exist no values without an appreciation of these values, and that "good" is nonexistent apart from the act of preferring one thing to another.

He says explicitly: "In appreciation, in preference lies the root and the essence of all excellence."[18] He appeals here to Spinoza's dictum in his *Ethics* that we do not desire something because it is good; rather, it is good only because we desire it. Santayana is correct to call his value relativism an "axiom," since all he does is assert it without offering any kind of evidence for it. He does not take the trouble to genuinely investigate the facts, the data; he introduces an axiom that does not correspond in any way to the facts. He makes no distinctions of any kind in the realm of what he calls "emotional." He fails to distinguish between a value judgment and an affective response to a value, and appeals to a thesis that Spinoza himself asserts in a completely arbitrary manner, without demonstrating it in any way.

Here, however, we must look at the various possible interpretations of this theory.

There is nothing new about the thesis that the importance of a being is derived from its ability to meet and satisfy the needs, desires, and longings—subsumed under the term *appetitus*—which are present in the nature of the human person. We find the beginnings of this theory as early as Aristotle, and it is further developed by Saint Thomas. Fortunately, however, it has never been applied with complete consistency. And when Thomas takes up the topic of moral value, for example, the moral value of an action, this attempt to derive all values from the satisfaction of an *appetitus* moves into the background; it is instead the *secundum naturam* (that which is "in accordance with nature") that occupies the foreground. The derivation from the *appetitus* is abandoned, objectively speaking, when Thomas affirms that the moral commandments of God, unlike the positive commandments, do not merely flow out of His will,

18. Santayana, *The Sense of Beauty*, 18.

but correspond to His being. In other words, the moral values of the human person are implicitly understood as a *similitudo Dei* (a "likeness to God").[19]

We need not discuss in detail the error which asserts that all importance is derived from the satisfaction of an *appetitus.* I have already done this in chapter 8 of my *Ethics*, and in still greater detail in chapter 1 of my book *The Nature of Love.* Although this thesis fully acknowledges the transcendence of the human person in knowledge, it completely overlooks this very transcendence when it turns every value-response into an *appetitus.* Something that is genuinely present in the case of thirst—namely, that water becomes important to the thirsty person because of his thirst, but that it loses at least *this* importance once the thirst is quenched—is extended to the utterly different situation in which we rejoice at the liberation of an innocent captive or at a heroic moral action performed by a human being. In the case of thirst, thirst is the *principium* (the cause) and the importance of the water is the *principiatum* (the effect); but in the case of joy or enthusiasm over the moral action of a human being, the moral value is the *principium* and our response the *principiatum.*

Reality is turned completely upside down when the importance of value is made to consist in its capacity to satisfy a need or a striving which is present in human nature. The autonomous existence of values is an unambiguous fact, as is their importance-in-itself—in these facts there is nothing to justify such a view. One does violence to the facts in order to justify the general principle that *ens et bonum convertuntur.*[20] For according to this principle, it is only through its relation to an *appetitus* that *ens* becomes a *bonum* and thus is elevated above its neutral quality so as to become important—it is important only in view of an *appetitus.* One has said everything about the *ens* as such as soon as one knows that it is a being. However, this proposition is not evident, nor is it in any way proven. The *appetitus* theory is the attempt at an oversimplified answer

19. Cf. Saint Thomas Aquinas, *Summa Theologicae* I, q. 80; I-II, q. 62; q. 93, a. 6, ad 1; q. 94, a. 2.

20. Cf. Saint Thomas Aquinas, *Summa Theologicae* I, q. 5, a. 1 and q. 16, a 3 ("Good and being are convertible").

to the great metaphysical problem of the relationship between being and value.[21]

As I said, I have shown this in other writings; what we must emphasize at present is that according to the *appetitus* theory—in contradistinction to the value relativism of Santayana, Ralph Barton Perry, Dewey, and innumerable other modern philosophers—the object does possess a quality that corresponds to the *appetitus* that is present in the essence of the human person. In other words, it possesses the ability to satisfy this *appetitus.* The traditional convertibility doctrine does not in any way deny the objective validity of a value judgment. All it does is reduce all importance to one specific form of objective good for the person; but it does not intend to derive all importance from what is merely satisfying to me—something that varies from person to person.

The *appetitus* theory is false, and it completely misunderstands the essence of value, of the important-in-itself, although it continually presupposes this in a tacit manner. But this theory is not in any way a value relativism which makes "value" into an expression of a desire that can vary from one person to another.

At this point, we encounter once again the equivocal element in the concept of "relative," which designates *both* an objective relationship between one thing and another *and* a denial of objective validity, the affirmation that something "just seems so to us." Aristotle pointed out this central distinction long ago. We have already pointed to the objective relatedness to a possible knowledge that characterizes a premise in an argument. This is a classic example of the complete objective validity of relatedness to a personal spirit—in this case, to knowledge. The premise provides, in an objectively valid manner, a basis for possible knowledge, and this function distinguishes it from everything that "merely appears to be so." The achievement of the premise in an argument, that is, to guarantee the existence of another fact for possible knowledge, is itself not relative to a human mind. It exists completely objectively in itself.

21. See Josef Seifert, "Die verschiedenen Bedeutungen von 'Sein'—Dietrich von Hildebrand als Metaphysiker und Martin Heideggers Vorwurf der Seinsvergessenheit," in *Wahrheit, Wert und Sein,* 301–32.

We could also express this point by saying that the judgment that one fact constitutes the basis for knowing another fact is itself objectively true. In its truth it is not in any way true only "for" a personal mind.

In the false *appetitus* theory we find something analogous to this objectively valid relatedness to the human mind, but this theory does not, like modern value relativism, argue for the dissolution of all values.

The subjectivization and relativization of beauty (Spinoza)

Spinoza made a disastrously erroneous claim, which has been quoted again and again, namely, that we do not desire something because it is good, but that something is good only because we desire it. This entails a much further-reaching subjectivization of value than in the *appetitus* theory. Like this theory, Spinoza transfers the source of the importance from the object to the human person, but behind this subjectivization in his philosophy there lies a general idol of neutrality, an anti-qualitative attitude, which finds clear expression in the fact that for him (unlike for Saint Thomas) God is not the embodiment of all values, of all goodness and holiness, but lies beyond good and evil. This radically separates his understanding of values from the *appetitus* theory. Spinoza's thesis entails a dethroning of values that comes much closer to modern value relativism. Similarly, his view of love as a pleasure that we feel when confronted with an object displays a radical misunderstanding of all intentionality. Love is merely a feeling of pleasure evoked by an object. Santayana does not adduce any arguments in favor of Spinoza's thesis, nor does he seek to demonstrate it; he does not offer any unprejudiced analysis of the data. At most, we find a deduction from general principles that are neither evident nor proven.

We must distinguish here two elements which often go hand in hand, namely, subjectivism and relativism. The subjectivist theory denies that beauty is a quality of an object, and declares it to be something existing in the mind, a feeling, or a mental satisfaction, etc. Relativism goes further, by refusing to recognize any kind of objective validity in beauty. Any judgment that ascribes beauty to a being is relative to exactly the same degree as the judgment, "I like the taste of beans." Indeed, there are even some who deny that a value judgment can in fact be called a genuine proposition. According to Ayer and Carnap, a value judgment is in reality nothing other than an exclamation, like the cry "ouch!" when someone steps on your foot. In other words, it is the pure expression of a feeling.

All I wish to do here is to draw a distinction between the subjectivization and the relativization of beauty, since the assertion that something is an experience lived in me or by me has *per se* nothing to do with the question of objective validity. The grief that I feel at the death of a beloved person is subjective in the sense that it is of its essence something that exists as conscious, as the act of a human being, as something lived in a personal manner. As such, it is not only a complete and real entity, but also a higher form of reality than any physical process such as the movement of a body, the flowing of a river, etc. The existence of grief is not relative to me like some impersonal object that only seems to exist but has no objective existence. It is of course true that the grief presupposes my person, because it is enacted by me. It is a part of my conscious being—but in its existence, it is completely objective in the sense that it does not exist "for me" like some appearance, or like some subjective aspect. In addition, if the object objectively demands and deserves *this* response, the grief is the objectively *correct* behavior. The value of this correctness is not in the least relativized by the fact that we are speaking of a mental act. It is not difficult to see that the values adhering to an act are completely objective (for example, the moral value of an act of forgiving).

Santayana's erroneous distinction between value judgments and judgments of fact

We encounter total value relativism in Santayana when he says that all value—which for him means what I call "importance," since he does not have the true concept of value as distinguished from what is objectively good for the person and what is merely subjectively satisfying—has its origin in the immediate and inexplicable reactions of vital impulses, and in the irrational part of our nature.[22] This section of his book on the rational and irrational parts in the human person teems with completely "dogmatic" assertions and confusions. It is also here that Santayana's epistemological relativism and his pragmatism come to full flower, but we shall not discuss these topics here, since we find much more interesting what he says about the essence of beauty. First we find an indubitably correct proposition: "It is evident that beauty is a species of value."[23] It is true beyond any doubt that beauty is not something neutral or indifferent but rather something important. But when he immediately goes on to say, "what we have said of value in general applies to this particular kind,"[24] the observation (in itself correct) that beauty is a kind of value becomes a great error, since it then contains the assertion that beauty is not important-in-itself but is only something subjectively satisfying for me; it is supposed to be a product of immediate, irrational impulses. In a word, it is not a value in the true sense of the term, since Santayana holds that there are no values in this sense.

It is even more remarkable that he adduces concrete, correct facts as proof of his erroneous thesis about beauty. Thus he is correct to say, "If we approach a work of art or nature scientifically, for the sake of its historical connexions or proper classification, we do not approach it aesthetically. The discovery of its date or of its author may be otherwise interesting; it only remotely affects our aesthetic appreciation by adding to the direct effect certain associations." This observation is in itself correct, but it is employed as an argument for the assertion that "[t]o substitute judgments of fact for judgments of value, is a sign of a pedantic and borrowed criticism."[25] This last sentence displays yet again the erroneous idea (to which I have already drawn attention) that facts are essentially neutral and are therefore different from value judgments. I have already said that although the observation of neutral facts is different

22. Santayana, *The Sense of Beauty*, 19.
23. Ibid., 20.
24. Ibid.
25. Ibid.

from the perception of values, value is something that really exists. Similarly, the observation that something is beautiful refers to a fact, to something that exists in reality. Here Santayana adduces facts such as the year in which a work was produced or the name of the author, as if such facts were the only possible objects of perception, and he infers from this that all perceptions are irrelevant to the beauty of a painting or a piece of music, and that there is no objective perception nor any true judgment about the beauty of a work of art, no judgment that refers to the fact—this is what is decisive for us at present—of the beauty of the painting, no judgment that can be true or false.

His emphasis on the immediacy of the "impression," which is decisively important for the perception of beauty—in contradistinction to many things that we only know about a work of art—would likewise be correct if he had not understood "impression" as a mere "effect" upon us, and the perception of values as a subjective reaction.

It is very interesting to note that while false or at least insufficient evidence is often adduced on behalf of great truths, here, by contrast, correct observations are adduced on behalf of an error.

It is completely unjustifiable to deny a fact on the grounds that the evidence of its existence is insufficient. The insufficient arguments cannot prove the truth of a proposition—nor can they demonstrate its falsity. The affirmation of the immortality of the soul is not refuted by the fact that some of the arguments put forward in favor of this proposition do not hold water. And even when observations which are correct (although they include some unclarities and equivocations) are adduced on behalf of an incorrect thesis, we must not allow ourselves to be dazzled by the correctness of these observations, which are not in any sense a proof of this thesis, nor allow ourselves to be disposed to view it favorably.

The perception of beauty and the value-response to it, as opposed to a projection

We shall now concentrate on the situation that is genuinely present in every perception of values, including the perception of beauty.

We have already drawn a distinction between the value of the object, in the full sense of this term, and the value-response that we make to the good to which the value attaches. We have seen that the perception of a value is an explicit frontal "consciousness of," not something that is lived laterally (like the responding to the value). I am joyful, I experience joy; but I have a consciousness of beauty, I discover it, it reveals itself, it discloses itself to me on the side of the object. Every attempt at equating the two, by interpreting beauty itself as an emotion that is only projected by us onto the object, contradicts the facts.

As Reinach correctly emphasized,[26] the best way to recognize the difference between things is to ask what we can predicate of one object but not of another. C. S. Lewis has rightly pointed out[27] the absurdity of the assertion that when we say a landscape is sublime, what we are really affirming is an emotion that we experience when seeing the landscape and that we merely project falsely onto the landscape itself. This absurdity is revealed by the fact that the emotion felt in looking at the landscape is not itself sublime. Rather, we feel humility and reverence in the encounter with the sublimity of the landscape. And consider this: we can indeed say that our enthusiasm over the beauty of a piece of music was greater the last time we heard this music than it is today; but it is obvious that we cannot meaningfully say that the piece of music itself was more beautiful a week ago than it is today.

26. Adolf Reinach, "A Contribution Towards a Theory of the Negative Judgment," trans. Don Ferrari, *Aletheia* 2 (1981): 33.

27. In *The Abolition of Man* (New York: Collier Books, 1962), 14–15, Lewis quotes from a school textbook in which the authors (whom he presents under the pseudonyms "Gaius" and "Titius") write: "When the man said *That is sublime,* he appeared to be making a remark about the waterfall. . . . Actually . . . he was not making a remark about the waterfall, but a remark about his own feelings. What he was saying was really *I have feelings associated in my mind with the word 'Sublime,'* or shortly, *I have sublime feelings.*" Lewis takes this theory *ad absurdum* when he goes on to write: "Even on their own view—on any conceivable view—the man who says *This is sublime* cannot mean *I have sublime feelings.* Even if it were granted that such qualities as sublimity were simply and solely projected into things from our own emotions, yet the emotions which prompt the projection are the correlatives, and therefore almost the opposites, of the qualities projected. The feelings which make a man call an object sublime are not sublime feelings but feelings of veneration. If *This is sublime* is to be reduced at all to a statement about the speaker's feelings, the proper translation would be *I have humble feelings.* If the view held by Gaius and Titius were consistently applied it would lead to obvious absurdities. It would force them to maintain that *You are contemptible* means *I have contemptible feelings,* and in fact that *Your feelings are contemptible* means *My feelings are contemptible.*"

Every attempt to present beauty as a product of our own response is a clear contradiction of the facts. Value-responses always presuppose the perception of a value on the side of the object. As we have seen, value-responses are a personal reality, something that exists consciously, and are thus objectively distinct from the values to which they respond. They can never be generated without a "consciousness of" the values on the side of the object. Enthusiasm over the beauty of a melody is essentially a response. More precisely, it is an affective and intentionally meaningful response to the beauty that one has recognized.

Clearly, however, Santayana does not have in mind the meaningful, intentional responses. All the value relativists move within their own unphenomenological constructions; they are much too little concerned about the facts to be able ever to discover such intentional meaningful responses. They are blind to the difference between intentional meaningful responses such as joy, enthusiasm, and love, on the one hand, and purely physical states such as depression, a cheerful mood, pleasure, and pain, on the other. This emerges clearly in Santayana when he emphasizes the irrational character of everything "emotional"[28] and speaks of mere "reactions" which are more or less a matter of chance. However, these emotional reactions are not responses which presuppose the value of the object: they can be conditioned by purely physical factors, for example, the cheerful mood which comes from drinking alcohol, or the depression which comes from too little sleep. These states are psychic realities. They are something that exists consciously, whereas the beauty of the Farnese Palace in Rome or Michelangelo's *Dying Slave* does not in fact exist in the onlooker's mind, but possesses a completely different form of existence. This beauty reveals itself unambiguously as something adhering to the object and not as a mental state which takes place in us. We can formulate predicates about these states, but such predicates become meaningless when we apply them to the beauty of the objects. Is the reaction evoked in us by a beautiful object merely the effect of some cause (as when the sight of something nauseating makes us want to

28. Santayana, *The Sense of Beauty*, 17–18.

vomit), or is it merely a chance coincidence in time between the perception of an object and a state which has quite different causes? Obviously, the latter alternative would be even more absurd.

At this point, however, the value relativists would object that while of course the beauty appears in the object—a point that no one denies!—it appears only as the consequence of a projection. We project the emotion of pleasure or displeasure that the object evokes in us, or that we at any rate experience when we look at the object, onto the object itself. The positive or negative importance that the object thereby acquires derives exclusively from the pleasure or displeasure that we feel, since by definition this distinction between positive and negative comes into existence only through our feeling pleasure or displeasure.

We must look more closely at this celebrated "projection" of our "emotions" onto the object, and the best way to undertake a critical examination is to begin with those cases in which we genuinely find something like a projection.

It may, for example, happen that, thanks to a state of sheer depression which is brought about by physical causes, the whole world is bathed in a gloomy light. Everything that we must do, all the events that lie ahead of us, appear to be objectively difficult and unsettling. Something that is in reality free of risk appears dangerous; something that is easily attainable appears insuperably hard. Are we really projecting the depression onto these objects? No. Our depression makes it impossible for us to evaluate the objects objectively. We attribute to them qualities that they do not possess—but qualities that they can in principle possess, such as "difficult," "dangerous," etc. Because of our mood, we see things in a false light. But we are not projecting our experience into the things: what we project are qualities that could be motives of our depression. The term "to project" is used here in an analogous sense. Obviously, all the products of these projections disappear as soon as the mood changes, or as soon as someone recognizes that he is depressed and has diagnosed his state as exclusively physical, or as conditioned by the repression of an earlier negative experience. For then he sees clearly that his judgment about the things, tasks, and events around him was a prejudice, and that these objects do not possess qualities of that kind, but are either neutral or else easy, pleasant, etc. This so-called projection is indeed a possible source of deception, to which some persons are more prone than others. It is, however, always clearly distinct from those cases in which someone grasps a genuine quality of objects and his judgment is not clouded by this source of deception.

It is needless to add that the same thing can happen in a euphoric mood. This can make every object and one's present situation in life appear in a rosy light, so that things appear at the moment in a manner that does not correspond to reality.

Another type of much more literal projection occurs when I project my experiences into another person. Because I am on edge, the other person seems to me to be on edge, his attitude seems to me to be unfriendly, or, to take a widespread illusion, because someone is in love, he projects his own feelings into the other, and then the words of the other, as well as her behavior toward him, appear to him to be an expression of the requital of his love. This type of projection differs from the previously mentioned type in that what is projected into the other is essentially of the same type as the projecting experience, namely, a personal act. I ascribe to the other person what I myself experience, I have the impression that he feels the same as I do. But this certainly need not be the case. The justified observation that the other person loves me, because he manifests this in word and in deed, is by contrast not in any way a projection. But even here it is possible for a projection to be a source of deception, which is clearly distinct from the true observation of a fact. This projection lies behind many cases of wishful thinking.

A projection in the true sense of the term occurs when, for example, I assume that another person is acting out of the same motives as I myself. A money-grubbing person cannot imagine that someone does something for any other reason than to make money. But this is not a true understanding of another person. How often do we learn of motivations that we ourselves have never previously experienced, for example, a heroism of which we were never capable (at least, up to now)? We must realize that our normal supposition of motives in another person does not derive from a projection, but from understanding the meaningful relation between the value (or the other kinds of importance) of an object and the appropriate response to this object, a relation that is grasped intuitively.

When we understand why someone who has lost his mother, to whom he was very devoted, is sad, we make neither an inference from ourselves to the other person nor a supposition derived from our personal experience. This meaningful motivation was presupposed by Freud, too, when he discovered the phenomenon of repression. The insight that a trivial event or a neutral object cannot be the reason for tremendous excitement or grief led him to the idea that this conscious object to which the response is made cannot be the true reason for the behavior of this person: it must be a "representative" of something that has been repressed into the unconscious. It is only this that explains the impact on the person.

Another type of genuine projection occurs in "phantom pains," for example, when someone's leg has been amputated and he feels pain in that foot. Here the projection takes place not from a subjective process into an objective process, but from a physical pain to a place where it does not in fact exist. There is a physiological reason for this false localization of the pain. This is in one sense the objectivized form of the deception, and it continues to exist as an impression even when I know that it is a deception.

The decisive point is that in all true projections a possible deception occurs. With the exception of the last instance, however, this is clearly different from the normal, genuine perception of the object and its qualities.

We need only compare this genuine act of projection, which can be observed as such, with those instances in which there is no projection but rather a genuine "consciousness of"—more specifically, the recognition of a quality, a specific characteristic, of the object, of a value attaching to it—in order to see clearly how impossible it is to interpret every act of the apprehension of value as the projection of an emotion onto the object. It is only against the background of genuine perception that the act of dreaming can be seen for what it is. Similarly, it is only against the background of a genuine knowledge of the object that we can recognize the act of projection.

The attempt to explain beauty by means of association

The attempt to explain beauty by means of association is similar to the explanation by means of projection. "Association" is one of those terms to which the words of Goethe's *Faust* truly apply: "For precisely where concepts are lacking, a word turns up at the right time."[29] As soon as it is a question of a relationship which demands a genuine act of understanding and a deeper penetration into it, thinkers very often take refuge in "association." The attempt is made to explain the relationship between the word and the object to which it refers, the profoundly meaningful relationship of signifying and denoting, by means of "association." Or it is claimed that the knowledge that the lily is white, and has a particular shape and a particular fragrance, is attained through association. Or it is asserted that the music of Mozart's *Don Giovanni* does not give expression to the figure of Don Giovanni; it is only by means of association that we link the idea of this personality with this music. Every link between word and music is said to be built exclusively on association, and the beauty of a piece of music is said to be linked to this music only by means of association. We associate pleasant feelings with a piece of music. We could go on in the same vein for hours, if we wanted to list all the instances in which philosophers (or at any rate, those who think they are philosophers) take refuge in association. Here too it suffices to reflect on genuine association in order to recognize the completely equivocal use of this term, and to see that in all the other instances in which people take refuge in association there exist relationships that are radically different from genuine association.

A typical case of genuine association is the purely subjective linkage between two contents, a linkage not based on their specific character. For

29. Goethe, *Faust*, part I, verse 1995.

example, when we are falling asleep, one image follows another, without there being any meaningful objective linkage between them. It is typical of the state of distraction that we hear a word, and our consciousness is suddenly withdrawn from the object to which this word refers, or from the matter to which the sentence refers, and we begin to think of completely different things, for the sole reason that this word sounds like the other word of which we now begin to think.

Or we are accustomed to one particular sequence of words when we have learned a poem by heart. The fact that the next word automatically appears once I have spoken the previous word is a process of association, unlike the interconnectedness of the words which we join together in a sentence when we make a statement. The mechanical, automatic character of the association when we recite something that we have learned by heart is also expressed in the fact that the automatic process which leads us from one word to the next is suddenly interrupted when we get stuck at one word, or say a different word at some point. A rational reflection on the meaning of the missing word will not necessarily restart this process; usually we have to go back to an earlier point in the previous passage in order to get back into this automatic process. Similarly, there is a risk, once we have learned by heart a poem in which the same words occur as in another poem, that we will suddenly append to these words in the first poem something that follows the same words in the second poem. In other words, we are caught up in the irrational, mechanical process of purely habitual association. Memorization is a deliberately produced association. We attempt, through the frequent repetition of a literary passage, to establish a functioning association.

Something similar occurs when we learn a foreign language and continually repeat a word in this language in association with a word which meaningfully designates an object in a language we already know. There is a world of difference between the relationship of meaning [*Bedeutung*], on the one hand, and every association, on the other.

Nor is association involved when I grasp that the French word *cheval* means *horse* in English. The person who teaches me French informs me of the fact that *cheval* in this language means *horse.* This is a meaningful piece of knowledge which is completely different from any association. But let us suppose that my aim is to speak intelligibly in French in such a way that whenever I aim with my conscious intention at *horse*, I will not need to search laboriously for the correct word, nor ask someone for information: the word *cheval* will then automatically occur to me. In that case, I will try to establish a completely automatic process of association between *cheval* and *horse*, so that this word occurs to me as soon as I need it for purposes of communication or assertion.

Here we have an association that we ourselves have explicitly created. Its only function is to serve our intellectual life. In the other examples mentioned above, for example, when we are falling asleep or distracted, we are not dealing with associations explicitly created by ourselves, but rather with associations that have arisen by custom or by some accidental external similarity or by a frequent simultaneous experience of two things, etc. This unintentional, more or less "wild" association is the antithesis of every meaningful, objectively based link with the object; it is even the antithesis of everything that we ourselves consciously link with it.

There are completely absurd associations, as, for example, when some people link one particular color with a number. Often quite arbitrary links to images resonate in the background when we speak meaningfully of an object. For example, when Napoleon is mentioned, our minds see the famous image of him with his arms crossed. But as Reinach (from whom this example comes) said, this image which surfaces in our minds must be clearly distinguished from the person of Napoleon, which is the only object of our intention. Although this merely associative resonance is not absurd (like the link between the color red and the number three), it is radically different from every meaningful link. It does not even serve a meaningful process, like the mechanism of association in learning a text by heart, or the memorization that goes with learning a foreign language. As I have said, it is a "wild" association.

A melody can remind us of one specific period of our life, perhaps the beginnings of love or some other great, intense experience, or perhaps a country in which we lived at one time and its particular atmosphere.

Much more is entailed here than a mere association. There is of course no objective affinity between the melody and this or that experience; such an affinity can doubtless exist, but it need not. This is why we shall concentrate on those cases where no such affinity of a qualitative nature exists.

What we see here is no naked association, but a kind of "investing." In one particularly important period of our life, we often heard the melody, so that a certain "investing" of this melody in that time took place. The melody entered the total atmosphere, or else we ourselves "invested" in that melody a relationship to that particular period. In some sense, the melody has become for us a representative of that period. When we hear it at a later date, it transports us in an intensive manner back into that period and evokes in us a specific kind of presence of what we experienced then.

As I have said, there is more here than just an association. Nevertheless, this "investing" is a boundary case which has much in common with association, even as it is very unlike every other form of perceiving, coming to know, meaningful thinking, etc. Association is a purely immanent psychological process, unlike all objective meaningful relations and every transcending act whereby we apprehend something.

What I wish to do here is to demonstrate the impossibility of deriving the beauty of the Gulf of Spezia, or San Marco in Venice, or the beauty of the adagio in Beethoven's "Harp Quartet" (opus 74, the string quartet in E flat major) from associations of any kind. We do not associate with them any feelings of pleasure, or mental states of any kind, nor any particular situation from our life into which they transpose us; for their beauty reveals itself clearly and unambiguously as a quality of these things. Similarly, the clear insight that one painting is beautiful, while another is insignificant or trivial or tasteless, has nothing at all to do with associations.[30] We do not associate any feelings of pleasure or displeas-

30. I cannot accept the objection that there are in fact many persons whose relationship to works of art is constituted in part by association, or at least by non-aesthetic sources. I do not in the least wish to deny this fact, and I shall speak in detail in the second volume of this work about the substitutes for the authentic relationship to works of art. Santayana too admits this difference between aesthetic and extra-aesthetic motives; he refers to it in passing in his discussion of the distinction between value judgments and judgments about facts (*The Sense of Beauty*, 20)—a distinction in his thinking which, as I have already said, is highly dubious. Although he adduces it as evidence in support of his unfortunate theory, he has at any rate seen the difference between aesthetic and extra-aesthetic criteria in the evaluation of a work of art.

ure with them; nor do they need to remind us of anything else, in order to reveal themselves in their value or disvalue.

Someone might object that it surely cannot be denied that beauty makes us happy. It may not be linked by way of association to a pleasurable experience on our part, but the link does nevertheless exist. The answer to this objection is: But of course; it is a quality of all values, and especially of beauty, that they affect us in a specific and unique manner. We do not only perceive beauty and grasp the value of beauty: our heart is touched by it. The perception of beauty's value and the perception of beauty itself are a typical "consciousness of." But while being-affected doubtless presupposes a "consciousness of," it goes beyond this, since it activates in our soul something that exists in a personal manner, something with a specifically affective nature.

Being affected by beauty

I have written in detail in Part I of my book *The Heart*, and in even greater detail in my book *The Nature of Love*, about what it means to be affected. Accordingly, I limit myself here to discussing the specific way

Once, however, we have seen in a clear and fundamental manner this distinction between aesthetic and extra-aesthetic perspectives, my assertion is confirmed that associations play no role of any kind in one who unambiguously perceives the beauty of a work of art.

As I have said, this does not exclude the possibility that many people deceive themselves about the reason why they are affected by a melody. There are reasons unconnected with the aesthetic dimension which make people interested in objects and find pleasure in them, and such reasons block their access to aesthetic values. We will speak in greater detail in volume II of these extra-aesthetic elements. Here I wish only to underline that some people enjoy a melody because they are reminded by it of happy times in their lives. This melody can affect them, touch them, make them happy, etc., in a variety of ways. But it affects them not through its beauty, but merely through its ability to transpose them back into those times. It has then a purely instrumental function. What *really* affects them is the happy time. We can make this point more precise: their experience of being touched and made happy is a fruit of their recalling the happy time, and the melody helps them recall it. Even primitive persons who lack any marked aesthetic sensitivity seldom extol and praise such a melody as "beautiful." Rather, they like to hear it, and it helps them have the experience of becoming moved. They take pleasure in it, but they scarcely come to the point where they speak explicitly of its beauty. Above all, someone who has a relationship to the piece of music, and is capable of perceiving its beauty or lack of beauty, will draw a clear distinction between this beauty or lack of beauty and the importance that a melody acquires through its ability to remind him of a particular period, an experience, or a person. He will be perfectly aware that this value of remembrance has nothing to do with the beauty of the melody.

in which one is affected by beauty and by its opposite. When we hear a beautiful melody, we not only perceive its beauty: it takes hold of our heart and makes us happy, it infuses something into our soul. It touches our heart and fills our soul with a particular happiness. Beauty can take hold of us and move us to tears; it can fill us with light and with confidence; it can enthrall us, take us into the depths, and draw us *in conspectu Dei* ("before the face of God").

This experience of being-affected is fundamentally different from every mere "effect." There is no causal relationship, such as exists between a loud noise and my being startled, or between joviality and the state of being slightly drunk, the so-called being merry with wine. In the experience of being-affected, there exists an intentional, meaningful relationship. In its intentional character, it is comparable to motivation, but in another sense it is typically different from this.

Being affected not only presupposes a "consciousness of" the beauty of the object; it also shares with this "consciousness of" a receptive character that distinguishes it from all stances of the person, including all responses (and especially all value-responses). When I am affected, the object speaks to me and I receive the "word" of beauty. It penetrates my heart. It generates a particular affective experience in my soul, an experience full of joy. But this experience of being-affected is clearly distinct from the beauty of the object on the object side. It is ontologically and qualitatively very different from the beauty. The "emotion," the happiness, being led into one's depths, being raised up above oneself—all of which are conscious experiences, psychological-mental entities that are generated in my soul by the beauty which affects me and are gifts or fruits of being-affected (or, as we might also say, *modes* of being-affected)—these are clearly qualitatively different from the beauty. They are not a conscious enacting [*bewusstes Vollziehen*] of the beauty, since that is an impossibility. Their qualitative content is not beauty, but happiness, being profoundly moved, etc. They are personal entities belonging to the psyche and the spirit; they are not apersonal entities like beauty.

This is why it is completely impossible to appeal to the experience of being-affected in order to make beauty a product of the happiness which beauty itself generates and nourishes. The specific character of being-affected shows us clearly the ontological and qualitative difference between beauty and its "effect" in our soul. It also shows that beauty is the *principium* (that which originates), and our being profoundly moved by beauty is the *principiatum* (that which is originated). It is precisely this most intimate touching of our soul by beauty, through the experience of being-affected, that shows us how impossible it is to make beauty a product or a projection of the experience that beauty awakens in us, and that can be awakened only by beauty.

The act of perceiving the beauty of an object, and the experience of being-affected by this, are also clearly different from all those processes in our soul that the beautiful object can set in motion in us *apart from* its beauty. When we hear the melody that draws us back into a happy period and therefore touches and moves us, we are completely aware that this does not make the melody beautiful: this effect is engendered by non-aesthetic qualities.

Beauty essentially possesses the importance of value

Let me once again insist as forcefully as possible: the importance that beauty possesses is eminently the importance of value in the true sense of this term. It is not merely an objective good for me; even less is it something that is only subjectively satisfying for me.

There can be no doubt that beauty is *also* a lofty objective good for us, but this is because of its value. When we say that beauty, or rather those things that are the bearers of beauty, are objective goods for the person, we mean that these belong to that category of objective goods for the person in which things of intrinsic importance, or value, superabundantly overflow into objective goods for us. But beauty does not derive its importance, that which raises it above the indifferent, from what it can achieve *for me*, for my existence, my happiness. Unlike something like health, or the minimum amount of money required to sustain our life, or safety from persecution, beauty is not in the first place an objective good *for me.* Unlike these, its importance is not an importance "for." It is not constituted by this character of benevolence, of being a gift for me. I have discussed this in detail in my *Ethics* (especially in chapter 3).

It is a fundamental and decisive difference that we find between, on the one hand, all experiences of pleasure, all non-intentional states of a positive kind, and all immanent self-centered happiness, and on the other hand, the transcendent happiness that has its source in the existence of goods having objective values. Until this is recognized, the path to understanding values and their intrinsic importance remains blocked.

This means that any conclusion about the essence of beauty is unfounded, or built on sand, if it is derived from this fundamental misunderstanding of the essence of value. When Santayana says: "A beauty not perceived is a pleasure not felt, and a contradiction,"[31] this merely begs the question. It is indeed true that psychological-mental entities do not exist if they are not conscious, or are experienced in some form: a joy that is not felt can indeed not exist! But when Santayana transposes this onto beauty, and indeed onto all values, this assertion is completely false. The moral value of an action remains fully real even when no one knows about it and even when the agent himself does not become explicitly aware of this value. Besides, a value can never exist as a consciously lived psychological reality. As we have seen, it can only adhere objectively to specific conscious acts as its bearers. Accordingly, the conclusion begs the question; or we could say that it is meaningful only if one's starting point is the total misunderstanding of the essence of value whereby value is arbitrarily equated with the happiness that it can bestow on us.

Uti (using) and frui (enjoying)

At this point we must ask: What kind of contact takes place between the objective and the subjective when we enjoy the beauty of a landscape or of a piece of music? What do we mean by the verb "enjoy"? Is not enjoyment something explicitly subjective, a matter of pleasure?

31. Santayana, *The Sense of Beauty*, 45.

There is no doubt that enjoyment is an experience had by a person. Unlike *non*-enjoyment, it is a unique, conscious entering into the positive content whether of a feeling of a bodily or mental kind, or of some object. Enjoying something is the opposite of merely making use of it. It was Saint Augustine who discovered this central difference in our attitudes and elaborated it clearly in his *De doctrina christiana* by means of the two verbs *uti* (using) and *frui* (enjoying).[32] He shows that *frui* means entering into something for its own sake, whereas *uti* means using it only as a means for attaining some other good. Eating food because it tastes good is an instance of *frui*, but eating it for the sake of nutrition is an instance of *uti*. Similarly, taking medicine is a pure *uti*. We could also say that in *frui*, the focus is on the positive content; in *uti*, the focus is on this content only to the extent that it is a means to attain something else.

The difference between these two basic attitudes is repeated at every level in the hierarchy of beings. We can enjoy a good wine or the company of another person or the rare beauty of a piece of music; or else—and this is *uti*—we can drink the wine only to warm ourselves us up, or in order to get drunk so as to escape the thoughts that oppress us. We can seek the company of another person only because we hope to get information from him about something that interests us keenly. We can listen to beautiful music only because we must study it for an examination.

Here, however, we must distinguish between two different situations. In the one case, the question is whether an object is of such a kind as to appeal to *frui* or to *uti*. In the other case, the question concerns our behavior toward the object: do we enjoy it, or merely make use of it? A good wine appeals to *frui*, a knife appeals to *uti*. The company of someone we love appeals to *frui*, but the train or airplane that will bring me to him appeals to *uti*. We could make this point as follows. Our first question is posed from the standpoint of the nature of the object: What is its "theme," what is its *raison d'être*? Does it exist for the sake of *uti* or *frui*? Our second question is: How does someone relate to it? For a child a rattle can be an object of *frui*. Some people enjoy traveling by train

32. Saint Augustine, *De doctrina christiana*, chaps. 3–5, 22, 27–33.

without any particular goal for their journey, and others enjoy flying for its own sake.

In the case of all those things that are bearers of a high value, *frui* is not their *raison d'être*; this, rather, lies in their value. But they are most definitively *fruenda*, "things to be enjoyed." One *ought* to enjoy them. One ought to be interested in them for their own sake. One ought to make their value the theme, not merely make use of them as a means to attain something else.

The completely conscious experiencing of beauty presupposes the objectivity of beauty

The antithesis between *uti* and *frui* is not the only relevant distinction here. For example, we can say, "Unfortunately, I could not enjoy the concert so much, because I had a headache," or "because I was deeply worried by a number of things," or "We were not able really to enjoy our meeting with this person; it was too short, too hectic, etc." When we speak here of "enjoying," we mean the ability to enter into something valuable, to become absorbed in it. We mean the conscious experiencing of the happiness that the beautiful piece of music, or the time spent with the person whom we love, awakens in our soul. Here the act of enjoying means that one allows oneself to be affected by the value. In this explicit, total absorption in that which is valuable, the focus is wholly on the value and its intrinsic importance; at the same time, however, its character as an objective good for me thanks to its value, and its character as a gift, are fully experienced and appreciated. The failure to enjoy, or the failure to enjoy sufficiently, means that one is not sufficiently absorbed in this value: one has not attained the contemplative attitude that is always required if a value is to become fully thematic for us. Without this contemplative attitude, it is impossible to be truly affected by a value and to experience fully in our soul the happiness that the value bestows.

When we say that this happiness, too, is experienced with full consciousness in the act of enjoyment, we do not in any way mean that we look at the happiness and that this becomes our genuine focus, for that would destroy everything and would be the greatest foe of true enjoyment. Once again we encounter the fundamental difference between a value and something that is merely satisfying for myself, or between goods that bestow happiness and goods that bestow only pleasure. In the case of objects that are important only because they engender pleasure in me, I can indeed look at the pleasure when I enjoy them. But in the case of values, of the bearers of those values that are a source of the true happiness that always includes a dimension of transcendence, it is wrong to accord primacy to happiness over the value. Indeed, this means the death of this happiness, and thus also the death of the only kind of enjoyment that is possible in this context.

The antithesis between a full, conscious experiencing and a less full, conscious experiencing is characteristic of the act of enjoying. This full consciousness includes all the following elements: entering into the object and its beauty, experiencing the full thematicity of the beauty, fully allowing oneself to be given the gift of the beauty, being affected by it; it also includes the completely distinct thing of the happiness that is experienced laterally, the happiness that beauty kindles in our soul.

This full conscious experiencing of all the elements—each in its own place, in the correct hierarchy of thematicity—also contains a full experience of the present moment. We emerge from the tension toward the future, a tension that permeates our life in general. This act of enjoyment contains not only the total thematicity of the bearer of the beauty, and especially the beauty itself, the total concentration on this beauty, and interest in it *propter se ipsum* (for its own sake), but also the contemplative element of standing still and opening oneself entirely to this object. The act of enjoying is very significant and certainly signifies a close union between the person and the object. Nevertheless, we cannot deny the difference between the objective beauty that one enjoys, and everything that this beauty actualizes in our soul—all the emotion, the happiness, the joy, the experience of being drawn into one's depth. In the act of enjoying, the beauty does not itself become a conscious being, a psychological or mental entity that takes place in my soul and is a part of my person. Nor is that which I experience when confronted with the beauty, when it affects me, projected onto the object and made into a quality of the object. Nor does the beauty derive its importance from the potential happiness it causes a human being when it affects him. The beauty of the object always remains the *principium*, and everything that its enjoyment brings forth in our soul is the *principiatum*. The special kinds of experiences that are kindled in our soul, such as emotion, elation, or happiness, necessarily presuppose the beauty of the object and a clear perception of this beauty, a "consciousness of" the objective beauty. Equally, the experience of being made happy that is involved here necessarily presupposes the perception of the importance-in-itself of value, and it is clearly and distinctly a world apart from every purely immanent, self-referential experience of feeling happy.

We must conclude this section with the observation that general value relativism is nothing other than a prejudice. It has never been proven, but is either introduced dogmatically as an axiom, as if it were self-evident, or else is backed up by lazy and superficial arguments. As soon as one analyzes the facts without prejudice, one sees unambiguously the profound difference among the various basic types of importance. One discovers the undeniable existence of that which is important-in-itself, namely, values and their real essence. One also discovers that we presuppose values at every step; that they play an undeniable and fundamental role; and that they belong to those ultimate primordial facts (such as being, truth, and knowledge) that one tacitly presupposes whenever one denies them.

This is why we find nothing of any serious interest in all those analyses of beauty that take their starting point in this general value relativism. They declare with an illusion of correctness that "Beauty is a value," but all that they mean by this affirmation is that beauty, like all value, is merely relative and a product of our emotional impulses.

Ross's equivocation with the concept of objectivity

We turn to the question whether it is possible for beauty to exist in a world without a spirit which perceives it. The question is raised even in thinkers who are on an incomparably higher philosophical level than

Santayana. I have in mind here not Kant and Schopenhauer, for whom beauty is universally valid even though it is not a quality of the object, but William David Ross.[33]

Unlike Kant, Schopenhauer, and many others, Ross recognizes the concept of objective value in ethics. When he speaks of beauty, however, he raises the question whether this does not in fact presuppose a spirit which perceives it and rejoices in it. This is the beginning of an infelicitous chain of specious reasoning in which he sees himself increasingly compelled by false arguments and equivocations to deny the objectivity of beauty. This is not a dogmatic denial of the objectivity of beauty—quite the opposite! At the beginning, he seems to see this objectivity, but at the end, he feels himself compelled by a number of confusions or equivocations of the concept of objectivity to deny to beauty even the character of an objective value.

This tragic lapse on the part of such a profound thinker, who was not in the least a relativist or immanentist, is particularly interesting in the present context because of the confusion of various issues connected with the question of objectivity.

Ross takes his starting point exclusively in the beauty of the visible and audible, and in fact he limits the concept of beauty to this type of beauty.

He begins by observing that beauty is indefinable. This observation can mean various things, such as that beauty is a primordial phenomenon: I cannot derive it from anything else, all I can do is perceive it in intuition. From the epistemological perspective, this indefinability is certainly no disadvantage. It is completely erroneous to say that the ideal of knowledge is the ability to define something, and this for two reasons. First, the intuitive penetration of a datum that possesses a genuine essence, as well as the knowledge of its essential characteristics, are a much higher form of intellectual penetration, of true knowledge, than the act of making a definition. Secondly, it is impossible to define any

33. William David Ross, *The Right and the Good* (Oxford: Clarendon Press, 1930), 124–31.

primordial phenomenon. Just as I can never learn by means of a definition what red is, or what color or space is, so too I can never learn by means of a definition what value (the important-in-itself) is.

But it may be that when Ross thinks of the term "indefinable," he does not have in mind a datum with an immediate givenness that can never be replaced by a mere definition. Rather, he may wish to point to a kind of inability to be grasped, something that eludes our knowledge, that slips through our fingers as we attempt to grasp it. In any case, he draws from the indefinability of beauty the conclusion that the only way to draw near to beauty is to take one's starting point in the kind of enjoyment it gives to the human spirit.

According to Ross, "beautiful" denotes that which brings about one particular kind of enjoyment in our spirit. He justifies this indirect definition of beauty by asserting that whoever calls something "beautiful" must also experience this kind of enjoyment.[34]

Here, of course, he makes an irreparable mistake. A factor that is in fact not more easily definable, namely, aesthetic enjoyment, is made the starting point for getting to know the essence of beauty and for achieving after all a kind of definition of beauty.

Apart from this erroneous starting point (which, as we shall see, drives Ross into a completely unjustified subjectivism), he confuses the question of the objectivity of beauty as a value with the question whether the bearer of beauty is independent of the human spirit. He says that since it is questionable whether colors and sounds truly belong to the object rather than merely *appearing to us* to belong to the object, it is also questionable whether the beauty that adheres to the visible and audible exists independently of our spirit.[35]

It is extremely important to see that the objectivity of beauty as a value, its importance-in-itself, has nothing to do with the question whether the so-called secondary qualities exist independently of a human spirit.

It is possible to grasp clearly the fact that beauty is something impor-

34. Ibid., 127–28.
35. Ibid., 126–27.

tant-in-itself, rather than something that offers a merely subjective satisfaction—indeed, that beauty is not even merely an objective good for me—when we reflect on the essence of beauty. I have already mentioned that it is meaningless to say, with regard to the beauty of a landscape or a melody, that they are "beautiful for me." We need only reflect on what is given to us and what reveals itself to us when we hear, free of prejudice, Handel's *Largo* or Bach's *Air*, or look at the dome of the cathedral in Florence: for then we will have no difficulty in perceiving that the beauty which we see inhering in these things is a value, something that bears its importance in itself, independently of how anyone reacts to it. We also grasp that the appropriate response must be made to this beauty, and that there is an objective disharmony when the beauty is not perceived and the appropriate value-response is not made. We realize that just because other persons do not perceive the beauty that we ourselves clearly perceive does not turn that beauty into something that merely satisfies. The importance-in-itself, the value character of beauty, is obvious to us, as is the radical difference between this value character and the character of being merely satisfying to us. Indeed, this is independent even of the question whether the object is truly as beautiful as it appears to us. When we speak of beauty, we mean *unambiguously* a value, something important-in-itself, not merely something that satisfies us. This fact, rooted in the very essence of beauty, is completely independent of the question of the extent to which we err when we take something to be beautiful that is not beautiful in reality—just as the question of what truth is, of what belongs to its essence, is independent of whether something that we take to be true is really true.

But quite apart from what beauty essentially is, this new question—whether the beauty of an object can exist in such a manner as to be given to us with full evidence—is extremely important for the objectivity of beauty. In the case of truth, it is indisputable not only that we can perceive its essence as something evident, but also that we can recognize many facts as absolutely evident. This is why the truth of all those propositions that affirm an essentially necessary, extremely intelligible, and evident fact excludes every possibility of falsehood. These propositions present absolutely certain truths. We shall return later in this chapter to the exceedingly important question whether a judgment that ascribes beauty to an object can possess an absolute certainty analogous to the judgments that formulate an evident essential law. We can also formulate this question as follows: Is it possible for the beauty of an object—the fact that it is genuinely beautiful—to be given to us with full evidence?

The human aspect of the external world and the objectivity of beauty

Before we take up this extremely important question, we must once again emphasize that the value character of beauty as such is completely independent of whether the bearer of beauty presupposes a human mind, or exists independently of such a mind. Beauty does not cease to be a genuine value in the case of a beautiful mirage or a landscape in a dream. Even if the visible world were to exist only for one human mind, beauty would not cease to be a genuine value. It would not thereby become merely something that brought me satisfaction, nor would this relativize the fact that something that appears only to me is objectively beautiful.

Here we must recall another question, namely, whether something is a part of the human aspect of the external world, or is a mere illusion.

In my book *What is Philosophy?* I have written in detail in chapter 5 about the human aspect of the external world. Many things are completely independent of the human mind, for example, all the laws that govern the essences of things, the existence of one's own person, of the external world, of other persons, etc. But there are many things that, while not possessing this kind of independence of the human mind, nevertheless have a completely valid reality and are not in any sense a mere illusion. Still other things possess only the minimal existence that consists in being the object of a "consciousness of," for example, the house of which one dreams or the thunderstorm that is only a hallucination.

Color is a primordial reality. Every color—red, yellow, green, or blue—possesses a genuine essence that no human being can invent. Colors are bearers of a genuine value. Of their very essence they presuppose a two-dimensional sphere in order to unfold their being. Their form of existence is essentially different from any conscious existence. There is a world of difference between their ontological structure and that of a psychological state, an intentional state of being-affected (for example, being deeply moved or shocked by something), or an affective response (for example, joy or enthusiasm over something). They are given to us as qualities of physical objects. The grass is green, the earth in some regions is red, some garments are blue, and canaries are yellow.

When we go on to ask whether the colors adhere to an object in the same way as its size or its weight, or whether they presuppose a human being in order to constitute themselves, we must underline from the very outset that the answer to this question can never turn a color into something in the human mind, or into something that exists consciously. Even if we admit that the color presupposes a human mind in order to constitute itself, it nevertheless remains a quality attaching to the object, and its dependence on the human person never makes it a mental entity. Colors can never be a mere illusion. They can never be merely what an equivocal expression calls a "content of the consciousness." This has several reasons. First, they play a great role in the image of the external world that is formed by all human beings who are not colorblind; and the same things possess the same colors for all human beings. Secondly, they are obviously not an "illusion" like the stick that seems to be broken as it lies in water: as soon as we take it out of the water, we can see that this was only an "illusion." Thirdly and most importantly, the colors are so meaningful, they are such a central factor for the external world as this is given to the human person, and they are bearers of such beauty, that their dependence on the human person can never give them the character of a deception that is not only general but also existential.

If someone objects that "in reality" all we have here are electromagnetic waves, he is forgetting that although the colors do belong to the human aspect of the external world, they present something much more meaningful, much more important than these waves. Ultimately, we must say that the electromagnetic waves exist for the sake of the colors. If we determine the rank of an object by means of the message from God which it contains, by means of the depth of the *vestigia Dei* (the "traces of God") in it, surely no one can doubt that colors contain a much profounder message and that they image God much more significantly than electromagnetic waves.

Naturally, we cannot in any way equate this kind of dependence of the human aspect on the human person with what Kant called the *phenomenon*. The human aspect is not an image created by our mind, something distinct from the true objective "thing in itself." No, the human aspect is that aspect of the complete, real external world which does not cut us off from the "thing in itself" nor cover it over; still less does it falsify this object. Rather, it is a great gift of God, an act whereby we see the objects as they *ought* to appear. It contains a much deeper and more real message from God than those aspects of the physically real external world with which physics and chemistry are concerned. For Kant, the objects studied by physics and chemistry are only *phenomena.* I have explained elsewhere[36] how erroneous and unjustified the whole Kantian immanentism and its distinction between *noumenon* and *phainomenon* are. To make the distinction between a reality that is independent of its being perceived by the human mind, and the human aspect of the external world, has nothing to do with adhering to his transcendental idealism.

Here is the point that we have to grasp. The fact that the bearers of the beauty of the visible and audible belong to the human aspect does not in any way diminish the value character of beauty, nor does it diminish the objective validity of a proposition such as, "The *Dying Slave* of Michelangelo is beautiful" or "Beethoven's Quartet opus 130 is beautiful." Even less does this fact turn beauty into something mental or something consciously lived. Neither beauty nor the bearers of beauty are turned thereby into something that exists inside myself, that is, into a real part of my lateral consciousness.

We have seen how unjustified, indeed how false the widespread thesis is that beauty, since it is something important and not neutral, cannot exist as a quality of an object. We also now see that there is no basis for any of the ways of denying that beauty is an objective quality of an

36. In my *What is Philosophy?* chap. 5.

object (a denial also found in Kant): for even if the bearer of beauty is a part of the human aspect of the external world, it nevertheless remains on the side of the object and objectively grounds the beauty. This beauty belongs to its bearer, independently of our being affected by it and of our response to it. It is the *principium*, and our being-affected—including both the aesthetic enjoyment and our value-response of admiration and enthusiasm—is the *principiatum*.

Since Ross fails to draw distinctions among all these things, he slides from the first false thesis—that beauty is what generates aesthetic enjoyment—more and more into relativism, until he finally declares that one must give a negative answer to the question whether beauty is a genuine value, something important-in-itself. For him beauty is not a value like the morally good; it is only something that satisfies us.

The evident givenness of the beauty of the visible and the audible

We now turn to the question mentioned above: Can the fact that something is beautiful be given to us in an evident manner? Although the value character of beauty as such is given to us in an evident manner, and we can perceive with absolute certainty that beauty is important in itself (that is to say, a value) rather than something merely subjectively satisfying or important only to me, we must still answer the question whether the fact that one concrete object is beautiful and another object is not beautiful (or is indeed the bearer of an aesthetic disvalue) can possess the same evidential character as the absolute certainty we have that humility is morally good and arrogance morally bad.

Naturally, the beauty of that which is visible and audible in individual concrete entities, for example, in Michelangelo's *Pietà* in Florence or in the Farnese Palace in Rome, cannot be compared to general virtues such as humility. The corresponding example in the moral field would be specific moral behavior such as that of Saint Martin, who gave the beggar half of his cloak, or the prayer of Saint Stephen for his murderers. The moral value of these concrete actions is evident, and we can grasp their sublime value with absolute certainty. Is this equally true of landscapes such as the Gulf of Spezia, or of architecture like that of San Marco in Venice?

Naturally, the fact that many persons do not grasp an evident state-of-affairs is not an argument against the objective truth of the proposition that registers this evident state-of-affairs. The truth of a proposition depends exclusively on whether the state-of-affairs which it affirms exists—not in the least on how many persons grasp it. One cannot establish truth by means of a majority vote.

This is why the fact that many persons are blind to moral values says nothing against the possibility that the knowledge of moral values can be evident, nor against the evident state-of-affairs that justice is good and that martyrdom (for example, of Saint Ignatius of Antioch) is the bearer of a sublime moral value.

Ross makes the following objection to the absolute truth of an aesthetic value judgment: whereas we can expect of every human being a perception of moral values, and blindness to moral values is always in some way an individual's fault, only some persons have an organ that allows them to appreciate aesthetic beauty. He derives from this fact an argument against the absolute objectivity of the beauty of an object.[37] But it is clear that this argument does not hold water. Why should the objective validity of beauty, or the fact that one object is beautiful and another not, be put into question just because a special organ not possessed by everyone is required in order to perceive beauty? Behind this argument there somehow lurks the fallacy that objective truth depends on recognition by all human beings.

The fact that certain organs are required in order to perceive something has no influence of any kind on the objective validity of that which is perceived. We have to reject as untenable all those arguments on behalf of relativism that are based on the fact that there are all kinds of various and indeed contradictory judgments. The fact that something is objectively valid, that it is true, does not in the least demand that everyone should be able to grasp it.[38] Ross is indeed perfectly correct to draw a dis-

37. *What is Philosophy?* chap. 4.

38. Here we must also emphasize that there is no genuine antithesis between seeing something and not seeing it. If one person says, "I see a snake over there," and another person says, "I see no

tinction between blindness to moral values and blindness to aesthetic values,[39] but he is wrong to assert that this means that the aesthetic values are relative. On the one hand, every human being possesses a sense for moral values, with the consequence that all blindness to moral values is a perversion and therefore often a person's own fault; on the other hand, the aesthetic values require a special organ that is sometimes called "good taste," something that not everyone possesses, something that is not bestowed on the human being as such. But this fact is not in the least an argument for the relativity of the aesthetic values.

There is another important difference between the moral sphere and the sphere of the beauty of visible and audible things. The way in which the moral value is rooted in an action or in some kind of behavior has a much more rational character than the way in which beauty is rooted in certain forms, colors, and proportions of visible things, or rooted in a melody. The term "rational" must be understood correctly: I mean a kind of intelligibility that is present in all the beauty of the moral realm, in all the beauty that is a reflection or a fragrance of other values, or is a *splendor veri* (a "splendor of that which is true"). I shall discuss this metaphysical beauty in the second and third chapters. The way in which it is rooted in other values possesses this same full intelligibility.

This is just what is lacking in the case of the beauty of visible and audible things, which for Ross and for many others makes up the whole of beauty. As we shall see, the way in which visible and audible things ground beauty is completely different; we do not need to know anything about this relationship of grounding in order to perceive the beauty of something visible or audible. The artist is doubtless aware that if some particular melody is to be beautiful, it has to go up at the end and not down, or down and not up. But in order to perceive the

snake," it is clear that there is only a contradiction between seeing and not seeing, but not a contradiction with regard to the fact that a snake is over there. If one person says, "Impurity is morally bad," and another person says, "I cannot see that," this too is only an antithesis between seeing and not seeing—not an antithesis with regard to the fact that impurity is a moral disvalue. An antithesis would be present if someone were to assert that he saw clearly that impurity was an explicitly moral *virtue*. Clearly, this assertion is completely different from the mere observation, "I cannot see that impurity is morally bad." See the essay by Alice von Hildebrand, "On the Pseudo-Obvious," cited above.

39. *What is Philosophy?* chap. 4.

beauty of the melody, we need know nothing of this. The artist knows which means he must employ in order to make a movement appear poetical, or in order to bestow a profound, noble expression on a human face. We do not need to know any of this in order to perceive the beauty of the painting.

It is much less easy to understand, and much more mysterious, that certain forms, colors, proportions, etc., have just this or that effect. I refer here not to their effect on our mind but to what they determine on the side of the object, to their role in giving rise to beauty.

With regard to the intelligibility of the reasons why something visible or audible is beautiful, then, there is in fact an important difference between the moral and the aesthetic spheres.

But we must make a distinction between this difference with regard to the intelligibility of the aesthetic and the moral values, and the question whether the beauty of something visible or audible can be determined with absolute certainty, or in other words, whether the fact that this or that object is beautiful can be given with full evidence.

Let us begin with the general difference between the evidential character of essential laws and the evidential character of an individual fact. The essential laws always refer to something general. "2 x 2 = 4" refers to the essence of these numbers. "Colors presuppose extension, a two-dimensional space, in order to be able to unfold." "Moral values can adhere only to persons, never to apersonal entities." "A proposition cannot simultaneously be true and false." "Justice is the bearer of a moral value." "Every 'appearance' presupposes a conscious spirit to which it appears." All these essential laws are of a general nature. Although they govern every corresponding real entity, they do not entail the positing of any individual real entity. We do not need to discuss here the evidential character of the essential laws; I have already treated this question in detail in chapter 4 of my book *What is Philosophy?*

There also exists a form of absolute certainty in the knowledge of concrete individual states-of-affairs, although it is beyond dispute that this is completely different from the evidential character of the essential laws.[40] The extraordinary absolute certainty that Saint Augustine states in his marvelous *si fallor, sum*, or the indubitable certainty of the real existence of my person that Descartes takes up anew in his *cogito, ergo sum*, is naturally a unique case. Its evidential character is guaranteed on the basis of essential laws. In a completely different way, we can perceive with absolute certainty the reality of the external world. Here we find neither the evidential character of the essential laws nor that of the *si fallor, sum*. Absolute certainty is here attained not by means of an immediately intelligible and intuitive evidence, but indirectly.

A completely new case is the insight into the moral value of specific behavior. Since the general fact that forgiveness is morally good, and repentance morally valuable, is an essential law, it can be perceived with the same evidential character as every essential law. In the case of the behavior of an individual human being, the fact that he has truly forgiven or genuinely repented is of course not an essential law; nor does this fact ever exist with the same absolute certainty as the *si fallor, sum*, or even the existence of the external world as a whole. Here it is in principle possible to err. But this is not just the same possibility of error that exists in every concrete perception, that is, the possibility of dreaming, or hallucinating, or having an optical illusion, etc. The question is not only whether this morally noble conduct has in fact taken place, as when we ask whether it is perhaps only the protagonist of a novel or some figure in a saga who behaves in this way, or whether it was only a mistaken report in the newspaper, or something in a dream. The issue at stake here is the real existence of this conduct, and this is naturally an extremely important question. There is an immeasurably great difference between a genuine deed of high moral value and a deed that is only imaginary. All this concerns the real existence of the bearer of the deed, and through this existence, the realization of the moral value of the deed.

But in these cases there is an additional possibility of error: the possibility that although this was in fact the conduct of a real human being and

40. *What is Philosophy?* chap. 4. 71ff.

not something dreamed, this conduct only appeared to be an act of forgiveness or repentance. We cannot perceive the act of forgiveness or of repentance in the same way as the color of a house, the size of a room, and so on. The words in which an act of forgiveness or repentance is proclaimed and the appropriate facial expression may be given, but this need not mean that the inner attitude is present in full genuineness, depth, and reality.

This possibility of error,[41] present in principle in the case of cognizing human beings, is not present in the case of works of art. Not only does the beauty of Michelangelo's *Dying Slave* exist unambiguously; the fact that this concrete figure possesses great beauty is also evident. And so we arrive at this definitive affirmation: we can know with absolute certainty that aesthetic values belong to a work of art, a landscape, a human body, or an animal. We can speak here of real evidence. It is true that if beauty, especially the beauty of works of art, is to be perceived, a specific organ is required that not everyone possesses; but as we have seen, the question whether something can be perceived by every human being has nothing to do with the question whether, for those who do possess the necessary organ, something is given with complete evidence and thus can claim complete objective validity.

As we have clearly seen, the beauty in nature or in a work of art is neither the projection of a bodily sensation of pleasure nor of a mental state nor of the value-response to such a sensation. Nor does the beauty derive its importance from the affective experiences it awakens in us when it affects our soul. Rather, these experiences show unambiguously that they presuppose beauty as something important-in-itself.[42] And this implies two things. First, it implies the difference between beauty and all that is purely neutral. If we affirm that a melody consists of twenty notes or

41. I do not wish in any way to deny that it is also possible for the virtues and the moral situation of a human being to be given with full evidence—quite the contrary! All I wish to do is to point out that with the concrete individual act of observation there exist possibilities of error that are not present in the case of the aesthetic values. In the present context, space does not allow me to demonstrate that it is also possible to overcome these possibilities of error with regard to the moral values of an individual person.

42. [The German text is garbled here (p. 74 of the German original). Several lines containing mere sentence fragments had to be passed over. Fortunately the paragraph still has a clear and unified meaning even without these. JFC]

tones, this affirmation concerns a neutral fact. But if we state that this melody is beautiful, we are not affirming some neutral fact. We are not saying something neutral about the melody, but something important in our special sense of that word. Secondly, it implies not only the difference between neutral and important, but also the equally significant difference between objective importance-in-itself and the kinds of importance *for* the person—whether the importance of the objective good for the person, or the importance (radically different from this) of what is merely subjectively satisfying. If we fully realize these implications of the fact that beauty is a value, we will also realize that this first characteristic of the essence of beauty is of fundamental significance and provides the indispensable basis of every true aesthetics.

The two concepts of "important-in-itself"

Before we turn to the question of beauty as the fundamental value of the aesthetic sphere, and to the two basic kinds of beauty, there is one further view of the value of beauty that we want to deal with. This lies on a much higher level than all the subjectivisms and relativisms that we have refuted up to this point.

G. E. Moore[43] says that there is no doubt that the entire aesthetic experience possesses an "intrinsic value," a genuine value, something important-in-itself. Since he makes no distinction between "value" and "good," we can express his thesis in our own terminology as follows: There is no doubt that the entire aesthetic experience is a good, the bearer of a genuine value. Moore emphasizes that this aesthetic experience is an organic whole, made up of the object that we call beautiful and our being affected by this object, our "feeling" of its beauty. Clearly, this feeling encompasses both what I call "being-affected" and what I call "value-response." While Moore does not make this distinction, he does distinguish between the act of recognizing beauty and the act of "feeling" beauty, enjoying it, indeed being made happy by it. He does however

43. G. E. Moore, *Principia Ethica* (Cambridge: Cambridge University Press, 1903), chap. 6.

assert—while keeping the two things distinct—that if it were possible for an act of recognizing beauty to exist without being affected and without being made happy, the value of the authentic aesthetic experience would be diminished. These must always occur together, so that the value of the entire aesthetic experience may be present. This necessarily includes a feeling of the value. But note that he does not employ the term "feeling" in the sense of Scheler's "feeling of value" [*Wertfühlen*], which is a form of the act of knowing.

The interesting point in Moore's position is that he clearly recognizes that there is a meaningful relationship between the beauty of an object and our response to it, even though, as I have said, he does not distinguish from this response the experience of being affected by and enjoying the beauty. This relationship entitles us to speak of an appropriate response and an inappropriate response. He thus grasps the exceedingly important datum that I have discussed in chapter 18 of my *Ethics* under the name "due relation." Moore goes on to say that a genuine value is present only when the object is of such a kind that it deserves a positive response and when this response is in fact given. Here the object and our attitude toward it form an organic whole. If the appropriate response is not given to the beautiful object, or if no response whatever is made, or if a positive response is given to an ugly object, the value disappears, or a disvalue is present; more precisely, we can say that the positive good, which is the bearer of a genuine value, is not realized.

These remarks by Moore certainly contain important insights that go far beyond the general level of writing on aesthetics. At the same time, however, we must note a problem.

The term "intrinsic value" contains a grave equivocation. It means, on the one hand, that what is involved is a direct value, not an indirect value. Naturally, this is a very important distinction. Does something have importance in its own right, or is it important only as a means to something else? In the terminology of Saint Augustine, are we seeking something *propter se ipsum* ("for its own sake") or only as a means to something else? I have written in detail about this distinction at the end of the third chapter of my *Ethics*.

This meaning of *important-in-itself*, as opposed to *important only as a means to something else*, is found in all three of the categories of importance that I distinguish. A compliment that someone pays me is, as such, subjectively satisfying; it is directly pleasant. If, however, I go to a party because I hope to receive compliments, this party is attractive to me only as a means or a potential occasion to receive compliments for my dress or for my jokes. The pleasure I receive from good food or good wine is an end in itself (a term we can also apply to what is directly important); but the purchase of the wine is important only as a means.

The distinction between directly and indirectly important, which we see here in the sphere of that which is important only for me, is found also in the sphere of the objective good for me, and above all in the sphere of value. The life of a human person is directly valuable, while the medicine with which he can be saved when he is gravely ill is indirectly valuable. It attains its value through its ability to be an effective means to save his life.

Now it is easy to see the difference between the two meanings of *important-in-itself* or *intrinsic value.* First of all, *important-in-itself* means directly important. In other words, the object possesses its importance in itself and not because of its function as a means to something else. Importance-in-itself is meant in the sense of an end in itself, and the term refers not to the kind or category of importance but to the relationship of the bearer to its importance. Secondly, *important-in-itself* denotes a kind of importance itself and does not involve the question whether the bearer possesses this importance of itself or borrows the importance, so to speak, from the end that it serves as a means. Unlike that which is only important for me, value is important in itself; that which is only important and satisfying for me derives its importance from a relationship to my satisfaction.

It is of course a great mistake on Moore's part that he employs the expression *intrinsic value* to denote both the end in itself and also the kind or category of importance. This use of the term has particularly unfortunate effects on his ethics.

Moore's thesis of the "organic whole" (beauty and its appropriate appreciation)

There is a lack of differentiation in Moore's thesis that is even more interesting for our analysis of aesthetic enjoyment. In reality it is not only the organic whole of which he speaks—made up of the object and our appropriate appreciation—that is a valuable good or a bearer of a value. We must also draw the following distinctions between certain values, or between certain valuable goods. First of all, there is the beauty of the object, for example, of a landscape or a work of art. The beauty adheres to the object as a quality, independently of whether or not someone understands it, reacts appropriately to it, or enjoys it. This beauty of the object is an unambiguous value. It is something important-in-itself, not something that is satisfying only to me. And the object—the landscape or work of art—is a valuable good, one that is not only indirectly valuable, but also directly valuable.

Secondly, the appropriate appreciation that is realized on our part when we are affected by beauty and respond with enthusiasm is the bearer of a genuine personal value. Being moved by a genuine beauty and giving the value-response of enthusiasm are themselves noble modes of conduct by a person, and they possess a real value. For example, when we see how someone is moved, touched, and taken hold of by a great work of art and how he responds to it with enthusiasm, we rejoice at this noble, beautiful attitude and clearly perceive its value. Moore is completely correct to point out that the true beauty of the object is presupposed, in order to make the attitude of enjoying its beauty valuable. It is also commendable that (unlike most writers on this subject) he sees the meaningful relationship between the specific character of the object which we enjoy and our appreciation of this object. But he is wrong to see this relationship as the two organic parts of one whole; or, more precisely, he fails to see clearly that we have two completely different values here. The one value is the beauty, which attaches exclusively to the object (in the case of the landscape and the work of art, to the apersonal object); the other value is the nobility that attaches to the conduct of a person who understands the beautiful object, is moved by it, and makes an appropriate response to it.

Finally, we have something completely new in the value of the state-of-affairs that a person is moved, touched, elevated by something objectively beautiful, and is enthusiastic about it in the appropriate manner. *This* state-of-affairs is something completely new, although it presupposes the two other bearers of value, that is, the object and the appropriate attitude.[44] It seems that Moore primarily envisages this state-of-affairs and has this in mind when he speaks of the organic whole. We are about to point out that still other values are present here as well.

Let me sum up our result. There is first of all the value of the beauty itself, a specifically aesthetic value that adheres to the object. In order to make a philosophical analysis of the value of the beauty, we need not examine the state of being-affected and the value-responses which are made to the beauty. We must concentrate totally on the object, although this naturally presupposes that we have experienced the beauty, have directly perceived it prior to all philosophical analysis, and are deeply moved by it. Already at this point there is a state-of-affairs value [*Sachverhaltswert*] that must be distinguished from the beauty itself; I refer to the value that belongs to the existence of the beautiful landscape or work of art, that is, to the fact that it exists.

There is secondly the value of the human person's attitude. Being moved by a genuine beauty, as well as the value-response of enthusiasm to the beauty of a work of art or to the beauty of nature, are themselves bearers of genuine personal value.

Thirdly, there is the state-of-affairs value that belongs to the fact that a human person perceives something truly beautiful, is moved by it, and makes the right response to it.

We must now distinguish several other values. First, there is the very general value of the state-of-affairs that an objective good is given to a human person and he is made happy. Whenever a person is made happy,

44. See my *Ethics*, chap. 18.

this is always something valuable (assuming of course that he is made happy in a morally unobjectionable manner). This value is all the greater, the nobler, deeper, and purer this happiness is. Naturally, the value belonging to the state-of-affairs that someone attains eternal bliss is the highest value of this kind.

The value belonging to the fulfillment of due relation is completely different from this general value of the state-of-affairs of a person being made happy in a legitimate manner or participating in a genuine objective good (a value that of course is also present in the enjoyment of genuine beauty, and is all the greater, the more sublime the beauty is and the more deeply it moves him). As I have shown in chapters 17 and 18 of my *Ethics*, everything that is valuable deserves the appropriate response on our part when we come into contact with it. An appropriate response *ought* to be made to that which is valuable: in other words, it ought to affect us, touch us, and move us. A response of rejection *ought* to be given to that which is a disvalue. If no response whatever is given because a human person remains totally obtuse even when he sees something that is morally affecting, this state-of-affairs is the bearer of a disvalue. There is an objective disharmony. Here I am not thinking of the disvalue of the behavior as such; I am thinking of the metaphysical disvalue in the state-of-affairs that no response is given to something of disvalue, or an inappropriate response is given, as when someone is filled with enthusiasm over kitsch, and I am also thinking of the corresponding metaphysical value when an appropriate response is given to the value (in the present instance, to beauty) that one encounters.

Finally, we must add that there is a value in the state-of-affairs that beauty, especially the beauty of the visible and audible, is perceived by human beings. We mean that it is objectively a pity when a glorious landscape or a great work of art is not seen or a wonderful piece of music not heard. Beauty appeals to us to be received: it speaks to the spirit of the human person and contains a message for us. The fulfillment of this appeal, the fact that the beauty is perceived and understood by a human spirit and makes an "impact" on this spirit, is the bearer of a new value.

This value is not only the general value of the state-of-affairs that a human person receives an objective good, that is, it is not one of those values that are very profoundly connected with the happiness of the person, namely, the value that a person is happy (in the true sense of a legitimate happiness). Rather, it belongs to the fulfillment of beauty, to a tendency inherent in beauty, that it be perceived, grasped, and understood. This does not contradict the fact that the beauty belongs to an object whether it is perceived or not, and that it is important-in-itself and does not derive its importance from the effect it has on a human spirit—in other words, that it is a genuine value. The object does not cease to be objectively beautiful even if no one were ever to perceive it; but it is a characteristic of the value of beauty, and of its specific delectability, that it (unlike a moral value) "demands" to be perceived, and that it undergoes a new fulfillment when it is perceived.

Perhaps Moore too has this in mind when he speaks of the value of the object and of its being appreciated, its "effect" on our soul, as an organic whole. As we have seen, his view of this unity of elements as being an organic whole which alone bears a value and (to use our own vocabulary) is an objective, direct good, an end in itself, fails to register all the relevant distinctions, and especially to acknowledge beauty as a genuine value of its own. Nevertheless, he may have seen this ultimate value, this value of fulfillment; and this too, like his important recognition of due relation, is a significant merit of his.

CHAPTER TWO

The Realm of Aesthetic Values: Metaphysical Beauty and the Beauty of the Visible and the Audible [Sinnenschönheit]

NOW THAT we have recognized that beauty is a value, and hence differs both from all neutral qualities and from the other types of importance—such as the objective good for the person, and *a fortiori* from that which is merely subjectively satisfying—we must consider the question: To which particular value family does beauty belong?

The differences among ontological, technical, and aesthetic values

In earlier books, I have drawn attention to the variety of "value families."[1] The most important and most decisive difference is that between ontological and qualitative values. There is also a third type of values that we call technical values or values of perfection.

It is easy to recognize that aesthetic values, including beauty, are not ontological values. We need only think of particular ontological values,

1. See especially my *Ethics*, chap. 10, and my *Graven Images* (New York: David McKay Inc., 1957), chap. 5.

for example, the value that the human person possesses and an animal does not, in order to see that beauty does not belong to this type of value. Ontological value, which has its foundation in the being of the human person, belongs in an equal manner to all human persons. There is no hierarchy, no "more" or "less," within ontological value. There may indeed exist distinctions among people with regard to their qualitative values, and it is exceedingly important to recognize the hierarchy that exists from a qualitative point of view; but the ontological value that the human person possesses as a conscious, rational, free being, and that the animal lacks, belongs equally to the good and to the bad, to the clever and to the stupid. It belongs to the human being as a person, that is, to a being with an immortal soul.

Ontological value has no opposite. There is no positive disvalue that is opposed to the ontological value of the human person. It can only be missing, as in the case of the animal. The animal too possesses an ontological value, which is much less, however, than that of the human person.

It suffices in the present context to point to these characteristics of ontological value, in order to see that beauty, and indeed all the aesthetic values, are not ontological, but are typically qualitative values, like the moral and "intellectual" values.

Not only is it possible for one thing to be more or less beautiful than another; it can also possess a higher and more sublime beauty than another object. Above all, the opposite of beauty is not only an absence of beauty but also a pronounced disvalue, namely, ugliness, that is something positively present. One and the same ontological type, for example, a house or a picture, can be beautiful or decidedly ugly, crude, and repulsive.[2] This alone suffices to show that beauty and all the aesthetic values are qualitative values, not ontological values.

Nor are they the kind of values we have called technical values or values of perfection. These are found when we say, for example, that someone has a strong will, an acute intellect, or a good memory. The will has

2. Without offering any arguments in support of his position, Santayana denies that there exist aesthetic disvalues in the strict sense of the term, and that ugliness is the contrary opposite of beauty. He does indeed accept an antithesis between what is morally good and evil, but he asserts that the only antithesis of beauty is a lack of beauty (*The Sense of Beauty*, 49–50).

a high ontological value, and the good will bears a qualitative value—but the energetic, strong will is the bearer of a value of perfection.

The basic value [Grundwert] within families of qualitative values

It is easy to see that beauty is not an ontological type of value but a typically qualitative type of value; but the question of the relationship between beauty and other qualitative value families is more complicated. To begin with, it is obvious that the aesthetic values and their central value, namely, beauty, form a specific value family that is clearly distinct from the realm of both the moral and the "intellectual values." All the moral values—for example, just, generous, truthful, pure, or kind—share a fundamental theme that is different from beautiful, lovely, or poetical. And it is clear that the theme of beauty and all the other aesthetic values is completely different from that of the family of "intellectual" values, such as clever, gifted, endowed with genius, and so on. What, then, are the characteristic traits of the aesthetic value family, in contradistinction to the moral or "intellectual" value families, and to many other families of qualitative values? What is the relationship between aesthetic values and other qualitative value families?

The individual value families are distinguished from each other first of all by the nature of their theme. They are all genuine, qualitative values, but they are distinguished by their theme, by their basic qualitative note. This is most clearly expressed in the family of the moral values. The moral question is a theme of a very special kind that is sharply distinct from the theme of the truth, but also from the theme of the depth and appropriateness of knowledge, genius, and many other things. I have written in detail in chapter 15 of my *Ethics* about the characteristics of the moral value family in contradistinction to all the other families.

Let me here emphasize only that the quality of the morally good and the morally bad or evil unambiguously encompasses all the various moral value qualities. Fidelity, generosity, honesty, truthfulness, or purity: all these are morally good. Avarice, infidelity, cowardice, untruthfulness, mendacity, or impurity: the predicate "morally bad" fits all of these. "Morally good" is the basic value that permeates the entire family in a uniform manner, and "morally bad" is the basic disvalue that encompasses everything negative in this sphere.

It is essential that we grasp that not all the members of each qualitative value family must necessarily be united in one basic value, so that one value would represent, as it were, the genus of this family of values, and the other values would have the character of species within this genus. There is a great danger in philosophy that one is inclined to transfer the essential characteristics that one has discerned in *one* sphere to related, analogous fields, and to transfer not only those characteristics that indeed apply to the other spheres, but also those that are valid only in *one* particular sphere. This is why we must be on our guard when we look at the other value families, lest we assume *a priori* that everything in those families is analogous to the situation in the moral value family. This applies above all to the question whether we find in the other value families what we find with moral values, namely, the presence of a basic value that explains the unity of the theme of the value family.

The family of artistic and creative personal values

In earlier works,[3] I have contrasted the families of the moral and the vital values, on the one hand, and the "intellectual" personal values as a specific family, on the other. I grouped together in this value family qualities such as clever, gifted, endowed with genius, etc. Now, however, I must emphasize that the expression "intellectual" can be inappropriate or even misleading. Besides, this "family" breaks down in reality into several value families. It is obvious that the quality of an artistic talent is very different from that of a great philosophical gift. Clearly, the "intellectual" value we admire in Aristotle differs from the value we admire in Mozart. It would be completely inappropriate to call the latter value "intellectual."

Let us think of the breadth and fullness of a mind, or of its profundity; or of what we call intelligent; or of the nobility of mind that a man like Plato possessed to such an extraordinary extent; or of the genius of a

3. Dietrich von Hildebrand, *Metaphysik der Gemeinschaft* (Regensburg: Habbel Verlag, 1955), chap. 6.; *Ethics*, chap. 10; *Graven Images*, chap. 5.

great artist. We see that an analogous theme, that of the intellect, is present everywhere; but there is no basic value of which these values would be the differentiations. There is a qualitative difference between artistic genius and philosophical genius.

In the case of these values, of course, we are speaking only of values that belong to the person and, although they manifest themselves above all in the works of the person, are nevertheless wholly distinct from the value of the work itself. The value of Mozart's works is an aesthetic value, but this is not the case with the genius of his artistic gift. We can ascribe beauty to his music, but not to this artistic gift. Similarly, it is clear that the value of Aristotle's *Organon* is qualitatively different from the value of the gift that enabled him to have such insights into objective being. The value of the *Organon* belongs to the truth of what its author discovered and to an objectivization that possesses an extraordinary philosophical clarity and insight. But Aristotle's genius, the depth, clarity, and acuteness of mind that distinguish him as a thinker, are a completely different kind of value.

We see, then, that among the personal values, the value family that I had too generally characterized as "intellectual" breaks down into several personal value families, all of which are distinctly different from the moral value family. The personal values of the artistic-creative gift form a family on their own, to which the genius of Beethoven belongs no less than the genius of Michelangelo and Shakespeare. This is the family of the artistic creative power in every sphere of art.[4]

4. It is indeed true that the quality of talent also varies in the various spheres of art. It varies according to the type of bearer of artistic values that the artist produces. At the same time, however, we can take these personal values of artistic creativity together, despite their variety, and place them in one family, just as the values of the works of art in literature, music, and the visual arts possess a uniform character as aesthetic values. The theme is one and the same: beauty, artistic depth and greatness, especially in the works but also in the values of the artistic talent that empowers the artist to create these works. In this "theme" we encounter the difference between the personal values of great philosophers such as Plato, Aristotle, and Augustine, on the one hand, and of great artists such as Beethoven, Michelangelo, and Shakespeare, on the other. In the gift of the philosopher, the theme is not beauty, but truth. Besides this, the principal bearer of the value is knowledge, or the ability to know, and the next most important bearer is the ability to formulate and objectivize what one knows; in all works of art, on the other hand, it is the invention, the shaping, and the creation of something new that is in the foreground.

As long as we are speaking of general value qualities such as having stature [*bedeutend*], great, gifted, and endowed with genius, we can predicate these *both* of great philosophers *and* of great artists; but these value qualities are not found in the realm of moral values. A person may be simultaneously a genius and morally good, but one can never call him a genius or gifted on the basis of his moral values. In the same way, it is only by analogy that one could say that his moral values possess the quality "having stature."[5]

The fact that these general value qualities, which are not present in the realm of moral values, are present in many value families does not, however, prevent the personal values that characterize the artist and the philosopher from belonging to different value domains.

Surgeons, inventors, scientists, technicians, statesmen, and generals can likewise be bearers of these general qualities, such as having stature, being endowed with genius, or being gifted. It appears thus that there exists a large domain of personal values that is clearly distinct from the realm of the moral values, and also from that of the vital values such as vitality, good health, a strong temperament, etc. In an earlier book, we characterized this inexactly as the domain of the "intellectual" values. In reality, these constitute different value families.[6] But in comparison with the differences between the moral and vital values, they are relatively cognate.

Aesthetic qualities that are not forms of beauty

We ought also to undertake an individual investigation of the other qualitative value families, such as the vital personal values, with regard to the degree of qualitative unity, the identity of the theme, and the presence of a general basic value that embraces all the individual values of this sphere.

5. We see clearly how impossible it is to apply such predicates to the sphere of the moral values when someone says, "I am morally ungifted."

6. Since we lack an exact expression, we shall continue to speak of "intellectual" values. But it must be borne in mind that the expression "intellectual" does not designate a genuine genus. This is why it is put in quotation marks.

But such an investigation belongs in a general study of the qualitative value families. In a work on aesthetics, we cannot discuss this in detail.

This makes it all the more necessary to discuss the family of the aesthetic values from this perspective. We can say that all the moral values are embraced by the basic value of the morally good; but when we look at the aesthetic value family, we soon see that its unity, the common element that justifies us in speaking of a family of values, does not allow us to say that all the aesthetic values are embraced by the basic value *beautiful* in the way in which all moral values are embraced by the basic value of the morally good.

The concepts of "aesthetically valuable" and "beautiful" are not coextensive, for what is meaningfully denoted by the term *aesthetic* extends further than the primordial reality to which we refer by means of the term *beautiful.* We can also put this as follows: there are explicitly aesthetic values that are not subspecies of beauty, even if we understand "beauty" in a very comprehensive sense. Despite all the differences within beauty, including even the differences between the beauty of virtue and the beauty of a flower, or between the beauty of genius and the beauty of a color or a face, there still exist valuable aesthetic qualities that are not subspecies of beauty. As long as we are speaking of what is lovely, exalted, graceful, sublime, or poetic, it is clear that we are dealing with special kinds of beauty. When we move on to the elegant, we see that this is no longer a typical subspecies of beauty, and it is clear that qualities such as well-made or brilliant are not subspecies of beauty at all. A trivial piece of music devoid of all beauty can be brilliantly made. There are well-crafted pop songs that not only completely achieve their goal of popularity, but can be real "hits" (which merely makes their triviality all the more aggressive). We will speak of this in detail in chapter 12.

In order to work out the specific character of the aesthetic value family, we must realize from the outset that it is more comprehensive than everything that can be subsumed under the primordial phenomenon of beauty. Not all the aesthetic values are subspecies of beauty, although beauty is the queen of all that is aesthetic.

Despite the fact that there also exist aesthetic values that are not subspecies of beauty, we shall begin with beauty, the queen in the realm of the aesthetic, as we now turn to the specific character of the aesthetic value family, its difference from the other qualitative value families, and its links to them. Here beauty is the highest value, the aesthetic value *par excellence,* since the formal essential characteristics that we first discern through the contemplation of beauty apply to all the other aesthetic values too.[7]

The first characteristic of aesthetic values: they are found in the most various realms of being

One first characteristic of the aesthetic values is that, unlike the moral values and many other kinds of personal values, they do not presuppose one specific genus of being as their bearer.

Moral values, like many other values among those listed above, can adhere only to a person. Only persons and personal acts can be bearers of moral values. No apersonal being can be kind, pure, or generous. It is obviously absurd to speak of a just stone or to predicate purity or generosity of a tree. Not even a dog can be just, truthful, or humble.[8] There are of course states-of-affairs, such as laws, which we describe as just or unjust. But the predicate "just" is not identical in this case to the same predicate applied to a human being (although it is profoundly related to this predicate).

The same is true of other values. It is only of a person that we can predicate a deep and penetrating mind, genius, wisdom, or artistic talent. On the other hand, even a stone, a tree, or an animal can be beautiful. Beauty is to be found in the most various domains of being. We can speak of the beauty of a virtue, of the beauty of an action, of a rich and profound mind, of a book because of its truth-content, etc.

When we think of aesthetic values we of course have in mind above all the beauty of the visible and the audible, rather than the beauty of purely spiritual entities; but there indubitably exists a genuine beauty of

7. We speak of the aesthetic values that are not subspecies of beauty later on in the present chapter, in chap. 4, chap. 5, and in chaps. 17, 18, and 19.

8. Cf. *Ethics*, chap. 15.

virtue, genius, and other general personal values, such as the beauty of courage, just as there exist aesthetic disvalues such as the wretchedness and specific ugliness of cowardice. The attitudes and actions of the person can likewise possess an explicitly aesthetic quality: pettiness is ugly, and stupidity and intellectual shallowness also have a negative aesthetic value. This finds clear expression in the fact that some people are at risk of seeing human actions and attitudes largely in an aesthetic light.[9]

We shall look in detail later at the various kinds of beauty in the individual domains of being, and especially at the difference between the beauty of visible and audible things, on the one hand, and the beauty of purely spiritual things, on the other. At this point, the important thing to see is that beauty, unlike moral values and other values mentioned above, does not presuppose a person as its bearer, but can belong to various things and can be found in the most diverse domains of being. It is not difficult to see that, unlike moral values, the entire family of aesthetic values is not exclusively tied to persons as bearers. It is rather the case that one is tempted to limit beauty to the domain of the visible and the audible (rather than to the domain of the personal). Let us consider why that too would be a mistake.

When Alcibiades said of Socrates that he was the most beautiful of men although his face was pronouncedly ugly, this statement was entirely in order. Socrates's personality possessed high beauty and greatness of spirit; his virtue, moral nobility, and luminous mind are not merely beautiful in some analogous sense. This beauty differs in many ways from the beauty of the visible and audible, but it is a genuine beauty in the full sense of the word.

This beauty is also expressed in the very important Greek word *kalokagathon* (the beautiful, the good, the perfect). In Plato and Plotinus, the superiority of the beauty of spiritual things to the beauty of the visible and the audible is emphasized, although both philosophers explicitly acknowledge the latter in its value (especially Plotinus in the ninth *Ennead*).

9. Cf. *Graven Images*, chaps. 2 and 6.

Saint Augustine discusses the beauty of the visible and the audible in a number of his writings, especially in the *De musica.* But he also emphasizes the beauty of virtue and of truth. Above all, he speaks of the infinite beauty of God. How glorious are the words in the twenty-seventh chapter of the tenth book of the *Confessions*: "O beauty, so old and ever new!" He sees so deeply the justification for speaking both of the beauty of the visible and the audible *and* of the beauty of spiritual things, such as of virtue and truth, and above all of God, that he summons us to rise up from the beauty of the physical things that manifests itself to us through our senses, to the beauty of spiritual things, and on to the infinite holy beauty of God.

We shall return to all this; here I wish only to show how wrong it would be to limit the phenomenon of beauty—of this unique type of value—to the sphere of the visible and the audible and to see in the expression "the beauty of virtue" only a very analogous use of the term "beauty," or even merely a manner of speaking.

The specific beauty of all values, and the specific ugliness of all disvalues

When we investigate the relationship of the value family beauty to other value families, we discover one essential fact: that all the other values possess a specific beauty, and all the disvalues a specific ugliness. This is most striking in the case of moral values. The virtues of purity, humility, and truthfulness possess a special beauty of their own. Impurity, arrogance, and mendacity are ugly in a specific manner. The beauty of the virtues and the ugliness of the vices seem to be an irradiation of the moral values and disvalues. This does not mean that one and the same attitude is simultaneously morally good and beautiful, but that the beauty has its foundation in the moral value and the ugliness in the moral disvalue, and that this relationship of "foundation" is unique. This beauty is, as it were, the reflection, the irradiation, the fragrance of the moral value. The same is true of the relationship between the ugliness and the vice: it is a stench of the moral disvalue. We could say that this beauty is the noble face of moral value, and this ugliness the hideous face of moral disvalue. Here we have what we might call a metaphysical dimension based on how something "looks."

The metaphysical dimension of "outward appearance," delightfulness and fruendum

When we speak here of an outward appearance, we certainly do not mean only appearance in the sphere of the visible, but a primordial dimension of being, namely, that which shines out in the beauty of moral value, the morally good, and the individual virtues as *splendor*, as fragrance, as an irradiation of the moral value. This dimension of the outward appearance addresses itself in a special way to the person: it has the character of a self-revelation, a speaking to the person. And this is also expressed in the fact that every beauty is a *delectabile*, something delightful. Of course, beauty does not derive its importance from its capacity to give us joy, for then it would no longer be a genuine value. Beauty does not belong to the *bona delectabilia* as opposed to the *bona honesta.*[10]

It is important to see that the importance-in-itself of beauty, its genuine character as value (in our special sense of "value") is in no way diminished by its "delightfulness." It belongs to the essence of beauty and its metaphysical dimension of outward appearance that it is delightful thanks to the fullness of its value. The beautiful calls us to apprehend it, to be happy in it, to take delight in it.

This is why beauty plays such a fundamental role in love. Love responds to the overall beauty of the person who is loved. The highest love, the love for Christ, responds to the divine holy beauty of Jesus. It is not for nothing that one of the last invocations in the Litany of the Sacred Heart of Jesus says: *Cor Jesu, deliciae sanctorum omnium* ("Heart

10. I have pointed out in detail in my *Ethics* the inadequacy of the distinctions among *bonum utile, delectabile,* and *honestum* (the useful, the delightful, and the worthy good). This inadequacy, however, does not in any way nullify the profound insight of Aristotle that underlies this distinction.

of Jesus, delight of all the saints"). It is characteristic even of a purely natural love for a person, which is always love for the person as a whole, that it is a value-response to the beloved person's overall beauty,[11] which also contains the reflection of all moral and spiritual values. How profound and significant it is when Tristan, in his vision in the third act of *Tristan und Isolde*, cries out the ultimate word that sums up everything, the deepest word of love: "Isolde, how beautiful you are!"

This role that beauty plays in love, however, must not in any way be understood to mean that beauty is the theme of love. There is a radical difference between the value-response of love to a person and the value-response to a work of art, for in this latter case the beauty is indeed thematic. The beauty of the beloved person is, as it were, an irradiation of all his or her other values. It is these (the moral, "intellectual," and vital values of this person) that are the theme. The metaphysical beauty which is their irradiation does not interfere with the thematicity of these values; on the contrary, it gives them particular prominence. Love would be undermined if one were to make the "glory" of the other values, the beauty that emanates from them, the theme. In addition, the love refers to this real individual person and embraces this person in his or her totality. This is why one cannot take the same attitude to a beloved person that one takes to a work of art; such an attitude would be utterly incompatible with the essence of love.[12]

The important point here is to see that beauty belongs to the sphere of glory and is a *fruendum* ("something to be enjoyed"). This is true not only of beauty, but of all the aesthetic values, albeit in an analogous manner: all the aesthetic values possess this dimension of outward appearance, and all are delightful. Naturally, the delightfulness of the comic cannot be compared to the delightfulness of sublime beauty, nor above all to the sublime beauty of holiness; but the comic too is characterized by the dimension of outward appearance. It appeals to us to apprehend it. It addresses us and is a typical *fruendum*. One could perhaps see these

11. Cf. *The Nature of Love*, chap. 1.
12. Cf. ibid., chap. 2.

two characteristics—the dimension of outward appearance[13] and the delightfulness—as the traits that bind together all the aesthetic values (both beauty as thematic, as for example in art, and beauty as a superabundant gift) to form one single value family.

Metaphysical beauty as the irradiation of other values

We return now to the relationship between aesthetic values, especially beauty, and the sphere of moral values. The aesthetic value of morally positive value, or the aesthetic disvalue of moral disvalue, is a necessary and profoundly important irradiation, but it is never the theme. The moral value, which is completely different from the aesthetic value, is the theme; its aesthetic value is a superabundant gift. This aesthetic value, this beauty, lacks all the special characteristics that define the moral value family.[14] At the same time, the link is so close that this beauty of the morally good is inseparable from the moral value. It is the beauty of the moral value—its "face," its "appearance." It announces the moral value. We can apprehend this beauty only when we have grasped the moral value in its specificity, only when it forms the primary theme for us, only when we understand the unique primacy of moral values and the moral question. Then, however, the full apprehending of the beauty of the moral value is one particular stage of understanding this value and encountering it. Its beauty demands a value-response; and this is equally true of the ugliness of the moral disvalue.

The special beauty of holiness and the demonic ugliness of sin are more unambiguously given to us than any other beauty or ugliness.

13. The dimension of outward appearance is understood here in a very broad sense. It is not limited to the sphere of sight, especially since we are dealing above all with metaphysical beauty. When we speak, for example, of the metaphysical beauty of purity or of justice, it is the moral values that are the true reality. Their beauty, fragrance, and irradiation belong to the sphere of the "outward appearance" of these values. What is involved here is a perception with the mind, not in the least a seeing with the eyes. Likewise, in the case of the beauty that is mediated by the senses (both the more primitive beauty and the high spiritual beauty), this dimension of the outward appearance is not limited to the act of seeing. It is found just as much in the beauty of the audible and in the beauty of that which is mediated by words. The dimension of how things look extends to all beauty in nature and art.

14. Cf. my *Ethics*, chap. 15.

The "intellectual" values, too, irradiate their own specific beauty. The depth and stature of a mind is something beautiful, and genius has a captivating aesthetic value. Intellectual limitation and banality [*Plattheit*] in particular are aesthetic disvalues. The disvalue of banality is triviality, and the disvalue of superficiality is tediousness and boringness. The fullness and richness of a mind, the unlimited unfolding of a gift, have an aesthetic fascination that we call brilliant. Similarly, the quick and sure functioning of a mind, or its wittiness, are often brilliant. All these aesthetic values and disvalues are irradiations of the "intellectual" values and disvalues.

In the sphere of the technical values, or values of perfection[15] such as energy, willpower, etc., which are neither moral nor "intellectual" values, we can likewise speak of specifically aesthetic values.

Many personal values that are not specifically moral, such as courage[16] and fearlessness, likewise bear a clearly aesthetic value. Courage is something beautiful. Unlike the wretched puniness of timidity, courage possesses an aesthetic attractiveness.

Here, however, a question is often raised: Does there exist primarily an aesthetic value that attaches directly to these qualities and attitudes of the person, or does physical courage possess a value of its own that bears the aesthetic value but has a theme of its own, a theme of a different kind? Are we really guilty of aestheticism if we concentrate on the aesthetic value of great physical courage, as shown in a bullfight or in diving into the sea from two hundred meters at Acapulco in Mexico? We do not wish to explore this question in greater detail here;[17] it suffices to see that we encounter in courage an aesthetic value of a particular kind that presupposes a personal attitude and is not just the beauty of the visible of which we can say, *visum placet* ("it gives delight when it is seen").

15. *Graven Images*, chap. 5.

16. Ibid., chap. 5.

17. Naturally courage takes on a high moral value when it is at the service of realizing a morally relevant good, such as the saving of a life. But it is clear that this courage is something completely new in relation to the purely vital courage that finds expression above all in athletic achievements.

Similarly, the vital values of health, vigorous life, or an especially tender vital structure, all have a specific aesthetic value, just as their opposites have a specific aesthetic disvalue.

At this point let it suffice to point out that there exists a genuine beauty outside the sphere of the visible and the audible. This beauty adheres to spiritual entities, but not directly: it is an irradiation of other values that belong to these entities. This beauty, which has its basis in other values in the uniquely intimate relationship of foundation that we call the irradiation, fragrance, and glory of those particular values, is a broad, comprehensive realm of beauty. We will call this genuine beauty by the name of metaphysical beauty.

It is easy to see that the height or rank of this beauty depends entirely on the rank of the value of which it is the irradiation. The beauty of the values that belong to a higher value family is always an even greater and more sublime beauty. Moral values are even more beautiful than vital values, and holiness is even more beautiful than all other values.

The hierarchy within a family of values also determines the rank of the irradiated beauty. The higher a virtue stands in the hierarchy of the morally good, or the greater the moral value of an action, the more beautiful is the virtue or the action.[18]

Before we discuss various questions related to metaphysical beauty, we must demarcate it from the beauty that is called a *transcendental property of being*.

Are being and beauty coextensive? Maritain's thesis

In the philosophy of Saint Thomas Aquinas we find the view that *ens et bonum convertuntur*.[19] The character of *bonum* belongs to every being *qua*

18. According to a striking utterance of Lacordaire, the virtues become captivating and draw us by means of their example only when they are also beautiful. Does this affirmation entail that the virtues become beautiful only from one particular level onward, only when they are fully formed? Or does it mean that beauty shines out, becomes "visible," only when certain other conditions are fulfilled?

19. Cf. chap. 1 above, n. 20.

being. *Bonum* is called a transcendental property of being because it belongs to being as such, independently of the genus and the species of the being. Just like being, *bonum* possesses an analogous character that includes all genera but is not itself a genus. The same affirmation is made of *pulchrum*.[20] The beautiful too is understood as an aspect of being *qua* being.

Maritain, as a strict Thomist, adopts this thesis of Saint Thomas and draws a distinction between beauty as a transcendental property of being and "aesthetic" beauty, by which he means the beauty of the visible and the audible. He expresses this clearly in his book *Creative Intuition in Art and Poetry*, when he says "that this category of the ugly has no sense for a pure spirit, and no sense for God. Because a pure spirit sees everything in a merely intellectual, not sensitive manner. Ugly is what, being seen, displeases: where there are no senses, there is no category of ugliness."[21] We see that when Maritain speaks of "aesthetic" beauty and ugliness, he is thinking only of visible and audible things.[22]

20. Cf. *Summa Theologicae* I, q. 5, a. 4.

21. Jacques Maritain, *Creative Intuition in Art and Poetry* (New York: Meridian Books, 1954), 126.

22. It is exceedingly astonishing that Maritain assumes that since they have no senses, pure spirits such as angels can apprehend less of being than we human beings. It seems that Maritain views the extremely important human aspect of the world and all the beauty of nature as a kind of illusion, and that he treats the objects of physics as the more genuine reality which is independent of our consciousness. Quite apart from the unjustified "metaphysicization" of the objects of physics—waves, movements, electricity, etc.—one should surely suppose that a spirit apprehends more of being, the higher, more comprehensive, and more unlimited the spirit is. One should not suppose that a great and important part of reality would remain closed for this spirit because he has no body. Does Maritain really intend to assert that colors, sounds, etc., are not important contents that represent an image of God and a special message from God? Does he not see that in their character as a message from God, they are much more important than mere waves? Does he not see that they possess a higher value? I have written above in detail about the human aspect of the world and its objective validity, and in *What is Philosophy?* chap. 5; here I must limit myself to a reference to those passages. Let me, however, underline at this point that Maritain's view takes on a grotesque character when he extends this absence of the human aspect as far as God, the omniscient, the Creator of heaven and earth. It is nonsensical to suppose that God, who after all created and intended the beauty of visible nature, cannot apprehend it! This beauty is a message that proclaims Him and elevates us to Him, a summons to human beings, a natural revelation addressed to them that contains in itself a praise of God.

In the eyes of God, according to Maritain, none of this plays any role: for Him, it is only naked being *qua* being that counts.

Is it not the case that one who knows only physical processes, but not the rich, colorful, shaped, resounding world, would possess a much more primitive knowledge than the one who apprehends this message, this deeper and more genuine reflection of God that is contained in the human aspect of the exterior world?

But we also see clearly that the distinction between beauty as a transcendental property of being and the beauty of the visible and the audible —which he calls "aesthetic" beauty, asserting that it is only this beauty that has an opposite, which he calls the "category" of the ugly—is not in the least identical with the distinction I have drawn between metaphysical beauty and the beauty of the visible and the audible. Above all, what I call metaphysical beauty is certainly not identical with Maritain's transcendental property of being. Metaphysical beauty, far from being a quality of being *qua* being, is a beauty that has its foundation only in the values of various things. A purely neutral being is not a bearer of metaphysical beauty.

When Maritain limits ugliness to the sphere of the visible and the audible, he does astonishing violence to the facts. It is difficult to suppose that he fails to see the terrible ugliness of sin, the abysmal ugliness of evil. He attempts to correct this in a footnote by conceding that in the eyes of God the "nothing" that lies in the free act of a human being is ugly; but he emphasizes that nothing which exists can be ugly, appealing to Angelus Silesius for support.[23] Clearly, however, the assertion that moral evil is non-being is a completely artificial construction. Unfortunately, moral evil is a monstrous reality.[24]

Must we not assume that the light waves and sound waves were created for the sake of the colors and sounds, just like the human eye and ear? Or should we instead believe that these waves are a much more serious reality, in metaphysical terms, that was created for its own sake, whereas the colors are a subjective phenomenon conditioned by the facts that the human being has a body and that his knowledge is bound to his senses? Is cognition through the senses really less deep and valid than the cognition by a purely spiritual being?

If God does not see the ugliness, it follows that he does not see the beauty of his creation either. The manner in which God knows, recognizes, and apprehends everything cannot be compared to our knowing and apprehending. But this does not mean that He of whom Jesus says that no sparrow falls to the ground without God knowing it (cf. Matthew 10:29) would fail to apprehend a high value that we apprehend and that also expresses a special message from Him to us.

23. Angelus Silesius, *The Cherubic Pilgrim* (1674):

> *"Man, nothing is imperfect; the gravel is equal to the ruby,*
> *The frog is just as beautiful as the seraphim." V, 61*
>
> *"God pays just as much attention to the croaking of the frog*
> *As to the trill that the lark brings forth for Him." I, 269*

24. It is difficult for a Christian to harmonize the idea that moral evil is non-being with the idea that God is offended by sin, and especially with the death of Christ on the cross as the expiation for sins. Can the terrible momentousness of sin, to which the mercy of God responded through the expiatory sacrifice of His Son, be regarded as a mere "non-being"? And is the devil a "nothing"?

It is true that moral badness, or evil, has been interpreted not as pure non-being, but as a lack (*privatio*) of the being that belongs to the will of the human person. But this too can at most explain the imperfection of a being, never the evil in it. A weak will, or an absence of the will in situations in which a person ought to will, or the absence of energy or a virtue, could indeed still be interpreted as the lack of something that belongs to the meaning and essence of a being; but moral evil, hatred, rebellion against God, envy, or resentment can never be interpreted as a lack of being.

This whole view of evil is based on an "axiom" that is not in any way evident and has never been proven, *ens et bonum convertuntur.* From this axiom the inference is drawn that all disvalue must be a lack of being. But an unprejudiced look at the facts shows unambiguously the difference between neutral being and the being that is valuable and important in itself. The relationship of the value to being is much more complicated, as I have pointed out in chapter 12 of my *Ethics.* Josef Seifert has worked out this relationship in a very profound analysis.[25]

Maritain also fails to recognize the important difference between ontological and qualitative values. As long as we are speaking of ontological values, the only opposite is the simple absence of these values, not beings that would be an antithesis to these values. In the realm of the qualitative values, on the other hand, there exist definite disvalues that are the true opposites of values. The disvalues belong to really existing bearers: they are no mere lack, but a real qualitative character of these bearers. In the realm of the qualitative values, we find good and evil, beautiful and ugly: these are genuine, real antitheses. It is indubitably correct to say that no substance *qua* substance has a negative value, but accidents, if we extend—this extension is questionable—this concept to cover even the attitudes of persons and the quality of these attitudes, are

25. Josef Seifert, "Die verschiedenen Bedeutungen von 'Sein'—Dietrich von Hildebrand als Metaphysiker und Martin Heideggers Vorwurf der Seinsvergessenheit," in *Wahrheit, Wert und Sein.*

equally genuine beings. I have discussed all these questions in my *Ethics*, chapter 10.

We can now see that Maritain's assertion that ugliness exists only in the realm of the visible and audible is clearly false. Many spiritual attitudes and spiritual entities can be not only beautiful but also bearers of ugliness. For example, all the attitudes that are bearers of moral disvalues are ugly in the full sense of a qualitative aesthetic ugliness, and, as we have shown, the same applies to the bearers of other disvalues. It is also clear that Maritain's distinction between beauty as a transcendental property of being and as "aesthetic" beauty is not at all equivalent to our distinction between metaphysical beauty and the beauty of the visible and the audible. Metaphysical beauty is not in the least a transcendental property of being in the sense that this term possesses in Thomistic philosophy.

Neutral being that possesses no other value than the value of existence

The value of being *qua* being—the mysterious dignity that being possesses as opposed to non-being and to all illusion and fiction—is an exceedingly important datum. We do not notice it as long as we only pretend that something exists. But this value does not abolish the distinction between neutral being and valuable being, since this value of being *qua* being is clearly different from the ontological value of one *particular* kind of being, and *a fortiori* different from the qualitative values. I have written about this in my *Ethics* (in the Prolegomena and in chapter 12).

In many cases qualitative values are such that they completely overshadow this value of existence as such. It plays a role in the qualitative values only in the sense that everything that is good ought to exist and that this existence is in turn the bearer of a new value. Here too, however, it is also true that everything that is morally negative ought not to be, and that the existence of something morally evil such as hatred, envy, or delight in other people's misfortune is a new disvalue. In moral evil the mere value of being *qua* being is completely covered over by the qualitative disvalue.

In my *Ethics* I pointed out that this value of being *qua* being is seldom apprehended as such and is seldom thematic. In the case of neutral being, that is, a being that possesses no ontological value on the basis of what it is and *a fortiori* possesses no qualitative values, this value emerges only when we concentrate in a special way on its pure being, that is, when we abstract from the whole of its essence and think only of the dignity that it possesses in comparison to non-being. But the beauty that goes with this most general value of existence and reflects the value remains a very abstract beauty. Normally it moves into the background when compared to the beauty of a being's ontological values, and above all when compared to the beauty of its qualitative values.

This value of existence takes on a new splendor when we relate it to ontological and qualitative value. We do this, for example, when we think of the value of the state-of-affairs that such a noble person exists or that such a glorious landscape exists. The existence of the valuable and non-neutral is of course always something thematic, something luminously valuable. This value of existence is, however, replaced by a terrible disvalue in the case of a major bearer of qualitative disvalues. In this case we have to say: "If only this had never become real!" The existence of dangerous ideologies is a great evil; the existence of Communism and of National Socialism is a dreadful evil in itself. It does not matter whether such evils, through the mercy of God, can in the course of history come to serve something valuable that is the exact opposite of their essence and intention. In exactly the same way a murder remains a sin even when it becomes a *felix culpa* (a "happy fault"). Not only does it remain something disvaluable in itself, a terrible sin that offends God; the state-of-affairs that a murder was realized and that a human being fell so low also remains a disvalue. God has the power to "overtake" this disvalue through something positive and to give this event a completely new meaning through its consequences—consequences that are opposed to its essence and indeed bestow a new value on it—but this does not change the fact that its existence is as such an evil.

The beauty of ontological values and of technical values

It is not only the qualitative values which have an aesthetic value that is, as it were, their *splendor*, their irradiation. The ontological values too irradiate a metaphysical beauty, for example, the dignity and nobility of the person, the ontological value of the living in the realm of fauna and flora, or the ontological value of each individual type in the hierarchy of the animals and plants (that is to say, not the value of the being *qua* being, but the value of one particular being on the basis of its particular essence), and the dignity of inanimate matter.

We must also mention the aesthetic value that attaches to the category of values that we have called the values of perfection or technical values. All such values (for example, strength of power, energy, good memory, or mental acuteness) have an aesthetic value, a modest radiance, a positive aesthetic outward appearance. This is for the most part not real beauty; rather, we find here more modest aesthetic values that are not subspecies of beauty but by their quality tend rather in another direction. We cannot find any proper name for the aesthetic value of acuteness of mind, nor even of a good memory, but it would clearly sound wrong if we were to speak of beauty in these instances. Both are impressive, and we admire them. There can be no doubt that not only the value of perfection is present, but also an aesthetic value that has an outward appearance that is delightful in some way.

The will, the ability to will, and above all the freedom of the will, all have great ontological value. The will is an extraordinarily precious gift, a primordial element of personal being. It is *as such* the property of all persons. Its freedom can be inhibited only by madness or mental retardation. There are, nevertheless, more and less energetic persons—there is in this regard a vast difference between a Peter the Great of Russia and an Oblomov.[26]

Energy, strength of will, and the ability to resist one's own instincts and tendencies, to fight them and emancipate oneself from them, are potentially contained in the gift of free will. But the actual unfolding and

26. The protagonist in the novel of the same name by Goncharov.

development of these things is something new. It is clear that this type of value, a value of perfection, is completely different from the qualitative value of the *good* will. It can be found both in bad persons and in good ones. It intensifies the good will in a certain sense, and it intensifies the bad will. In itself, strength of will is a value that also possesses its own irradiation and outward appearance. As long as it is not distorted by the qualitative disvalue, its aesthetic value is also a *delectabile.*

Greatness and stature [Bedeutendheit]

Above all, there is a whole range of definitely aesthetic values that are the irradiation of general personal values such as great stature, intellectual brilliance, etc. This class of values differs from the values of perfection, which refer to the extent of the perfection of an ontological value.

If we say of someone that he is a personality of stature, or that he is a kind of genius, we are clearly speaking not only of the unfolding of an ontological value but of something much less formal, a specific gift, something qualitatively new. It is not a matter of qualitative values like moral values or like intelligence or intellectual depth. As I have shown above in the case of the "intellectual" personal values, these values concern something found in various spheres. Someone can be significant as a personality because of his great human stature. But he can also be significant in some particular respect, significant as a general, like Alexander the Great, or significant because of his greatness as a philosopher, like Plato, Aristotle, or Augustine; he can also be significant as a scientist, researcher, inventor, artist, and so on. Though this value quality can be manifested in various fields, there are many professions in which this is not possible. We find everywhere that people can perform their professional work very capably— this is true of a cobbler, a baker, a train driver, or a notary—but one can scarcely speak of authentic significance and stature in the case of even the best cobbler, baker, or notary. Balzac's father wanted him to become a notary, but he was quite correct to say to him: "No, I want to become a great man!" A notary can never be great, no matter how capable he may be.

Naturally, the greatness or significance that someone has because of his great human stature is completely independent of the kind of professional work he performs. Here we must bear in mind, on the one hand, that values of this kind (such as stature, greatness, great intellectual power, etc.) are not mere values of perfection, but something qualitative; and on the other hand, that they are also formal values that can manifest themselves in various fields, doubtless always with a specific qualitative manifestation. They do not, however, form a thematically united qualitative family of values. Nor are they tied only to persons. One scientific book can be significant, while another is insignificant; the same applies to works of art. Similarly, one happening, one event can be significant, while another event is insignificant.

Here, of course, we exclude that significance which is nothing other than a consequence of quantity. If we speak of a significant sum of money, we do not envisage any value, but something completely different, something quantitative. If, however, we say of an historic moment, for example, the battle of Actium or Charles Martel's victory over the Arabs at Poitiers, that it is significant, we mean significance in the true sense of the word. We are referring to a value that this event possesses. The question whether this significant historical event was fortunate or catastrophic, whether the victory *qua* victory has value or disvalue, is irrelevant here. The value of the significant, in comparison to the insignificant, is a quality *sui generis.*

The genuine "greatness" of historic moments demands more than that an event has great consequences. It need not be a fortunate event—the victory of the good or the birth of a great saint, in short an event that is rich in other values—but a genuine greatness must be present, and not just the victory of mere mediocrity (what Kierkegaard calls "being trampled to death by geese"). Thus an event is not great that is indeed far-reaching and momentous in its consequences, but is in reality the victory of mediocrity, of base propaganda, indeed of stupidity. No, the phenomenon of the greatness of an historic moment is a quality of a specific kind, and it presupposes a number of things. The swindle of the fire in the Reichstag in 1933, which made it possible for the Nazis to abolish the rule of law in the German state, has the character of a cheap trick, a bad farce, although its consequences were subsequently to cost millions of people their lives. The invasion of Greece by the Nazis, who planted the swastika flag on the Parthenon, was even less an event of greatness. It was an embarrassing, pathetic piece of theater that is impressive (if at all) only thanks to its dreadful irony. There was no greatness of any kind in the wretched spectacle whereby the Parthenon, this symbol of genuine greatness of mind and the noblest beauty, was desecrated by the brown shirts and the mendacious symbol of the swastika. The victory of the anonymous mechanized power of the German convoys lacked every element of the greatness of the elemental force that we see in Attila, or of the brilliance of a victory by Napoleon.

We just saw that true greatness and stature possesses a particular aesthetic value, irrespective of the field in which it manifests itself. In many cases, however, the very thing that possesses greatness can simultaneously have great disvalues of another kind, for example, moral disvalues. In that case the aesthetic value of the greatness stands alongside the grim ugliness of sin, and in fact serves to increase it. Thus it would be a repulsive, indeed a sinful aestheticism, if one were to concentrate on the aesthetic value of the greatness. In the world of the imitative arts, however, in which everything is transposed—especially in literature—the aesthetic value of greatness, even the greatness of a wicked person, can serve the artistic beauty of the whole.

We find a completely different coupling of greatness or stature with disvalue in the case not of moral disvalue, but of events that are calamitous and bring much harm in their wake. Although the greatness is not poisoned here in the same way as when it is paired with the morally bad, here too the aesthetic value of the greatness must never be detached, still less enjoyed on its own, because the theme (as in the combination with a moral disvalue) is clearly something different.

We have already seen that the metaphysical beauty of moral values must never be the main focus of our attention, and that this sublime beauty is of its essence a superabundant epiphenomenon. It is meant to make us profoundly happy, and we are meant to "enjoy" it in the highest sense of this term. But if we were to fail to understand the thematicity of the moral, and were to attempt to make this beauty the theme, we would not only fall at once into an aestheticist attitude, but this beauty would melt away and become invisible. In the case of the aesthetic value of some other element, for example, of stature, which is not the reflection of a moral value, this aesthetic value must never be "enjoyed" when it is coupled with a moral disvalue, because the theme is a moral one, and it would be a terrible aestheticism to ignore this theme. This applies by analogy also to those cases involving the greatness of a calamitous event. The thematicity of the calamity prohibits a *frui* of the greatness.

There are many other value qualities analogous to stature and significance. These too are bearers of aesthetic value. They do not belong to any qualitative value family, but they can manifest themselves in certain qualitative value families and can be coupled with moral or with "intellectual" value.

We leave open here the question whether the link between these aesthetic values and these value qualities is precisely the same as the link in which metaphysical beauty has its foundation in moral, "intellectual," and vital values. In the present context it suffices to point to the type of aesthetic value that is found in these general value qualities, which for their part belong to mental or spiritual entities or to things such as events, facts, and communities, but of course also extend to the sphere of the visible and audible.

If we look at the aesthetic value qualities that are usually categorized as subspecies of beauty, qualities such as delightful, sublime, graceful, or poetic, it appears that the aesthetic value sphere displays no more variations than the moral value sphere. If, however, we think of the immeasurable number of aesthetic values resulting from the fact that all the other kinds of values (such as the ontological, the technical, and all the qualitative value families) possess a special quality of beauty that differs in accordance with the specific bearer, and if we think of all the aesthetic values like the value of stature, of greatness, of grandness, and so on, we gain some insight into the inexhaustible wealth of aesthetic values. There is an immense differentiation in this domain of values, which as such is always a qualitative domain, even when the aesthetic value is not the reflection, the fragrance, or the outward appearance of qualitative values, but grows out of ontological and other types of values.

We shall speak in later chapters of other qualities to which metaphysical beauty can belong, such as qualities of blossoming (in chapter 8); of power, solidity, and immovability (in chapter 9); and of the joyfulness of the sky, the quality of the morning, and other beauties of nature (in chapter 14).

The fundamental difference between metaphysical beauty and the beauty of the visible and the audible

Now we wish to turn to the following fundamental difference within the world of aesthetic values. On the one hand, we have the metaphysical beauty that has its foundation in other values and is the splendor, the fragrance, the irradiation of those values; and on the other hand, we have the beauty of the visible and the audible. As we shall show in chapter 6 below, we must distinguish in the case of the latter between two very different types, namely, between a more primitive beauty that (for want of a better term) we call the beauty of sensible things [*Sinnenschönheit*][27] or beauty of the first power, and a high spiritual beauty that we shall call the beauty of the second power.

Up to now, we have spoken primarily of the first form of aesthetic values (metaphysical beauty). Now we wish to turn to the beauty of the visible and the audible.

The beauty of an ornament or the capital of a column, or the beauty of the sound of a flute, is not the fragrance or irradiation of another value but belongs directly to this object. A melody, just like the ornament or the column, is a direct bearer of beauty. The primary theme is not some other value, but the beauty itself. Irrespective of whether the bearers of

27. [With *Sinnenschönheit* Hildebrand refers here to one kind of beauty of the visible and audible, namely the kind he calls beauty of the first power, or primative beauty; but in other palces, as in the title of this chapter, he refers with Sinnenschönheit to all beauty of the visible and audible, including the beauty of the second power. JFC]

beauty also possess another importance, are useful, or serve some other practical function, this beauty does not have its foundation in other indirect values that may or may not be present. It depends on completely different factors, for example, on color, form, or proportion in the case of the visible. It is the main value that belongs to these visible or audible entities. As we shall see below, this difference in the relationship to the bearer and to the factors on which the beauty depends is of central importance.

But both metaphysical beauty and the beauty of the visible and the audible are the same type of fundamental value. They belong to the same qualitative aesthetic value family. The great hierarchy and differentiation within beauty is found in metaphysical beauty and indeed in all the aesthetic values of spiritual entities, as well as in the beauty of the visible and the audible. This latter entails a specific problem that we shall consider in detail in a later chapter. The difference between metaphysical beauty and the beauty of the visible and the audible goes in a different direction than the qualitatively different types of beauty and the various levels of beauty.

We have distinguished metaphysical beauty from the beauty of the visible and the audible, while at the same time emphasizing their qualitative kinship that justifies us in calling both of them "beauty" in the full sense of the term. We shall now proceed to investigate how metaphysical beauty is given to us in experience, and then how the beauty of the visible and the audible, which presupposes the senses, is given to us.

CHAPTER THREE

How Is Metaphysical Beauty Given in Our Experience?

THE QUESTION how metaphysical beauty is given to us presupposes the question how moral, "intellectual," vital, and ontological values are given to us. I have discussed this question in several of my books;[1] here let me only mention the following principal types of the apprehension of value.

Stages of the immediate apprehension of values

We can apprehend the moral values of actions when we look at the qualitative character of particular actions in general. If we consider what a murder, theft, deceit, or rape is, we can immediately apprehend its moral disvalue, unless we are blind to moral values. The moral disvalue has its foundation in this type of action. When we visualize the specific quality of an action, its moral value or disvalue is immediately given to us. If

1. *Ethics*, chaps. 10 and 15; *Sittlichkeit und ethische Werterkenntnis*, reprinted together with my *Die Idee der sittlichen Handlung* by the Wissenschaftliche Buchgemeinschaft (Darmstadt, 1969); *The Nature of Love*, chaps. 1, 2, 5.

someone suggests that we should take part in a fraud, the moral disvalue is immediately obvious to us. Our conscience warns us against getting involved in any way. Likewise, when a life is saved, the moral value is immediately present to us. The essential point we must see here is that it suffices to understand the essence of a particular action or of a person's behavior in order to grasp the specific quality of this behavior and apprehend in an intuitive manner the moral value or disvalue of the behavior.

There are no doubt many gradations of the givenness of this value or disvalue; it need not always be an immediate givenness.

If we know what is morally right or wrong only because an authority has told us this, we may perhaps believe that it is in principle morally wrong to do certain things, or morally good or even obligatory to do certain other things; but we need not understand this. *A fortiori*, we do not need to understand, or to grasp intuitively, the specific value or disvalue of some particular behavior. We cannot speak of the intuitive givenness of value.

Another form of knowledge of the moral value or disvalue of something is given when we have indeed once grasped and understood that a particular conduct is morally good or bad, for example, that almsgiving is morally good or that lying is morally bad, but at present we simply draw on this earlier insight so as to remember it without re-enacting it. Thus we remain at a distance, having no intuition of the value or disvalue. It is mere knowledge (albeit absolutely certain) of a state-of-affairs, namely, "This is bad" or "This is good."

A completely new form of the apprehension of value occurs when we hear of a concrete action, for example, when we hear of someone who heroically saves another's life at the cost of his own, such as Saint Maximilian Kolbe in Auschwitz[2] or Mother Maria Scobtsova in Ravensbrück.[3] The moral greatness and the moral nobility of such a deed are immediately given to us.[4] We do not need to discuss here other grada-

2. Maria Winowska, *The Death Camp Proved Him Real* (Libertyvillle, Ill.: Marytown Press, 1971).

3. Sergei Hackel, *One, of Great Price. The Life of Mother Maria Scobtsova, Martyr of Ravensbrück* (London: Darton, Longman & Todd, 1965).

4. See my *Die Idee der sittlichen Handling*, part 2, chap. 2, 74ff.; *Sittlichkeit und ethische Werterkenntnis*, part 1, 2b, 131f.; *The Nature of Love*, chaps. 1 and 2.

tions, for example, the distinction between "apprehending a value" and "feeling a value," which we have set out in other books. The only relevant point here is to see that it suffices to think of some particular action, and that it is not necessary to have the action intuitively given to us in order to have its moral value or disvalue intuitively given to us. Even when the contact with a moral action is only indirect, as when someone tells us about it or we read about it, its moral value or disvalue can be intuitively given to us. We will speak in detail about how events, actions, and the modes of conduct of persons become intuitive, when we discuss in the second volume of this work the means employed by the arts in literature. Here it suffices to mention that with regard to the apprehension of the moral value, there is no decisive difference between being a witness to an action and only hearing or reading about it. In such cases, the moral value can be given to us with just as much intuitive presence and can just as profoundly affect us, take hold of us, and move us.

The ways in which metaphysical beauty is given

When moral value is intuitively given, its beauty too shines out. The senses, the eyes and ears, do not play a decisive role when metaphysical beauty now appears, since it does not appear in visible and audible entities but is a purely spiritual givenness, analogous to the immediate givenness of an essence in rational intuition. Although rational intuition is analogous to, rather than identical with, the intuition of metaphysical beauty, the two modes of presence have the character of a purely spiritual intuitiveness. This is one of the fundamental ways in which metaphysical beauty discloses itself to us. It suffices that the moral value be intuitively given to us—given when we reflect meditatively on the virtue of purity or humility, or when we learn about a concrete action, some specific behavior, by being told about it or by reading about it, or when we ourselves witness such a deed.

A second fundamental way in which metaphysical beauty can be apprehended is seen in the sphere of the visible and the audible: I refer to the case of a virtue being expressed in a person's face, when his face and his whole being bear witness to his kindness, his purity, his humility. In this case, metaphysical beauty reaches by means of this expression into the sphere of the visible and audible, and we encounter a new kind of givenness of metaphysical beauty. Here we touch something that fills us with marveling: the *mirandum*, or wonder of bodily expression. We shall discuss this in detail in chapter 5.

There is a third fundamental way in which metaphysical beauty is present: when the personality of someone discloses itself through many different kinds of channels. A person whom we know and with whom we live together discloses himself not only in his face, in the way he laughs and walks and moves, in his "bodily feeling," in his voice, but also in a completely new way in what he says, in how he says it, and above all in the position he takes with regard to all objective values. What are his interests? How deeply does the sphere of the beautiful in art and nature speak to him? How significant is his intellect? How burning is his love for the truth? How great is his potential for love? Does he have a sense of humor, and so on? All this reveals itself when I am in his company, sometimes more quickly, sometimes more slowly. Through which channels do I experience this? How do I form an impression of the quality of his personality? As I have said, the content of what he says plays a great role here: much is reflected in this.

First of all, the fundamental statements, when they are meant with full seriousness and are not the mere capricious assertions of a moment, reveal much about his understanding and depth. If these are fundamental statements about moral questions, they also reveal much about his basic attitude.

Secondly, the way in which he speaks about deep questions, his style, lets us recognize something of his personality. When we see something beautiful together with him, beautiful nature or architecture, or listen to beautiful music with him, what he says about this and his value-response disclose much to us about his being. The same is true of his value-response to literature and to all the visual arts.

Thirdly, his being discloses itself in things great and small: in the kindness with which he meets someone, in his patience or impatience in many situations, in the small ways in which he shows consideration to others, in his inclination readily to pay for others or rather to let others pay for him, and so on.

Here I wish only to point to the role played by words, actions, and conduct in the disclosure of a personality. The specific quality of this personality is thereby made intuitively accessible in a quite different manner than in the expression of the face, voice, and movements—in a word, in things visible and audible. It is of course true that we must in fact hear what the person in question says and not be deaf. We should perceive the way he deals with other persons, whether this reveals kindness, consideration, and love, or whether it reveals indifference, impertinence, arrogance, and malice. If we were blind and deaf we would be incapable of apprehending any of this. Nevertheless, the senses do not play the same role here as in the apprehending of expression.

Expression, too, can of course play a role in all these instances. For example, a person's deep emotion vis-à-vis a great work of art can express itself in his face; his kindness, love, and so on can find expression in the way he looks at others. It is not in the least my intention to downplay the role that expression plays in the disclosure of a personality through many other channels. All I wish to do is to show that there are many other ways in which, despite the continuously shifting facial expressions, the specific quality of a personality, his character, his basic attitude, and his spirit disclose themselves.

What a personality says or writes reflects his being primarily through the content. The tone of voice and the face that accompanies the words convey the other to us through expression in the full sense of the term. But what we learn about the essence of this personality through the meaning of the words that we understand, through the content of what is said, no longer passes via the channel of expression; and the same applies to what we learn of the essence of the personality through his deeds. We can hear of these deeds from other people, we can learn of them through a letter or from the personality himself, or, in the case of an historical personality, we can read his own words. If the person in question is unkind to someone and we are witnesses to this conduct, there is an additional factor in the face that he makes, the tone of voice in which he shouts at someone. These are mental attitudes expressed in visible and audible data. If we are not present as witnesses, the fact that they are expressed plays no role.

The fact that someone has committed adultery or a base swindle, or conversely, has helped another person most generously, or magnanimously forgiven another, discloses something of his essence in a completely different manner than the expression of his inner life in the realm of the visible and the audible.[5] The former is an indirect form of disclosure through a strictly intellectual-spiritual understanding [*durch das rein geistige Verstehen*] of the quality of the attitudes and actions. As we have said, seeing and hearing play a completely functional, indirect role here, which is why we cannot say that they express personal qualities in the world of the visible and the audible, or that these qualities "appear" in visible and audible things.

We see, therefore, that the metaphysical beauty of moral values, "intellectual" values, general personal values, and vital values can be intuitively given. It manifests itself not only through that expression (in the narrower sense of the term) through which metaphysical beauty becomes present to us in the sphere of the visible and the audible, but also through strictly intellectual-spiritual channels. Although the senses do play here a subordinate role, metaphysical beauty does not appear in visible and audible things but is conveyed to us by way of acts, modes of conduct, and statements, or by means of the character of the person.

5. Even when we are witnesses to a killing or a base act of heartlessness, or see how someone refuses to help another who is in need, we do not perceive the action in the same way as we perceive the facial expression of the person. Without discussing this purely epistemological question in further detail, I wish only to emphasize that the indirect path through which we learn about what has been said and done does not affect the intuitive presence of the values that attach to the actions, nor those values of the personality that make themselves known through one's fundamental principles, one's basic attitude, and what one says. Along with the intuitive givenness of the various values of this personality, the metaphysical beauty of these values is also intuitively given.

A completely new dimension of the disclosure of the personality of a human being, of his inner essence, opens up when it is a question of statements by which this person "declares" certain stances [*verlautbarte Stellungnahmen*] toward me [such as a declaration of love]. I have written in detail about the specific quality and the very special role of such "declarations" in my *Metaphysik der Gemeinschaft* (esp. in chaps. 1 and 4). Declarations are a revelation *sui generis* of the being of the speaker.

In a similar way, the metaphysical beauty of a profound truth exists for us immediately in the strictly intellectual-spiritual act of knowing, grasping, and understanding the truth, or every time we realize this truth.

At this point we must emphasize that the question of the mode of givenness of the beauty of the visible and the audible is identical to the question of the function which the various senses have in the constitution of this beauty. The mode of givenness of this beauty of the visable and the audible is not as such a problem of its own, analogous to the mode of the givenness of metaphysical beauty. But the difference in the role played by the individual senses is definitely a *mirandum*, a wonder. When we take up this question in the next chapter, the mode in which the beauty of the visible and the audible is given will also emerge clearly.

CHAPTER FOUR

The Role of the Senses in Apprehending Beauty

As we have seen, there exists not only that beauty which is the irradiation and fragrance of other values, and which we have called "metaphysical beauty," but also the beauty which adheres directly to material objects because of their form and color. It is this beauty that Saint Thomas has in mind when he defines it as follows: *Pulchra enim dicuntur, quae visa placent*.[1] We now turn to the question of how this beauty is present to us.

The beauty accessible to the senses, for example, the beauty of a color or of a sound, adheres to something visible or audible. Can it also adhere to other sensuous data—to the fragrance of a flower, or to the taste of food? And can we speak of beauty and ugliness in the case of those qualities which disclose themselves in the act of touching? Clearly, the other senses do not communicate beauty to us in the same way as the eye and the ear, as seeing and hearing. We must investigate why this is so, what

1. *Summa Theologiae* I, q. 5, a. 4, ad 1 ("For things are called beautiful when the sight of them gives pleasure"). Cf. I-II, q. 27, a. 1, ad 3.

aesthetic value qualities are communicated to us by the other senses, and how these differ from beauty.[2]

The beauty which is given through seeing

Let me point to the following essential traits of seeing. First, that which is seen is an objective datum which is clearly distinct from all mere sensory impressions. Here we are not interested in the question of the extent to which a color is a quality completely independent of our mind. What interests us is the fact that the color presents itself unambiguously on the object side as a quality of an object; that it stands at a distance to our own eyes; and that a clear "consciousness of" is present. This is quite the opposite of the sensation of burning in one's eye, or the sensation of being blinded by a light that is too strong, and so on. No other sense communicates such an objective datum to us as sight. No other sense, not even hearing, helps us to such a degree to achieve a clear knowledge and apprehension of something objective.

If we see the color of a green meadow or the yellowish-white color of travertine, this color does not imply a lived relationship to our eyes. We do of course know that we no longer see the color once we close our eyes. But when we see the color, this relationship to the eye is not given in the sense of being a specific experience of the eyes as such. The color communicates to us something about the object, not about our eyes. This is obvious when we compare the seeing of a color with the sensation provoked in our eyes by an excessively glaring light. In the latter case, our eye is the theme. We experience something unpleasant in our eye. This is clearly the opposite of the objectivity of that which is seen.

Likewise, in the attempt to see something which we cannot distinguish because of its distance or because of our near-sightedness, it is our seeing and not the thing seen that is thematic in the experience of unclarity, of

2. In his essay "The Nobility of Sight," in *The Phenomenon of Life: Toward a Philosophical Biology* (New York: Harper & Row, 1966), Hans Jonas underlines the unique role that seeing plays in our lives and its great superiority to the other senses.

not getting through to the object, and of making a laborious effort to see. We do not indeed experience any unpleasant sensation in our eye, considered as a part of our body. But the inability to see the object clearly means that we experience a limitation in our seeing, a sensation of failure which includes becoming conscious of the function of our eyes. Even when our eye is directed toward an object, the unpleasant sensation of effort and failure is not something that is seen. The sensation does not possess the objectivity of that which is seen, of the color and form of the object.

In addition to this transcendence of the act of seeing, and to the dignity it confers on the act of seeing, there is a second important factor. The perception which is bestowed on us through the eye is not in the least limited only to sensory data in the strict sense, such as colors and forms—that is an utterly sensualistic prejudice. When we open our eyes, a rich world of variegated things stands before us. For example, we look at a landscape and perceive mountains in the background. In the foreground is a piece of land with several different kinds of trees, some closer to us, others farther away. The two-dimensional space is immediately present to us, just like the colors; the three-dimensional space is immediately present to us, just like the forms of the trees and the mountains. We are not interested here in the question of the various experiences that are presupposed, if one is to understand what is seen. The only point that interests us is that the immediate perception of all these things—unlike those things which we only know about—comes about through the act of seeing, and that it is impossible for a blind person to have this immediate contact with the rich world of visible things.

The sphere of the visible not only encompasses objects of various kinds. There also exists an organic structure, from the most primitive sensory data such as colors, forms, and shapes up to entire situations. We encounter this structure as something objective. The two-dimensional space is necessarily linked to colors. These are always given to us as colors of something, as qualities of objects. We not only see a hill, a mountain, a meadow, the grass in the meadow, a tree, a group of trees, an alley, or a brook; mostly, these present themselves to us as a whole, unified thing. Naturally, we can look at them individually and apprehend them in their form and shape, their color and movement; but for the most part, the immediate experience is an overall impression. The same is true of a house, of a street with houses, of human beings and animals (such as dogs and cats), or of animals in a field (such as cows or sheep). The essential point is that the world of the visible is a world of wholes of every kind, differentiated rich wholes which are distributed in space in various ways and often come together to form an organic total picture, for example, a landscape in the typical sense of the term.

All this is found only with sight. As soon as we realize this, we apprehend the unique role that the visible can play as a bearer of beauty. Let me express this by means of an apparent paradox: the sense of sight is the most spiritual of all the senses.

The distinction between the act of seeing and sensation [Empfindung] in the genuine sense of the term

There exists a clear distinction between the act of seeing and a "sensation" [*Empfindung*] in the genuine sense of the term, that is, the impinging of the external world on our body. The sensations in the eyes, even the experience of completely unhindered seeing and the experience of hindered seeing, are clearly distinct from the qualities of that which is seen. This is why there is a clear-cut difference between a pleasant or unpleasant sensation in the eye and the aesthetic value of that which is seen. The beauty of marvelous weather, when the sky is a blue vault high above us, and the splendor of the light, are objective data. Even the experience of being affected by this beauty is an experience of our mind and spirit, not a bodily sensation of pleasure. When we are touched by the beauty of something visible, our mind and our heart are touched, but this is not an experience in our eyes. It is impossible to overlook the world that separates the quality of that which is bodily pleasant and unpleasant from the value quality of the beautiful and the ugly, the quality which adheres to the object that is seen.

It is nevertheless meaningful to say of certain visible data that they are "a delight to the eyes" [*eine Augenweide*]. There are some things, such as a velvet green meadow or the bright green of the trees in springtime, which "caress" our eyes, so to speak. This is a very specific phenomenon, which is clearly different from the typical sensations of the eyes. We say that one particular strength of the light or one kind of light is pleasant to our eyes, while another kind of illumination blinds us, is too garish, or hurts our eyes. It is obvious that these are bodily sensations, localized in the eye. The "delight to the eyes" is clearly something different from these typical bodily sensations; but it is radically different from the beauty of a mountain or of a tree. Unlike this beauty, which adheres completely to the object, the "delight to the eyes" implies an explicit relationship to our body. We feel that a color like this does good to our eyes, but this "good" is linked in a completely different manner to the object and its quality. The good it does is expressed, not in a bodily feeling of pleasure which can be detached from the object, but as the effect that the quality has on us. This effect can be called the delight of seeing, but it does not appeal to our mind, nor does it give joy and delight to our soul in the same way as beauty.

We need not speak in detail here of this very specific and isolated phenomenon, since we can clearly grasp that the fact that one and the same visible object can be (but certainly need not be) both beautiful and a delight to the eyes is no argument against the radical difference between the beauty of a visible object and a bodily sensation in the eyes, whether pleasant or unpleasant. It holds in general in every sphere of reality that radical differences between things are not abolished, or even diminished, by phenomena which lie between them.

That which is heard in its link to other perceptions

When we turn to the sphere of the audible, the picture is different in many ways, but we shall soon see the dignity that belongs to the sense of hearing and raises it, with sight, above the other senses. The various sounds, noises, and tones do not possess the clearly distanced objectivity that we find in colors, space, and visible things, but they too present themselves as objective data, as something that exists outside ourselves. Hearing is likewise a typical "consciousness of," and that which is heard is not something half-subjective, like a pain in one's finger.[3]

That which is heard can be linked in various ways to the corresponding objective occurrences in the external world. A sound can be a sign of something. I hear the sound of thunder and infer that a thunderstorm is drawing near; I hear a bang and infer that someone nearby has fired a shot. Obviously, this link to an occurrence is not present in an intuitive manner—we do not hear the occurrence, but only infer the occurrence from the kind of sound we hear. This link is completely different from the link in the case of seeing, which leads to an intuitive presence of things, occurrences, etc. (irrespective of how many experiences are necessary in order to understand what one has seen).

The hearing of words that another person speaks to me involves even less of an intuitive presence of what the other communicates to me. I do not exactly hear the sense and meaning of his words—I "understand" them on the basis of the words that I hear.[4]

It is certainly true that we hear the song of the birds, the babbling of the brook, the trotting of the horse, the barking of the dog, the meowing of the cat. If at the same time we also see the birds, the brook, etc., an intuitive presence comes into being with the help of the sense of sight. We perceive the song of the birds, the babbling of the brook, and so on.

3. We call the pain in the finger half-objective and half-subjective because it is clearly a sensation localized in my finger, a sensation which belongs to me, rather than an objective datum, something that represents a typical "consciousness of." On the other hand, it is not fully subjective in the manner of my joy over something—for this joy, which I enact and, as it were, *am*, is not something that I have, whereas I *have* the pain in my finger. Joy over something is enacted laterally, it is not something that I have (cf. my book, *The Heart*, part I, chap. 2).

4. We prescind here from this function of hearing words or sentences, and *a fortiori* from the function of seeing when we read the words or sentences; this function plays a role both in the relationship to other persons in various fields and above all in literature. The understanding of the words and sentences is always the real theme here. This is a highly intellectual process through which we learn something about the existence of states-of-affairs, facts, and entities of all kinds. We will speak in detail in the chapter on poetry (in volume II of the present work) about the act of understanding words, and also about the question whether it is possible to achieve an intuitive presence of some kind through that which has been learned by means of words and sentences. Let me only emphasize that when we refrain here from speaking of this indirect function of eye and ear, this does not mean that we overlook this aspect of human life.

But the quality which is grounded, for example, in the song of the birds, is much more important. Doubtless, it is grounded not only in the tones and sound, but also in the fact that it is the song of birds, which we recognize as such. A special poetic charm adheres to it, an explicit aesthetic value; and the same is true of the babbling of the brook. We could list many examples in which what is heard possesses a poetic character which is present in a completely intuitive manner. This beauty is immediately given and is every bit as clearly distinct from all bodily sensations of pleasure as the beauty of that which is seen.

Here too we find something that is radically different from a bodily sensation of pleasure. This completely objective beauty adheres, not to something that takes place in our soul, but to an object which we apprehend in a "consciousness of," for example, to the singing birds or the babbling brook. This beauty enchants our soul, not our ear, and the response to it—joy in it, enthusiasm over it—is something that we consciously live through, but it is not in any way a merely half-subjective experience, like a bodily sensation.

Up to now, we have spoken only of that which is heard. This unites with other perceptions, above all with sight, and is a part of an overall impression, of a comprehensive objective datum. It is the role that the audible plays in nature.

Hearing the human voice and its sound

Within the category of the audible the human voice occupies a very specific place. To begin with, there is its sound, its distinctive character in speaking. There are beautiful, noble voices, and ordinary, vulgar voices. The voice takes on another aesthetic importance in singing. For then it is clear that the sound of the voice can be the bearer of a completely new beauty—but also of a pronounced ugliness.

The phenomenon of expression is another important factor in the singing voice, and even more in the speaking voice. We shall discuss expression in detail below; here let me only underscore that the voice of a human being is also an element of the expression of an individual personality. The voice discloses his essence and characterizes him in some manner. Through expression the audible acquires a link to mental and spiritual contents and is once again linked (but in a way that is completely different from the link between word and meaning) to something that far transcends the audible.

In an analogous manner, the voice—for example, crying out—can express profound happenings in the soul: great pain, fear, horror, joy, exultation, etc. This means that the ability of the audible to be a bearer of aesthetic qualities goes much further still.

Apart from the audible which is embedded in the whole perceived external world, and even apart from the entire dimension of the expression of the personal mental processes and qualities, the audible in the narrower sense of the term—that is, the sound—has the ability to bear aesthetic values, and indeed to be the bearer of an emphatic beauty. The sound of a violin, flute, horn, trumpet, or trombone is as such something beautiful. The sound of poor or badly played instruments can be directly ugly. The same is true of the human voice, even when we prescind from every expression. Similarly, there are some birds whose voices sound beautiful and others whose croaking is in itself not beautiful. We say "in itself," because it is of course perfectly possible for the voice of a raven, as an element in nature, to contribute to the beauty of a total impression. The barking of some dogs is likewise ugly. Sounds as such can be bearers of beauty and ugliness in a manner analogous to colors. This too is important for the rank of hearing in relation to the other senses.

The hearing of music and of notes

It is, however, above all in music that we discover the decisive and exceptional role of the audible in the realm of the bearers of beauty. The notes, which are one special type of the audible, have the ability to join together to form a new unity, new well-shaped structures, wholes. This is most pronounced in the realm of the audible and is a further difference from the visible. One particular sequence of notes can form a melody, something that is completely new and much more important than the individual note. Indeed, the notes are oriented to the melody in such a way that it is only in the melody that they unfold their full aesthetic potential. In the case of the melody and the notes, one could speak of a certain analogy to the proposition and its individual words. These words do indeed already have a meaning, but it is only in the proposition that they are capable of positing an existing state-of-affairs, that is, of meaningfully asserting the existence of this state-of-affairs. Naturally, this applies only to propositions which affirm something, not to those that express questions or commands but do not possess a thetic or positing character. Even in such cases, however, we see that the words are oriented to the proposition, and they come alive in it, so to speak. It is only of the assertion that we can say it is true or false; we can say that a questioning proposition is meaningful, important, and deep, or meaningless, superficial, and unimportant; we can say that a sentence of command is valid, just, ethically unobjectionable, etc. These predicates cannot be applied to one individual word.[5]

This analogy is intended to show the potential that lies in sound. One particular kind of sequence of notes generates a completely new and incomparably more important structure: a melody. Through a different combination of notes—not a sequence of notes but a simultaneous sounding of notes—something else completely new comes into being: a harmony. Both together can constitute a structure of higher art: a movement or even a sequence of movements in a symphony, quartet, trio, sonata, etc.

We need not mention here all the other factors which are responsible for the beauty or lack of beauty of a piece of music: the rhythm, the differences between presto, adagio, and andante, staccato or legato, the orchestration, the sound and the combination of sounds. We will take all this up in volume II when we speak about music. Our concern here is only with the dignity of the sense of hearing and with the relationship of

5. This is not at all meant to deny the existence of some important predications applied to individual words. We shall discuss in the second volume the differences between noble and base, trivial and poetic, dramatic and reserved words. None of these differences relates to the specific function of meaning.

the world of the audible to beauty and the lack of beauty. Here our task is to elaborate the unique importance which hearing and seeing possess for beauty, in comparison with the activities of the other senses.

It is not difficult to grasp that tones (in the musical sense of this word) which possess a clearly elaborated character and are limited in number, are different from noise of any kind. They are also clearly distinct from the quality of the sound.[6] Only notes are capable of building up a melody and a harmony. They have an inherent power not only to appear in one particular combination, not only to take their place in one comprehensive perception, but to build up a new structure, a new entity, that is, the melody, an enduring new formal structure. Not only are they able to do so; they are in fact objectively oriented to such a structure. They themselves take on a completely new importance, a new life, when they appear as members of this new higher unity. The melody, this important structure, can only be built up out of notes.

The aesthetic qualities of smells

The superiority of seeing and hearing, their dignity, the potentiality of the visible and the audible from an aesthetic perspective, emerge clearly when we now turn to the other three senses: smell, taste, and touch. It is clear that seeing and hearing disclose to our mind a world that is incomparably higher, more spiritual [*geistig*], and more real. Above all, that which is seen and heard, the audible and the visible, is the home of beauty —and this is not true of the data of the other senses.

In the realm of smell, there is likewise a clear distinction between positive and negative. We typically call the smell with a positive value "good," and the smell with a negative value "bad"; we do not speak of "beautiful" and "ugly" smells. When we say that something "smells good," it is clear that this "good" has nothing to do with the morally "good." Nor does it have the meaning of the noun "a good." It is nothing other than the des-

6. When we discuss music in the second volume of this work, we shall speak in detail of the distinction between notes taken in the narrower sense and sounds. We shall also speak of the role played by height and depth and by the quality of the vowel sounds.

ignation of a positive value quality as distinct from a negative value quality. But it is characteristic that we do not speak here of "beautiful," as when we speak of sounds or colors.

This way of speaking is based, not on a merely arbitrary custom, but on the fact that value qualities other than beauty come into play in the sense of smell. We can understand this better when we realize that the transcendence found in seeing and hearing is not present in the sense of smell. It is doubtless true that the smell which we apprehend is not a sensation like a pain in one's finger. It does not belong to the category of things we have described above as half-subjective. But as Hedwig Conrad-Martius has shown in her important study *Zur Ontologie und Erscheinungslehre der realen Außenwelt* (Ontology and phenomenology of the real external world),[7] smell does not register a mere quality of an object, like the color of a tree. Rather, in the smell there is also an impinging of the external world on our body: it *affects* us. We perceive it only when it affects us. When a stench comes to meet us and offends us, the bodily sensation of displeasure is much less clearly distinct from the quality of the stench than the bodily sensation of displeasure is distinct from the ugliness of a color or the ugliness of a noise (for example, of an excessively loud din) which we experience as a shock in our ears.

It is true that the stench is the bearer of a disvalue which is certainly not reducible to the bodily sensation of displeasure; but these two are much closer to each other. Something analogous can be said of the positive value of a fragrance. This is certainly something distinct in itself, but it is much closer to the pleasure that we thereby experience than is a color or a sound. We say that this is only analogous to the stench, because the aggressiveness of the stench with regard to our body is much more pronounced than the experience of being surrounded by fragrances; for example, the stench can induce nausea in us.

It is in general false to assume that the distinction between positive and negative in every field does not also entail formal distinctions. The

7. Hedwig Conrad-Martius, "Zur Ontologie und Erscheinungslehre der realen Außenwelt," in *Jahrbuch für Philosophie und phänomenologische Forschung*, 345–542.

state of things need certainly not be the same, although the positive and the negative are clearly and unambiguously opposed to each other and form a definite antithesis.

Although smells in themselves have a character that is much more related to the body than the visible and the audible have, and are less spiritual [*geistig*] in a formal sense, we find clearly objective values in this sphere too. The fragrance of a flower—of a lily or a rose—possesses something enormously noble and sublime. The quality I have in mind when I say "noble" is certainly a high aesthetic value, although it is completely different from beauty; and we are fully conscious of this difference in our experience. This quality of the sublimity and nobility of a fragrance far transcends the quality of merely smelling good (as opposed to smelling bad). We shall return to this point when we discuss other formal aspects of the way in which various facts of the world around us disclose themselves through the sense of smell.

We want to note that smells cannot build up a new entity in the manner in which notes can build up a melody. One can combine smells, but the individual olfactory qualities can never build up a completely new structure. This is why they can never play a role analogous to the audible or the visible.

To say that several olfactory qualities can never form a new, higher unity is not to deny that the combination or rather the mixture of various smells can produce a qualitatively new smell. This process plays a great role in the invention of new perfumes. But such a structure is not an ontologically novel structure in relation to the individual olfactory qualities which are used in the mixture. Just like the individual smells which are used in the mixture, the result of the mixture is itself one particular smell. It is not a new, ontologically higher structure like the melody in comparison to the individual notes.

Connections between smells and other aesthetic phenomena

In nature there is an important collaboration between smells and visible forms. The smells are attached to a whole: for example, the fragrance is attached to particular flowers and blossoms, and the smell of the air is attached to the whole phenomenon of springtime. This link with visible forms makes for an important and organic contribution: the smell contributes to the beauty and the poetry of the whole.

The sublime fragrance of the lily belongs to the beauty of its form, and indeed is especially appropriate to this. The fragrance of the rose fits the rose uniquely; it is not by chance that the rose does not have the fragrance of the lily. I do not wish to claim that this is a necessary connection; but it is certainly a meaningful connection. The special smell is one element in the structure of the overall beauty of these particular flowers.

In another manner, the smell of the air in springtime or on a sunny winter day in the mountains, the smell of hay in the summer, or of many strong herbs on a hot summer day, or of burning wood in the countryside, the fragrance of linden and acacia trees in a promenade—these make their contribution to the overall aesthetic phenomenon. This element plays an important role in the emergence of a strong atmosphere, of a poetic "world."

It suffices here to think of how the smell of incense is appropriate to a church building and how the quality of this smell corresponds to the sacral atmosphere of the church, of the great "world" which the interior of the church irradiates.

Naturally many people will say that the connection between incense and a church is based only on association: we have often experienced this smell during a solemn Mass, and this is why we connect it via association with the sacral atmosphere of church. This is incorrect. I do not assert that this olfactory quality has in itself the quality of the sacral; but I do assert that it is appropriate to the sacral. If one were to sprinkle eau de cologne instead, this smell would not make the organic connection to the sacral. The fragrance of incense objectively suits the sacral, but this is not the case with the fragrance of eau de cologne. This is not to deny that frequent experience of incense in a church intensifies our sense of this appropriateness.

The smell of the air in springtime is not only associatively linked to the spring: in its quality, it is appropriate to this season. There is a deeper connection between the two than merely the association born of the frequent simultaneous experience of this smell and of the overall atmosphere of springtime.

This important role of the sense of smell, this meaningful link between smells and individual visible forms or total phenomena in nature, is, however, clearly distinct from the way in which notes are capable of building up a melody, and from the building up of visible data through visible forms.

Like certain melodies, certain smells can remind us vividly of particular situations, although the quality of the smells is not related in any way to the content of these situations. Smells and melodies have a special ability to transpose us in a very intensive manner back into particular situations and to remind us of all that we experienced in those situations. This is more than a meaningless association. It is something much deeper, just as the act of remembering something experienced earlier in our life is different from the mere mechanical process of association which comes into being through frequently experiencing two things simultaneously. This act of remembering is in fact even more opposed to such association than is the experience of being reminded of something by a smell.

We must, however, clearly distinguish the role of smells in the sphere of recollection from the qualitative relationship of smells to particular things. The smell of springtime is more than this external connection. Similarly, the fragrance of the rose, the hyacinth, or the lily is not bound to these objects only through the fact that we experience both together. The fragrances are characteristics of these structures, organically linked to form and color.

When we look at the special relationship of the olfactory quality to its bearer, we can observe that the olfactory qualities appear as the smell of something. They present themselves as the emanations of particular things. For example, the fragrance of a lily not only has a very specific quality, but it also presents itself as the fragrance of the lily. It speaks of the essence of the lily and unites itself in a unique way to the form and color of the lily. The lily (not from the perspective of physiological botany, but as a type which exists in the human aspect of nature) has not only the slender form, the glorious blossom, and the white color, but also its specific, differentiated smell. There exists a profound organic connection between the datum of the smell and the visible flower.

The analogy proper to smells

The role of the analogy which is proper to smell is particularly striking. The smell of an object, whether an outstanding fragrance or a stench, presents itself to such an extent as an emanation of the being of the object that we encounter here a universal metaphysical category, which is found in an analogous manner in many spheres in which there cannot be any smell to impress itself upon the senses. It is not by chance that one speaks of the fragrance of holiness and the stench of sin. Every kind of irradiation of the essence of a thing which is not a presentation of the pure characteristics of the thing, but is something ethereal that diffuses itself outward, finds in smell a primordial analogy. This is an analogy to an irradiation which starts in the sphere of the visible. We have already made repeated use of this analogy when we said that metaphysical beauty is an irradiation of other values, the fragrance of these values. The unique form of the connection between the object and its smell is a primordial type which extends by analogy far beyond the sphere of smell. Although the connection to the object is looser than in the case of colors, it nevertheless claims to disclose to us something of the profound essence of the object. The rottenness of meat, eggs, or other foods makes itself known primarily in the smell, often much more so than in the outward appearance. The smell is a symptom which tells us what is going on in many events.

In relation to smell, therefore, we must draw a distinction between two different dimensions. First, the smell can be united in an important manner to visible objects, for example, to a flower, as a characteristic trait of such a structure. As we have seen, the fragrance of a lily belongs to its morphic essence, and in such cases the fragrance even claims to communicate something of the essence of the structure to which the fragrance adheres and which, so to speak, breathes out the fragrance.

Besides this, the smell can be the bearer of a value or a disvalue: in other words, it can be a noble fragrance or a stench. There are also neutral smells which bear neither a value nor a disvalue. These values or disvalues belong to the family of the aesthetic values or disvalues, but as we have seen, these particular values are not subspecies of beauty.

The second dimension of smells is their ability to link up in a meaningful manner with other structures in the external world. In that case, the smells are not enduring characteristics of such structures, but link up with them in one particular situation and make an essential contribution to the beauty and poetry of a total situation. For example, the smell of burning wood in the countryside, or the fragrance of linden or acacia trees in a promenade of a particular town, or the smell of the springtime air—such things are irreplaceable factors for building up the "beautiful world" of a landscape and make a unique contribution to its atmosphere.

But although their role in nature is so great and they possess many values, smells are never in themselves bearers of beauty in the way that colors or sounds are.

Smells cannot contribute to the construction of a work of art

We must begin by stating that smells cannot play a role in the world of art. As we have already seen, they are not capable of building up new forms. Unlike the act of seeing, smells do not disclose to us a rich world full of varied things, that is, the external world which surrounds us. This explains entirely why smells play no role in art. Whenever the attempt has been made to unite smells and music—obviously, this is so utterly impossible with a statue or a picture that the attempt has not even been made—the result is devoid of artistic importance. Smells can neither intensify the beauty of music nor link up with music in any organic way. They remain something juxtaposed to it in a completely accidental manner. They cannot link up with a piece of music as they can with a flower. Melodies have no smells, and the attempt to combine melodies and smells has never resulted in anything more than what we experience when a lady wearing a strong perfume sits beside us in a concert or theater.

No work of art can be constructed out of smells alone. The element of composition which is present even in a landscape, and *a fortiori* in a work of art, is not possible with olfactory qualities, even though, as we have seen, these can make an important contribution in nature.

The qualities of taste

As in the sphere of smells, so too in the sphere which we apprehend by means of our organ of taste, and which refers more or less to things that can be eaten and drunk, we typically do not speak of "beautiful" and "ugly." We say, "That tastes good or bad," just as we say, "That smells good or bad." It is true that some people in northern Germany say, "That tastes beautiful," but this is at once felt to be very inadequate.

There are definite values in the world of tastes. A wine can be the bearer of a sublime, noble taste, while other drinks can have a base taste; a fruit can have a delicious, noble taste; a well-cooked and delicious meal has a different quality from a bad meal which is poorly cooked. Nevertheless, it is obvious that this is a completely different value than that of beauty. Like smells, these values and disvalues form a contrast to the merely bodily sensations of pleasure or displeasure that one feels when eating some particular food.

Despite these and other similarities, to which we shall return very shortly, there is a difference between smells and tastes from an aesthetic perspective. The bodily sensation of pleasure plays a greater role in tastes than in smells. Many people notice scarcely or not at all the value differences between noble, fine, exquisite, and base; rather, the subjective occupies the foreground. The expression, "I like this taste," is typical of this subjectivity. For many people, and especially for people who devour their food, the question whether they like the taste is so central that that they utterly fail to apprehend the objective value and disvalue qualities—noble, exquisite, base, vulgar. A special gift is needed to discern these. This gift is a distant analogy to the much higher organ which enables us truly to understand the beauty of the visible and the audible, which we encounter above all in the field of art.

Something similar applies to smells. There are people who cannot "stand" the noble smells, such as those of the gardenia and the tuberose.

One needs a certain understanding of these objective value qualities, for example, of the nobility of a smell. For many people, the central question is whether they subjectively "like" a smell.

With smells, and even more with tastes, many factors of a completely subjective nature play a role and influence our relationship to them. Some people find the substance of some food to be abhorrent, for example, when it has a slimy texture. They cannot eat eggs which are very soft-boiled, and they find the very idea of eating something as good as oysters repulsive; or certain tastes which fill others with delight move them to nausea. Similarly, the thought of eating the meat of animals which disgust us makes it impossible for us to eat them, quite irrespective of the taste.

If we once experience that a particular food makes us ill, this can spoil it for us. I do not think that in this instance we are afraid on rational grounds (that is, that the food could actually harm us); rather, an instinctive aversion against the food is activated. The decisive point is that in the case of the smell, and above all of the taste, the apprehending of a quality goes hand in hand with a pronounced bodily sensation, and that the unique distance of objectivity possessed by the visible and (in another way) by the audible is lacking. The apprehending of the taste of a food cannot be separated from an intimacy with our body. There is a special perfection of intimacy in the way in which our body is affected and the food is received into our body, but there is lacking here the thing that distinguishes the visible and the audible, namely, the glorious objectivity of the spirit.

We have already spoken of the analogy that the fragrance and the bad stench possess with properly spiritual contents: we have spoken of the fragrance of virtue and the stench of sin. Something similar is present in taste. The intimate, direct sensing of a content, the *sapere* ("tasting") which, unlike *videre* ("seeing"), finds its sensuous expression in the act of tasting, exists by analogy in the sphere of the spirit. Here I have in mind one particular way of being affected by a value. There are not only many stages of the knowledge of a value but also many degrees of the intimacy with which one is affected by this value. *Sapere* is often used both in poetry and in the liturgy to designate this intimate experience of being-affected.

This formal intimacy of tasting and (in yet another way) of eating does not, however, alter the fact that the subjective element of the bodily sensation of pleasure plays a great role, and that in fact for many people it completely predominates. This is why the values which a taste, too, can bear are often not apprehended; and even when they are apprehended, we do not always concentrate our attention upon them as such.

There are two kinds of enjoyment. One is related entirely to the subjective "I like this taste," that is, to the bodily sensation of pleasure. The other is primarily oriented to the value quality of the noble, the fine, the exquisite. This kind of enjoyment contains a value-response. One rejoices at the nobility of the taste of a wine or of a fruit. One is not only absorbed by eating and drinking, by the pleasure in consuming these foods and drinks: one reaches to their values and makes a response to them. At the same time, precisely the objective appreciation of these values confers a completely new character on the intimate act of consumption.

Like smells, tastes too can be bearers of objective values. These are not subspecies of beauty, but they form a special subspecies of aesthetic values. Their antithesis is the disvalues of the base and vulgar qualities of taste.

Like smells, tastes are not able to construct a new totality which belongs ontologically to a higher level. Certainly the combination plays a much greater role in tastes than in smells. Some vegetables go better with particular kinds of meat, some wines go better with one particular food. Different tastes have a definite relationship to each other: they harmonize, just as some colors that match each other in a garment are enhanced by their combination. In the sphere of taste, the role played by combination goes beyond matching each other, belonging together, and improving the total taste: in a perfect meal, the harmony between the various courses is very important. A first course can match the main course in such a way that there is a total harmony and an intensification of the entire culinary value. The same applies to the sequence of wines, to the dessert, and so on. The art of cooking is manifested not only in the preparation of one individual dish but also on a higher level in the harmony of an entire meal, including the appropriate wines. There undeniably exists a composition of the various tastes which lends a unity to the entire meal. Nevertheless, it is not difficult to see that this unity is not a new structure on an ontologically higher level, like the melody in its relationship to the notes. The individual tastes are clearly bearers of specific positive or negative qualities; they are not colorless like the notes. The meal, this "symphony" of tastes, is indeed an intensification in the sphere of taste, but it does not rise *above* this sphere. It does not offer any qualitatively new type of content. And so while it is true that the combination of tastes in the meal constitutes an important intensification, tastes can never build up an ontologically new and higher structure, an enduring object like a melody.

Tastes in their combination are undeniably an achievement of the culinary art. But it is surely not necessary to demonstrate that the word "art" has a different meaning here than in architecture, music, or literature. Although the culinary art, widespread in countries such as France and Italy, is definitely a cultural element, and fine cuisine belongs to the sphere of culture just like the wines in Germany and France, the fact remains that we can speak of "art" here only in a wholly analogous sense.

The tangible

The tangible, or everything that is disclosed to us through the sense of touch, occupies a position all its own. In her study *Zur Ontologie und Erscheinungslehre der realen Außenwelt* (Ontology and phenomenology of the real external world) mentioned above, Hedwig Conrad-Martius has correctly pointed out that the qualities hard, soft, smooth, rough, etc. are both sensations (in the strict sense of the word) and also traits of physical objects. There exists a pleasurable feeling of touch, where the relationship to our body stands in the foreground. How something feels is every bit as much a bodily sensation as the effect on us of the heat or the cold. But soft, hard, smooth, rough, etc. also present themselves as definite qualities of physical objects. As such, they are a completely objective datum, in contradistinction to those cases where they appear as sensations which are specifically related to the body.

This distinction emerges clearly when we reflect that we can also *see* the smoothness or roughness of a surface, and that such qualities are given to us when we look at the surface of a table, although the bodily tactile experience is completely absent, and the eyes would never be able to instruct us about how something feels to the touch.

Of course, the following objection has been made to this thesis: We do not really see the roughness of the surface but only know from experience, after we have taken hold of a rough thing and have also observed the specific appearance of its surface, that this appearance permits us to infer roughness or to associate it with the visible data. Once again, however, we have a typical case of being content with a shallow explanation, instead of penetrating more deeply into a surprising phenomenon and analyzing it without prejudice.

To answer this objection, it suffices to realize that no one will claim to infer, from looking at a lump of sugar, that it is sweet. Although this experience is of a very elementary nature, the sweetness of the lump of sugar never presents itself in such a way as to be immediately given to our vision. No association is capable of grounding an immediate intuitive givenness.[8]

In the case of the objective qualities of objects which are apprehended in touching, such as the smoothness or hardness of an object, and which we can often perceive with the eye, it is clear that we encounter something that can bear a value and can make a significant contribution to the beauty of an object. But it is embedded in the world of the visible when it plays this role. Thus, the smoothness of the marble is one element of its beauty, and the roughness of the surface of certain objects, such as moss or some stones, is a trait belonging to these objects which also forms part of their beauty. The sea is very beautiful when it is smooth as a mirror—and also when it surges wildly. It belongs to the beauty of certain parts

8. [The argument here seems incomplete. I surmise that if completed it would go like this. In the case of sugar we find the very situation posited by the objection: we cannot see the sweetness of the sugar, so we have to connect what we see with what we have previously experienced in tasting sugar. It becomes apparent by contrast that the smoothness of marble is not only felt but equally seen, so that no such work of connecting is necessary. JFC]

of the human body that they are firm, and to the beauty of other parts that they are soft. We do indeed apprehend these qualities by touch, but they possess their great aesthetic importance only in their visual appearance. Although aesthetic delight can under certain circumstances be intensified by touching the objects which bear these qualities (for example, smooth steel or soft velvet), it is impossible to detach the beauty of these qualities from their visual presence. They can be bearers of beauty only as a trait of an object which appears to us as a whole in the visible world. The sensation of touching itself, the experience related to the body which plays a role in the world of taste too, is definitely not a bearer of beauty or of the lack of beauty.

The sense of touch plays a completely different kind of role as an element of the contact with objects. It grants a particularly direct and intimate contact with things, with animals and plants, and above all with other persons. One seeks this form of contact with beautiful and attractive things: one wants not only to see them, but to touch them. In many instances this entails an intensification of the contact, as we see especially in the desire not only to look at a relic but also to touch it. One puts one's hand on the wall of the tomb of a saint, one kisses the relic. The touching, the bodily contact, becomes the symbol of a particularly intimate contact. One expects that a touch will be enough to bring healing. Here we may recall the woman who touches Christ's garment in the Gospel (Matthew 9:20-22).

Touching takes on an importance all its own in the sphere of tenderness. Even in the case of pets which one loves dearly, such as dogs, cats, or horses, one has the need to caress them. It is very remarkable that this touching has a special function, namely, to express an affectionate, kindly attitude. Naturally, this function unfolds fully only in our attitude to human beings whom we love.

The bodily contact which we experience through the sensation of touch is a unique fulfillment of the *intentio unionis* (the desire for union) which is proper to every love apart from the love of neighbor. The *intentio unionis* takes various forms, depending on the kind (or category) and the degree of love. One such form of bodily contact is already present in a handshake. In a conventional form of greeting, for example, vis-à-vis a person who has just been introduced to me, one cannot yet speak of tenderness. The handshake is an expression of a friendly attitude and a certain approach to the other, indeed of an acknowledgment of the other as a person who has now been welcomed into the circle of our acquaintances (though certainly not into friendship) and is lifted out of the anonymous mass of unknown people. The handshake becomes something incomparably more important when we shake a friend's hand, especially when this takes place not only as a form of greeting when we meet him again after an absence, but as a pure expression of our unity and love.

The meaning of the handshake, and *a fortiori* of holding hands, is completely new when we are speaking of a spousal love, for then the sensation of touch unfolds its special function as the expression and fulfillment of the *intentio unionis*. This is intensified in the embrace, in the kiss of greeting, and finally in the kiss on the lips.

When we think of the function of the sensation of touch in the sphere of relationships to other people, namely, to be an expression and a fulfillment of the *intentio unionis*, one cannot deny that the sensation of touch too can be a bearer of high values. But these values belong to a completely different family than the aesthetic values. They belong to the realms of the *intentio unionis*, love, and community. Their analysis does not belong in a treatise about aesthetics, but in a study of philosophical anthropology or the philosophy of community.

Smells, tastes, and tangible things bear aesthetic values in the broader sense

Let us summarize. There is no doubt that smells, tastes, and even qualities which we apprehend with the sense of touch can be bearers of values. The nobility in the fragrance of a lily, a lily of the valley, a hyacinth, or certain roses is not only subjectively satisfying, but is a definite value. The same is true of the bouquet of a noble wine or the taste of glorious fruits and many foods. Similarly, the smoothness of certain stones such as marble, or the solidity or softness of the bodies of certain animals, and especially of the human body, is not only pleasant, but is the bearer of a value. These values, which must be distinguished from what is merely subjectively pleasant,[9] are devoid of significance in art but play a great role in the beauty of nature—for example, the smell in springtime or the fragrance of a sunlit meadow in summer, the fresh mountain air in winter, etc. They make an important contribution to the beauty of life and to the poetry of many situations.

But neither the smells nor the tastes nor the sensations of touch can form a new totality which belongs to a higher order of meaning in the way that notes can construct a melody. This first step to a structure of a completely new kind is excluded; and the same applies *a fortiori* to all the further steps, such as that from melody to harmony and then to a musical totality, whether a movement, a symphony, or even the uniting of sounds and words.

It is clear that the values in the sphere of smells, tastes, and sensations of touch [when these values are taken by themselves] are not to be subsumed under beauty. The fragrance of the lily is not beautiful in the same way as its form, but it makes a unique and essential contribution to the total beauty, to the poetry of the lily. In a broader sense, therefore, these values do belong to the family of the aesthetic values.

Thus we see that the eye and the ear have a unique position from an aesthetic perspective in comparison with the other sense organs, and that it is above all the visible and the audible that are bearers of beauty. Only visible and audible data (such as colors and sounds) can as such be bearers of beauty. Only sounds are capable of constructing a melody, a structure of a higher kind. Only the eye enables us to apprehend immediately a rich world of things and their qualities [of beauty].

9. In my *Moralia* (vol. IX of my *Gesammelte Werke*), I discuss in greater detail these kinds of values which adhere to objects where the subjectively satisfying quality occupies the foreground. As genuine values, however, they are clearly distinct from this mere pleasantness.

CHAPTER FIVE

The Beauty of the Visible and the Audible [Sinnenschönheit] in Its Relation to Expressed Metaphysical Beauty

The collaboration between these two types of beauty in the human face

IN ORDER to investigate the question how expressed metaphysical beauty and the beauty of the visible and audible collaborate with one another, let us first examine in detail their collaboration in the human face.

There are undoubtedly faces which are definitely beautiful because of the form of the nose, the mouth, the eyes, and the entire face, as well as the colors. Likewise, other faces are ugly because of the unfortunate form of nose, mouth, or eyes.

This beauty of the visible and the audible tells us nothing about the personality. For it is an aesthetic value which attaches directly to the visible, in this case, to the face. It is not grounded in other values. It appears directly on the face as a quality of this visible structure, which is, however, the face of a human being, and indeed the face of a man or a woman. For the face is not just a bodily structure. One aspect of the beauty of the form of a foot is the fact that it is the foot of a human being rather than of an animal, but only to the extent that the inherent formal principle of the human foot is presupposed. If a person is stupid, petty, or boring, this does not in any way mar the beauty of his or her foot; for the personality does not express itself in the foot. In the face, however, there is always an expression of the personality; if it were devoid of all expression, it would be a mask.

The face needs expression. Although the beauty expressed in the face is dependent in its visible manifestation on purely visible factors, it is itself the beauty of a human person, and hence a metaphysical beauty. Both beauties, the expressed metaphysical beauty and the beauty of the visible, are wedded to form a total beauty, without, however, denying their different provenances. The beauty of the visible involves no other reality than that of the forms, colors, and material. The character of a person does not alter this beauty in any way.

If the person is not as he appears to be, the expressed metaphysical beauty nevertheless remains. If someone appears to be kind or to be a person of stature, without in reality being so, the expressed metaphysical beauty which is grounded in the supposed kindness or importance nevertheless adheres to his face. But the discovery that he is neither kind nor a person of stature makes this expressed metaphysical beauty a mere sham, whereas the beauty of the visible remains completely untouched by this. In this case, we will say, "He appears so kind or dignified—what a pity that he is not so in reality! What a pity that it is only an illusion!" If all that is present is a beauty of the visible, and if the person's expression bears witness rather to narrowness, stupidity, or wickedness, we will say, "What a pity that the ugliness of narrowness or of stupidity contradicts the beauty of the visible, so that no total beauty of the face is achieved!" But we will also make the corresponding remark if the person merely appears to be stupid, without being so in reality.

Let us sum up: The human being who appears to be dignified or kind does not cease to look like this if he is not so in reality. But although the expressed metaphysical beauty does not cease to exist, it sinks down to a mere sham, because it purports to say something about the person which is not really the case. The deceptive expression does indeed remain beautiful, but it can no longer make us happy, for the simple reason that it is a sham. The beauty of the visible and the audible does not pretend to state anything about the essence of the personality. Its home is exclusively the sphere of the visible and the audible. Irrespective of how the human being is as a personality, this beauty will never become a sham. But without the expressed metaphysical beauty, the beauty of the visible remains incomplete, a mask; it never attains a full overall beauty.

The overall beauty, in which there is an organic unity between the beauty of the visible and the expressed metaphysical beauty, continues to exist even when the metaphysical beauty is only a sham.

The overall beauty of a face and the difference between the two sources of its beauty

In order for the total beauty of a face to be realized, it is not necessary that all the positive personal values be expressed in this face. It suffices that positive traits such as a noble fullness of life, intensity, freshness, or spirited playfulness are expressed there, and that these are wedded to the beauty of the visible and the audible. In order for the overall beauty to be realized, it is not necessary that the face express stature, kindness, or depth. But if an overall beauty is to be realized, the face must not bear witness in its expression to certain disvalues, such as narrowness, pettiness, stupidity, frivolity, or boredom. The metaphysical ugliness of these traits makes the realization of an overall beauty impossible, even where the beauty of the visible and the audible is very great.

The way in which the overall beauty is limited by the expressed metaphysical ugliness varies in accordance with the specific disvalues which are present in each case. The metaphysical ugliness of narrowness, pettiness, stupidity, impurity, impudence, or irreverence prevents the realization of the overall beauty in another way than the expression of wickedness, hard-heartedness, or cruelty. This brings us to a very interesting but difficult problem, to which at present we can make only brief reference.

One fact is very important in our present context: the visible factors on which the kind of expression depends—which forms of nose, forehead, mouth, and eyes determine a face to look clever, kind, or noble, or to look stupid, narrow, evil, or base—are not the same factors on which the beauty of the visible and the audible depends. Both of these sets of factors are visible elements, proportions, forms, and colors; but they are not identical. The decisive difference is that the beauty of the visible is determined by certain visible factors and adheres directly to these, whereas metaphysical beauty adheres to spiritual entities. This latter beauty is a fragrance, a radiance of personal, moral, and vital values. These manifest themselves in the visible, and in this way let the beauty become visible. Visible factors allow these inner attitudes to appear in the face and are responsible for the expression. The expressed metaphysical beauty always remains the radiance of values that adhere to the inner personal realities; it always depends on these values, which are responsible for metaphysical beauty in the same way as the corresponding disvalues are responsible for metaphysical ugliness. But metaphysical beauty or ugliness are intuitively given in the face as a result of the fact that the bearers of beauty and ugliness (that is, values or disvalues of various sorts) express themselves in the face and are thus intuitively given.

There are faces which are outstandingly beautiful because of the proportion, the form of the eyes, nose, mouth, chin. In their combination, all these parts mysteriously form a totality which is beautiful even independently of the expression of the face, and which strikes us as something beautiful. On the other hand, there can be faces which lack this beauty of form but are beautiful through the expression of goodness, purity, or intellectual stature. A look from eyes in which playful charm is linked to kindness and purity can possess a high aesthetic value.

The human face is created for expression: so true is this, that a boring expression greatly limits even the greatest beauty of the visible and audible. A face may have an extremely beautiful form, but if it looks emphatically stupid and narrow, or evil, cold, and heartless, the beauty of the face becomes soulless. The face loses its full beauty. On the other hand, a face like that of Saint Vincent de Paul, which fascinates through its expression of kindness, love, and humility, is not beautiful in the full sense, since the beauty of form is completely lacking; indeed, the forms are somewhat ugly. In this case, however, the contrast between the lack of beauty of visible form and the presence of beauty of the expression actually gives the face a touching quality.

Once again, the important point in our present context is not that the beauty of the expression is meant to complement the beauty of visible form, nor that it is a more sublime beauty than the beauty of visible form which is deprived of all beauty of expression; what we wish to show clearly is the difference between two sources of beauty. One source adheres directly to visible forms, the other to the personality and to his or her soul, and manifests itself in the face through the expression. The manner in which the expressed characteristic of the person is a bearer of beauty is clearly different from the manner in which the forms bear beauty. The beauty of the expressed purity, nobility, or kindness is the *splendor*, the fragrance, the irradiation of the moral values. The face's beauty of visible form is not the *splendor* of another value but adheres directly to these forms.

It is indeed a very remarkable phenomenon that many visible and audible forms are bearers of such a definitely aesthetic value as beauty, and that forms, proportions, colors, sounds, etc. can directly display beauty. But it is even more astounding that certain forms in the face condition the expression of a spiritual reality, and concomitantly of the metaphysical beauty (or lack of beauty) of this reality.

The mystery of expression in the human face

This phenomenon of expression—the fact that someone makes a face at one moment which allows his joy to become visible, and later another face which allows his grief to become visible—is a great mystery.[1] This is of a completely different kind of mystery than the union of body and soul in the human person (itself likewise an extremely mysterious matter). Here we have the union of physiological processes with inner psychic and spiritual processes; these sometimes have a causal effect on each

1. See Gabriel Marcel, *Being and Having* (New York: Harper & Row, 1965), 116–23, 145–46. See also Josef Seifert, *Leib und Seele*, 201ff.

other, but in such a way that the physiological process and many other relations do not constitute the cause of the spiritual but only one of its presuppositions. In the facial expression, we find something new: the ability of some visible change in the face to permit something that belongs to a completely different sphere of being to become intuitively present.

This would not be particularly remarkable if all that we had here were an inference. For example, we have often noted that someone makes a particular face when he expresses his anger in words, and we therefore deduce from his communication what is going on inside him. This leads us to infer that this particular face is a sign of his anger. And we continually draw such inferences from data of one sphere of being to data belonging to another sphere of being.

But the immediately intuitive givenness, the self-manifestation in a human face of something in a person's psychological or even inner personal life, the fact that this manifestation is linked to particular faces which this person makes and that the personal element manifests itself intuitively in and through these faces, this is something extraordinary, a *mirandum*. This is most remarkable in the case of the eyes, or the look. A look may be hostile or friendly, happy or sad, in love or indifferent, scornful or reverential. Especially mysterious is the fact that it takes only a slight physical alteration of this little organ for something so significant and personal to come to light, and with such a highly differentiated quality. This applies all the more strongly to the enduring expression in the face of specific characteristics, virtues, and personal qualities of all kinds. The forms of the face and the look express these personal qualities and allow them to become visible, so that they can be apprehended intuitively.

We see that the expressed metaphysical beauty and the beauty of visible form collaborate in a unique manner in the human face in order to constitute the overall beauty of the face. This collaboration is unique, because the human face is meant to possess an expressed metaphysical beauty, and this means that the beauty of visible form on its own never suffices to ground the overall beauty of the face. An expressed metaphysical ugliness can even undermine from within the beauty of visible form.

Refinement [Die Feinheit]

Some personal values and disvalues find expression in the whole bearing of a person, in the way someone speaks, in his choice of words, etc., but especially in the face. Here we have in mind the value of refinement and its antithesis, the disvalue of vulgarity.

Refinement is not a moral value, nor does it belong to the family of the "intellectual" values. It is closest to the sphere of the vital values, but it also reaches into the specifically personal sphere. Like all values, this value quality possesses its own specific metaphysical beauty, although no beauty in the narrower sense of the term [the beauty of the visible and the audible] is present here, just as it is not present in the case of the metaphysical beauty of moral, "intellectual," and other values.

As I have said, the refined and its opposite, the vulgar, are expressed in a particular manner in the face, but also in the entire bearing of a person, the way someone speaks, the ring of the voice, the choice of words, and many other things. Refinement is a quality that unfolds above all in the sphere of the external appearance and expression, although it is an internal quality of the human person. It can appear in an analogous manner in certain animals, and in another analogous sense it can also appear in art.

We limit our considerations to the value of the refined and to the disvalue of the vulgar in the human being.[2] Even here there are various interpretations: a purely vital refinement in distinction to one that moves more into the properly personal sphere, or a deeper refinement in distinction to a more conventional refinement.

We cannot make a thorough analysis of this value and of the disvalue of the vulgar, since that would be the task of a philosophical anthropol-

2. The term "refined" can refer to other personal value-qualities too, that possess no more than a certain analogy to the "refined" mentioned above. We can use this term to allude to the considerate, tactful character of a person and to the differentiation in this character. In that case, its antithesis is not vulgar but inconsiderate, tactless, or coarse.

ogy. We are interested only in the aesthetic value that is in itself the reflection of a personal value and finds its expression in the external sphere.

Our primary question is: What is the relation between the aesthetic value of the refined and beauty? What role does *this* aesthetic value play for the aesthetic value of the external appearance of a human being? Some faces are distinctly refined. We also call them "aristocratic," although many non-aristocrats have refined faces, and it is certainly not true that all aristocrats have refined faces. If someone has a refined face, this is indubitably a high aesthetic value, but it does not *per se* make the face beautiful in the typical sense of that word. The refinement is no more a guarantee of beauty of visible form in the face than does the expressed metaphysical beauty that is the reflection of kindness, purity, or humility.

In order to be beautiful, as I have said, the face needs expressed metaphysical beauty: the beauty of moral nobility, of spiritual stature, etc. But refinement, which is also an expressed vital value and the bearer of an aesthetic value, bestows a particular aesthetic value on a face. When beauty of visible form is present in a face, refinement helps to intensify the overall beauty. However, unlike the expressed metaphysical beauty of moral and "intellectual" values, refinement is not essential to this overall beauty. The "marriage" between the expressed metaphysical beauty and the beauty of visible form is one thing; the "marriage" between refinement and the beauty of visible form is another.

There are faces which are beautiful both because of their beauty of visible form and because of their expression, in which the refinement is, as it were, superseded; although we will not call these faces specifically refined, the terms "unrefined" or (even worse) "vulgar" are inappropriate here. We do not miss the expression of this vital value; the spiritual quality is so explicit and beauty so sublime that the refinement is quite simply superseded. Such faces are refined *par excellence.*

In other faces, however, the refinement is not superseded, but their beauty is not impaired by the mere absence of the refined. It does not in fact occur to us to look for the refinement; we do not even miss it.

But as soon as the face appears vulgar, its beauty is severely impaired.

A face may possess a beauty of visible form that shows itself in its shapes, color, and skin, but the expression of vulgarity robs this face of its aesthetic value and corrodes from within its beauty of visible form.

It is assuredly not only in the face that refinement and vulgarity find expression. Refinement can be seen in a person's bodily posture, his comportment, his voice, the way in which he speaks, the words he uses when he is enthusiastic, and especially when he is angry.

There is of course a quality of "good manners," which is much more external than refinement but nevertheless belongs to it. The refined person has good manners. When we speak of refined persons, we naturally mean people who genuinely possess this quality, not those whose faces merely look refined—for the facial expression can be misleading. There are people who look clever but in reality are stupid (and *vice versa*). But when a personality is refined, this will be expressed in his entire outward appearance: in the way he speaks, his "style," his laughter, the ring of his voice, and also his good manners. However, the person who is a conventional member of society can also possess good manners without being refined.

This refinement of the truly refined person is attested in a unified manner in all the spheres mentioned above (face, movements, voice, language); it must be distinguished from the refinement which is manifested in only one sphere, namely, in the ring of the voice or in the face or in the bearing of the person. Each of these spheres on its own, without the others, can express the quality of refinement. A person can have a face that does not express refinement yet possess refinement in his voice. Similarly, one who is refined in his face can bear himself in a slovenly way and have bad manners.

The true opposite of refinement is vulgarity. I said above that "refined" is not in itself an aesthetic value, but a vital value (we might call it a spiritualized form of the vital), and that "vulgar" is not an aesthetic disvalue; but this does not mean that the metaphysical beauty of the refined is not an aesthetic value, nor that the metaphysical ugliness of the vulgar is not an aesthetic disvalue. We are, however, conscious that the refined does not possess metaphysical beauty in the way that moral values possess it.

The refined possesses an aesthetic value of a different kind, one that represents the irradiation of the refined. This expressed reflection of the refined is an aesthetic value, and the expressed reflection of the vulgar is a distinct aesthetic disvalue. We must remain content with pointing to the significance of this aesthetic value or disvalue in the external appearance of a person, and with bringing to light the specific character that distinguishes it from the rest of metaphysical beauty or ugliness.

The beauty of the human body

In many cases where expressed metaphysical beauty and the beauty of the visible and the audible work together, the beauty of the visible and the audible is able on its own to constitute the overall beauty, although the expressed metaphysical beauty can intensify this. One example is the human body.

Forms, proportions, colors, and material, which determine the beauty of the visible in some visible entity, depend on the specific essence of the entity's form. If the entity is to be beautiful, its formal principle may be neither breached nor infringed. This will become particularly clear when we speak of plants in chapters 8 and 12 below; even more, when we speak of the higher animals; and above all, of course, when our point of departure is the human form.

The ontological character of human beings and their special ontological value have an extremely significant influence on the beauty of the human body. Naturally, the entire outward appearance of the human being, the "invention" of the human structure, is based on a formal principle. In order for the beauty of the visible and the audible to be achieved, specific proportions, colors, and materials must be present. In addition to this beauty the metaphysical beauty of the ontological value of the human being is of great significance for the beauty of the human body, although differently than it is for the beauty of the human face. As an entity equipped with understanding and free will and possessing an immortal soul, the human being is the bearer of an eminent ontological value. This ontological value possesses great metaphysical beauty (it is not only qualitative values that possess beauty). There is a deep and meaningful connection between the essence of the person and his or her visible form. One could devote an entire section of a treatise on philosophical anthropology to this topic. For example, the upright gait of the human being is profoundly significant; and one could list many other things that are an expression of the essence of the human person. We limit ourselves here to pointing to the metaphysical beauty which is a reflection of the ontological value of the human person. This value finds its expression even in the form of the human person. It makes a significant contribution to the beauty of the human body.

The beauty of the ontological value of masculinity and femininity

I have pointed out elsewhere[3] that the difference between man and woman is not only a biological difference. Rather, we have here two basic types of the human person, both of whom possess all the attributes of a person, but with differences that reach deeply into the soul of each. The expressed metaphysical beauty of the ontological value of masculinity and femininity plays a great role in the overall beauty of the male and female body. The female body expresses the specific character of the woman in a special way—just as the male body expresses the specific character of the man. The psychological as well as the innermost personal essence of woman or man influences the essence of the form and of the formal principle. The well-shaped female body is also beautiful thanks to the expressed metaphysical beauty of her femininity; naturally, the same can be said of the masculinity of the male body.

We have up until now, whenever we have spoken of expressed metaphysical beauty, almost always spoken of the beauty which is grounded in qualitative values. But of course there also exists a beauty that is the splendor and fragrance of ontological values. Metaphysical beauty, as the

3. See my essay "Friendship Between the Sexes," in my collection *Man and Woman* (Chicago: Franciscan Herald Press, 1966). This is a partial translation of my "Die Bedeutung von Mann und Frau füreinander außerhalb der Ehe," in *Die Menschheit am Scheideweg* (Regensburg: Habbel Verlag, 1955). See also my *Metaphysik der Gemeinschaft*, chap. 5, pp. 62–64.

reflection of the ontological value of the human being, is extremely significant for his external form. This is true also of the metaphysical beauty of the female and the male. This spiritual quality plays a decisive role in the beauty of the body. But this ontological character of the beautiful object and the metaphysical beauty which is grounded in it is of a quite different kind from the metaphysical beauty of purity, modesty, or an unaffected manner. The metaphysical beauty that is grounded in ontological values is a presupposition for the beauty of the visible and the audible, whereas the metaphysical beauty that is grounded in qualitative personal values is a factor that complements the beauty of the visible and the audible.

Now we understand the difference between the way metaphysical beauty and the beauty of the visible and the audible work together in a face, and the way they work together in a body. The human body can be the bearer of a very high beauty of visible and audible form. The beauty of the total proportion and of the individual parts such as the legs, and in the female body the beauty of the breasts, work together and can attain one of the highest levels of the beauty of visible and audible form. When it is perfect, the body as such can possess a high spiritual beauty, purity, and poetry; indeed, we shall call it a beauty of the second power. A perfectly constructed body does not have the ability of the face to express either stupidity and mediocrity, or the many kinds of moral values and their metaphysical beauty. At the same time, however, elements of expression, for example, the refined and the vulgar, also play a significant role in the body. The "body feeling" of a human being, that is, how he "feels" in his body, can have a very varied quality, and can accordingly have a very positive or negative value. This applies, however, not so much to the pure outward appearance of the naked body as to the way in which someone presents himself, to the rhythm of his movements, and indeed to his entire bearing.

The fact that the beauty of the human body—which by the way is rarer than the beauty of a face—can possess a poetry that moves the onlooker is often obscured by the fact that the naked body also possesses a specific sexual charm. In particular, the naked body of the woman possesses this sexual charm for the man, and it is certainly both legitimate and positive. It is definitely a value, something mysterious and intimate; but it is oriented in such a way to love and to the ultimate mutual act of becoming one that as soon as it is isolated, it is pushed out by an evil, brutal sensuality.

The beauty of the body and the charm that appeals to the senses

Many somewhat primitive persons have no understanding whatever of the beauty that the body can possess, but see only the legitimate sexual charm or only the brutal sensual power of attraction. But even those who would in fact be capable of apprehending this beauty tend to regard the beauty of the body as sub-personal [*ungeistig*], because of its charm for the senses. We cannot speak in detail here of the value and nobility of sensual charm, of its link to love and, through love, to the world of the spirit. I have discussed this subject in several other books, especially in *Purity*. In the present context, the only thing that matters is to draw a distinction between the beauty of the body and its sensual charm. The latter is present even when the body is not beautiful, and this holds both for the noble charm of the mysterious and the intimate in true spousal love, as well as for the brutal, base sex appeal experienced by debauched men. This is not to deny that the beauty of the body intensifies the attractiveness of the noble charm: in that case, the one who loves experiences this charm as a special gift. For debauched men the beauty of the body is an intensification of sex appeal. But we must affirm very decisively that the beauty which a body can possess is as such completely independent of every kind of sensual charm, and that every attempt to reduce beauty to this charm is utterly absurd. The beauty of the human body is a definite, genuine beauty, a high beauty of eminent aesthetic value.

The expressed metaphysical beauty or ugliness that is grounded in qualitative values does not play the same role in the human body as in the human face. It is true that the expressed metaphysical beauty of purity, modesty, or noble "body feeling" confers on a dignified and worthy personality a significant intensification of his or her overall bodily beauty; but even if no expression of this kind is present, the beautiful body does not become a mask like the face does under certain circumstances. If, however, an insolent wantonness is expressed in the naked body, this clearly mars its overall beauty, but the marring is not nearly as bad as it is in a face that expresses the same wantonness.

Here I am speaking only of the real body as found in nature, not of its representation in works of art. As we shall see in the second volume of this work, the situation changes completely through the artistic transposition, and expression then acquires a much greater significance.

The beauty of animals
Expression in a broader sense

We find in animals too that the beauty of the visible and the audible works together with expressed metaphysical beauty. "Expression" in animals is of course understood in a broader sense than in the case of human beings, and especially of the human face.

Does not an expression of the characteristics of a higher animal, for example, a horse or a German shepherd dog, play a role in its beauty? It is indeed true that the animal is not the bearer of moral values. It is not a person. But the various animals have their various characters. It makes good sense to call a horse—unlike a rat—a noble being. It is well known that the eyes of a dog can express joy or misery. But is the general "character" of an animal expressed in its outward appearance? We can certainly say of one particular dog, "He looks fierce, or nasty, or aggressive," and of another dog, "He looks good-natured and trusting." In that case, we are referring to the qualities of one individual animal which are expressed in its outward appearance. But the question is whether the dog really is the way he looks. There is often a gulf between the expression and the real character of the animal.

We should note that the beauty of an animal is largely independent of its expression. The beauty of a well-built horse, a zebra, a German shepherd or Newfoundland dog, a sheep, a deer, etc. is primarily a beauty of the visible that is grounded in the forms, colors, and so on—for example, in the coat of the animal. Above all, they look beautiful.

On the other hand, there are definitely ugly animals, such as the toad or the hippopotamus, whose forms directly ground a certain ugliness. An octopus has a hellish ugliness; a lion, especially the male lion, is definitely beautiful, as are the tiger and the black panther; but the hyena is ugly.

In most instances, the expression of feelings in a higher animal is not primarily a bearer of beauty. The dog's eyes move us by its fidelity, its sadness or joy, its devotion to us, rather than by the beauty of these expressed values. When we say of a dog or a horse, "How beautiful this animal is!" we are not referring primarily to the expression of some particular experience in these animals. It is not so easy to apprehend the "character"—itself a more analogous type of expression—as the expression of one individual dog, cat, or horse; but the general character of a kind of animal is a significant factor. The grace and elegance of the cat's movements are not an expression in the genuine sense of that term; rather, its external bearing is an essential component of its "character." These qualities are found even on the level of the visible. Similarly, the sweetness and beauty of the nightingale's voice do not belong to a reality which lies *behind* the level of the audible and merely manifests itself on this level; rather, they belong to this level itself. No matter how great the role of expression in the broader sense may be, the world of the beautiful which is given to us in the animal realm, as well as the ugliness, is grounded directly in the visible and the audible; this beauty and ugliness are conditioned in a mysterious manner by forms, colors, and proportions.

Accordingly, although the beauty of the visible and the audible is much more independent of expressed beauty in the animals than in the human face, it is also the case that there is in the beauty and poetry of the animal world a working together of both kinds of beauty, that is, the beauty of expression in the broader sense and the beauty that is directly conditioned by certain forms, colors, proportions, etc.

CHAPTER SIX

The Riddle of Spiritual Beauty in the Realm of the Visible and the Audible

"WITHIN the hierarchy which runs through the universe, the sublime beauty of visible objects and of music stands out in a surprising, puzzling way. The lofty spiritual beauty irradiated by the Coliseum, the landscape of Tuscany, or Mozart's Quintet in G minor, has a quality that towers high above the ontological dignity of the sphere of sense objects as such, and confronts us with a puzzle."[1]

The two different kinds of beauty that adhere to the visible and the audible

"This problem has often been evaded, either by regarding the beauty of the visible and the audible as a qualitatively lower form of beauty and by opposing this to the higher beauty of spiritual contents; or else by believing that the root of this beauty could be found in something

1. Dietrich von Hildebrand, "Zum Problem des Sichtbaren und Hörbaren," in my collection *Die Menschheit am Scheideweg* (Regensburg: Habbel Verlag, 1955), 409.

purely spiritual that was linked to the visible and the audible only in our thinking. But reality resists these attempts at explanation. There is no doubt that a mountain or a bay flowing into an ocean can have a lofty spiritual beauty, and that this beauty does not adhere to some 'idea' that would be merely 'represented' by the mountain or awakened in the imagination by it. On the contrary, the beauty adheres immediately to the mountain, prior to all the ideas associated with it."[2]

This brings us to the central problem of all of aesthetics: the mystery that is entrusted to the visible and the audible, namely, the ability to be the bearer not only of beauty that appeals to the senses, but also of sublime spiritual beauty. This spiritual beauty goes far beyond the ontological rank and dignity of the object to which it adheres, even as it also transcends the qualitative values that this object as such possesses. In order to deal adequately with this problem, we must first realize that two very different types of beauty adhere to the visible and the audible. Both types deserve the name "beauty," not only in some analogous sense, but fully. We have called the first and more primitive type the beauty that appeals to the senses, or beauty of the first degree; we have called the second type, the lofty spiritual beauty, beauty of the second degree.

When we speak of the beauty of an ornament, a color, or the pleasant melody of the flute, we are in reality referring to something quite different from that which we praise in the beauty of the Coliseum in Rome, the landscape of Tuscany, or Mozart's Quintet in G minor. It is very important to understand that visible and audible things can be the bearers of two qualitatively very different types of beauty. Both the beauty that appeals to the senses and the sublime spiritual beauty in nature and art presuppose the senses—the eye and the ear—and both kinds of beauty, in contrast to metaphysical beauty, appear directly in the visible and the audible and are not the splendor and fragrance of other values. The way they appear is conditioned by visible and audible factors. The beauty that appeals to the senses is indeed very significant and represents a great gift from God, but it does not have the specifically spiritual element possessed by the beauty of the Gulf of Naples, or the view from the

2. Ibid.

Capitol to the Campagna and the Sabine Hills, or San Marco in Venice, or Beethoven's Quartet opus 59 no. 1, or Schubert's Quintet opus 163.

But whereas the difference between metaphysical beauty and the beauty of the visible and the audible has always been seen, for example, by Plato and Plotinus, the distinction within the beauty of the visible and the audible was not seen.[3] Either the necessary involvement of the senses (eye and ear) in the case of all beauty of the visible and the audible was taken to imply the impossibility of visible and audible things ever possessing spiritual beauty such as we find it in the virtues or in truth; in this case one inferred that all beauty of the visible and the audible was unspiritual and was nothing other than what we call the beauty that appeals to the senses. Or else the attempt was made to salvage the spiritual quality of the higher beauty in nature and art by showing that it did not really adhere in any way to the visible and the audible but was associated with it only in our thinking it. This was nothing other than an attempt to evade the problem. The spiritual beauty that can appear in visible and audible things is an undeniable fact. It is immediately linked to the visible and the audible as intuitively given and not merely as linked by association with other spiritual entities.

Erroneous attempts at explaining the spiritual beauty of the visible and the audible

We shall speak in detail below of the difference between the beauty that appeals only to the senses and spiritual beauty; here it must suffice to

3. In the first part of Kant's *Critique of Judgment* ("Critique of Aesthetic Judgment"), division 1, book 2, "Analytic of the Sublime," he draws a distinction between the beautiful and the sublime. He regards the sublime as something much higher and more exalted than beauty. But it is unlikely that he understands by "beauty" what we call the beauty that appeals to the senses, or by the "sublime" what we call specifically spiritual beauty. It is certain that in Kant the sublime is regarded as much more spiritual, and beauty is seen wholly as the beauty that appeals to the senses. The distinction he draws refers clearly to two completely different qualities. He does not indeed deny that something visible can be sublime, as we see from his famous dictum that there is nothing more sublime than the starry sky above us and the moral law in us (cf. *Critique of Practical Reason*, conclusion of the second part, and *Critique of Judgment*, part 1, division 1, book 2, "General Remark upon the Exposition of Aesthetic Reflective Judgments"). Nevertheless, the way he presents the beautiful and the sublime does not in any way permit us to equate this distinction with our distinction between the beauty that appeals to the senses and specifically spiritual beauty.

affirm that the beauty of a color or an ornament or a sound, such as that of the violin or flute, does not pose the same problem that we encounter in the specifically spiritual, transfigured beauty of a landscape such as the area around Florence or Siena, or in the beauty of Beethoven's "Harp Quartet" or Bach's "Air on the G-string."

The most primitive form of dismissing this question is to have recourse to association, that "jack of all trades." One of the most popular, but also one of the cheapest and most mediocre, attempts at explanation is to derive something from association. Thus we are told that the beauty which captivates us in the landscape is linked to the landscape only by means of association: either it reminds us of pleasant experiences, or else it generates associations with ideas that make an impression on us. The same attempt is made all the more with music. But this explanation is so impossible, so utterly far-fetched, that we need not dwell on it; it suffices to recall what we have said about the objectivity of values, and our demonstration that beauty is a value. As we saw already in the first chapter of the present book, such arguments are basically nothing more than empty words.

We must take much more seriously the attempts to explain the spiritual quality of this sublime beauty of the visible and the audible in terms of deeper intellectual links between the visible and the audible, on the one hand, and something spiritual, on the other. For example, a theologian once said to me, "When the beauty of a mountain range captivates us, what moves us is basically not what we see, but the idea of God's creative power. Understandably, this lofty spiritual datum captivates us deeply. We then apprehend an ultimate"—in our terminology, a metaphysical—"beauty, that of God's unlimited creative power, for which the mountain range is but a sign, a symbol. We need not therefore be astonished that something visible leads us to the enjoyment of such a spiritual beauty—for it is only a symbol of something infinitely higher. Through the visible datum we are reminded of God's creative power."

We want now to respond to this attempt to evade the problem posed by the spiritual beauty of the visible and the audible, and we want to begin our response with an investigation of the basic kinds of possible links that sense data can have with spiritual contents. This investigation will show us clearly the impossibility of all attempts at circumventing the problem of the spiritual beauty of visible and audible things. We shall then investigate the levels of beauty, from the beauty that appeals to the senses, to the spiritual beauty that can adhere to the visible and the audible, in order thus to clear the path for understanding the great mystery that is contained in the spiritual beauty of visible and audible things.

CHAPTER SEVEN

The Various Ways in which the Visible and the Audible are Linked to Non-material Contents[1]

Sign and meaning

THERE ARE many ways in which the visible and the audible are linked to non-material contents. The first and most external link exists when some visible or audible datum functions as a sign for a non-material reality. A color or a sound can be a sign of a state-of-affairs that itself is not of a visible nature. A red light is a sign that a motorist is not allowed to continue driving, and a green light is a sign that he is allowed to do so.

This sign is of a conventional nature. One must *know* that the color red has been chosen as a sign for stopping and the color green as a sign that the road is clear, that is, as a prohibition or a permission to drive on.

1. [One may wonder why we rendered *geistig* in the previous chapter as "spiritual," and here as "non-material." In that chapter Hildebrand is speaking about a kind of beauty which is better called spiritual beauty than non-material beauty. In the present chapter the things called *geistig* are not forms of beauty at all; for the most part these things are better called non-material than spiritual. *Geistig* is one of those German words that has no English equivalent and has to be translated differently in different contexts. JFC]

It would have been perfectly possible to have chosen green for the prohibition and red for the permission.[2]

We prescind here from all those signs that are not a form of the link of visible and audible things with immaterial realities, but are only an indication of the presence of other processes of a material nature. For the problem that interests us in the present context is: How is it possible that visible and audible things can be bearers of a lofty spiritual beauty? We shall therefore briefly analyze all the possible links of visible and audible things with immaterial contents, in order to delineate clearly between the link of spiritual beauty with visible things in nature and the visual arts as well as with structures of sound in music, on the one hand, and every other possible link, on the other hand.

The term "sign" is employed to designate relationships of various kinds. First of all, we employ it for everything that entitles us to infer from one thing to another. We say, "The path is wet. This is a sign that it has rained." When we see footprints, this is an indicator that someone has passed by. In these cases the term "sign" is grounded exclusively in a causal relationship, that is, it does nothing more than designate something that guarantees our knowledge of a thing. The wetness is a guarantee of my affirmation that it has rained, and the presence of the footprints is a guarantee of my knowledge that someone has passed by. Here there is no transition from something visible to something immaterial. The wetness and the state-of-affairs that it has rained, or the footprints and the state-of-affairs that someone has passed by, belong to the same realm of being; at any rate, the second state-of-affairs in each of these examples is not an immaterial reality.

Something visible or audible can entitle me to infer the presence of something that belongs to the immaterial realm. For example, I hear in a neighboring room the well-known voices of my neighbors shouting at each other in great agitation. This is an indicator that a quarrel is taking

2. "... For the sign exists only for the one who knows that it is a sign; and in the strictest sense it exists only for the one who knows what it means; for anyone else, the sign is only what it is in its immediacy." Søren Kierkegaard, *Practice in Christianity* (Princeton: Princeton University Press, 1991), part 2, "The Categories of Offense, that is, of Essential Offense," 1: "The God-Man is a Sign."

place among them and that they are excited, annoyed, etc. Although I draw an inference to something immaterial from what I hear, the latter remains merely an indicator. In other words: one state-of-affairs justifies me in drawing a conclusion about another state-of-affairs. This form of linkage of the cause of knowledge presupposes an ontological causal relationship in which the effect is a guarantee for us of the cause. This is the important point here.

Secondly, the relationship between a word and the object meant by it has often been regarded as a sign. Indeed, many positivists reduce the relationship of meaning to a mere association or at best to a pure indicator. In scholastic philosophy, "meaning" is understood only as a species of the *genus* "sign," but without being equated with "indicator."

In reality, however, as was shown by Edmund Husserl in his *Logical Investigations*,[3] by Alexander Pfänder in his *Logic*,[4] and by Adolf Reinach in several essays,[5] the relationship between the word and its intended object is not a species of the *genus* "sign," but rather something completely different. We begin this chapter by speaking about this specifically immaterial and intellectual relationship of meaning, because this is often confused with the relationship of a sign. A thorough analysis of this relationship belongs in a work on logic or epistemology, not in a work on aesthetics; accordingly, I shall discuss it only briefly here. When we speak of literature in the second volume of the present work, we shall discuss it in much greater breadth, though from a different perspective.

This relationship of meaning [*Bedeutung*] is actualized above all in acts of the person: first, in the act of intending [*Meinen*], of referring meaningfully [*sinnvolles Abzielen*] to an object by means of a word and of its meaning; and secondly, through the understanding of the word which is only spoken or read by us. An exact analysis of these acts brings out clearly the unique essence of "meaning" [*Bedeuten*]. Naturally, this

3. Edmund Husserl, *Logical Investigations*, trans. J. N. Findlay (New York and London: Routledge, 1970), vol. 1, First Investigation, 181–233.

4. Alexander Pfänder, *Logic*, trans. Don Ferrari (Frankfurt: Ontos Verlag, 2009), 143–45.

5. Adolf Reinach, "A Contribution Towards the Theory of the Negative Judgment"; and Reinach, "Concerning Phenomenology," trans. Dallas Willard, appended to Reinach, *The Apriori Foundations of the Civil Law* (Frankfurt: Ontos Verlag, 2012), 143–65.

meaningful [*sinnvoll*] link between the word and the object to which it refers plays a decisive role when we affirm a proposition.

We must distinguish between two things here: first, the relationship between the word and the intended object; and secondly, the relationship between the phonetic structure that we call a word and its meaning, or in other words, between the word and the conceptual entity by means of which we refer to the object.

Concepts [*Begriffe*] are unities of meaning [*Bedeutungseinheiten*] and must be distinguished from the real object to which we refer when we speak. Their form of "existence" is radically different not only from that of the real objects, but also from all ideal entities such as essences. They belong to a world of their own, where the various types of propositions are also to be found. Just as the proposition differs from the state-of-affairs to which it refers, so too the concept differs from the object to which it refers. Concepts are in fact "media" through which our spirit meaningfully refers to something that exists. This is why the relationship between the concept and the phonetic structure which we call a word is different from the relationship between the concept and the object to which the word refers.

Naturally, when we investigate the essence of a concept, we make the concept too an object, to which in turn we refer intentionally by means of other concepts; but this possibility does not abolish the fundamental character of the concept as a medium. The concepts are at home, so to speak, not in the act of knowing in the strict sense, but in the acts of affirming what one has come to know, of communicating this in every intentional act of reference, and of understanding what has been said or read.

Above all, we wish to show that the act of meaning [*Bedeuten*] is not a subsection of the sign, but far transcends the signitive relationship. It is much richer in meaning [*Sinn*] and much more differentiated than the signitive relationship.

The link between the phonetic word and its meaning, that is, the concept, is always a link between something sense-perceptible and something immaterial, even in the case of the concept of something material or physical, since the concept as a meaning-unity is never of a material nature. These are the most important points to be made about the essence of meaning [*Bedeutung*].

In the sphere of signs we make a distinction between conventional signs and natural indicators. The latter are based on a causal relationship which is known to us; their character as signs is something very like a guarantee for our knowledge and is clearly distinct from the underlying causal relationship. In the relation of meaning [*Bedeutung*] we cannot draw the distinction between what is conventional and what exists naturally. The choice of a word for an object, which is different in every language, never exists as already given, given in the way some guarantee for our knowledge is given. On the other hand, the meaning of a word is not the result of a convention, of a conventional selection. There are indeed technical terms which are the results of a definition undertaken in one or several countries; for example, the degrees of temperature are named after the men who introduced them, Celsius, Fahrenheit, or Réaumur. Not only the technical term (here a sort of name) is different, but so is the unit of measure on which the measurement is based. There is thus—and this is the important point for us here—a conventionality analogous to what we see in conventional signs.

Unlike the technical term, however, the genuine natural word is something that has grown up organically. The fact that a word such as *love* or *amour* has been chosen for this primordial phenomenon is a problem posed afresh in every language, and it is something extraordinarily mysterious and opaque. At most, one can "justify" the "choice" of this phonetic entity for the concept of an object in the case of onomatopoeic words; but in general there is no choice, and this makes it impossible to grasp why one word has precisely *this* particular meaning in *this* language. All that is certain is that the relationship of a phonetic entity to a concept, to its meaning, comes about organically and is not the result of a conscious convention.

I mention this only in passing, because the relationship of meaning [*Bedeutung*] as such, which is clearly different from the mere sign or indicator, is of course present both in the onomatopoeic words and in the technical terms. In all these cases we can see an expression [*Niederschlag*] of the act of meaning [*Meinen*].

We surely do not need to demonstrate in detail that the link between visible and audible entities, on the one hand, and their immaterial beauty, on the other, is not the same as the link between a word (as a phonetic entity consisting of vowels and consonants) and the meaning or concept by means of which we aim with our intention at an object. It is obvious that the lofty beauty of the Gulf of Spezia is not its "meaning" [*Bedeutung*]. Such a construction would clearly be absurd.

Accordingly, we shall turn to other relationships between immaterial contents and visible and audible things, where the attempt to derive the sublime immaterial beauty of the visible and the audible from these relationships is indeed mistaken, but not *a priori* absurd like the reduction of these relationships to that between word and meaning. We encounter above all the relationship of the symbol to what is symbolized.

The symbol in the classical and the Freudian senses

The expression "symbol" is frequently employed for very different things. We limit ourselves here to the classic symbolic relationship that is found in religious symbols or in symbols in the public sphere of state and nation.

A visible thing represents a reality belonging to the immaterial world, whether a person, an office, or a community. Thus, the flag is a symbol of a nation, the crown a symbol of royal dignity, and the fish a symbol of Christ.

One first essential characteristic of this relationship is the existence of a link that must be explicitly set up. We must be informed about it in order to know it or to know about it; it is completely impossible to apprehend it simply by looking at the symbol. There exists no objective ontological relationship [of one thing symbolizing another]; all we have is a relationship defined by the competent authority. The symbol shares this trait with conventional signs.

The difference between the symbol and the indicator emerges clearly in the second characteristic of the symbol: representation. The indicator shows us the presence of something else; but the symbol, for example, the paschal candle that symbolizes Christ, is not in any way an indicator of the presence of Christ. It is rather the case that it represents Christ. We could say that it is treated as if it were Christ, the risen Christ. The genuine symbol has an "ambassadorial" function. The ambassador represents the head of state or the nation in such a way that to insult the ambassador is to insult the state or nation; this is how the symbol represents what it symbolizes. The symbol is treated with the respect demanded by what it symbolizes. The symbol stands for what it symbolizes.

Thirdly, in the case of a genuine symbol, what is symbolized stands on a much higher level and possesses a much higher dignity than the symbol itself. In terms of its dignity, what is symbolized cannot be compared to that which functions as a symbol. There is a relation between symbol and symbolized that does not appeal to our knowledge of the symbolized; nor does it draw our attention to the symbolized. It demands, rather, that we give a particular response to it. On the one hand, we know clearly that the symbol is not in any way what it symbolizes; we know that a world of difference lies between the two. On the other hand, we treat the symbol as if it were what it symbolizes. Our relationship to that which is symbolized finds expression in our behavior toward the symbol.

Through this function the object that serves as a symbol acquires a quality that it does not in any way possess in its own right, independently of this function; it acquires a dignity that far transcends the ontological and qualitative rank that accrues to it in its own right. But it does not acquire this dignity as something belonging to its own self even if it were to cease to function as a symbol. On the contrary, it possesses it only in its function as a symbol.

It is obvious that the symbol in this classical sense has nothing in common with the "symbol" that plays a prominent role in Freud's psychoanalysis. In Freud one thing symbolizes another not because it has been consciously set up by a competent authority as a symbol of this other thing, but rather in a subconscious manner. A person does one thing but subconsciously intends something else. This symbol is a typical fruit of repression. What one really intends, that which motivates one's response and one's conduct, is covered over by something else. According to Freud's theory, many things that as such have nothing to do with the sexual sphere are symbols of something sexual. As in genuine symbols, there is a formal representation, but this has the character of something that obscures. Its characteristic is precisely that we are not conscious of this representation. We deceive ourselves by passing off one thing for another. We behave as if one had the symbol in mind, while in reality we subconsciously have in mind that which it symbolizes: it is this that motivates us, it is this that we intend, but without admitting it to ourselves, since we have suppressed the thing symbolized. In Freud the relationship between the symbol and what it symbolizes is exactly the opposite of a conscious, explicit relationship. This means that all the other characteristics of the classic symbol, that is to say, the official establishment of the symbolic relationship by a competent authority and the conscious focus of the symbol on what it symbolizes, are eliminated.

Much more significant in the present context than the difference between the classical symbolic relation and Freud's use of the term "symbol" is the difference between the symbol and another fundamental relation between visible, physical entities and immaterial entities, namely, the relation of analogy.

The qualitative analogy and its various levels

By "analogy," we mean here qualitative analogy, that is, neither the mere *analogia proportionis* (the analogy of proportion) nor the *analogia attributionis* (the analogy of attribution). The universe is permeated by qualitative analogies of the kind we have in mind, for example, the relation of light to truth, or of darkness to error, and the analogy of "above" and "below," and of "high" and "low," to the hierarchical ranking of goods and values. We are continually compelled to make use of these analogies when we speak of immaterial entities and their specific character by means of words whose primary meaning refers to contents of the external physical world that surrounds us, to visible and audible things, and to all the data supplied by the senses. The qualitative analogy, this relationship of correspondence between contents that are radically different and belong to completely different spheres of being, is a very central and extremely significant relationship. Unlike the relationships of indication, meaning, and symbol, it is a relationship which exists intuitively, independently of all official declarations and conventions, and is grounded in the very essence of the terms of the relation. It reveals itself to our mind as soon as we get to know the essence of the two things; for example, once we have understood what truth is, we also apprehend the analogy of light and truth.

The observation of natural scientists that there is no "above" and "below" in the universe independently of human beings is irrelevant to this qualitative analogy. The phenomena of the physical "above" and "below" are primordial realities for our immediate experience, determined by our upright posture. This immediate datum is the basis for the qualitative analogy to the immaterial world. Accordingly, if we say that the qualitative analogical relationship is based on the essence of the two contents between which this analogy exists, we encounter no obstacle in the fact that the concepts of "above" and "below" are limited and relative to human experience and to the human aspect of the external world. The analogy is between this primordial datum within the human aspect of the world and some metaphysical reality.

This correspondence of two things that we find in a qualitative analogy as well as in the *analogia proportionis* is entirely different from membership in the same *genus*, as when we speak, for example, of the "foot" of a mountain. We do not in the least believe that there are two species of feet, one with which we designate the foot of a human being or an animal, and another with which we designate the foot of a mountain, and that these two are species of the one *genus* "foot"! The feet of human beings and of animals are two species of the *genus* "foot," distinguished by a *differentia specifica*, that is, a trait which makes for a species; but this is not true of the feet of the human being and the foot of the mountain.

The foot of the mountain is not a real foot. All that we envisage when we use this word is the function played by one part of the mountain for the mountain as a whole, which is in a limited sense analogous to the function played by real feet for the body. Analogy is a unique form of similarity, which is completely different from every form of membership in one and the same *genus*.

The same applies to the deeper, much more significant and intimate qualitative analogy of which we are speaking. For example, when we speak of the blazing glow of love, we envisage something to which the blaze of a fire—unlike a weak flickering—offers a qualitative analogy. But nothing would be more absurd than to think there was a *genus* "glow" that could be dissected into the two species of physical glow and immaterial glow.

We shall return in the second volume to speak in detail of this qualitative analogy. We will examine the artistic means employed in literature, for this qualitative analogy plays a great role in poetry and indeed in the phenomenon of the poetical as such.

Here we present the qualitative analogy as only one of the various possible relations between immaterial things, on the one hand, and visible or audible things or for that matter any other sense-perceived things, on the other. These relations are clearly different from those involving an indicator, a meaning, or a symbol. The fact that some symbols latch onto a qualitative analogy should not blind us to the specific character of this extremely significant relation of qualitative analogy, or blind us to its difference from the symbol. In the paschal candle, for example, there is not only the officially posited symbolic relationship to Christ but also the qualitative analogy of light and truth, since the light forms a qualitative analogy to Christ who is *the* truth and who says of himself, "I am the light of the world" (John 8:12). Accordingly, the Church in the Easter liturgy speaks of the *lumen Christi.* There is another qualitative analogy at work in this symbol: the burning candle, unlike an extinguished candle, reflects the resurrection of life and the risen Lord.

In many cases qualitative analogies are chosen and employed for the symbol; but this does not alter the fact that the symbolic link is completely different from the qualitative analogy. One chooses as a symbol something that possesses a qualitative analogy to the thing symbolized and brings it thereby into a completely new and different relationship to the thing symbolized, to which it was previously linked only by means of a qualitative analogy. The qualitative analogy may be a motivating factor in the choice of *this* object as a symbol, and it is likely that this is very often the case. But in order to establish the relationship between the symbol and what is symbolized, one is not obliged to choose an object that relies on a qualitative analogy to what is symbolized. The symbol of the fish for Christ possesses no qualitative analogy of any kind: the early Christians made use of the very abstract and accidental fact that the initial letters of *Iêsous Khristos Theou huios sôtêr* ("Jesus Christ, God's Son, Redeemer") form the word *ikhthus* ("fish") in order to conceal what was symbolized from the eyes of the non-initiates. Similarly, the choice of particular colors for the flag of a country need not in any way be determined by a qualitative analogy, and in fact this is very seldom the case.

At any rate, the fact that one thing possesses a qualitative analogy to another, and that it was chosen as a symbol for this reason, must not lead us to confuse the qualitative relationship of analogy with the symbolic relationship. These relationships remain radically different, even when one and the same thing is linked to another thing by both relationships. This must be explicitly emphasized, because the expression "symbol" is often used for a qualitative analogy, as when light is described as a "symbol" of truth.

There are various levels within the qualitative analogy. We wish to point here to one principal difference. Let us compare the analogy between light and truth, mentioned above, with the analogy between the physical power in a mighty waterfall and the immaterial power in a dominating personality. In the analogy between light and truth, the relationship to truth is not an element that is already present in the act of seeing the light, in such a way that we would somehow be obliged to think of truth: we can enjoy the beauty of the light without in the least thinking of truth, and it is only when we think of both truth and of light that this qualitative analogy occurs to us. This involves not only radically different spheres of being, but also a profound qualitative analogy that does indeed exist objectively but must be discovered at some time. It is understood as soon as someone makes use of it, but it is not given along with the phenomenon of light. This phenomenon on which the qualitative analogy is built does indeed exist, but the objective analogy itself (that is, the relation to the truth) is not given along with it.

On the other hand, if we are impressed by the power of a waterfall, it is not indeed necessary to think of the analogous power of a strong personality, but the analogy is much closer. Nevertheless, there is no ontological link of any kind between the physical power of the waterfall and the power of the will or the personality. We can indeed say that the physical strength of an animal or a human being is ontologically related to that of the waterfall, for here we have a *genus* of physical power, one species of which is represented in the waterfall, while another is represented in the bodies of animals and human beings. But this cannot be affirmed of the physical power and the immaterial power. It would never be possible in the course of evolution for the one to become the other. This is one of the many philosophical errors of Teilhard de Chardin, who speaks of energy as a *genus* which is split into physical and immaterial energy; indeed, he asserts that the one kind of energy can become the other kind. There is no ontological bridge between physical and immaterial power. There does exist, however, a quality of powerfulness that is given in both cases, and that possesses a special metaphysical beauty.

Now this qualitative analogy has a different character from the one between light and truth. The quality of powerfulness is a common element in the two different and ontologically unbridgeable cases; but we must go deeper if we are to discover the analogy between light and truth, since these two things do not possess any common quality of this kind.

On the other hand, there exist many poetical qualitative analogies which a poet can employ, as when Goethe says: "O love, oh, lovely / So golden fair / Like morning cloudlets / On that hill there!"[6] Here the poet

6. Goethe, *Mailied* (*May Song*). English translation by John Sigerson, homepage of The Schiller Institute.

captures a distant qualitative analogy, but one that is not present as a permanent element in the structure of the cosmos. It is an illustrative analogy, very loose and tender, which does indeed capture something objective, but only in the way of a glance.

In our present context this brief discussion of the various levels within qualitative analogy must suffice. The most important thing here is to demarcate the qualitative analogy clearly from the other kinds of linkage between physical and immaterial things.

Expression
The analogical inference theory

A completely new relationship is present when we speak of "expression" in the precise sense. Obviously I do not mean "expression" in the same sense as Husserl, who equates the meaning of a word with "expression" in his *Logical Investigations*.[7] What I have in mind is the relationship that can be apprehended in a completely intuitive manner when we say of someone that his face expresses kindness, nobility, purity, or meekness, or when we say that one sees in his face how furious or how joyful he is. I have in mind the unique relationship that exists when visible data, whether the unvarying forms of a face or the shifts of the countenance from moment to moment, express immaterial qualities or processes in a person. We speak of the expression of the eyes, etc. This is a very remarkable fact, a relationship that demands a philosophical *thaumazein* ("marveling"). This link between immaterial and visible or also audible things is all too often explained away, in order that one may not be forced to confront this mysterious datum.

There are two well-known attempts to "explain" the remarkable fact that the kindness and purity, or the anger, joy, and pain of a human being are expressed in his face. The one is the analogical reasoning theory, which was particularly widespread in scholasticism, and the other is Theodor Lipps's theory of empathy.

7. Edmund Husserl, *Logical Investigations*, vol. 1, First Investigation.

How is it possible that we see the visible traits of someone's face and say of him that he looks very excited, profoundly sad, or radiantly happy? Thanks to the face, we learn something about what is going on in his soul at this moment, whether a psychological event, or, as sometimes happens, an experience rooted in the spiritual person. The theory of analogical inference explains this as follows: what we see are particular contractions of the muscles in the other person's face. These occur in our own face when we are sad, happy, or excited. We too make such faces then. Since we are very familiar from our own life with the connection between these muscular contractions and certain emotional states or attitudes, we conclude, as soon as we perceive these contractions in the face of another person, that he too is having analogous experiences. According to the theory of analogical reasoning, all that exists here is a simple inference; there is no special and certainly no mysterious link between the physical and the immaterial.

This "explanation," however, becomes utterly untenable as soon as one investigates the things themselves more closely; one sees then that there is no connecting link to the conclusion. What we experience when these muscular contractions take place in our face does not in any way tell us how we look. What we see in a face which changes through muscular contractions is a completely different datum from the physical feeling that we have from within of our own muscular contractions. We are very surprised at how we look when we weep or laugh, as soon as we see this in a photograph that someone took of us at precisely that moment, or when we happen to catch sight of ourselves in a mirror when we were weeping or laughing.

It is obvious that, in order for me to infer from someone's facial expression, determined by particular muscular contractions, to the fact that he or she is annoyed or contented, happy or sad, the outward appearance of the muscular contractions in someone else's face must be identical with the feeling of these contractions that I experience in myself; for then I would know from experience that I myself have the same muscular contractions that I see in the other. But this is not at all the case. Accordingly, this alleged analogical inference lacks the connecting link that would entitle us to draw the inference. From A, B follows. From B, C follows. But since B is employed with a different meaning in the two affirmations, it is obvious that we cannot infer from C to the presence of A.

One could present many other arguments against this alleged analogical inference. For example, let us picture the terrifying expression of a furious face and compare the inference drawn from it with another inference, namely, the inference that we draw from someone continually coughing and wiping his nose to the fact that he must have a cold. The coughing and the dripping from the nose are not expressions of having a cold, but its symptoms—and symptoms are not something apprehended intuitively, something immediately given, but rather premises ordered to a conclusion.

First of all, the expression of sadness, joy, or of other affective attitudes that appears in a person's face is something that is immediately given, something that can be apprehended intuitively. It is not an inference of any kind. Secondly, it is obvious that the experience of the muscular contractions which we make in our own face when we feel joy or sadness, or have any other affective experiences, plays no role at all for us. If we are happy we concentrate completely on the fact that motivates our joy, and we are completely filled by the experience of the joy itself. We are scarcely aware of the muscular contractions in our face that are conditioned by our joy. We sooner notice that our heart is beating more quickly than that we are drawing our facial muscles together in one particular manner. This is why we ourselves are scarcely aware of the connection between our joy and the physical feeling of the muscular contractions.

We need only think of what we experience when we weep because something hurts us or moves us deeply. Obviously, we are fully conscious of the fact of our weeping, of the physical feeling when we burst into tears; we experience this clearly and unambiguously. We do not indeed know what kind of face we are making when we weep, but we note "from the outside" that we are shedding tears, that our hands or our handkerchief is getting wet. We hear when we sob. Our comportment is present to us "from the outside." When we see someone else weeping, his weeping is likewise a symptom of the fact that he is deeply moved. This inference is possible; but the fact of his weeping cannot tell us by itself whether he is shedding tears out of joy or grief, whether from being touched or from anger. When he weeps, however, his face can express feelings such as deep pain, emotion, anger, or joy; his expressions are not themselves just symptoms (like the shedding of tears).

In this comparison it is important to see how little we notice of the muscular contractions that our emotions bring about in our face. It is clearly ridiculous to declare that here lies the key to the rich and great knowledge of the affective processes in other persons that is supplied by the expression—quite apart from the fact that, as I have shown above, the alleged analogical inference is impossible in this case.

Thirdly, the outrageousness of this conclusion by analogy emerges with particular clarity when we reflect on the terror that a little child already experiences when he sees a furious face. It is ridiculous to suppose that the child knows something about the connection between anger and the contraction of his own facial muscles, and that he is drawing inferences at this moment. Even more ridiculous is the idea that he knows from experience what kind of face he makes when he is angry.

We sometimes hear the objection that very small children are frightened and weep even when they see the friendly faces of people who are completely unknown to them. This leads to the conclusion that the friendly expression is not an immediate fact that can be apprehended intuitively. In reality, however, this objection does not hold water. First of all, the fact that the strangeness of the face has a stronger effect than the special expression of the face does not mean that the friendly expression is not something immediately given. All it means is that in some instances, the strangeness and unfamiliarity play a greater role than the expression. This, however, is only sometimes the case. Often a baby smiles when a complete stranger gives him a friendly smile, reacting unambiguously to the friendly expression. Besides this, the reaction we cited above is not that of a very small child. We have in mind above all the reaction of a child between two and four when he is startled and frightened by a fierce and furious face. A friendly face will scarcely make the same impression on such a child, even if the child is afraid of all the people he does not know.

But the untenability of the analogical reasoning theory can be seen most clearly when we think of the lasting expressions of faces, of kind, pure, gentle, or evil, crude, impure faces. The pseudo-analogy of muscular contractions, which are erroneously adduced as a connecting link, then loses all plausibility. One does not perform particular muscular contractions when one is gentle or pure, nor does one experience one's own gentleness or purity. Since these are lasting characteristics of our personality, they do not penetrate our consciousness. As soon as someone thinks that he is pure or gentle, the lack of humility that this entails corrupts these virtues and turns them into pseudo-virtues. These virtues of ours can safely come to consciousness only in the form of our love for purity and gentleness as such, and in our endeavor to acquire these virtues, to do nothing impure, and to commit no offense against gentleness. Apart from this, the possession of moral virtues makes itself felt in our consciousness through a particular kind of joy and peace. But we must never directly aim at this joy or peace.

This should be enough to show us clearly that we are never drawing an inference from some experience in ourselves to the presence of virtues in another person when we say, "He looks kind, gentle, or pure; his face expresses these spiritual attributes." No one who truly possesses these virtues will ever look at his own face in a mirror and say, "How pure, how gentle, how kind I look!"

The theory of analogical inference is a consummate specimen of the desperate attempt to explain away a phenomenon that is both surprising and mysterious.

Conventional signs as pseudo-expressions

The fact that expressions are immediately given and intuitively apprehensible emerges with particular clarity when we think of the conventional signs which function as pseudo-expressions. In Europe whistling is an expression of displeasure, of contempt; in America it is a sign of applause. In Germany the rustling of feet is a well-known form of protest, of rejection, especially in university lecture halls; in Hungary it is a form of applause. Obviously in such cases there is no expression in the genuine sense of this term. Neither clapping nor whistling nor stamping is an immediate expression of the opinion of the public. We must know the character possessed by a particular sign in the country or continent in question, if we are to learn whether the public is thereby making known its applause or its displeasure and protest. This is a typical sign that is linked only by convention to what it indicates, although it is intended by the persons who clap or whistle as an expression of their feelings and their attitudes. But this instrument of communication or proclamation, which they intend as the expression of their attitude, does not possess as such any quality which reflects the kind of attitude.

Words too can function as an expression of enthusiasm or displeasure, when the public cry out "Hurrah!" or "Bravo!" or "Boo!" or "Away!" One must know these words. One must know what they mean, since otherwise one will learn nothing about the reaction of the public. These words are not conventional signs; the relationship involved here is quite different from the relationship of the sign. In the present instance, the word is not used in its specific function of meaning but rather as a way of expressing ourselves.

It is indeed true that in these calls uttered in public, the voice, and above all its tone, can give expression to something, reveal assent or rejection, make a quality intuitively present. But this is a much weaker form of expression than exists otherwise, for example, when we hear a terrified scream or a voice filled with hatred.

The internal aspect and the external aspect of personal acts

We wish now to draw attention to something significant that far transcends the problem of expression, namely, the terrible immanence in which one confines the human person when one denies that we can ever apprehend something immaterial-personal that we have not already experienced in our own selves, in our own personal life. For when we get to know an exceptional personality, our eyes can be opened to a new world of attitudes, for example, a love of neighbor or a moral heroism, that we have never experienced in ourselves, attitudes that are completely new to us in their essence and quality. Behind this error lies the completely unjustified thesis that the world of the psychological and the personal-immaterial, that is, the mental acts of the person, can disclose themselves to us only in the lateral consciousness of our own living of these acts, but never in a "consciousness of" the actions, declarations, and expressions of other persons.

There are two accesses to actions and expressions: living them "from within" and apprehending them from without. The internal aspect is certainly something new, something different from the external aspect that we apprehend in a "consciousness of." In both aspects, the essence of one particular personal act discloses itself. The way in which we come to learn the essence of love when we ourselves experience this act is certainly different from the way in which the essence of love can disclose itself to us when we are loved, or in the love of another person for a third person. We can come to know the essence of love both in the internal aspect of loving and in the external aspect of the love of another person. In both cases, the essence of love can disclose itself to us in an original manner; we need not draw an inference from the "internal experience" to the "external experience," nor regard the former as a basis for apprehending the latter.[8]

Theodor Lipps's theory of empathy

Theodor Lipps's theory of empathy likewise evades the real phenomenon of the psychological and personal entities making themselves known in visible data. He rightly rejects analogical reasoning, and he emphasizes intuition rather than inference; but this theory holds fast to the erroneous supposition that it must be *our own* feeling that we project into the other

8. Cf. the Introduction to my book *The Nature of Love*, trans. John F. Crosby (South Bend, Ind.: St. Augustine's Press, 2009).

person. The theory also overlooks, or explains away, the specific character of the phenomenon of expression.

Lipps affirms that a human person is able to "feel himself into" the internal life of other persons. He does not mean the gift that some people have in particular situations of understanding how another person feels, for example, when someone says, "I know what you are feeling about the death of your mother." Nor does he mean what we have in mind when we say, "We can sympathize with what you are feeling." Rather he means an unconscious projection of our own experiences into something visible or audible, as when we call a piece of music joyful or tragic, or when we say that a person's face expresses profound sadness. The theory does not tell us why this projection takes place, why various people find that a face reveals sadness or joy. Does this mean that something we perceive makes us sad or happy, and that we then unconsciously project this feeling into the thing as a quality of it? It is well known that if one fills a room with red light, people become agitated, but that with green lighting they become calm. But no one would attribute to the red light a quality of agitation and say that we project this into the light.

Genuine joy and sadness can never be evoked in us by such a purely causal effect, but only by events about which we are informed and by which we are meaningfully motivated. They are responses to the nature of the events, whether good or bad for us. When we look at another person, why should we suppose on the basis of his face that he is feeling joy or sorrow? When a person's face does not express any joy or sorrow, the sight of it can never motivate our own joy or sorrow, unless we are happy that this person is still alive or that we can see him again, etc. But it is not the visible datum of his face at this particular moment that leads us to project our joy into him, so that we could say, "How joyful he looks!" So-called empathy must obviously be something else.

We must acknowledge the fact that visible and audible data can give immediate expression to something immaterial, that a specific quality of immaterial acts, and indeed the genuine presence of these acts in a person, can manifest itself in his or her face, just as a shout can be filled with fear or pain.

The expression of psychological processes and permanent qualities

In this context we must draw a number of important distinctions. First of all, the expression of a psychological or mental process in a person can manifest itself in his face, his voice, or even his gestures. We say that he is very angry, or that she is very happy or that she is very sad, very depressed, or that he looks amorously at a woman. What is expressed is not only an immaterial quality, but a real, lived mental act of a human person, an affective response, or simply a psychological state—but always something that exists really and consciously, something that takes place in the person's soul. From this we distinguish the case of a face expressing permanent qualities of a personality, qualities which may be moral virtues or moral vices, or intellectual qualities such as genius or intelligence, or humor or optimism. These immaterial entities are not concrete psychological or mental processes, nor do they have the specific character of personally conscious being. They are qualities of a personality, and they certainly presuppose intellectual and volitional stances or temperamental aptitudes. Although they are also personal realities, they have a fundamentally different structure from concrete processes in the mind and the spirit. They are not consciously existing things in the strict sense, although they are grounded in what exists consciously.

This difference in the nature of what is expressed must not only be emphasized *as such,* nor only because we have here two kinds of link between the immaterial and the visible-audible, but also because it is important for the understanding of completely new forms of expression—or better, because the second kind of expression just discussed serves as a bridge to the understanding of other forms of the relationship of expression.

When processes that are taking place at the moment in the soul of a person are reflected in his face or voice, or when his face reveals general traits of his personality, what is expressed always presents itself as something that genuinely exists. A face expresses genuinely felt agitation or anger of this person, and likewise his real kindness, refinement, or purity.

It is the manifestation of a real psychological, mental process, or of a genuine characteristic of this person.

At the same time, we must emphasize that although it can undoubtedly happen that a person looks angry or joyful, and likewise that his face looks as if he were kind, pure, or gentle, it is perfectly possible, and is sometimes in fact the case, that he is not angry; and it happens even more frequently that, despite his kindly appearance, he is not in fact kind. His face undoubtedly *expresses* these characteristics, but it is far from absolutely certain that what is expressed exists in reality. The possibility of an illusion does not prevent these visible data from actually expressing something immaterial; it does not mean that this person cannot truly look angry, or that his face cannot reflect kindness and purity and make these qualities visible. But if we are to know whether he was genuinely angry or only pretended to be angry, we need further information. In the case of a kind, pure expression, we need many confirmations of a quite different kind in order to be sure that this person not only appears to be kind and pure, but is so in reality.

What is involved here is not the general possibility of illusion, which exists, for example, in a dream or a hallucination; nor is it the error we make in our judgment when we go beyond what is really given to us. What is involved here is the difference between appearing so and truly being so. The appearance is completely real, and it is perfectly true that a face expresses something specific; but what is expressed need not really exist. It can be an illusion, although this is mostly not the case.

A swindler or a boastful person tries to make exactly those faces that will make him appear different from what he really is. He pretends to be happy or sad, he assumes a countenance that expresses something that completely contradicts reality. This shows us that the link between one particular immaterial quality and the visible datum in the face of a person is different from the link between the real affective response or the qualities of a person and the visible datum. The quality is unambiguously given in the face; but the real process, or the real traits, need not manifest themselves. What manifests itself may be a mere illusion. This does not prevent the facial expression in question from pretending to display a mental reality or the character traits of a particular person.

This fact can be seen clearly in the following. When a play is performed, the expression on the actor's face plays a great role in the service of the illusion that is necessary for the theater, the illusion that transports us totally into the play. We see the expressions of Romeo and Juliet or of Hamlet, and we do not believe that the actor who plays Romeo or Hamlet is joyful or sad as a private person. The actor's face genuinely expresses sadness and joy, but these are meant to represent the sadness and joy of the character he is playing, who may perhaps never have existed and who at any rate is different from the person of the actor. This means that there is no possibility of illusion. A genuine process in the soul of a human being is here being expressed, but this person is from the outset posited as not really existing. This is an exceedingly interesting case: on the one hand, we must live completely in the illusion, while on the other hand, we distinguish this illusion from reality.

We shall speak in detail in the second volume of this book about this fact, which is so significant for the presentation of dramas. Here we are speaking only of the phenomenon of expression, that is, of the difference between the expression of a human being in real life and the expression found especially in the case of an actor. Although it is not his intention to express something real, the expression of the immaterial quality and of a mental and intellectual process remains intact.

Something analogous occurs when we see the portrait of an unknown man and speak of the expression of his face. We do not ask whether the man was genuinely kind or sad or happy, because the theme that concerns us is completely different. The expression—whether happy, sad, noble, profound, or kind—plays a great role in the beauty of the picture. But the question of the extent to which the man who is portrayed here had these feelings or character traits— if indeed he ever lived—is entirely secondary.

All these modifications of reality, in which a face expresses mental, personal processes in the soul or expresses permanent, immaterial character traits of a personality, are still found in the context of a basic form of expression. The face, certain bodily postures, and the voice reflect a personal reality. In all these cases, the visible and the audible discloses something that lies "behind" it, a reality in which the close link between body and soul in the human being is manifested. It is this concrete human being whose face or whose voice expresses something of his soul. It is true that the modifications just mentioned—the actor or the portrait of the unknown person—represent very significant differences with regard to the claim to display something that really exists; but they remain within the framework of a face or voice expressing a psychological or personal reality of this human being.

An analogous form of expression is also found in higher animals, for example, when a dog whines or looks at us sadly or joyfully. This is analogous because a process which belongs to another sphere of being is reflected in a visible or audible datum. Naturally, there is no intellectual reality in the case of animals, and even the term "psychological" is inexact, because we are not speaking of a person. But this process is something that is "felt," and thus something essentially different from the visible and the audible entities; it is not a material process. In the higher animals, therefore, we find only an analogous expression. Nevertheless, it belongs to the comprehensive family of expression, in which something real that belongs to another order of being makes its presence known, expresses itself, and shimmers through in the visible and the audible.

Qualities proper to the appearance itself, such as the majesty of a lion

The situation is completely different when we say of a lion that it is majestic and that its great strength is intuitively given. These characteristics adhere to the special animal that stands before us. In the majesty of the lion there does not exist the difference—typical of every genuine expression—between the internal and the external. Naturally, there are phenomena of expression in the case of the lion too. Its roaring can express anger, its face can express fury. But this is obviously completely different from the situation where we speak of the majesty of the lion. This majesty, like its strength, is not something experienced by the lion itself. It is not an inner reality of its own which breaks forth, as it were, in the lion's external appearance. These are, rather, qualities which are directly grounded in its external appearance, traits of the visible itself. The lion looks majestic. This majesty is a pure quality, not the breaking through of another reality. One could be tempted to say, "This is analogous to the case where we say that a face expresses the kindness and purity of a person. There too it is not a psychological or mental experience that manifests itself in the face, but a quality." But clearly this would be a complete misunderstanding, since this goodness and purity are permanent, immaterial traits of a personality which manifest themselves in his or her face. They are characteristics of a reality of a completely different kind that lies behind the face. In the majesty of the lion, on the other hand, we have a quality belonging directly to the external appearance, not a manifestation of its character.

That which we call "majestic" is doubtless not a quality that belongs to the bodily sphere, such as length, breadth, height, color, weight, etc., but an immaterial quality. But it does not adhere to the form of the lion in the manner of an expression, nor does this link permit some quality of an inner reality to emerge. This kind of link of the visible-audible with an immaterial quality in the broadest sense of the term—with a certain aesthetic quality, as we could also say—is something new in relation to expression.

Objective qualities that are given intuitively, for example, the joyfulness of the blue sky

We must now draw attention to another very significant link between visible and immaterial qualities. This is often "explained" in an extremely banal way. I am thinking here of the blue sky illuminated by the sun. We speak of a joyful sky, a sky which radiates joy. Let us now put the unprejudiced question: What do we mean when we speak of the joyfulness of the sky? What is intuitively, immediately given to us when we look at the blue sky? Naturally, we do not mean that the sky "feels" joy. We refer only to a pure quality that also characterizes the human reaction of joy over something, but that does not only occur as a consciously "felt" joy. There exists a quality of joyfulness that indeed occurs primarily in the personal act of joy as a real, concrete, conscious being. But there also exists an objective quality of joyfulness that does not exist as consciously lived but is a quality that occurs only in some objects as a characteristic of these objects.

The attempt has been made to interpret the joyful blue sky as an *analogia attributionis*: just as we call a food "healthy" and mean thereby not that "healthy" is a genuine characteristic of the food but that it is healthy for us, so too the joyfulness of the blue sky is a manner of expression constructed on an *analogia attributionis*. When we look more closely, however, we see how untenable this interpretation is. When someone describes the blue sky with the sun shining brightly as "healthy weather," this is indeed a manner of expression constructed on an *analogia attributionis*. As soon as someone asked us, "What do you really mean by 'healthy weather'? Do you believe that the weather too can be healthy and sick, like a plant, an animal, or a human being?", we would reply, "No, we mean that it is healthy for human beings, that it fosters our health." If, however, someone were to ask us, "What do you mean by a 'joyful sky'?", we would not say, "All we mean is that it makes us joyful or awakens our joy." For although it will often be the case that we rejoice in the beauty of the sky with a joy that is a meaningful intentional value-response, or else that this weather causes in us a non-intentional joyful mood, this need not always be the case. In a time of great sadness, for example, when someone whom we have deeply loved dies, we can find the joyfulness of the radiant sky oppressive. The contrast between the festive splendor of the blue sky and the profound pain in our soul can disturb us, and it would be easier for us if the day were rainy. Thus the experience of a contrast between the quality of the sky and our psychological state shows clearly that when we speak of this quality, we have more in mind than merely the impact it makes on us.

Nor is this contrast like the one we experience when a happy piece of news arrives precisely at the time when our soul is filled with a deep pain.

The sad event and the happy event are here juxtaposed, and the more significant of the two, the event that affects us more strongly, will tip the balance. If the sadness is caused by a great disaster, we will not be able to give the full, appropriate response to the joyful event, which is less weighty. If our heart is running over with joy because some great happiness has come to us, we will not be really affected by the unhappy event, which is less weighty. In both cases, however, we will suffer from the contrast between the two events, or indeed wish, when we are full to the brim with sadness, that the happy event had never occurred.

Something completely different is involved in the contrast between the joyfulness of the sky and our sadness. There is no juxtaposition of two events, one of which is a reason for joy and the other a reason for sadness; nor do two feelings coexist in us. Rather we have, on the one hand, an event that justifies my sadness, and on the other hand, the objective quality of joyfulness in a thing. Or in other words, we have the sadness in me and the joyfulness of the thing.

The attempt has also been made to introduce here the celebrated but absurd theory of projection. We have already demonstrated its untenability in chapter 1 above. Since it keeps on trying to assert itself, we need not be surprised that it is adduced as an explanation of the joyful sky. The temptation to have recourse to the projection theory is much stronger than in the case of beauty, for this theory is much more plausible than in the case of beauty; after all, the quality of joyfulness is present above all in the personal experience of joy, whereas beauty is never a "feeling." In beauty there is no counterpart to the personal act of joy. As we have seen, beauty is always an objective characteristic of something. A noble, generous deed is certainly the bearer of a beauty, but it appears, like moral value, on the "back" of the deed or attitude (as Scheler would say) and is not the consciously lived content of the experience.

Similarly, in the case of the joyful sky, this alleged projection of our joy into the sky is not merely a pure hypothesis, undemonstrated and arbitrary; it is an untenable theory, lacking all cogency. In order to apprehend the joyfulness of the radiant sky, we need not feel joy over something else or even over the beautiful blue sky itself, nor do we need to be in a joyful mood. Someone may be annoyed at the fine weather, because it deprives him of a welcome excuse for not going to a boring or unpleasant meeting; but this does not make him incapable of recognizing the joyful character of the blue sky.

It is also impossible in this case to take refuge in an explanation in terms of a naïve personification. We are told that primitive peoples saw a threatening cliff and assumed that an evil spirit lived in it, and that they personified in this manner everything that was merely material. Xerxes had the sea whipped because his fleet was destroyed by the Greeks. In the same way, the joyful sky would be merely a remnant of the mythological personification of an earlier age, when the sky was understood as a personal deity: people saw fine and brilliant weather and assumed that the sky was happy.

Without noticing what they are doing, those who put forward this whole line of argument presuppose and thus recognize the phenomenon they seek to explain away. Why did the primitive peoples make an evil spirit out of a threatening cliff but not out of a soft and pleasant hill? Because they apprehended the threatening character as a quality of the cliff and interpreted this as the attitude of a person. It was precisely this intuitively given quality that was the precondition for interpreting the cliff as an evil spirit rather than a friendly spirit. The qualities of the threatening and the pleasant are not interpretations or the products of a naïve mythology; rather, the objective, non-personal quality is interpreted as a personal spirit. The intuitively given qualities are the starting point, not the product of this mythologization and personification. This means that even when every mythological interpretation is eliminated, the phenomenon of the joyfulness of the blue sky unambiguously remains.

There are two significant characteristics of particular interest about the kind of link between the visible and the immaterial that we find in the blue sky. First of all, it involves immaterial qualities that also occur as the content of a feeling, of a consciously lived personal response—there really do exist qualities such as an objective joyfulness. Secondly, it does not involve an expression of the kind we discussed at the beginning of this chapter, nor a normal predication, but a relationship of grounding that is highly mysterious, since there is a gulf, ontically speaking, between the visible object and the immaterial quality.

In evading this problem one has often taken refuge in the term "symbol." This is perhaps the term that is most frequently applied, in a great variety of meanings, in this context of visible or audible data and immaterial qualities or realities. Sometimes a qualitative analogy has been called a symbol; sometimes this term has been applied to an immaterial quality that adheres in some way to a physical object, such as the joyfulness of the sky; and sometimes a genuine symbolic relationship is involved, or else the beauty of the mountains, the light, or a church building. We need not say anything more about this equivocal use of the expression "symbol," which is a kind of escapism, because in all these cases the specific problem is explained away. Since we have spoken in detail in the present chapter about what a real symbolic relationship is, the reader will easily see that the relationship between the radiant blue sky and joyfulness is not a symbolic relationship.

It is also clearly different from every merely qualitative analogy. It is obvious that the relationship between light and truth is utterly different from that between the blue sky and joyfulness. Truth does not present itself as a vividly given quality of light. When we see light, the phenomenon of truth as something adhering to light is not in any way given to us. Truth is certainly not grounded in light. All that exists is a qualitative analogy between them. This is surely a very obvious analogy, and it is not difficult to apprehend it; but there may be people who do not recognize this analogy unless their attention is explicitly drawn to it. Besides, everyone sees light in all kinds of situations without thinking of the analogy with truth. In the case of the radiant blue sky, on the other hand, joyfulness is given as a quality grounded in the sight of the sky; one need not make the ascent into a completely different sphere, and we do not find that element of making a comparison that is present in every qualitative analogy.

Before we turn to a completely new link between lofty immaterial beauty and visible and audible entities, that is, before we proceed to the answer to the central problem posed in chapter 6 above, we must investigate in the following chapter different levels of beauty, looking at all the kinds of beauty that appeal to the senses, up to the lofty, specifically immaterial beauty. In this way its qualitative character in the realm of the visible and the audible will come to light. This investigation, too, is indispensable if our central question is to be answered.

CHAPTER EIGHT

Levels of Beauty

A SIGNIFICANT presupposition of beauty, and especially of the levels of beauty, is the fact that while some elements can combine organically to form a new whole, others cannot do so. Accordingly, before we turn to the levels of beauty, we shall briefly discuss the basic kinds of possible combinations of different elements, that is, what we might call a hierarchical structure of composition. It far transcends the sphere of the aesthetic but plays a special role in the world of the beautiful.

Meaningless, chaotic, inappropriate, ugly, and unfruitful combinations

First of all, some things are incompatible and inherently contradictory. For this reason, they exclude *a priori* every possibility of unity. We are familiar with such incompatible things in the sphere of logic, for example, the combination of words which do not form a sentence and contravene the most basic rules of a meaningful sentence, such as: "Cow, thirty-three, querulous." These things do not exactly contradict one another, and they can occur in a meaningful sentence; but this way of combining them contravenes the basic laws of meaningful sentences, and this prevents them from building up any kind of unity. Their combination is meaningless. If we affirm that the number three is red, we have indeed formulated a real sentence, but the state-of-affairs to which it refers is impossible, indeed meaningless. It is not only false, it is absurd. Another kind of meaninglessness is found when we affirm a proposition that is inherently contradictory, such as: "A is equal to not-A."

We present these various types of meaninglessness, absurdity, and contradiction only as examples of a radical incompatibility between certain elements. Above all, we have in mind the incompatibility that is chaotic, a conglomeration of things, of elements that are utterly incapable of amounting to any kind of unity. In these cases, the absence of any unity is caused by mutually exclusive elements. In other cases, it is indeed possible to unite elements, but this does not lead to a meaningful new thing or to any kind of enrichment. On the contrary, the uniting compromises the individual elements from the aesthetic perspective, since they do not fit together. When colors mismatch, we say that they clash, for example, when someone puts on a red tie with a shade that does not in any way match the red of his sweater.

Our concern at present is to make a clear distinction between the impossibility of uniting things and the clashing of things. The result of a clash is not chaos or sheer absurdity, but something definitely ugly, indeed an ugliness of a special kind, such as singing off-key, something "false." We do not only say, "How ugly!" We also say, "How impossible, what a dissonance!"

Ugliness is much more than a simple clash. There are things that clash and form a complete negative counterpart to things that match. Ugliness means more than simply the absence of the aesthetic-positive element of matching: it is the opposite of this aesthetic-positive element and contradicts it. The elements fight against each other to such an extent that the outcome is a downright disharmony and an embarrassing ugliness. In a certain sense, this fatal clash constitutes a radical antithesis to a genuine *contrast* (in the positive sense of this word). The contrast is a fruitful antithesis which throws things into relief. It can form a genuine unity, and in fact it can be a source of particular beauty.

A further level of combination, different from that of clashing elements, is the unfruitful and unnecessary combination that we find, for example, in a mere sequence of notes that is not a melody. One cannot say that the uniting of these notes is ugly as a result of them clashing. But it does not form anything new; it does not "give birth" to any new structured form, nor give rise to a melody. It is not an ugly or false combination, but an unfruitful combination.

We find something analogous in nature when trees, meadows, or brooks are juxtaposed without giving rise to a new landscape, a new structured form, or a new and higher unity. Though each one of these individual elements can be a bearer of the beauty that appeals to the senses, they gain nothing through this combination, and the beauty of the individual is not enhanced in any way.

This combination is not in fact ugly, nor does it involve compromising the elements of the combination, but apart from its unfruitfulness, it is characterized by arbitrariness and randomness, and in a certain sense by meaninglessness. And usually it is rather boring.

The two types of necessary, fruitful combinations

After looking at this unfruitful combination, we must now look at the contrast provided by a decisively new level of combination, namely, the fruitful composition that comes into being when a sequence of notes gives birth to a melody, or a piece of nature presents a real landscape.

Here we have a first level of necessity, since a meaningful "form" comes into existence, in contrast with the meaningless, random, unfruitful unity. Nevertheless, this is a very low stage of necessity, as we are about to see. It is indeed a genuine composition, and the new unity is capable in a completely new way of bearing aesthetic values and disvalues. But the value possessed by the birth of a new form, of a composition, though it surpasses the mismatch, the poor match, and the unfruitful combination, does not guarantee any kind of positive aesthetic value. The melody may be trivial, weak, or boring; the landscape may not be trivial, but still desolate and boring. The coming into existence of a form, of a genuine unity, does not in itself guarantee any beauty; the inner necessity may be very weak. We can say of a melody or a landscape, "It need not have been thus—it could also have been otherwise. Nothing would be lost, if it did not exist." It may possess only a very low level of necessity. There are thus very different levels of necessity in the realm of composition, of the fruitful combination of elements that gives birth to a new whole.

With regard to these levels of composition it suffices to distinguish two levels of necessity. First, there is the primitive necessity that is linked to the birth of a new essential unity, of a structured form; every melody and every landscape possesses this necessity. Secondly, there is the lofty artistic necessity that has a number of dimensions. We shall speak of this especially in the second volume of the present book.

The formal beauty of "being something at all"

After this brief reference to the various kinds of combination, extending from the impossibility of combination up to the fruitful composition, and also to the two types of necessity, we now turn to the levels of beauty.

We have spoken in chapter 6 above of the profound qualitative difference between the beauty proper to the visible and the audible, on the one hand, and the immaterial beauty that appears in the visible and the audible, on the other. This difference is the point of departure for the central problem of aesthetics, namely, the *mirandum* that visible and audible things can be bearers of the highest spiritual beauty. In distinguishing the two kinds of beauty we have called the second one beauty "of the second power." In qualitative terms, it is comparable to metaphysical beauty insofar as this is the splendor and fragrance of the highest kinds of values.

When we speak of the levels of beauty, we can mean different things. First of all, the levels can refer to kinds of values that are so dissimilar that the term "beauty" possesses only an analogous character. In that case, the word "beauty" is being used in a sense different from ours. Secondly, one can start with types of objects that are potential bearers of beauty, and keep in mind the hierarchy of the beauty that some particular object is capable of. Finally, we can start with the purely qualitative levels of beauty that we have in mind when we call one piece of music more beautiful than another or one landscape more beautiful than another. In this case, we refer to a purely qualitative hierarchy.

The first difference is so radical that we can no longer speak of a difference of level. We have already spoken (in chapter 2 above) of the transcendental beauty that is a splendor of the value of a being *qua* being. We emphasized the extremely mysterious value of existence; it is the value which what truly exists possesses in contrast to all sham, all illusion, everything that does not exist.

Now we wish to point out the similarly transcendent value of "being something," the *ens nominale*, and the beauty of this unity in contrast to chaos. In my book *What is Philosophy?* (chapter 4, section 3, A-C), I have investigated the various primordial types of essence, starting from the very random unities and reaching to the necessary, intelligible essences. In the present context, the significant difference is the one between everything that has some kind of essence, and the absence of any unity, the pure chaos that cannot exist because it does not possess any kind of essence. Every genuine essence possesses a certain beauty because of its "being something," because of its unity, which is the splendor of the most general value, the value of being as such. Although this transcendental beauty increases, in keeping with the higher level of the essence, in the direction that we have just indicated, it is nevertheless a wholly formal beauty. When in this work I call some object beautiful, I have in mind something completely different.

The aesthetic disvalue of the chaotic

Chaos cannot in the true sense be the bearer of a complete ugliness, like the ugly in the realm of the visible and the audible. Nor can it be the bearer of a metaphysical ugliness such as sin, falsehood, or error, since chaos has no essence. Nevertheless, it is meaningful to speak of the ugliness of chaos, the absence of all unity, the lack of all "essence." The chaotic is not ugly; it is simply incapable of bearing any concrete positive aesthetic quality. As such, it generally has an aesthetically negative quality. A definite disvalue adheres to it—not a disvalue of the aesthetic kind, but a disvalue of hostility to all being. The chaotic is a destructive principle similar to the terrifying emptiness that evokes the *horror vacui* (the abhorrence of total emptiness). It is hostile to God. This transcendental disvalue of the chaotic possesses an ugliness all its own.

This ugliness of the chaotic and of total emptiness is in fact much more distinctly given than the beauty that adheres to being as such and that belongs to every being as the irradiation of the special value that "being something" possesses in contrast to nothing, that is, to "not being something." This is easy to understand. That which is something has the potential for infinite differentiations; it provides the necessary basis for beautiful and ugly, for aesthetic values and disvalues. The chaotic does not provide any such basis. In order to be beautiful, or even just pleasing, a being must have a particular structure. Everything that does not fit organically into this structure, everything that contains a contradiction of this principle, is ugly and displeasing, and drowns out the beauty of the wholly formal value of being something. We can speak of an irregularity only within something that possesses an essence. It is obviously meaningless to speak of an irregular chaos. All ugly things possess an essence. They are something, and thereby bear the formal value of "being something" as such; sometimes they also bear the formal transcendental value of existence along with the beauty of existence. But this formal value does not come to evidence as an aesthetic value. It is rather like the ontological value of the will, a value present even in an evil will, where it is completely overshadowed by the moral disvalue. I say "rather," because this is only an analogy: the moral disvalue is incomparably more significant and negative than the ugliness that is grounded in the breakdown of the organic formal principle.

That which is pleasing [das Wollgefällige] as the most peripheral type of beauty

The lowest level in the realm of the visible is a completely different beauty from the transcendental beauty of "being something." This is a beauty in another sense of the word, but it forms an analogy to the transcendental beauty of "being something," since it is a regularity [*Regelmässigkeit*] grounded in a visible unity. It is unnecessary to state that it stands *per se* on a much lower level than the transcendental beauty. We began by speaking of the beauty of "being something" and the repulsiveness of the chaotic, but this was intended not as beginning with the lowest level, but as beginning with the most general, most formal beauty, where beauty is found as a specifically aesthetic value only in an analogous sense.

Now, however, we begin with a beauty where this term still has an analogous character. The pleasing is not only the most formal type of the beauty of the visible and the audible, but also the lowest and most peripheral type of beauty altogether.

There is a completely peripheral kind of beauty and ugliness that is connected with regularity and harmony. A triangle or a circle has an aesthetic pleasingness that a completely irregular structure with an arbitrary form does not possess. Pleasingness—a more appropriate expression for this phenomenon than "beauty"—is determined by a particular order. The wholeness, the meaningful unity, the harmoniousness that the circle and the triangle possess and an arbitrary form lacks—all this is the bearer of aesthetic value. These types of form possess a kind of clarity, an element of meaningfulness and non-arbitrariness, that is the bearer of a very formal but genuine aesthetic value. They contain an element of repose, harmony, and meaningfulness, thereby forming a kind of antithesis to everything that tends in the direction of the chaotic.

Is there anything analogous in the realm of the audible? Are there analogous sounds that possess such an inherent unity and clarity? This is certainly the case with every pure musical tone as opposed to an impure tone, or with a pleasing sound such as that of the waves beating against the shore, as opposed to the shrill sound that is created by scraping a knife across a glass. This negative quality has even less of a full aesthetic character than the positive quality. The displeasing stands entirely in the foreground. The negative quality is much more related to the senses and has an unpleasant, distressing impact on the senses. It does not constitute the real counterpart to the clarity of a sound or to the expressive roaring of the sea, since the antithesis of the pure sound is the impure sound. The antithesis to the roaring of the sea or the babbling of the brook is an unformed banging.

We now move from this formal beauty, which constitutes only a formal analogy to real beauty, beauty in a qualitative [*material*][1] and much fuller sense. We begin with a second kind of gradation, which is oriented to the bearer.

Beauty of color, material, and sound

Within the realm of beauty in the full and true sense, the lowest level is constituted by the pure beauty of a color, a material, or a sound. A color can possess an intrinsic beauty which far transcends the pleasingness of that which is formed and clear (what distinguishes the circle from a completely irregular figure).

Usually we see colors as properties of things. The beauty of these things often works together with the colors. But perhaps we are enthusiastic, not about the beauty of the green of the trees in the spring, or the beauty of the green color of a meadow, or the beauty of the faded leaves in the fall, but about the red or green of a cloth. Naturally, the beauty of the material—wool, silk, satin, or damask—will add something, but now we are concentrating only on the color. One color can possess a great beauty, another can lack this. We do not dispute that all the colors—red, orange, yellow, blue, green, even white and black—have their own special beauty. But many nuances lie between a noble red and a gaudy red, or a noble green and a boring green, etc.

1. [The German word is *material,* but it would be misleading to translate it as "material," since this is the natural translation for the German *materiell. Material* expresses a contrast to *formal,* and so we render it as "qualitative." JFC]

We must pay attention to three factors here. First of all, considered on its own, a color already possesses a genuine beauty, not a mere pleasingness in a formal sense. A color already has a qualitatively filled and explicit beauty.

Secondly, this beauty of the color becomes much more significant as such when the beauty of the material to which it adheres, the cloth of the garment, the curtain, or the quilt, unites with it. The beauty of the color is incomparably more significant and belongs to another level of beauty when it is one of the elements at the service of the total beauty of an object, for example, the color of flowers, trees, the lawn, the sea, the sky, rocks, or the color of the eyes, skin, and lips of a human face. We will have to speak of this in the second volume of the present book, as well as of the completely new function of color in painting, a function that cannot be compared to any other function of color.

Thirdly, it is clear here that a visible datum is the bearer of this beauty. But does the beauty that a color can determine by itself already contain such a spiritual character that it could ever be compared, as to its quality, to the beauty of virtue or truth? Obviously not! We are still dealing here with a beauty that appeals to the senses, that is, a beauty in which there is not a total discrepancy between the bearer, on the one hand, and the beauty that is manifested by means of the bearer, on the other—and it is this discrepancy that touches the core of the problem we posed in chapter 6.

A level of beauty similar to that of colors is also the beauty of material as such, for example, of a stone, whether sandstone, travertine, or marble. There can be no doubt that these stones bear a definite beauty even in the visual appearance of their tangible qualities. It is indeed true that like colors, they attain a much greater beauty in combination with other elements, for example, their color, and especially in the totality of a landscape or in a building; but in themselves, like colors, they possess a genuine beauty that appeals to the senses. The same is true of materials such as bronze and other metals, and of fabrics such as linen, wool, and above all satin and silk. These all possess a definite aesthetic value simply on account of their material.

Likewise, sounds are bearers of beauty. The sounds of a violin, flute, oboe, cello, horn, trumpet, or trombone each possess a particular beauty. The nobility of the sound of a violin, the sweetness of a flute and even more of an oboe, the richness and power of the sound of horns, the brilliant festiveness of a trumpet and the heroic sound of a trombone already possess by themselves a definite beauty, comparable to that of colors. On the other hand, there are ugly, base sounds: the sound of a poor violin, of a strident or screaming voice, or of a man who squawks when singing. How beautiful and how ugly the sound of a human voice can be, and how beautiful the voice of the nightingale!

Unlike sounds, tones are not as such bearers of beauty and ugliness. It is meaningless to say that a C is more beautiful than a G. As long as one takes each tone all on its own, in isolation, it is aesthetically neutral, apart from the formal beauty (mentioned above) of the pure tone as opposed to the impure tone.

The beauty of the form as "invention" or as fulfillment of the form principle

We now turn to a higher level, the second level within beauty in the full sense of this word. The beauty of trees, flowers, animals, and above all the human body is higher than the beauty of colors, materials, and sounds that appeals to the senses. The beauty of their form as such is a higher level than that of colors, materials, and sounds. Initially we are thinking only of the beauty of plants and animals on the basis of their form; naturally, we must add to this the beauty of the colors and the material of plants and animals. We begin by concentrating on the beauty that appeals to the senses and that adheres to the form in the broadest sense of this term.

When we speak of levels of beauty, we must not forget that the levels of the fullness of "invention," of that which is interesting, are linked to these levels. Similarly, the question of which entity displays a greater invention plays a large role here. The aesthetic value of the invention is so significant that even the ugly animals such as the toad, the octopus, and the hippopotamus possess an aesthetic value despite their ugliness. From the aesthetic point of view, the world would be poorer if they did not exist. This aesthetic value of invention must be seen clearly, and without overlooking or underestimating the beauty that appeals to the senses and its meaning, as by deriving this beauty from a mere primitive regularity and harmony.

Naturally, we are not yet speaking of the artistic beauty that, for example, a mask can have in combination with many other things. We shall discuss this in detail in the second volume of the present work. We are thinking only of those animals that are as such ugly, unlike other animals that have a noble and beautiful form.

When we now turn to a higher level of the beauty that appeals to the senses—to the beauty of a flower, tree, dog, horse, etc.—we notice that the bearer of the beauty is a specific form, to which colors and material (for example, of the leaves or blossoms) are an additional element.

What interests us here in this new level of beauty is above all the role played by the form, not in the sense of a mere unity of form as in the formal primitive level of the beauty of the triangle or the circle, but in a much deeper sense where the form constitutes one particular invention in ever new variations, such as the form of a pine tree, a cypress, a chestnut tree, a weeping willow, a birch, or a poplar. Naturally, the form and color of the leaves and of the trunk also belong to the invention which each of these trees presents. All these trees are bearers of a high beauty that appeals to the senses and that far transcends the beauty of a color or sound.

Flowers occupy a particular place in the realm of these bearers of beauty. In flowers, the beauty of the form is completely interwoven with the beauty of colors and material; in many flowers, their perfume is an additional element. It is on this level that the collaboration between the expressed metaphysical beauty and the beauty that appeals to the senses begins. Ontologically, the flower is a precious entity. In addition to the beauty that "appears" in it, it possesses a beauty that speaks of it as an entity, namely, the metaphysical beauty of blooming. This has a special ontological position in the realm of the plants. How beautiful, how noble a rose, a lily, or a lily of the valley can be!

This shows us what level is already attained by the beauty that appeals to the senses, and how profound this beauty can be: for despite the expressed ontological value and its beauty, and despite the expressed metaphysical beauty, it is the beauty appealing to the senses that stands in the foreground, and it does not speak of the essence of this entity but rests in a mysterious manner on this essence—on its form, its color, and the material of its blossoms. We grasp this clearly when we recall how much more beautiful a lily is than a worm, although the worm occupies a much higher ontological position.

There is no doubt that one kind of tree is more beautiful than another. For example, a cypress is more beautiful than a spruce. Accordingly, there exists a hierarchy of the beauty of these entities. One kind of tree is more potent as an invention, and more beautiful as a form, than another kind. The same is true of flowers.

In addition to this hierarchy, there is the hierarchy that concerns the complete realization of the specific formal principle in one and the same exemplar and that leads us to call one cypress more beautiful than another, one rose more beautiful than another, or one horse more beautiful than another. What we mean is that within one type of tree, flower, or animal the inherent formal principle of this particular form unfolds without any kind of disturbance, and that ugliness results from some kind of interruption of this formal principle.

The visible essence of the form of a horse as such is a divine invention. This essence is the root of the special formal principle that must be realized, and it determines which proportions must be present. The more this special formal principle is realized in one individual horse, the more beautiful that animal is.

It is interesting that one and the same form appears inappropriate in one instance and perfectly fitting in another, depending on the structure intended by the specific nature of one particular form, which displays innumerable variations. The same nose that makes a cat's face especially beautiful would be a severe limitation on the beauty of a human face. Even within one species of animal, such as dogs, there are many inventions of the most varied kind, such as the German shepherd, the Finnish spitz, the poodle, the dachshund, etc. In the one type, short legs or a proportionately large head do not disturb; on the contrary, they are required. In another breed, this would disturb us and would entitle us to call such an animal ugly.

Strangely enough, the more a species can attain a greater beauty *qua* species, the more seldom do we find a perfect individual exemplar of this species. Horses are more seldom perfectly built, that is, flawlessly beautiful, than trees or flowers. And certainly, a human being in his own form is more seldom perfectly beautiful than a horse in its form.

The aesthetic quality of form is thus a higher kind of beauty than that of colors, materials, and sounds. This kind of beauty is grounded in the formal principle that governs the special form.

The beauty of the species; other qualities of animals

There also exists a beauty that appeals to the senses and that does not depend on the realization of the formal principle of a species: its bearer is the species itself. The species of the horse is as such beautiful, unlike the species of a tapeworm. We see this most clearly when we look at those animals whose species is a bearer of ugliness. In the ugliness of a toad, an octopus, or a hippopotamus, we see not the ugliness that is determined by the non-fulfillment of the formal principle inherent in this essence, but an ugliness that is determined by much more general laws of composition.

In those forms which are intrinsically beautiful, the question whether or not something contradicts its formal principle plays a much greater role than in those forms which are intrinsically ugly. Thus the difference between the individual toads or hippopotami is much smaller than the difference between the individual horses or German shepherds—to say nothing of the difference between individual human faces—and from the aesthetic point of view the question of the extent to which the inner principle of the former is fully realized is far less central than the question of the extent to which the inner principle of the latter is realized.

Even within those animal species which *qua* species possess a definite beauty of form, there are not only great differences, but also very different value qualities. The unique charm and poetry of the donkey, the tremendous invention which this animal presents, is a different positive aesthetic value from the aesthetic value of the noble and beautiful horse. Dachshunds do not have the beauty of the German shepherd, the mastiff, or the Newfoundland dog, but they have an aesthetic charm all of their own, just like little Pekinese dogs. The originality of the form, the special invention that lies in such animal forms, the richness of the invention—this is a specific kind of aesthetic value that is completely different from the beauty of the proportions that marks out certain species of animals. The existence of camels, giraffes, kangaroos, and frogs makes the world much richer even from the aesthetic point of view, although these species of animals do not attain the beauty of the horse, the lion, or the stag.

As we have seen, the beauty which is directly grounded in the form and color of the animal is much richer in content than the beauty which is based on other values. This beauty is not the *splendor* and fragrance of other values, but is grounded directly in particular forms and colors and is conditioned by their quality and specific character.

Many other elements combine with this beauty and are closely interwoven with it: for example, an analogy to expression (though assuredly very different from genuine expression) and a manifestation of the animal, of its way of life, and of certain qualities that go beyond the pure beauty of its form [*Gestaltschönheit*].

We have spoken of this expression in the preceding chapter. For example, the dove looks gentle, the spider looks evil, and the snake looks cunning and malevolent because of the way it moves; but it is more than doubtful whether we can affirm that these animals possess these qualities, even in a merely analogous sense. Nevertheless, their external appearance expresses these qualities. It is quite a different question, how far these qualities contribute to their beauty or ugliness. But certain characteristics of these animals—the behavior of dogs, their vitality, the way they jump for joy; the peaceful way of life of sheep and lambs, their unity with the nature that surrounds them; cows at pasture; the silence and elegance of cats' movements, the aristocratic trait that distinguishes them from many other animals; the flight of birds, their singing, the relationship between many birds (for example, swallows) and the various seasons of the year—are bearers of a poetic quality and contribute to the beauty that animals possess because of their form and color. Indeed, they unite with this beauty in an intimate manner. Thus, many animals are the bearers of a high poetic beauty because of the background of the nature which surrounds them, and they attain thereby a much higher kind of beauty.

The form and beauty of a melody

We find bearers of this higher beauty at a much earlier stage in the realm of the audible. In the form of the melody that can come into being through a particular sequence of notes, we have already a bearer of eminent aesthetic values, quite apart from the role played by harmony and by the development of the melody in a piece of music. A melody can be the bearer of a sublime immaterial beauty, but also of an aesthetic disvalue that possesses a wholly new dimension. Some melodies are trivial and base, and counteract the high value of beautiful melodies in a quite different way than typical ugliness counteracts beauty.

Handel's *Largo,* the "Liebestod" in *Tristan,* the Gregorian *Kyrie eleison* of Eastertide, or the Alleluia in the Easter Vigil Mass: these open up for us a sublime immaterial world, a profoundly significant immaterial beauty.

Here we encounter for the first time the type of beauty that in its spiritual dimension and depth can be compared only to the beauty of high virtues, or even of a saint. We encounter the true mystery, namely, that the visible and the audible are entrusted with a beauty that we otherwise find only in high metaphysical beauty. There is a total discrepancy between the ontological dignity of these bearers of beauty and the beauty which appears in them. First of all, this immaterial beauty far transcends in its quality all the kinds of beauty mentioned above, such as the beauty of colors, material, and sounds; indeed, it is a beauty of the second power. Secondly, the relationship between this beauty and its bearer is radically different from the bearer-relationship in the case of every beauty that is a reflection of other values, a *splendor veri*, *splendor boni* ("splendor of the truth, splendor of the good"). The beauty of a virtue is an irradiation of its moral value. The higher this is, the more beautiful the virtue. There is an intelligible connection, a profound organic connectedness between this beauty and the moral value of the virtue. The link between a melody, a structured form composed of individual notes, and the profound, immaterial beauty is not in the least an intelligible connection; rather, it is a mystery. The connectedness is much looser.

This brings us back to the central question that we posed in chapter 6 above, and that will finally be answered in the next chapter.

CHAPTER NINE

The Solution to the Riddle: The Mystery of the Immaterial Beauty of Visible and Audible Things

Demarcation of the immaterial beauty of visible and audible things from symbols and from bodily expressions

WE HAVE already seen that we find in the world of the visible and the audible not only expressed metaphysical beauty and the beauty that appeals to the senses, but also a specifically spiritual beauty such as the beauty of a glorious landscape (for example, the Alban Hills seen from the Palatine, or the Gulf of Naples) or of the adagio from Beethoven's "Harp Quartet." This beauty is not only incomparably superior to the beauty that appeals to the senses, it is not only a much higher and more sublime beauty of the second power; in addition to this it towers in its spiritual quality far above the world of visible objects and audible entities by means of which it makes its appearance. In qualitative terms, it is much more closely related to lofty metaphysical beauty.

Here we see the full meaning of the question how a physical object such as a rocky mountain can possess in a certain light a beauty that is comparable only to the metaphysical beauty of high virtues.

It is not difficult to understand the failure of every attempt to derive the manner in which this sublime immaterial beauty adheres, for example, to Michelangelo's *Dying Slave*, to the adagio in Beethoven's ninth symphony, or to the Florentine landscape as seen from Bellosguardo, from the kind of link that exists between the symbol and the symbolized and is also found in signs, word-meanings, analogies, and bodily expressions.

We have already said that there is no highly intelligible link here, like the link between a word and its meaning, since the immaterial beauty of a melody or of a landscape is a completely intuitive givenness. The beauty is no less immediately given than the melody or the landscape.

Similarly, we need not discuss how the link between the immaterial beauty of the visible or the audible and its bearer differs from the link between all signs or indicators and what they indicate. In the latter case, what is indicated is not intuitively given. Something intuitively given, such as a red traffic signal, refers to the command to stop; but this command itself is clearly not intuitively given. Since it does not in any way appear in the signal, we cannot call the signal its bearer in any sense.

For this reason, the attempt has usually been made to interpret as a symbolic relation this appearing of the immaterial beauty in something incommensurable with the beauty, namely, in something visible and audible. But it is obvious that this too is a completely false thesis, an interpretation that flagrantly contradicts reality.

First of all, the symbolic link is not intutive. Secondly, it presupposes a special act by means of which one thing acquires the character of being the symbol for another thing. As with all conventional signs, if we are to understand the symbol, we must be informed about this act whereby the symbol is established. The symbol can refer to what is symbolized only if we know that it is specifically designated as a symbol. The symbolic relation lacks the immediate intuitive link that exists between the melody or the landscape and the immaterial beauty—a link that does not presuppose any knowledge. Thirdly, the melody or landscape does not *represent* the beauty. Rather, it bears the beauty, and the beauty appears by means of it. Here there is no ambassadorial relationship. Fourthly, what is symbolized is not intuitively given. It does not stand before me as something present in its own reality, nor is it perceived in the broadest sense of this word. But this is precisely what happens in the case of this lofty spiritual beauty of the visible and the audible.

Nor can the relationship of the melody or the landscape to lofty immaterial beauty be derived from a qualitative analogy. For example, the relationship between light and truth is indeed intuitive, and it does not presuppose, in order to be known, any knowledge of some act that connected light and truth. But it is certainly not of such a kind that when we see the light, the essence of truth is also immediately given to us; on the other hand, when we hear the melody or perceive the landscape, the beauty is no less immediately given to us than the visible and the audible entity. Everyone who hears the melody or perceives the landscape will somehow apprehend this beauty, unless he or she totally lacks any organ for beauty.

The qualitative analogy is one particular phenomenon, a unique qualitative "similarity" between two completely different things; it is a typical relationship between two completely different realities. In order to apprehend it, we must know the two objects independently of one another; only then do we discover this remarkable relationship. This is in contrast to the beauty of a melody.

It is bodily expression that comes closest to the relationship between visible and audible entities, on the one hand, and the lofty spiritual beauty that appears in them, on the other. But it would be a great error to confuse the two things. One might be tempted to say, "The face of a human being takes on its full and deep beauty only thanks to its ability to express the spiritual qualities of this personality. The same applies to all those visible and audible entities that are bearers of lofty spiritual beauty. The beauty that is grounded in other values and is, as it were, their irradiation and fragrance, itself becomes visible thanks to the fact that this visible entity, the face, expresses the nobility of the soul, the brilliance, the depth of the person."

It is indeed true that the beauty of the human face, insofar as it is conditioned only by forms and colors, never achieves the rank of a lofty spiritual beauty apart from some expression. But it is impossible to reduce in principle the sublime spiritual beauty of visible and audible things to expression, or in other words, to assert that this lofty immaterial beauty is always metaphysical beauty, that is, is always a beauty that is an irradiation of other values (whether ontological or qualitative), such as the fragrance of moral values (kindness or purity) or of "intellectual" or vital values that manifest themselves in a human face.

In most of the instances where the lofty spiritual beauty of visible and audible entities takes hold of us deeply, there is no question of an expression in the strict sense. But not even the phenomenon of expression in the broader sense can offer an explanation of the miracle of this spiritual, sublime beauty appearing in visible and audible entities.

We have already mentioned (in chapters 5 and 7) various kinds of expression in the broader sense. One of them occurs when certain qualities of an object become visible in its external appearance. This kind of expression entirely lacks the dimension of the breakthrough of a personal quality in the appearance, since it involves not persons but apersonal entities. But that which finds expression in its visible appearance transcends its material and physiological elements. As we have mentioned, when one sees a mighty waterfall, one is impressed by its power; when one looks at cliffs and mountains, one is impressed by their solidity and immovability. These qualities of their essence—power, solidity, immovability—are not as such of a purely visible nature. Although they are not immaterial qualities, and still less personal qualities, they far transcend phenomena such as large and small, loud and quiet, red or green. Not all the things that contain some power express this quality in their appearance. This quality recurs in an analogous manner in the most various spheres of being. Here we have a type of special qualitative analogy. Certainly, this power, this immovability, is a bearer of beauty; in this case, of metaphysical beauty, for the bearer is the irradiation of the value of the power, of the immovability.

The beauty of a mountain is obviously not limited to this beauty. The aesthetic qualities of a particular mountain—its form, its color, the light that rests upon it, its surroundings—clearly transcend by far the visible expression of the essence of this being. They adhere directly to the visible aspect.

Apart from those things that express this immovability and strength, there are other great variations in beauty that are conditioned by the special form, color, or surrounding landscape. This shows us clearly that the lofty spiritual beauty that attaches to them is completely different from expressed metaphysical beauty. We can see clearly that the sublime beauty of Vesuvius in the Gulf of Naples cannot be derived from the metaphysical beauty of the strength, the solidity of the mountain.

There is yet another completely different type of expression in the broader sense, namely, the joyfulness of the radiant blue sky—a phenomenon that can be called an "expression" only in a wholly analogous sense. Here too there is something different from the immaterial sublime beauty of Handel's *Largo.* The pure quality of joyfulness, which does not in any way pretend to be an experienced personal joy, is a pure quality, nothing that is enacted by a person; it does not possess the form of being and the level of reality that belong to the personal attitude of joy. It too is the bearer of a special beauty, but this beauty of joyfulness is not the unique beauty of a blue sky that is completely lit up by the rays of the sun. The joyfulness is one of many factors that ground the sublime beauty of the sky. The important point in our present context is to see that the way in which joyfulness adheres to the blue sky is not identical to the way in which the beauty appears in the sky. Although the link between a visible content and a spiritual content (for example, the quality of joyfulness), when compared to the link between something visible or audible and its sublime spiritual beauty, is closer to this link than to all the previously mentioned kinds of link, the two links are not identical. Above all, it would be mistaken to take this kind of immaterial quality (for example, joyfulness, impending disaster, tragedy, etc.) as the basis for interpreting the lofty spiritual beauty of the visible and audible. It is a similar, analogous kind of link, but it does not contain the same mystery that the relationship between a lofty spiritual beauty and a visible or audible entity bears in itself.

The mystery of the sublime spiritual beauty of the visible and the audible, and its relationship to the beauty that appeals to the senses

We have seen above that the sublime spiritual beauty of the visible and the audible is clearly distinct from expressed metaphysical beauty. At the same time, it collaborates with the expressed metaphysical beauty in a significant manner. This beauty of the second power adheres to its bearer in a manner similar to the beauty that appeals to the senses: just as immediately and intuitively, but in a much less intelligible way. It is already remarkable, and indeed very hard to understand, that the appearing of the beauty that appeals to the senses depends on the quality of the colors, the specific character of the material, and the forms and proportions of an object; this becomes a great natural mystery in the case of sublime spiritual beauty. The discrepancy between the conditions within the visible and the audible for the appearing of sublime spiritual beauty, on the one hand, and the depth, importance, and immateriality of this beauty of the second power, on the other hand, is so great that we are truly confronted by a unique *mirandum*, a wonder.

Although we must draw a sharp distinction between this beauty of the second power and the beauty that appeals only to the senses in all its gradations, it must be explicitly underlined that the former presupposes the latter. Without the beauty that appeals to the senses, the other beauty could not appear in things visible and audible. The beauty that appeals to the senses is an essential presupposition, although it plays only an ancillary role in the appearance of the beauty of the second power.

The existence of the beauty that appeals to the senses was never denied. Expressed metaphysical beauty likewise remains mysterious, but it does not contain the mystery of the beauty of the second power within the realm of the visible and the audible.

Not only the independence of beauty from the ontological hierarchy which we have observed even in the beauty that appeals to the senses, but above all the gulf that separates the exceptional depth of the specifically spiritual quality of this beauty from its bearer, show us that it is mistaken to assert that no beauty appearing in visible and audible things could ever attain the height of metaphysical beauty. Plato and Plotinus inferred that it must be so because it was impossible for visible and audible bearers to possess a beauty similar to that which adheres to pure spiritual entities. How could a material thing such as a mountain, its color, and a particular play of light on it possess a beauty equal in rank to the beauty that adheres to a virtue or to the truth? This is impossible, they thought.

This argumentation would be correct if the relationship between the bearer and that which it bears were the same in the case of this beauty of the second power in the realm of the visible and the audible as in the case of metaphysical beauty. If this transfigured beauty of something visible or audible were a reflection of the essence of its bearer, as the metaphysical beauty of humility is a fragrance, a reflection, of the moral value, then it would be impossible for a mountain in one particular light, or an entity built up of notes, harmonies, and sounds like the adagio of the "Harp Quartet," to be just as sublime and spiritual as the beauty of humility. But in this beauty of the second power, which appears in visible and audible things, the relationship between the bearer and that which it bears is radically different from the relationship involved in the beauty of humility.

The visible object or the composition of many visible objects, or the audible musical entity such as a movement in a quartet or the quartet as a whole, has a completely different function in relation to its beauty than moral virtues have in relation to their metaphysical beauty. The visible or audible bearer is only a pedestal on which this beauty mysteriously appears. It does not draw up its bearer to the level that the beauty itself possesses. This beauty speaks not of the essence of its bearer, but of something incomparably higher.

The human person is raised up by the moral value of his behavior. He shares fully in this moral value, through which he acquires a new preciousness. This is why he is clothed in the beauty which is the fragrance, the *splendor* of this moral value. It adorns him—it is his beauty.

But this does not happen with the beauty of the second power that belongs to the mountain. The mountain, as a real entity, is not clothed with this preciousness. When we discover the beauty of someone's soul, this beauty speaks of his essence and proclaims it; and we yearn for fellowship with him, with this real person. Doubtless, we are happy to spend time at the mountain; when we are far away, we yearn to see it again. But this beauty does not proclaim the mountain as a real entity; it does not make known this particular mass of stone. It proclaims much higher realities. It kindles in us a yearning for the world of lofty immaterial realities. Basically, this is a longing for that which is "above us," *quae sursum sunt* ("the things above," Colossians 3:1); it draws us upward.

With regard to music, Cardinal Newman made this point in these marvelous words:

> There are seven notes in the scale; make them fourteen; yet what a slender outfit for so vast an enterprise! What science brings so much out of so little? Out of what poor elements does some great master in it create his new world! Shall we say that all this exuberant inventiveness is a mere ingenuity or trick of art, like some game or fashion of the day, without reality, without meaning? We may do so; and then, perhaps, we shall account the science of theology to be a matter of words; yet, as there is a divinity in the theology of the Church, which those who feel cannot communicate, so is there also in the wonderful creation of sublimity and beauty of which I am speaking. To many men the very names which the science employs are utterly incomprehensible. To speak of an idea or a subject seems to be fanciful or trifling, to speak of the views which it opens upon us to be childish extravagance; yet is it possible that that inexhaustible evolution and disposition of notes, so rich yet so simple, so intricate yet so regulated, so various yet so majestic, should be a mere sound, which is gone and perishes? Can it be that those mysterious stirrings of heart, and keen emotions, and strange yearnings after we know not what, and awful impressions from we know not whence, should be wrought in us by what is unsubstantial, and comes and goes, and begins and ends in itself? It is not so; it cannot be. No; they have escaped from some higher sphere; they are the outpourings of eternal harmony in the medium of created sound; they are echoes from our Home; they are the voice of Angels, or the Magnificat of Saints, or the living laws of Divine Governance, or the Divine Attributes; something are they besides themselves, which we cannot compass, which we cannot utter,—though mortal man, and he perhaps not otherwise distinguished above his fellows, has the gift of eliciting them.[1]

1. Blessed John Henry Newman, *Fifteen Sermons Preached before the University of Oxford* (Westminster, Md.: Christian Classics Inc., 1966), sermon 15, pp. 346–47.

Comparison with the sacraments—the discrepancy between the bearer and that which it bears

Here we encounter a *mirandum*, namely, the mystery that the visible and the audible are entrusted with the possibility of permitting a beauty to appear, of making present a beauty that far transcends the ontological rank of these entities and all their qualitative values. The best way to characterize this *mirandum*, this natural mystery, may be to compare it to the tremendous supernatural mystery that for Catholics is contained in the sacraments. The distance and difference between the two is indeed very great, but both have an analogous discrepancy between the bearer and that which it bears. It is an extraordinary thing that a new supernatural life is implanted in the one who is baptized through the pouring of water over his head and the words which accompany this act. It is incomprehensible that this great and sacred event should be so linked to these modest things that, according to the doctrine of the Church, they are made, as it were, preconditions for the infusion of the life of grace. Since a certain analogy in relation to the discrepancy between the bearer and that which it bears, or in relation to the modest role of the bearer, is to be found in the beauty of the second power of visible and audible things, we can call this a quasi-sacramental beauty. It goes without saying that this discrepancy is incomparably greater in the sacraments, where it spans the difference between the natural and the supernatural. In the beauty of the second power, the discrepancy only spans the difference between material and immaterial within the natural.

Our only reason for drawing attention to this comparison is in order to show the humble ancillary role of the visible and the audible in the appearing of beauty, and the mysterious link binding something much higher to certain seemingly inessential conditions. If one were to use rosewater or wine for baptism, it would not be valid. If one changes something in a melody—a few notes,[2] the tempo—the beautiful, exalted melody can become much less beautiful and important. Indeed, under

2. Cf. Schopenhauer: "How astonishing that the change of half a tone, the entrance of a minor third instead of a major, at once and inevitably forces upon us an anxious painful feeling. . ." Arthur Schopenhauer, *The World as Will and Idea* (London: Kegan Paul, 1909), I, paragraph 52, p. 340.

certain circumstances all its beauty is destroyed and it lapses into triviality and tastelessness.

This discrepancy between "cause" and "effect" is incomprehensible—but it is in fact not a genuine cause. These factors do not generate the beauty. They are only conditions that permit it to appear, conditions to which beauty's possibility of appearing is bound.

When we reflect on all this, we understand why it is not impossible for a beauty to adhere to visible and audible things that is qualitatively no less sublime than the metaphysical beauty of high virtues; but the adhering to the bearer and the relationship to the bearer are very different in the two cases.

In qualitative terms, this beauty of the second power is more closely related to the high metaphysical beauty than to the beauty that only appeals to the senses. The beauty that appeals to the senses has a completely different relationship to its bearer than metaphysical beauty, which is the splendor and fragrance of other values. The beauty that appeals to the senses is likewise independent of the ontological rank of its bearer, and adheres only to the external appearance of the bearer. But unlike the specifically immaterial beauty of the second power, it does not rise up above the whole natural, physical sphere.

We see thus that the relationship of grounding vis-à-vis its bearer is the fundamental difference between metaphysical beauty and the beauty of the second power in the realm of the visible and the audible. The metaphysical beauty of purity, which is its fragrance and reflection, is a full characteristic belonging to the pure person and speaks of this characteristic. But the sublime spiritual beauty in the realm of the visible and the audible does not speak of its bearer: it appears by means of the bearer, which is only its pedestal, so to speak. It speaks of something completely different, something higher.

This beauty reveals the world above us

What is this "higher" thing of which it speaks? Our answer must point both to what it makes known and to the way in which it proclaims or speaks, which is clearly distinct from the grounding of metaphysical beauty in those values of which it is the reflection. The beauty of the second power speaks of the world of higher goods and their values. It is a word of the whole world of values which surrounds us, rising up to the infinite beauty of God. This beauty appears in a certain sense in visible and audible things, of which however it does not speak. It is different from metaphysical beauty, the reflection of other values, which is qualitatively different, depending on the value in question. We have already seen that the link between metaphysical beauty and the value on which it is based is very intimate. It does not speak of the value: it is its reflection, its fragrance, and in order to apprehend this beauty, I must first apprehend the value of which it is the reflection. The same is true of expressed metaphysical beauty.

In the case of the beauty of the second power, on the other hand, the relationship to the world of goods and values is completely different. First of all, this beauty is not a fragrance or reflection of these values: it only "speaks" of them. Secondly, this is a "speaking" of this world in general and an indeterminate, hazy reflecting. Thirdly, we need never think of the world of values and goods in order to apprehend the beauty. On the contrary, simply by virtue of its own specific quality alone, this beauty raises us up into the world of values, of spirit, of truth.

There is a hierarchy in the beauty of the second power. The higher and more sublime this beauty is, the more it draws us through its quality alone into ever sublimer heights, until we enter before the face of God, *in conspectu Dei* ("before the face of God").[3]

The beauty of the second power that is found in the visible and the audible speaks of the world of God, the world above us. Newman

3. It would be impossible to present in detail this world of higher values, of which the beauty of the second power of visible and audible things speaks. The situation is different in music as soon as there is a link to the word, for then it is possible for the beauty of the second power to unite in a unique manner with the "expression." In *Fidelio*, the sublime joy of seeing one another again after all the suffering finds a moving expression in the words: "*O namenlose Freude!*" ("O nameless joy!"). Certainly, the beauty of the music as such is determined by factors other than those which "express" the joy, but the music is wholly at the service of the expressed metaphysical beauty of the joy. The direct beauty of the piece of music and of the metaphysical beauty of the noble, sublime joy that is expressed in the piece of music converges here in an incomparable manner.

expressed this wonderfully in his words about music, quoted above. Above all, however, it speaks of the world of natural values, of the fullness and the richness of life, of happiness, of *joie de vivre*, ascending to the profound happiness of love and to existence as a person. It "speaks of" this; it "does not express it." The beauty of the second power speaks of all this only in a purely qualitative manner and in very general terms.

CHAPTER TEN

The Spiritual Plentitude of the Beauty of the Second Power

IN ORDER to investigate further the unique quality of the spiritual beauty of the second power, we shall indicate a number of important value qualities which are inherent in a unique way in this beauty.

The value qualities inherent in the spiritual beauty as antitheses to specific disvalues

Let me explicitly underline at the outset that this inhering must be clearly distinguished from the irradiation which we have observed in the relationship between metaphysical beauty and the values on which it is based. The inhering means that the beauty of the second power contains certain value qualities which are characteristic of it. It is thus a completely new kind of link, which must first of all be distinguished from the irradiation that occurs in metaphysical beauty. In the inhering, these value qualities are contained in the beauty, without themselves forming the theme of the beauty. In a certain sense, the beauty possesses these value qualities *per eminentiam.* Nor is the inhering the relationship which this beauty has to the world of values and which it proclaims in a very general manner through its quality. The value qualities to which we wish to draw attention here are not those into which we enquired in the last chapter: Of what does the spiritual beauty of the second power speak?

No, it is rather elements of this beauty itself that characterize it and are present in it. We point to it in order to bring out more clearly the quality of this beauty and to reveal its dignity, spiritual character, and depth.

When we investigate the beauty of the second power, however, it is necessary to point also to the disvalues to which it forms a specific antithesis. To put it briefly, if we are to do justice to this beauty philosophically, we must take a detour which may initially seem strange.

It is significant that the beauty of the second power, this lofty beauty which the visible and the audible can possess, forms an antithesis to various disvalues of a general kind. Also significant is the way this antithesis is inherent in the beauty of the second power, the way it possesses these values purely in their quality and without the bearers of these general values being present. We shall begin by listing the various disvaluable qualities which are opposed to this beauty, which for its part contains their positive antitheses.

Let me emphasize at the same time that these negative qualities are opposed not only by beauty but also by quite different values. The primary antithesis of these disvalues, their primary positive counterpart, is not this beauty but rather values which can also be found in objects in which the beauty is not thematic.

We have in mind disvalues such as the prosaic (in the sense of something with a negative value, of a dull sobriety), or the philistine, the bourgeois; the sentimental, the fake; the shallow, the mediocre, the flat. It is easy to grasp that, with the possible exception of the prosaic, these are not primarily aesthetic disvalues. In order to establish their specific character and especially their true primary antithesis, that is, the relevant value in each instance, we shall have to take as our starting point nonaesthetic objects or things in which truth is the theme, such as worldviews, philosophical works, and currents of thought. When we have investigated these values, which are to be found in a purely qualitative manner in the beauty of the second power (but not in such a way that their real bearers are present), we shall return to the second problem, that is, the way these values are incorporated in beauty, to the mysterious indwelling of these values in it.

The prosaic as an antithesis to beauty of the second power

We begin with the prosaic, a disvalue which is of a more aesthetic nature. All beauty is an antithesis to the quality of the prosaic, or, as one might also put it: all beauty sings!

When we say "prosaic," we do not invariably mean something with a negative value. There are two basic kinds of the prosaic: that which is neutral and indifferent from the perspective of qualitative values, and the prosaic in the sense of an aesthetic disvalue.

The prosaic in the first sense includes many practical things and activities which have a value of usefulness. They are indispensable, but from the aesthetic perspective they are completely indifferent, possessing neither an aesthetic value nor an aesthetic disvalue. Examples are getting dressed, washing one's hands, shaving, washing the dishes, or winding up a clock. When we say that beauty forms an antithesis to everything that is completely indifferent in aesthetic terms, we are stating a truism.

"Prosaic" has, however, another meaning; it refers to an aesthetic disvalue. We encounter this negative quality of the prosaic above all in the sphere of our practical life. It is the atmosphere that a factory or an office can have, the atmosphere radiated by typical philistines.

This dull, gray, depressing atmosphere is the uttermost antithesis of all that is brilliant and festive, of all that is abundant. In this context, the word "festive" might perhaps lead the reader to think that we have the "everyday" in mind when we use the term "prosaic." It is true that the expression "everyday" is sometimes used in the sense of "prosaic," but it would be a serious error to believe that a thing is somehow identical to the prosaic for the simple reason that it occurs every day and we encounter it every day. Sunrise and sunset are daily events, sometimes extraordinarily beautiful and sometimes less beautiful—but always the opposite of prosaic, and hence not "everyday" in the sense of "prosaic."

Similarly, one must not confuse the prosaic with the habitual. It is no doubt a tragic weakness of the human being that he is dulled by habit: his appreciation even of goods with high values will be blunted if he comes effortlessly into contact with them every day. But the only danger here is that *we* may become blind to the value of a thing: an unprosaic thing never becomes thereby prosaic. We may no longer fully apprehend its splendor, but we will never find it prosaic. The quality of the habitual, of that which one takes as a matter of course, is completely different from the prosaic in the sense of an aesthetic disvalue. There is nothing prosaic in nature. Even the least important object—a grain of sand, a drop of water—is not prosaic in this sense; the ontological dignity of all that exists excludes this *a priori.* The prosaic is a quality which can inhere in human abilities and activities when these do not take their place in our life as humble means which are at our service, but in their plain emptiness claim a thematic quality which does not belong to them.

Let us compare an oriental bazaar, a souk, with a modern department store. We are not thinking here of the aesthetic difference in the quality of the wares, the difference between genuine oriental carpets and modern imitations, etc. We are thinking of the organic atmosphere of the souk, filled with human life, of the way the wares are distributed and sold, in contrast to the mechanized, dehumanized, sober, dull atmosphere of a modern department store. The latter atmosphere is typically prosaic. Or let us compare the workshop of a craftsman, for example, a cobbler, with a factory. In the workshop, we often still find an organic life permeated by the human personal element; in the factory, we find the dullness of things that are purely mechanical, of the machine. Theodor Haecker has rightly drawn attention to the radical difference between a machine and a tool.[1] In the case of the tool, the human being is still the *causa principalis* (the principal cause), and the tool only the *causa instrumentalis* (the instrumental cause); but the machine is almost the *causa principalis,* and the

1. Theodor Haecker, *Was ist der Mensch?* (Munich: Kösel Verlag, 1948), 36ff.

human being who operates the machine is merely a *causa remota* (remote cause).

One could mention many such examples, but the quality of the prosaic emerges most clearly in certain human beings. The bureaucrat is specifically prosaic. The prosaic is a mechanization of the spirit, a mere soulless adhering to the shell of something. The philistine is even more prosaic than the bureaucrat. This person pays homage to a pseudo-realism for which things are real only in the sense of a naked, austere usefulness. He regards everything else as a "romantic" playing around, an illusion, a waste of time. People who see everything in a gray, austere light and believe that this austerity is the only valid and serious reality—the only reality in and with which they feel at ease, indeed the reality that they love—emanate a prosaic, oppressive, dull atmosphere.

The prosaic exists analogously in the world of the university. There is a specifically professorial dullness, a distressing pedantry which constitutes a special antithesis to the brilliance of a researcher or thinker, and to true personal culture. Goethe portrayed this marvelously in the figure of Famulus Wagner and expressed it in the words: "That visions in abundance such as this / must be disturbed by that dry prowler thus!"[2] Famulus Wagner is typically prosaic.

The prosaic stands out in contrast with the poetical as well as with the nobility and splendor of genuine intellectual culture, when it penetrates and disturbs the world of beauty and the world of those things which shine in their value. Then it happens that even those merely neutral and lackluster things which are prosaic in the first and general sense can become prosaic in the narrower sense of an aesthetic disvalue.

The difference between prosaic and unprosaic emerges most clearly when we reflect on how love, especially being in love, takes the prose out of everything that is lackluster, everyday, and practical. Purely practical activities such as cleaning a room and washing the dishes cease to be prosaic as long as we are doing them together with the beloved person. Love is so much the antithesis of all prose that washing the dishes with one's

2. *Faust*, part I, verses 520f. English translation by George Madison Priest.

beloved is no longer prosaic, because the atmosphere proper to these activities is completely covered over by the splendor of love, by the festive happiness bestowed by being together with the person one loves. The prose of these activities has been silenced by the song of love.

Here, however, it is only a question of the prosaic in the sense of the lackluster, the neutral, not of the prosaic which is an aesthetic disvalue. The light which derives from being together with the person one loves can draw objects which are merely neutral into the splendor of this situation, so that washing the dishes is no longer lackluster. But the prosaic as a definite disvalue, the dullness and the hurtful presumptuousness of the prosaic in the second and more genuine sense, is silenced only by the splendor of being in love. In that situation, one does indeed see the contrast to one's situation—one sees the dull, oppressive world of a prosaic person who is present, or the prosaic character of a department store—but the splendor of being together with the beloved and the poetry which his essence radiates are so powerful that the prosaic in the sense of a negative value is drowned out.

Some of the false antitheses to the prosaic are very instructive, helping us to see the sense in which beauty in its lovely sound, its character of gift, and its superabundance constitutes a specific contrast to all that is prosaic.

Pseudo-antitheses to the prosaic: the sensational and the exciting

There are people who flee from the boredom and dullness of the prosaic into the sensational. The excitement of a detective novel doubtless forms a kind of antithesis to the daily, the humdrum, and to boring work, but it is not in reality an antithesis to the prosaic. Pure excitement, the kindling of our expectations, the appeal to our delight in the sensational—whether a football game or a horse race, the cruel sensationalism of a Roman circus or of a boxing match, or whether a detective novel or film—are only a formal antithesis to the prosaic, not a qualitative antithesis. It is the antithesis of the sensational to all that is monotonously, uniformly, plainly prosaic; qualitatively speaking, however, it is much more the antithesis to the boring than to the prosaic. For all these things are as such themselves prosaic; they can never raise us up above the prosaic but are only palliative means to alleviate our boredom. And after the excitement, one relapses all the more into boredom. Being lifted out of boredom in this way never bestows the power to do without boredom the prosaic-everyday things which one must inevitably do. This is because one is not really raised up above the prosaic, but remains on the same level. The antithesis is of a purely formal nature.

We mention these effects on the person only in order to show that the sensational, this quality of the exciting and thrilling, is not a genuine antithesis to the prosaic.

We must however emphasize that not every excitement [*Spannung*] is sensational. On the contrary, there exists a noble and highly important excitement which plays a great role both in life and in art. It is a primordial element which possesses a great value and finds a specific expression in the dramatic dimension of life as well as of art, especially in literature. This excitement is never mere excitement. It is always grounded in the value of lofty goods and events. The dramatic construction in a work of art for example, the excitement found in the scene at the beginning of Dostoyevsky's *The Idiot*, when Natasha Filippovna is invited, or in the scene at the beginning of his *The Brothers Karamazov*, when the Karamazov father and Staretz Zosima meet—is grounded in a high aesthetic value. We will discuss all this in detail in the second volume of the present work.

The nervous excitement due to purely psychological factors which we find in a number of Dostoyevsky's characters is a negative quality in terms of the person and his or her health. But sensational excitement is not a mere excitement like the state of being excited for no reason (although such excitement is naturally not without some cause).

The sensational is a particular quality which is grounded both in the kind of object and in its effect on the human person. The thirst for the sensational is akin to curiosity. The sensational is *per se* disvaluable, but the disvalue naturally varies in accordance with the kind of object and its effect. If the sensational is nourished by looking at cruel, brutal things, this is of course much worse than the sensational in a detective novel. In the present context, the only important point is to see that the sensational, even in its harmless form, does not constitute an antithesis to the prosaic. Even the sensational can be prosaic; and this is in fact usually the case. Similarly, there is no specific antithesis to the prosaic in all those things which are harmlessly entertaining; they are certainly legitimate, and bring relaxation precisely by means of excitement. That which is entertaining need not be prosaic; but it is never the antithesis of the prosaic.

The festive

Another antithesis which must not be confused with the prosaic and its true antithesis is the antithesis between "everyday" and "festive." "Festive" is a definite value, a quality which can already appear in a relatively peripheral form and which reaches up into very great heights. It contains various elements: first of all *vacare*, being free from work, being raised above the necessity to work by the sweat of one's brow, being liberated from the compulsion to do only what is useful, being free for *frui* [enjoying something for its own sake]. Another element is that of splendor, of a bright light instead of a dull and somber illumination. This element has a specifically aesthetic character. Feasts are to be celebrated.

The first element, *vacare*, comes into its own in a sublime form in the Sabbath and on Sunday. It is an anticipation, a reflection of the *vacare* in eternity, of which Saint Augustine speaks in the noble closing words of *The City of God*:[3] *Ibi vacabimus, et videbimus* . . . ("There we shall be at rest, and shall see . . ."). Sunday is a holy *vacare*, a day which belongs to God in a special way and is dedicated to the praise of God. Connected with this element of the festive there is a second element of the luminous, a specifically aesthetic quality: the day of the Lord is to be celebrated in a festive manner.

A third element of the festive is the exceptional, such as the remem-

3. Saint Augustine, *The City of God*, book 22, section 30.

brance of an important event, whether the day of the event itself or the memory of the event. Usually this is the meaning and the motivation of the celebration of feasts, from the birthday of a member of the family, and the intimate feasts of a wedding and a silver anniversary, from the public feasts of a country, the days commemorating important events or the birth of a particularly important personality for a country, all the way up to the glorious sacred feasts which refer to the *magnalia Dei* (the "mighty deeds of God"), the *causae exemplares*, the archetypes of true feasts.

But there are also feasts which lack such a meaning, feasts without the element of commemorating some great event: feasts for the sake of the festive joy. They are indeed a much more peripheral type, but they have a particular interest from the aesthetic point of view, because the aesthetic element emerges completely naked in them. These feasts are an expression of *joie de vivre*. They are celebrated only for the sake of this *joie de vivre*, for the sake of enjoyment. This category includes the feasts of earlier times at the courts of kings, the carnival festivities in many cities such as Rome, Munich, Cologne, etc., in which everyone wears fancy dress and moves from the prose of everyday life into a bright world full of colors and sounds, a world in which people dance and all sorts of games and surprises are organized.

This form of the festive differs from the sobriety of everyday life in a peripheral but very definite manner. It forms an antithesis to the prosaic, but not the specific antithesis which raises us above the prosaic. This kind of anti-prosaic allows us to forget the prose of everyday life for a short period. It has above all the character of the exceptional, the extraordinary.

But beauty has always *a fortiori* the character of the festive. Even a modest beauty, not only the beauty of the second power, is festive: in this respect, too, it constitutes an antithesis to the prosaic.

The fantastic

Another false antithesis to the prosaic is the fantastic, an unreal world in which the classic structure of the cosmos is abolished, a world of the unreal in which everything is different, the world of the fairy tale, of the jack-o-lantern, of the brownies and dwarves. The fantastic is a quite different quality from the sensational; both share in the exciting and the extraordinary, but the two go in completely different directions.

Despite the etymological relationship of the word *phantastisch* ("fantastic") to *Phantasie* ("imagination"), the fantastic is certainly not a mere creature of the imagination. In other words, not everything brought forth by the imagination has the specific quality of the fantastic. The latter possesses the attractiveness of the unreal, the confusing, the impossible, of a world in which all the laws of nature are suspended. It forms the radical antithesis to the genuine miracle, in which God's omnipotence for one moment suspends purely natural laws (which are His own creation). In the genuine miracle, we are suddenly permitted to look into heaven; this has the profound meaning of a revelation, and at the same time in many cases it expresses God's infinite mercy. We affirm that the fantastic is the radical antithesis to the authentic miracle. In the latter, all the laws of nature are certainly not turned meaninglessly upside-down, nor are we transposed into an unreal, confused world. Rather, all the contours of nature are clearly preserved in their rationality; but above them shines the immediate intervention of God, the Creator of heaven and of earth, as a bright shining light in which all that is earthly and natural retains its full clarity. The proportions of the cosmos do not become a confusing chaos. Rather, when the absolute, the supernatural shines out, everything moves into its true position.

Clearly, it is not our task here to speak of the reality of miracles as such—neither to point out that the possibility of a miracle follows logically from the assumption of the existence of a personal, omnipotent, and entirely good God, nor to discuss whether miracles have or have not taken place in reality. It suffices to show that the phenomenon of the miracle and its glorious quality are not only radically different from the fantastic, but are its complete opposite. In the miracle the higher reality discloses itself to our eyes. The absolute reality of the miracle, which certainly does not transpose us from the world of the real into a world of phantasy, belongs to its essence.

We have just said that not all the creations of the imagination are fantastic. All that is fantastic is indeed a product of the imagination, but not every entity born of the imagination is fantastic. It is not necessary to draw a distinction here between the fantastic and the power of the imagination in the sense of an artist's invention, nor between the fantastic and the imagination which is required in the case of many discoveries in the natural sciences; but we must point out that even in mythology, the product of the imagination need not possess the quality of the fantastic. The world of Homer is not fantastic. The personification of primordial phenomena in nature, the portrait drawn of gods and goddesses such as Apollo, Aphrodite, Pallas Athene, Poseidon, and Ares is free of the illusory character of the fantastic. No doubt, an abyss separates the action of these deities from the miracle mentioned above; but their activity is free of the confusing twilight and the world of sorcery, and of the weirdness which adheres to the fantastic. Unlike many other mythologies, Greek mythology possesses a classic brightness in which the poetic element predominates.

When we call the fantastic a false antithesis to the prosaic, we do not intend in any way to assert that it possesses a negative value, as is largely the case with the sensational. We say only that it is not the true and correct antithesis of the prosaic, and the flight into the fantastic is not the way to overcome the prosaic. Above all, the fantastic is not the element which makes beauty anti-prosaic, nor the reason why beauty "sings." Nevertheless, it has its legitimate place in the life of human beings, and especially of children. The fantastic in a fairy tale has a definite value. The world would be poorer without fairy tales, especially those of the Brothers Grimm. But their value is not primarily the fantastic but rather the great poetry which is linked to the fantastic in these fairy tales. They give expression to profoundly human truths and transpose us into a beautiful "fairytale land" through a charming free play of the imagination.

And yet the fantastic, in the much more pronounced, more dangerous, and even more specific sense than it has in Romanticism, especially German Romanticism—whether in Tieck, in Eichendorff's *Ahnung und*

Gegenwart, or most clearly in E. T. A. Hoffmann—has a charm of its own and can make a contribution to the artistic value of certain works of art. The fantastic can also be linked to genuine poetry.[4]

The poetic, the true antithesis to the prosaic

The specific antithesis to the prosaic in its two forms is the poetic, an extremely important aesthetic value which we shall discuss in detail in chapter 11 below. The poetic is a primordial element in art, not only in the artistic genre of poetry as a branch of literature, but in all the literary genres, in music, in the visual arts, and to a special degree in nature.

The poetic also plays a great role in our life. It characterizes many situations and personalities, and it is a profound source of joy. Some personalities have a specifically poetic charm. The poetic can occur on many levels of their being: in the gracefulness of their gestures, their smile, the way they walk, the way they express themselves, up to the highest irradiations of their being. Let us point out only that this is the specific antithesis to the prosaic, and that here the antithesis to the prosaic goes in a direction completely different from the case of the fantastic—to say nothing of the merely apparent, false antithesis of the sensational.

If the poetic is the specific antithesis to the prosaic—an antithesis like that between black and white—it follows that every beauty (apart from the most primitive formal beauty of regularity) contains an antithesis to the prosaic. Beauty is essentially unprosaic. We do not mean that beauty forms the specific antithesis to the prosaic (this is the poetic), if only because it is an incomparably more general value quality. In another respect, however, it is the much more important opposite of the prosaic, both as the opposite of lackluster neutrality and of the absence of qualitative values, and as the opposite of one particular disvalue. The valuable as such is always specifically unprosaic. This primordial antithesis is seen

4. An interesting example of the difference between the fantastic in this sense and the atmosphere of Greek mythology is Eichendorff's short story *The Marble Statue*, in which the classical Aphrodite becomes a Romantic-fantastic Venus.

with particular force in metaphysical beauty, which is the fragrance and the splendor of the value in question.

We must understand that not only metaphysical beauty in the sense explained above, but also the beauty which appears immediately by means of visible and audible entities, contains this profound antithesis to all that is prosaic. This beauty too "sings" in all its various degrees of rank, although this element in beauty intensifies, the more sublime the beauty is.

The beauty of a rose, a hyacinth, a lily; the beauty of a landscape such as that of the area around Florence or the Apuan Mountains in Tuscany near Carrara or Sarzana; the beauty of Bernini's colonnades and the dome of Saint Peter's in Rome; the beauty of Michelangelo's Medici tombs, Giorgione's *Pastoral Concert*, Bach's *Air*, or the adagio in Beethoven's ninth symphony—all this is the enemy of the prosaic. This beauty is always the absolutely unprosaic.

Certainly, many of these objects also possess a specific poetry: flowers, the area around Florence, the *Pastoral Concert.* But neither the vista of the Apuan Mountains, nor the dome of Saint Peter's, nor the *Air*, nor the adagio in the ninth symphony is specifically poetic. One might say that they are poetic *per eminentiam.* Their solemn beauty, their moving seriousness extend beyond the poetical. At any rate, there are many beautiful things which possess the quality of the poetic both in their beauty and apart from it. There are other beautiful things which we cannot call "poetic"—not because they are unpoetic, for that is most certainly not the case, but because they are "super-poetic" and far transcend this quality in their beauty.

There are also beautiful things on a lower level than the specifically poetic things of beauty. Here the poetic element does not constitute the theme; their beauty goes in another direction, but without ever being "unpoetic."

The mediocre, the philistine, and the bourgeois as objective antitheses to beauty

A second element contained in beauty is the antithesis to all mediocrity, to the philistine and the bourgeois. In his book *L'Homme*, Ernest Hello says that there is nothing the mediocre person hates as much as beauty.[5] This insight is doubtless very profound; but what interests us here is not the position of the mediocre person vis-à-vis beauty, but rather the objective antithesis between beauty and the mediocre, and the quality of freedom and breadth which is to be found in every beauty (apart from the lowest form: the mere beauty of that which possesses some form as opposed to the chaotic). This special value of the freedom of spirit and breadth, which constitutes an antithesis to the quality of the mediocre, the philistine, and the bourgeois, is one of the elements contained in beauty, especially beauty of the second power. Naturally, this applies equally to metaphysical beauty. But it is remarkable that the beauty of the visible and the audible can also possess this fullness, height, and depth. This freedom and breadth live in the beauty of nature and of great works of art. They are the opposite of all that is mediocre, philistine, and bourgeois. This is why, as Hello says, the mediocre person hates beauty: he senses that it implicitly contains a verdict on the terrible disvalue of his attitude of mind. This disvalue is not primarily aesthetic; at least, it does not belong primarily to the family of the aesthetic disvalues. The theme of the mediocre, and of the philistine bourgeois, is not an aesthetic theme. Both qualities are personal disvalues which adhere primarily to the cast of mind of certain persons, but also to their products, for example, to theories and pseudo-works of art. These disvalues are not to be found in nature.

The remarkable and surprising thing is precisely that the beauty of the second power constitutes a qualitative antithesis to these disvalues, although its bearers are certainly not personal attitudes. Here we must at once warn against a misunderstanding. The expression "mediocre" can be understood in a broader sense or in a specific, narrower sense. In the broader sense, it denotes only an absence of greatness, for example, when a work or the spirit of a human being does not rise above a low level, but belongs to the weak average. We are not thinking here of this quality, but

5. Ernest Hello, *L'Homme* (Paris: Perrin, 1936), in the chapter entitled "L'homme mediocre," 59–60.

rather of the mediocrity which has an aggressive character and is a definite, dreadful disvalue. We shall now attempt to define mediocrity in the latter, narrower sense.

Obviously, the terms "philistine" and "bourgeois" are much more unambiguous. They always point to a very "positive" disvalue. Although the philistine, the bourgeois, and the mediocre in the narrower sense are not identical, we can study them together, since they all contain the opposite of freedom and breadth of soul. They are very closely related in qualitative terms. The philistine is always mediocre as well, and the specifically bourgeois always at least smacks of mediocrity.

In order to understand the common element in mediocrity (in the sense of the aggressive mediocrity), in the philistine and the bourgeois, we must of course take our starting point in the human being to whom we ascribe these predicates. This is the person who looks at values in a "diminutive" way: he does not deny them, but he interprets them in a way which deprives them of all greatness, of all that is absolute and unconditional. The mediocre person evades the demand made by values. He does not want to rebel against them, but he is willing to get involved with them only up to a certain degree. The philistine hates everything that is unconditional. He never wants to leave his warm nest or lose the solid ground under his feet. In keeping with his basic attitude, he regards all that is unconditional and heroic, all glowing enthusiasm, and the total gift of oneself as "exaggerated." He does not wish either to utter a promethean protest against the world of values—and ultimately against God—or to commit himself genuinely to them. He is not driven hither and thither by evil passions; he is no debauchee who squanders all his money on satisfying his lust, no one like the Karamazov father; nor is he the typical cheapskate like Molière's *The Miser* or Eugénie Grandet's father in Balzac's novel of the same name. He wants to remain on the golden middle ground in every sphere of his life. He wants to be "rational"—as *he* understands this term. He never wants to relinquish possession of himself to anything: he does not want to be swept off his feet by great passions, or to be touched in his innermost depths by lofty goods which are greater than himself. This is why he attempts to downplay moral values, the majesty of the moral commandments, and above all religion in such a way that he can evade their ultimate demand without an open conflict, without a breach. This mentality wants to relativize everything, not in the sense of a theoretical relativism but in the sense of downplaying the absolute, of an attitude which looks on the absolute as if it were relative. This is why this person draws no clear distinction between mere conventions (which are in fact relative) and the moral values and commandments.

It is in this mentality that we find the most radical opposite of Kierkegaard's marvelous maxim that one should simultaneously "take an absolute attitude to one's absolute *telos*" (final goal) and "a relative attitude to that which is relative."[6]

The mediocre person shuns all that is absolute. He draws no distinction between the absolute and the relative. But it is interesting to note that his treatment of the relative—especially of conventions, and especially of the bourgeois element of the "proper," respectable man—is not nearly relative enough. This mentality of the mediocre, the philistine, is a poison which corrodes the attitude to every high good. It is a creeping sickness, a terrible danger to religion, to the relationship to God. Kierkegaard aptly describes this danger to religion when he says that the Danish Protestant Church supplies the "faithful" with the necessary compromise, making it possible for them to live as pagans under the pleasant and expedient shield of the respectability provided by the Christian name.[7]

The beauty of the second power contains an antithesis to the oppressive, petty-minded atmosphere of the mediocre, the philistine. Although the specific antithesis to mediocrity lies in the atmosphere of genuine greatness, genuine breadth and freedom—although the saint who follows Kierkegaard's maxim is eminently un-mediocre, un-philistine, and un-bourgeois—it nevertheless remains important for our presentation of the

6. Søren Kierkegaard, *Concluding Unscientific Postscript,* trans. David F. Swenson (Princeton: Princeton University Press, 1941), 347–59.

7. See Kierkegaard's *Practice in Christianity,* part 1, objection, I; part 2, "The Categories of Offense, that is, of Essential Offense," 7; part 3, V.

spiritual plentitude of the beauty of the second power to see that this beauty contains a qualitative antagonism to the quality of the aggressive mediocrity and of the philistine.

We will understand this better when we now go on to draw a distinction between the specific antithesis to the mediocre, genuine greatness, and the false antitheses which have played a great role in the history of ideas.

False antitheses to the mediocre: Aestheticism [Schöngeistigkeit], high-flown idealism [Verstiegenheit], promethean rebellion (Nietzsche)

The first false antithesis is a high-flown idealism. Here we must draw a distinction between two forms. First, there is the shallow form known as aestheticism. This has an element of the ungenuine, not in the sense of falsehood, but in the sense of something not completely real. For example, an English lady who lived on Capri once said to me, "I could live without tea, but not without beauty." This is in itself a completely correct statement, since the elementary role that beauty ought to play in the life of the human being, and in fact plays for many persons—even for those who are not always aware of it—is of course incomparably greater and more important than the role played by a favorite drink which happens to be popular in one's country. But the tone in which this was said, the gnostic contempt for the body and for those things that are necessary for our daily life, the sentimental enthusiasm for all that belongs to high culture, the failure to pay sufficient attention to the decisive differences in value, are characteristic of aestheticism. Apart from the arrogance which is a factor in many of those who want to be one of the cultivated class, there is also an escape into a flimsy pseudo-culture which does indeed constitute an antithesis of the mediocre, but is a false antithesis.

The second form of an overwrought idealism is incomparably more noble and serious, and is much more important. It contains a genuine yearning for a *sursum corda* ("Lift up your hearts!"), a genuine idealism, but with a certain thinness that belongs to the idealism that is opposed to the classical truth about values and to the cosmos as seen in the light of God. This is a kind of spiritual culture which in itself is certainly noble and which contains an enthusiasm and an unconditional quality which make it an antithesis of the mediocre; but it is too flimsy, it is insufficiently constructed upon the true foundations. It lives too much from the mere affective momentum. This form of idealism can also be found in very noble spirits who are averse to and even despise the mediocre, the philistine, and the bourgeois.

When the frequently prosaic poet Richard Dehmel says, "Goethe went on foot, Schiller rode on Pegasus, and I ride my bicycle," this remark contains a great truth, although "I ride my bicycle" points to a prosaic naturalism rather than to the mediocre. But the contrast to Goethe's walking on foot and to Schiller's riding on Pegasus points to a difference which is crucial in this context. In Goethe's walking on foot, there lies a classic dignity of the human person; and riding on a real horse also has this kind of link with nature. But the unreal Pegasus which rises up into the air has the character of a certain high-flown enthusiasm. On the one hand, we have the classical cultural richness of Goethe, which is opposed to the mediocre because of the inherent fullness of its own content and its nobility; as a contrast, in a certain sense, we have the upward flight in Schiller's noble personality which leaps over the real path leading upward. In this contrast, we are not thinking of Goethe's worldview, nor primarily of his personality, but of the artistic spirit in his great works. The difference between Goethe and Schiller is related to the antithesis between a classical reality and a noble but overcharged enthusiasm.[8]

The second and much more dangerous false antithesis to mediocrity is the promethean rebellion. The gesture of protest becomes an end in itself. Every ordered structure, every noble measure, every law, every subordination under something, indeed every harmony is regarded as a bourgeois limitation and narrowness.

It is a typical form of false reaction when one makes the specific char-

8. This certainly does not mean that we wish to present Goethe as the specific, typical representative of the true antithesis to the mediocre, the philistine, or the bourgeois. We will speak of these typical representatives in the following passage.

acter of a gesture the main thing, because one ignores the reason for the gesture and therefore does not understand that the meaning, justification, and value of a gesture are completely dependent on its reason, that is, on the thing that motivates it. One does not get beyond a formal, apparent similarity, and one overlooks the depth which also separates the gesture in both cases.

In the present case, the greatness and dignity of the moral law is mistakenly equated with a conventional bourgeois narrowness; true and profound harmony is mistakenly equated with a philistine glibness, obedience to the moral law with a conventional lack of freedom, with adapting oneself to what "one" does. For this mentality only the so-called courageous rebellion against every authority—it is irrelevant here whether the authority is true or false—only the promethean gesture is free of all mediocrity, of all bourgeois, philistine pettiness.

In one point there is a certain analogy to this mentality in the bohemian mentality. The latter lacks the idolization of dynamism, the cult of the grandiose, which is characteristic of the promethean mentality, but the bohemian too makes an analogous confusion between convention and the moral law. He too pays homage to a pseudo-freedom. In his case, however, the emphasis lies on the opposition to the sphere of the law; above all, he overlooks the value of the legal sphere, acknowledging only the voice of the "heart." Besides this his understanding of the heart is completely false. He constructs an irreconcilable antithesis between the legal sphere and humaneness.[9]

Apart from the shared failure to grasp the difference between a noble and balanced measure and the idol of the golden middle way, the difference between convention and the moral law, the mentality of the bohemian is clearly distinct from the promethean mentality. In the latter, the cult of dynamism for its own sake goes hand in hand with an attitude to that which is morally bad. The promethean finds this uninteresting, as long as it does not assume a quantitative dimension. Then he actually sees it as something positive, something magnificent. His mentality is

9. See my work *Transformation in Christ*, chap. 10, "True Freedom," esp. 195.

such that he will not be shocked, saddened, or thrilled by an ordinary impure man—but it finds a Don Juan magnificent and attractive. The cult of the dynamic blinds him to the difference between the true greatness of morality and the pseudo-greatness that immorality achieves through sheer quantity. The idolization of protest, the pseudo-greatness of Prometheus, also blinds this person to the true greatness of all morality, of sacred obedience, of all humility and holiness.[10]

Nietzsche with his *Übermensch* is surely the most outstanding representative of this promethean mentality, which is the typical false antithesis to mediocrity. This finds the most concentrated, most apt expression in his words: "Light to all on which I seize, ashen everything I leave: Flame am I most certainly!"[11] He felt that he was the triumphant conqueror of all mediocrity. He believed that he had seen through mediocrity in a way never previously achieved, and that no one had hated mediocrity as much as he. This was a great illusion. Because he did not recognize the true antithesis to every mediocrity and to philistine, bourgeois narrowness, because he succumbed to a cult of promethean dynamism, he demonstrated unambiguously that he never apprehended the real evil, the true disvalue of mediocrity. He hated only formal elements of the mediocre; he did not recognize the real poison of mediocrity.

The true antithesis to mediocrity (Kierkegaard)

This becomes particularly clear when we think of the great and moving figure of Søren Kierkegaard, whose mentality is a prototype of the true antithesis to every mediocrity and to all that is bourgeois and philistine. Kierkegaard apprehended with full clarity the genuine antithesis to mediocrity. His entire personality and his entire oeuvre are permeated by deep faith, by an absolute dedication to Christ the God-Man.[12] He saw the

10. See my book *The Heart* (South Bend, Ind.: St. Augustine's Press, 2007), part II, chap. 1.

11. Friedrich Nietzsche, *The Gay Science*, trans. Del Caro (Cambridge: Cambridge University Press, 2001), 52. These verses are taken from the "Prelude in German Rhymes" with which the work opens.

12. Cf. Kierkegaard's Diaries from 1834–1835. Cf. also Walter Lowrie, *A Short Life of Kierkegaard* (Princeton: Princeton University Press, 1942).

true Christian faith as the uttermost antithesis to the mediocrity which he so hated, above all because it poisoned true Christianity. For him Nietzsche's *Übermensch* would have been an abomination. Kierkegaard never saw any kind of greatness in the open rebellion against Christ. Although his main fight was against the destruction of the specific essence of Christianity in Hegel and against the bourgeois imposition of mediocrity on Christianity in the Church of Denmark, he was always fighting against the real poison of mediocrity.[13] His concern was the disfigurement of the genuine ultimate greatness of the Christian religion by mediocrity, not the lack of the merely grandiose gesture of the dynamic.

Finding a similarity between Nietzsche and Kierkegaard is one of the most bizarre misunderstandings, a typical proof that one is incapable of separating the essential from the inessential. In this instance one has understood neither Nietzsche nor Kierkegaard, and one falls victim to a "false similarity." A purely formal external similarity prevents one from seeing a very profound difference. It is in general a specific feature of intellectual weakness that accidental similarities lead one to overlook the essential radical dissimilarities. Unfortunately, this has frequently occurred in the history of philosophy.

How Kierkegaard loved Socrates, about whom he wrote such glorious words![14] Nietzsche hated Socrates and praised the Sophists.[15] He had an astonishing similarity to Callicles in Plato's *Gorgias.* Most of what Nietzsche presents as a great discovery of the slave revolt in morality[16] is already placed by Plato on Callicles' lips.

Kierkegaard was the most enthusiastic supporter of objective truth[17] and a radical opponent of all relativism and skepticism. In Nietzsche, on

13. Cf. Kierkegaard's Diaries and also his *Book on Adler*, ed. and trans. Howard V. Hong and Edna H. Hong (Princeton: Princeton University Press, 1998) as well as his *Practice in Christianity*, chap. 4.

14. See Søren Kierkegaard, *Philosophical Fragments*, trans. David F. Swenson (Princeton: Princeton University Press, 1967), 11–16, to mention just one place where Kierkegaard praises Socrates.

15. See Friedrich Nietzsche, *The Will to Power*, I, trans. A. M. Ludovici (New York: Russell and Russell, 1964), the section entitled "A criticism of Greek philosophy," which is 345–68.

16. See Friedrich Nietzsche, *Genealogy of Morals*, first essay.

17. See, for example, *Christentum und Christenheit, aus Kierkegaards Tagebüchern ausgewählt und übersetzt von E. Schlechta* (Munich: Kösel Verlag, 1957), nos. 277, 767.

the other hand, we find perhaps one of the most diabolical forms of skepticism: a lack of interest in the truth.[18] "Truth is that kind of error without which one particular kind of living beings could not live."[19]

The thinkers who are the true antitheses of mediocrity and of the philistine, bourgeois mentality are Plato, Augustine, Pascal, and Kierkegaard. What a contrast to all mediocrity do we find in every Platonic dialogue, in the atmosphere of truth, of reverence, of the true *sursum corda*! This antithesis is particularly clear in the *Phaedrus* and the *Phaedo.*

Kierkegaard says that one attains to the true self in the true and wholesome losing of oneself which is the opposite of enslavement by the passions. This holy madness—unlike the sick madness—deals the deathblow to mediocrity, which is never willing to step outside its nice and neat, little warm nest.[20]

In the *Confessions* of Saint Augustine we are embraced by the breath of the true God, by ultimate greatness, breadth, absoluteness, and total gift of self, all of which are radical antitheses to mediocrity and philistine narrowness. This is why mediocre spirits nourish an especial hatred for this work and regard it as the prototype of exaggeration, of "knowing no boundaries," of "going too far."

In Pascal we find an explicit fight against mediocrity, against the philistinism of rationalism and the bourgeois mediocrity of the deists. This finds its expression in the moving, glorious *Mémorial*: "GOD of Abraham, GOD of Isaac, GOD of Jacob. Not of the philosophers and of the learned . . . GOD of Jesus Christ."[21] His work is permeated by the fight against all compromises, against every attempt to make light of serious things.

It is in Kierkegaard that the conscious fight against mediocrity, to which he opposes the true antithesis, reaches its high point.[22] This

18. On this see Josef Seifert, "Friedrich Nietzsches Verzweiflung an der Wahrheit und sein Kampf gegen die Wahrheit," in *Rehabilitierung der Philosophie* (Festschrift for Balduin Schwarz), 183–215.

19. Nietzsche, *The Will to Power*, II, 20.

20. See Kierkegaard, *The Sickness unto Death*, section 1, c; *Practice in Christianity*, part 1, IV; part 3, II.

21. Complete French and Latin text of Pascal's *Mémorial*, with English translation: www.users.csbsju.edu/~eknuth/pascal/html.

22. See, for example, *Christentum und Christenheit*, nos. 207ff., 221, 238, 247ff., 262ff., 272ff.

antithesis to mediocrity is the absoluteness of genuine devotion, indeed of the response to God, to the moral commandments, to the spirit of true freedom—the spirit which is just as opposed to every idolatry as to all that is distinctly mediocre. There is a primordial lack of freedom in the promethean mentality in which one is enslaved by pride or by the cult of making a gesture for its own sake, or in the titanic rebellion involved in succumbing to an idol and adoring false gods. The fundamental sovereignty of truth, which is expressed in Kierkegaard's words quoted above—that one should treat the absolute as absolute and the relative as relative, or that we should take account of this difference in our response—is the soul of true freedom and is the real antithesis to mediocrity.

In our present context it is important to grasp that the beauty of the second power also contains a qualitative antithesis to the mediocre, the philistine, and the bourgeois, since it irradiates an atmosphere of true breadth and true freedom. This is not only the case when this element plays a role in terms of content, as for example when the truth in a literary work of art or the elevating moral character of a figure in a drama contributes to this element of the anti-bourgeois, the anti-mediocre; it applies equally to the purely qualitative antithesis between the beauty of the second power and the oppressive atmosphere of the mediocre.

This beauty may occur in nature, in architecture, or in the union of nature and architecture, in music, sculpture, painting, or literature. The atmosphere of greatness, breadth, and freedom always lives in it—the uttermost antithesis of the oppressive quality of the philistine and mediocre. We find it, for example, in the view of the sea across the gardens and rocks before the Villa Rufolo and the Villa Cimbrone in Ravello, or in the view of the Grand Canyon in Arizona. We are spellbound on the Piazza San Marco in Venice when we look at San Marco and the Palace of the Doges, or when we stand behind the cathedral of Santa Maria in Florence and look up at Brunelleschi's unique cupola. We are raised up into this world when we look toward Florence from Bellosguardo and perceive the marvelous wedding between nature and architecture, between the city and its surroundings; or when we come from Montefiascone and catch sight of the city of Orvieto; when we stand before Santa Maria degli Angeli and see Assisi, or when the Alhambra in Granada stands out against the background of the Sierra Nevada. This atmosphere shines out in Titian's painting of Charles V in the Prado in Madrid, and in the frescos of Piero della Francesca in Arezzo. This atmosphere of greatness, breadth, and a freedom that makes us deeply happy, embraces us when we look at Michelangelo's *Dying Slave* or a relief from the Parthenon. Other examples are the opening chorus in Bach's *Saint Matthew Passion*, the first movement of Beethoven's ninth symphony with its mysterious density and depth, and Mozart's Quintet in G minor. In each instance, and each time in a new form, this world makes itself felt—a world which is the opposite of all that is mediocre and philistine.

Doubtless, no one who experiences this beauty will think immediately of the antithesis to those disvalues; but he will feel and apprehend the special quality which is the objective antithesis of the mediocre and the philistine, and it will take hold of him. He will apprehend the inexhaustible richness of spirit, the seriousness, and the greatness which lives in this beauty in purely qualitative terms. Our concern here is to point to this mystery: the spiritual beauty of the second power as found in the visible and the audible—though it has been regarded as qualitatively lower than metaphysical beauty because of its link to the senses and physical world—contains, purely as beauty, this whole range of spiritual values. We can describe these correctly only if we take our starting point in other fields, that is, in human beings, in their mentality and attitudes, beginning with the negative antitheses that we find in human attitudes to these values.[23]

23. Naturally, there are enormous gradations within the beauty of the second power. There exists not only the exalted beauty which we have listed in these examples, but also a delightful, more modest beauty, the magic of a play by Carlo Goldoni, of an opera like Rossini's *Barber of Seville*, etc. Depending on the level of beauty, the quality—the qualitative value which is the opposite of the mediocre, the bourgeois, and the philistine—emerges to a greater or lesser degree, and indeed in a variety of ways. The more modest, charming works of art are equally opposed to the mediocre and the philistine, but in a different way. They do not possess the specific quality of breadth and greatness, the intellectual freedom which constitutes the true antithesis to the mediocre. In them one is not touched by the breath which contains a special message from God, a breath which comes from on high, from above. The *sursum corda* does not live in them. Nevertheless, although they are not a specific antithesis in their charming poetry, they are not merely free of the oppressive world of mediocrity, but are in fact opposed to it.

The flat [das Platte], the cheap [das Billige], the shallow [das Flache] as antitheses to beauty of the second power

We turn now to another negative quality which is opposed by the beauty of the second power, that is, the quality of the shallow and the cheap. At first sight, one could think that these are identical to the mediocre, the philistine, and the bourgeois, but when we look more closely, we can see that they are a new kind of negative quality, a disvalue of another kind. Doubtless one can also understand the mediocre in such a way that it is coextensive with the flat and the cheap; but the specifically philistine and bourgeois is clearly different from the flat and the cheap. When we described the mediocre ethos, which is also philistine and bourgeois, we had something in mind which is not in the least coextensive with the flat and the cheap.

While the attributes "philistine" and "bourgeois" are the characteristics of an ethos, the flat, the shallow, and the cheap are at home especially in the world of the intellect, of its products and achievements. But they do not have their origin in a diminutive worldview, in downplaying things, in evading all absoluteness and devotion; nor do they have the tendency to avoid every risk and to look for protection through convention and through being anchored in this. They are not inclined to follow the norm of what "one" does, to choose the golden middle path, or to go along only up to a certain point. In the shallow, cheap mentality, we find not the *downplaying* of the moral sphere, of religion, and of everything that demands absoluteness and total devotion, but an attempt to *deny* all this. In every rebellion there is still a tacit acknowledgement of the greatness of that against which one rebels, but here a foolish arrogance asserts that everything higher derives from something lower. It is openly claimed, and without fear of falling into error, that "basically" everything higher is nothing more than well-known things belonging to a lower sphere. The flat and shallow person feels himself superior and declares impudently that love is basically only a sexual drive; that all intellectual acts are basically only chemical processes in the brain; and that selfless action is an illusion, that we speak of "selfless" action only because we forget that there are some people who find greater pleasure and more delight in making others happy than in pursuing their own interest, as Mandeville claims in his fable about the bees.[24]

This mentality is found above all in philosophical systems and theories, or better: in "philosophisms" such as materialism, positivism, pragmatism, behaviorism, and utilitarianism. It is the true antithesis of depth—much more so in fact than mere superficiality. The merely superficial person dreads the effort involved in penetrating the depths of being; he wants to remain on the periphery. He does not pretend to dethrone all that is great and profound; he passes with a light touch from one thing to the other. He prefers an elegant, witty chat about God and the world to an "academic" discussion. The specifically superficial person does not wish to deny the existence of greater and deeper things, and he does not wish to eliminate them. But he does not wish to move out into the depths that would make possible an appropriate response to these things. He is content with a witticism. The superficial person may be incapable of understanding deep things, and in that case, his superficiality is nothing other than a failure. But it may be that he is unwilling to get involved with them, and in that case his superficiality has a much more negative character. It moves us to protest. Even if it is accompanied by wit and by a certain brilliance, we nevertheless find it oppressive. After a while, it becomes definitely boring.

It is clear that the antithesis to depth which we find in the flat, the shallow, and the cheap is of a different nature than the antithesis we find in the superficial: it consists in the arrogant attempt to eliminate all depth. Such persons believe that they can rob the cosmos of all depth and greatness, of all true values, and especially of mystery—not in a titanic assault but with an apparently clear, sober reduction, an "explanation" that they hold in readiness for everything. The representatives of this mentality are full of self-satisfaction and of a primitive overestimation of their ability.

The mentality and the intellectual attitude of the flat and the cheap emanates an atmosphere which is disgusting and suffocating. Naturally, it is also the prototype of the boring and the depressing. But it is much

24. Bernard de Mandeville, *The Fable of the Bees: or, Private Vices, Publick Benefits* (1714).

more "positively" negative than that which is boring; it is nauseating. The quality of the flat is a terrible disvalue.

Although false philosophical doctrines provide the context where this quality is really at home, it is also found in pseudo-works of art, in kitsch of every kind—in paintings, novels, music. Indeed, it plays a prominent role in pseudo-works of art. People who believe themselves capable of creating a work of art, but without possessing the true gift, are especially prone to the temptation to produce something cheap. Unfortunately, they have a talent for finding cheap solutions, and they succeed brilliantly in producing cheap things.

In nature there are no bearers of the flat or the cheap. This category presupposes the human spirit and its capacity for perversion. The specifically shallow mentality and the cheap arguments are to be found in the intellectual products of the human person.

The beauty of the second power also contains a qualitative antithesis to the flat and the cheap. This qualitative antithesis to the flat is alive in all genuine beauty.

As we have indicated, the cheap can be found in poor works of art; "cheap" can be directly said of these works, and it can be used in the analysis of them. This is why the good work of art is a direct thematic antithesis to the cheap pseudo-work of art. It constitutes both a purely qualitative antithesis to the general quality of the flat and the cheap and a specific antithesis to the literal character of the cheap which characterizes the poor work of art.[25]

Pseudo-depth

We must point out that there is also a false antithesis to the shallow and the flat, namely, pseudo-depth. Beauty, in its simple truth, forms a specific antithesis to this too.

Once again, we encounter this pseudo-depth primarily in the sphere

25. The shallow, the flat, is not identical with the cheap. We have discussed these in one and the same section because all shallow and flat things are also cheap, and everything that is cheap is also shallow. Although they go hand in hand, they are not identical as qualities.

of the intellectual. It manifests itself when depth is confused with complicatedness, or indeed with incomprehensibility. This can even go so far that some authors employ incomprehensibility in order to create the impression of depth, and this can lead to intellectual imposture. But there are also self-deceptions where the author feels that he is immensely deep, thinking of the darkness of his confused and incomprehensible speculations as depth.

There is yet another form of false depth, namely, the tendency to import mysterious depths into everything that is not in fact deep, the tendency to "metaphysicize" everything. People who have this attitude see everything that happens as profound and important only because it takes its place in the rhythm of history and *de facto* occurs. They perceive in every event the breath of Hegel's world-spirit. In their eyes, even the most stupid movements in history possess profundity as soon as these movements become an historical-sociological reality.

This pseudo-depth is a great danger for the Germans. It is easy for Germans to take something that is done with frivolous cynicism in France and to treat it as profound. We need only compare the immorality on Montmartre with the "metaphysics of the abdomen" which held sway in Schwabing in Munich before the First World War, where one could hear a woman declaiming erotic poems such as, "I offered my body to the sun, so that it might become ripe for love." Another example is the pseudo-seriousness, the pseudo-solemnity in the rites of the German student corps. Unfortunately, the tendency to import mysterious depths into things—depths that they do not in fact possess—instead of calling things by their real name, is not confined to Germany, although it is a greater danger for the German spirit than, for example, for the French spirit. In America too there is the danger of projecting deep mysteries into things that are not in fact deep. I once heard the following words on the radio: "Today we want to discuss the problem of jazz and the depths that are contained in this kind of music."

Just as all genuine beauty contains in its truth and genuineness an antithesis to the shallow and the cheap, so too it contains an antithesis to pseudo-depth in all its forms.

Ungenuineness as antithesis to beauty of the second power. This brings us in a natural way to another central element which is possessed above all by the beauty of all true works of art, namely, genuineness. This forms the antithesis to the ungenuine.

Qualitative ungenuineness is likewise a disvalue *sui generis* which does not occur in nature but only in the human person and in the things which he produces.

Here we do not have in mind the very general meaning of "genuine," which refers either to the opposite of mere appearance or to the question of the extent to which something completely fulfills its essence. This fulfillment has been called "ontological truth."

When we speak of the "genuine," therefore, we do not mean that which truly exists as opposed to mere appearance. The genuine Dionysius the Areopagite was not the author of the celebrated work; Macpherson was not the genuine Ossian; muscovite [*Katzensilber*, "cat silver" in German] is not genuine silver [*Silber*]; and so on. The dialogue *Alcibiades* is not genuine, that is, not written by Plato. "Ungenuine" here means "spurious" and "apocryphal." Obviously, this spuriousness which the merely illusory possesses (as opposed to the genuine) is not a qualitative disvalue. Its theme is the contradiction of reality that lies in mere illusion. It bears the disvalue of all that is illusory.

This "ontological ungenuineness" is not the quality we have in mind here. We are aiming at something quite different, a falseness of a special kind. It must be clearly distinguished from mendacity. The mendacious hypocrite, a Tartuffe or an Iago, is certainly not spurious. Mendacity is a moral disvalue, a quality for which one is responsible. It is a grave ethical blemish. The Devil is "the father of lies."

Ungenuineness as we mean it, however, is not an ethical disvalue but a quite general disvalue for which one is not responsible and through which one incurs no guilt. The liar, the mendacious person, is aware that he is lying; but the ungenuine person is not aware of being spurious. The liar intends to deceive someone; the ungenuine person does not consciously want to deceive anyone. At most, he enjoys the role he is playing. Typically ungenuine are persons full of affectation: everything—their words, gestures, movements, laughter—has a ring of the ungenuine. It is not natural but artificial. We cannot take their words altogether seriously, and their gestures have an embarrassing quality. The ungenuine can also take on the form of the specifically theatrical; but this is a relatively harmless, somewhat ridiculous form of the ungenuine.

Another and worse form of ungenuineness is found in false pathos. Ibsen offers a masterly portrayal of this pathos in the character of Hjalmar Ekdal in his drama *The Wild Duck*, and it can also be seen in one particular type of French orator. It finds a clear expression in the intonation and in what is said, for example, in the words that Victor Hugo cried out to the sick Balzac and his wife after the events of 1848: *Il y a quelque chose de plus grand que le roi, c'est la nation* ("There is something greater than the king—the nation!"). One must be acquainted with the entire situation in order to apprehend the false pathos, to which Balzac was particularly averse, in this affirmation (which is not as such untrue). Another good example of false pathos is provided by the way in which some of Schiller's plays were staged around 1900. And which of us has never in life encountered people who put on display a false pathos?

Much worse, however, is the ungenuineness which permeates the entire essence of one type of hysteria. The enthusiasm of hysterical persons of this kind is not genuine; it rings a false note. Their love is not genuine, and they say many untrue things. They certainly do not consciously intend to lie, but they exaggerate out of all proportion the importance of the virtues of their spouse, their children, or the events that they have experienced.

The quality of the ungenuine deprives everything of its full validity. Such persons may be good, compassionate, helpful, and intelligent, but this all-pervasive ungenuineness undermines everything.

Shallowness is at home primarily in the intellectual sphere, but this ungenuineness is at home above all in the affective sphere. Ungenuineness is an illness of ethos rather than of logos. It is found in the expression of feelings and especially in the behavior of a person.

Besides this, ungenuineness is found in many products of the human spirit, as the false pathos in literature and music attests. Affectation can express itself in paintings and sculptures. An even more embarrassing ungenuineness holds sway in all bad art. We shall return to this in the second volume of the present work, namely, in our detailed discussion of the various spheres of art.

Here let us emphasize only that beauty in all its levels, and especially beauty of the second power, contains a profound antithesis to all ungenuineness. In order to understand this better, let us look briefly at the false antitheses to the ungenuine.

One widespread false antithesis to the ungenuine is a crude "honesty." There are many people who believe that they are not genuine unless they put into words everything that they feel. They feel that they are all the more genuine, the more blunt they are, the worse manners they have, the more they let themselves go. They believe that the basis of genuineness is the agreement between the feeling they happen to have at the moment and its expression—independently of whether their feeling is good or bad, justified or unjustified. They do not care whether their utterance may wound or harm another person. In other words, they silence the question: What ought to be the case? They do not ask what their behavior ought to be or what manners are good. Their only question is whether their behavior corresponds to their momentary inner disposition.

This false honesty, this false ideal of genuineness, which ultimately suspects the presence of something ungenuine in every external form that offers resistance to just letting oneself go, is often manifested in the religious sphere, namely, when people believe that they cease to be genuine as soon as they say words in prayers which do not correspond to what they feel (at least for the moment). They forget that in prayers, especially in the liturgical prayers, we find the formulation of what we ought to feel when we pray to God, not only the formulation of what we already feel. Clearly, it is a pseudo-genuineness that pays attention only to what we really feel and ignores everything that we ought to feel (and therefore also long to feel, or ought to long to feel), everything that is objectively the appropriate response, and everything that objectively expresses what we ought to pray for and the attitude we should have.

If we attempt with our will to force the appropriate affective response, we easily end up in ungenuineness. It is of course true that we ought to concentrate on God with our will, immersing ourselves in the unfathomable holiness of Jesus and thus indirectly preparing the ground for an affective response. But as soon as we attempt to generate the affective responses with our will—which is objectively impossible—the result is something ungenuine. The "valid word" of love, adoration, and repentance, like the act of the will, can indeed be posited by us freely; but the specifically affective fullness is a gift. If we attempt to generate it directly, the outcome is something ungenuine.

Our behavior will be even more ungenuine if we aim at the affective responses not for God's sake, that is, because they are due to Him, but because we want to enjoy the elevated temperature of our emotional life. This is how the specifically ungenuine feelings are born, deprived of their meaningful character as responses. There is no longer any true response here, but only a fatal self-enjoyment.

This ungenuineness poses a particular danger in the natural love for a human being. One wants to love with a passionate ardor, because it is so beautiful to love in that way. But there is a particular type of person who has not found the one who kindles this love in him, the one with whom he truly falls in love—and who then attempts to work himself up into such a love. When there is no kind of objective requirement—which is a pure gift, and in the case of real being in love is felt to be an inner necessity—this intervention by the will, which usurps the place of that which spontaneously comes into being, is a complete mistake and can only generate an ungenuine love.

In the second volume of this work we will see how false genuineness comes into its own in the sphere of art. For example, the attempt is made to achieve genuineness by means of dialect and Bavarian coarseness, in the belief that only one particular form of down-to-earthness, a dash of local flavoring, can bestow on a work the character of the organic, of the *genitum*, of that which has spontaneously grown, as opposed to the artificial. One seeks refuge in a stifling genre-atmosphere. All this is an affected genuineness. The genuine cannot be intended. An essential character of the genuine is that it comes about spontaneously. Artificial genuineness is a special subspecies of the ungenuine.

True genuineness implies that we are completely directed toward the object in our attitude. It is important that our response is the response required by the object. Genuineness is imperiled by every self-observation, every looking back upon our own selves, and above all by self-enjoyment at the moment in which a good summons us to give the appropriate response. Genuineness requires a healthy motivation, the healthy organic rhythm and unfolding of our inner life. On the one hand, it demands the complete, conscious lateral enactment of our response; but on the other hand, in many instances it demands that unconsciousness of which the Gospel speaks: "Your left hand is not to know what your right hand is doing" (Matthew 6:3). Above all, genuineness excludes any looking backward while giving the response, any self-observation, or any kind of seeing oneself from the outside that destroys the transcendence of the value-response.

Sentimentality and its false antitheses

The beauty of the second power in the realm of the visible and the audible also contains an antithesis to the sentimental. The term "sentimental" is often used wrongly, especially in America. Everything that is emotional is called "sentimental," and this naturally leads to a total equivocation. I use the term "sentimental" to refer to a perversion of the affective, a very quality of disvalue. I have discussed the quality of sentimentality in the true meaning of the word in my book *The Heart* (part I, chapter 1). Here I want to work out the essence of the sentimental in greater detail.

We must begin by distinguishing between sentimentality and exaggerated sensitivity. There are some people who make affective responses which go beyond what the meaning of the object calls for. But this exaggerated sensitivity is not present in every affective response of an inappropriate strength. The irritable person, the irascible person who flies into a rage over small things, is not overly sensitive. The "harsh" affective responses have a completely different quality. This disproportion is found in irascible, irritable, and timorous persons, in the unjustifiably optimistic and pessimistic, just as much as in those who are exaggeratedly sensitive. The exaggerated sensitivity is at home in the "soft" affective sphere. Not only is it exaggerated; it also bears the marks of an excessive softness.

At some periods this sensitivity was extremely widespread. People who were moved burst into tears all too quickly, and life in society was dominated by an elevated temperature of soft affectivity. This is true, for example, of Jung-Stilling's *Lebensgeschichte*, a work which is otherwise so beautiful and full of great poetry in many places. Similarly, Goethe's *Werther* is full of this exaggerated sensitivity, which is certainly the bearer of a disvalue; but this is a small disvalue, which rather prompts us to laugh at it. The exaggerated sensitivity makes it impossible for us to take with full seriousness the feeling in question and its expression. Although this exaggerated sensitivity may seem ridiculous, it is a relatively likable disvalue.

We must however emphasize very strongly at this point that there is a whole world of difference between this exaggerated sensitivity and the strength and intensity of the affective sphere. The affective responses of love, profound joy, and enthusiasm can never be too strong, provided that the correct relationship is maintained between the response and its object. The greater a person's potential for love, the better! The intensity, depth, and absoluteness of affective value-responses can never be too great. According to Leonardo da Vinci, "The greater the man, the deeper is his love." The exaggerated sensitivity is something negative because of its *inappropriateness* as a response, because of the disproportion between the response and its object. It is related especially to the exaggeration of the expression.

The sentimental is completely different from exaggerated sensitivity. It contains a false, perverted ethos and is the bearer of a definite and grave disvalue.

The characteristic of sentimentality is that the real theme is a certain softening, a delight in swimming in an ungenuine emotionality. The sentimental person never dedicates himself truly to the object. The object—

a particular event, the action of another person, or another human being —is not the theme but only a means to elicit a pseudo-emotion which the sentimental person enjoys. For him, the theme is this pseudo-emotion, which is a world away from genuine emotion. The quality of this emotion is ungenuine. It is a false, a qualitatively perverted affectivity, not at all an exaggerated sensitivity, and still less a mere predominance of the emotional vis-à-vis the reason and the will. It is an error that goes in a completely different direction.

Sentimentality contains a false self-absorption, the lack of a true affective response to something that is objectively sad or joyful, that is, the lack of a genuine affective value-response. In truth, the sentimental person is not too affective; rather, he is not affective at all in the genuine sense of this word. He enjoys his pseudo-emotion, a kind of softened ethos; the qualitatively perverted emotion is his goal. Naturally, the emotional softening is not always deliberately sought; usually, this misuse of the object takes place spontaneously. The sentimental person listens to a piece of music, hears of an event, or reads a book—and his reaction is this state of being "pseudo-moved," which he actually enjoys.

We must explicitly underline that only one particular kind of object prompts this false state of emotion. The sentimental person loves sentimental music and literature. But he will also use many things which are *per se* unsentimental as a means to attain the state of emotional softening; he does this by misunderstanding these things or interpreting them incorrectly.

All beauty, but especially the beauty of the second power, forms a definite antithesis to this perverted ethos of the sentimental. In order to understand the antithesis, this true opposite of sentimentality which is implied in the beauty of the second power, we must briefly mention some false antitheses to sentimentality which unfortunately play a great role in our lives.

The first false antithesis to sentimentality is the complete absence of the affective. We find this in the typical bureaucrat, or in a person who is completely absorbed in his intellectual interests, one particular type of professor who is dried up, as it were, from an affective point of view. We find it also in the low-brow for whom the category of the "useful" dominates everything else. He regards everything that is affective as a waste of time, a superfluous dallying with something that is unproductive.

A second false antithesis to sentimentality is the idol of "the new objectivity" [*die neue Sachlichkeit*] which we have discussed in detail elsewhere.[26] This is not the true antithesis to sentimentality, but the opposite of all that is affective, even of the great and glorious genuine affectivity.[27] This pseudo-objectivity, which confuses genuine affectivity with sentimentality, is itself the bearer of a disvalue which is just as great as the disvalue borne by sentimentality.

Another false antithesis to sentimentality is the idol of virility. There is an idol of manliness, of self-control, which looks on every occurrence of the affective as weakness. This has to be distinguished from the Stoic idol of *apatheia,* an anti-affective attitude which is based on completely different motives. Here it is not so much a question of despising the affective and of interpreting its noble gentleness as weakness and sentimentality. Rather the wish of the Stoic is to be independent of all the bonds which arise out of the response to an object which exists outside our own selves. The point is that in love one becomes dependent on the happiness of the other person, on his well-being, on his life. Similarly, in joy at something that makes one happy, and especially in sadness at something that is objectively sad, a dependency is generated by the meaningful confrontation with the object, with its quality, with its value or disvalue. Accordingly, one prefers to do without every true joy, in order never to become dependent on anything, and especially on anything sad. This is definitely an idol, grounded in arrogance, in a false "freedom" born of arrogance. As we have said, there is here a renunciation of all affectivity, not because of its quality but because of the idol of *apatheia.*

In the idol of manliness, on the other hand, the affective is avoided not because of the limitation on our autonomy but because of its quality, because it is a voice of the heart; and the man regards this voice as a weakness. For the adherent of the idol of manliness, every experience of being

26. See my essay "The New Functionalism in the Light of Christ," in my collection *The New Tower of Babel* (New York: P. J. Kenedy and Sons, 1953).

27. Cf. *The Heart, inter alia* in part I, chap. 2.

moved is a soft and contemptible weakness. Fritz von Unruh tells of a glorious sunset which he experienced as a cadet. When the major saw that Unruh was moved by this beauty and cried out to the other cadets, "How wonderful!" he shouted at him, "Hey! That is the language of a girls' boarding school, and let me tell you once and for all that I will not tolerate such expressions here."[28] Such words betray the utter ugliness of the idol of manliness. Its devotee regards as a contemptible weakness every affective emotion, even the noblest response to something that calls for this emotion, and even more every shedding of tears. Virgil's glorious words, *sunt lacrimae rerum*, are completely incomprehensible to him.[29]

This idol is the opposite of that genuine affectivity that we have called "tender" affectivity in my book *The Heart*, as distinct from the "hard, dynamic" affectivity of the passions. It is therefore no true antithesis to sentimentality, and for three reasons. First, the devotee of this idol does not see the difference between sentimentality and true affectivity; secondly, he does not recognize the true disvalue of sentimentality; and thirdly, he misunderstands the lofty value of true affectivity. This idol of manliness may perhaps be even more disvaluable than sentimentality; at any rate, it is certainly more repulsive.

The true antithesis to sentimentality is the genuine affectivity which we find, for example, in a great love like that between Leonora and Florestan in Beethoven's *Fidelio*, or between Tristan and Isolde in Wagner's musical drama; in a deep and grateful joy, whose highest form finds its expression in the aged Simeon's *Nunc dimittis* ("Now do you dismiss your servant, O Lord, depart in peace . . . ," Luke 2:29-32); in the deep and noble experience of being moved by a sublime beauty; or in the tears caused by repentance, a deep pain, or a deep joy.

The important point in the present context is to grasp that the beauty of the second power is incompatible with sentimentality, and that although this is not its theme, it contains an antithesis to all sentimentality. The interesting thing here is not only that the expressed ethos,

28. Fritz von Unruh, *Im Haus des Prinzen* (Frankfurt: Societaetsverlag, 1967), 48.

29. "These are the tears of things": *Æneid* I, 462. Cf. Theodor Haecker, *Vergil, Vater des Abendlandes* (Munich: Kösel, 1952), chap. 8, "Tränen."

where this occurs in a work of art that is supposed to be beautiful, must never be sentimental, but also that beauty as such contains an antithesis to the sentimental. This is why in nature, where the expression of a mentality does not occur, the beauty of the second power is also an antithesis to sentimentality.

After discussing sentimentality, this special form of ungenuineness, let us return to ungenuineness in general.

We will see in the second volume of this work that the quality of the ungenuine likewise plays a large role in poor works of art. Here it suffices to say that beauty includes a qualitative antithesis to all ungenuineness. And this is a significant element, because it also points to the mysterious connection between beauty and truth.

It is, however, very important to understand that there also exists "ungenuine beauty," a pseudo-beauty which is one specific opposite of the beauty of the second power: we refer to the trivial, to kitsch. Unlike the ugly, the trivial claims to be beautiful. The metaphysically ugly, which is the specific antithesis to the metaphysical beautiful and has the same relationship to this as the morally bad to the morally good, does not pretend to be beautiful. It contains a clear "no," a hostile attitude toward beauty. But the trivial, which plays a great role above all in art, is a pseudo-beauty. It "lies," it passes itself off as beautiful, but it rings false. Not only does beauty possess the qualitative antithesis to the prosaic, the mediocre, the shallow, and the ungenuine; the beauty of the second power in art is the thematic opposite of the trivial, in a manner analogous to the relationship between metaphysical beauty and metaphysical ugliness, or between the beauty that appeals to the senses and the corresponding ugliness. We shall look more closely in chapter 12 below at the extremely important phenomenon of the trivial, when we discuss the three thematic opposites of beauty.

Here our theme was to indicate the wealth of spiritual contents and elements which are contained to some degree in all beauty, but above all in the beauty of the second power. Our aim was to show the universal depth and the richness that beauty possesses, and to demonstrate its full seriousness, which often goes unrecognized.

CHAPTER ELEVEN

The Poetic

BEFORE we study the three antitheses to beauty, we shall look in detail at the special aesthetic value of the poetic. We have already spoken in the preceding chapter of the poetic as the true positive opposite of the prosaic. Now we wish to investigate this quality in its own right, for it is one of the most central aesthetic values.

Its hovering and delicate harmony [sein schwebender, hauchhafter Zusammenklang]

The poetic is a phenomenon *sui generis*, and indeed one that is difficult to grasp. We find it in the realm of human beings: some persons have a great poetic enchantment. It occurs in animals, many of which—such as the nightingale, horses, asses, and sheep—have a great poetry. We can discover poetry in all of nature which surrounds us, especially in particular landscapes, and animals often contribute to this poetry. The poetic appears naturally in all kinds of art.

Let us begin with the poetry that a landscape can possess. There are very beautiful landscapes that are not specifically poetic. Doubtless, as we have already seen, they contain an antithesis to prose; every beauty, and *a fortiori* every beauty of the second power, is unprosaic; it "sings." It is poetic *per eminentiam*, but unlike certain beautiful landscapes, it is not specifically poetic.

One typical form of the poetic is the phenomenon of the pastoral. The shepherd with his flock, especially with sheep or goats, has an aesthetic quality all its own. The closeness to nature, the contemplative element of his activity, the sight of the sheep with the sheepdog, their form, the peaceful, calm surroundings: all this unites to form a lovely unity that irradiates a very specific atmosphere. The loose unity of a placidly murmuring brook, a meadow, some trees, poplars, willows (including weeping willows), and a gentle hill in the background can possess an intense pastoral atmosphere. If we compare this pastoral landscape with a grandiose landscape such as the Grand Canyon, the Dolomites as seen from Lake Misurina, or the Jungfrau, Mönch, and Eiger Mountains as seen from Lake Thune, it is easy to recognize that such landscapes do not have the quality of the pastoral, and that it would indeed be incorrect to describe them as specifically poetic.

The difference we have in mind here is not the same as that between the lovely [*lieblich*] and the sublime [*erhaben*]. The phenomenon of the specifically poetic, of which the pastoral is only one special instance, can occur in the most various degrees and levels of the beautiful, and it is not in the least tied to a smaller, more modest format. There exists a poetry of an extraordinary depth and a moving beauty, especially in literature, music, and the visual arts. It suffices here to recall the poetry at the beginning of the eighth canto of Dante's "Purgatory" in the *Divine Comedy*, Faust's words during the walk on Easter day, the second part in the second movement of Beethoven's Quartet, opus 132, or Giorgione's *Pastoral Concert*.

Since the poetic is a primordial phenomenon, all we can do is point to some essential characteristics and appeal to the reader's intuition of it by means of examples.

The easiest way to apprehend one essential characteristic of the poetic, namely, its hovering and fragrant character, is perhaps to look at the poetic in nature and in particular situations. It is constituted by a harmony of factors which are not united by a really tangible connection. Let us think of the following situation: we arrive toward evening at a beautiful little town such as Terracina south of Rome, on the Tyrrhenian coast, or Altopascio near Lucca. The final splendor of the sinking sun transfigures the town and the surrounding landscape. The bells are ringing the Angelus, and people are going home after finishing their work. Perhaps a shepherd is driving his flock homeward. We are moved by the beauty of this situation, by its special poetry.

One who has no organ for poetry, such as the typically prosaic person, the philistine, will say, "What is supposed to be special here? It is all perfectly normal! The sun sets every day; the bells ring, because people are supposed to say some special prayer; the shepherd happens by chance to come back with his flock. These individual elements are perfectly everyday occurrences." The philistine does not perceive the unique harmony of these elements. All he sees are tangible connections of efficient or final causality. Everything else is a chance coincidence that does not interest him in the slightest.

Intermediary realm and "earthly" character

This unpragmatic, delicate harmony of different kinds of elements has a definitely objective character, even if it is constituted only for me because I come on the scene at precisely this moment. In this combination there shines out a quality that brings a message from a higher reality. Poetry, or the poetic, is an intermediary realm between eternity and earthly life. In the glory of eternity, where everything is perfect and all that is earthly is superseded, the ultimate and endless glory that is our joy will be the absolute and only reality.

The poetic is one form of the reflection of the higher world on this earth, but only a breath that brings a presentiment. Naturally, there are completely real witnesses to heaven, especially the saints. They are a full, substantial reality in the image of heaven they present; they are an anticipation. Another more distant level is constituted by moral values, by the highest natural truths, and by the metaphysical beauty of values.

However, the poetic has an "earthly" character. It speaks only indirectly, in the form of this "breath," of the world of values. It speaks, not of eternity, but of the abundance of the natural values; but it does so in the manner of an intimation, and in a form that makes it an "intermediary realm" between the earth and eternity. The poetic gives our soul wings—a special kind of wings. Plato rightly says: "When it looks on beauty, the soul acquires wings" (*Phaedrus* 249d). In the case of the poetic, the wings are of a different kind. They raise us up above the world of the actual, of the prosaic in the broader sense of the term. But unlike the highest form of beauty, they do not raise us up to God. There is an element of liberation in the poetic, but the "beautiful world" that it contains is realized only in the manner of an intimation. It does not have the reality that is possessed by the metaphysical beauty of real persons or the beauty in the visible and the audible that appeals to the senses; nor does it have the reality of the prosaic. Naturally, we have in mind above all the poetic situations, the poetic atmosphere, that result from the harmony of various things and events—an atmosphere that appears accidental when seen "from the outside."

On the other hand, the quality of the poetic that adheres to the essence of a person is completely real. Similarly, the quality of the poetic that a piece of music, a poem, or some work of art possesses is just as real as other high aesthetic values, indeed just as real as all the beauty of the second power in the realm of the visible and the audible, which only "appears" on its bearer.

Its completely real quality

It would be completely wrong to believe—like many people with a touch of philistinism—that the poetic is a lovely illusion and the poetic world of a situation a mere product of the imagination, a dream-world. No, it is completely valid, with its own special form of reality. It is not unreal, not a fairytale world: its existence is completely real and objective. Fairy tales can indeed be very poetic. But poetry, the poetic, is no fairy tale.

There are few aesthetic values that are so hard to grasp as the poetic. We must be content here with the little we have said about it; when we speak about literature and about poems in particular in the second volume of this work, we shall attempt anew to penetrate the essence of the poetic and of its bearers.

The beauty of the second power that belongs to the visible and the audible is equal in rank to the highest metaphysical beauty in terms of quality, but not in terms of the level of reality. The former, quasi-sacramental beauty only appears: it is not the radiation of an entity that is fully realized here on earth. But the poetry of particular situations has a special character, which we have called an intermediary realm between heaven and earth, because in this realm—unlike the tangible, real connections of a causal and teleological kind—there is a delicate harmony among elements that are ontologically quite independent of each other. From a "realistic" standpoint, this harmony is unreal, random, subjective; but in truth these elements in their harmony give birth to a profoundly meaningful and valuable light, to something that is objectively valid.

The striking thing about the poetic is the fact that meaningful and significant content comes into being out of the harmony between things that have no real connection, a harmony that is the utter opposite of every pragmatic link. This is why the poetic is also an antithesis to the *utile,* the "useful"; it is especially "useless."

On a beautiful night when the moon shines, the song of the nightingale in a silent valley can have a special poetry thanks to this harmony, above all if the landscape is completely uncorrupted by technological intrusions of any kind and already possesses a charm of its own. The eye of the philistine cannot recognize this connection. Typically, not only the visible and the audible collaborate: odors too can play a role here. The smell of the air, the fragrance of the blossoms and flowers, indeed even the freshness of the air which is no longer as cold as in winter, all make a contribution to the poetry of the spring, in which budding and blossoming, the beauty of the blossoms and flowers, the song of the birds, and the rustling of the brooks unite. This is that rare instance in which many senses are involved in order to ground a special aesthetic value, as we have shown in chapter 4 above.

The philistine will declare that this delicate harmony is based on sheer association. This is a grave error. There are very specific factors that make this delicate but completely objective harmony possible through their special quality. The individual factors are really present, and harmonize in our impression. They form a phenomenal unity on the object side that does not have the same reality as the individual factors but nevertheless possesses their kind of essential autonomy through its profound qualitative content. The ability to apprehend this harmony and its quality and value has nothing to do with association.

Association is a completely subjective, quasi-mechanical link, which can be utterly "wild" and meaningless. If someone hears birds singing and suddenly realizes that he has forgotten to feed his canary, this is a pure association. Naturally, there are innumerable forms of association. There are artificially acquired paths, as for example when we learn something by heart and one word, independently of its meaning, leads us on to the next. There are also sequences of images which occur all by themselves, for example, when we are falling asleep or dozing, or when the similar sound of one word suddenly diverts my thoughts away from the meaning of what I hear and toward a completely different object.

A link between various contents that is based on sheer association is as such never substantial or meaningful. It is never the bearer of a profound value, and never presents itself as something that exists on the object side independently of my own self, as a "message" of a special kind.

Certainly, an association can make some food repulsive to me. If someone speaks of something unappetizing, I can lose my appetite. An associative link between a beautiful thing and an oppressive experience in the past can depress me and prevent me from enjoying this thing. Obviously, this is completely different from the meaningful content of the poetic, which is constructed by the harmony among various elements.

An association can blur and disturb my experience of the poetic situation, but in that case I am aware that the situation objectively bore this poetic character. Similarly, a philistine can destroy my impression and my enjoyment of the poetic situation through his mere presence, and even more by his remarks. This makes it especially clear that the poetic is an objective datum: for the philistine is a "foreign body," who emanates a banal atmosphere that I experience as an annoying contrast to the poetic situation. This contrast to the poetic situation and the objective disharmony are clearly given to me. This is even more the case when the person in question is not only banal, but definitely trivial.

The phenomenon of poetry is illustrated by the crash from a poetic situation into a completely prosaic situation that is caused by an event that has a theme utterly opposed to the poetic, a theme to which one is obliged to turn.

The crash from poetry into prose in a poem is likewise very illustrative. Heinrich Heine often deliberately employed this, for example, in the following lines: "Could I but see thee once, one day, / And sink down so on my knee, / And die in thy sight while I say, / 'Lady, I love but thee!'"[1]

But it is even more important to draw attention to a false, cheap poetry, which is a much greater disvalue than all that is prosaic and banal. This pseudo-poetry presents a fatal untruth and untruthfulness, in a manner similar to the trivial, the specific antithesis to the beauty of the second power.

As we have seen, the poetic characterizes many situations which we experience. It is an aesthetic value that is not restricted to nature and art, and this means that we shall repeatedly encounter the poetic in chapter 15 below, when we study the role of beauty and the bearers of beauty in "lived life."

In what follows, we turn to the specific thematic antitheses to beauty, the forms of the un-beautiful, since it is an especial mark of beauty that there is not only one negative antithesis to it—like the evil *versus* the good, the false *versus* the true, or the stupid *versus* the clever—but three basic types.

1. Heinrich Heine, "Heimkehr," no. 25 in *Buch der Lieder*. English translation, entitled "Ad finem," by Elizabeth Barrett Browning.

CHAPTER TWELVE

The Three Antitheses to Beauty: Ugliness, Triviality, Boringness

Ugliness as the contrary opposite to every kind of beauty

THE CONTRARY opposite to metaphysical beauty, that is, to every beauty that is grounded in other values, as well as to the various levels of the beauty that appeals to the senses, is ugliness.

In the case of metaphysical beauty, this antithesis is most marked in the moral and religious sphere. The terrible ugliness of moral evil is the most typical example of this metaphysical ugliness. Indeed, we can speak of the "stench" of sin. Here we see the total contrary opposite of the exalted beauty of moral goodness. This applies all the more to the religious sphere. The monstrous ugliness of the hatred of God is the radical opposite of the transfigured beauty of all that is holy. And the ugliness of black magic, of the diabolical, is the contrary opposite of the beauty of all that is holy, of genuine miracles, of the supernatural, of the true liturgical sacrifice.

It is interesting to note the various levels of ugliness that distinguish moral evil from moral badness. The distinction between the morally bad and the morally evil is very significant and has a strong qualitative character.[1] We cannot discuss this in detail here, but we want to emphasize the new level of ugliness that evil possesses vis-à-vis badness. Evil is something monstrous.

Although the antithesis between metaphysical beauty and metaphysical ugliness emerges most clearly in the moral and religious sphere, it exists analogously in all the other value families. All the negative qualities to which we have drawn attention, such as the philistine, the mediocre, the shallow, and the ungenuine, are also bearers of a specific metaphysical ugliness that corresponds to metaphysical beauty as its opposite. This beauty constitutes by its real depth and freedom, its true greatness and genuineness, a contrary opposite to ugliness.

When one speaks of ugliness, however, one usually has in mind the opposite of the beauty that appeals to the senses, in its various levels. As long as this is only a question of the irregularity that is opposed to the most primitive beauty of form (that the triangle or the circle possesses), one cannot yet speak of "ugliness." In that case, the principal characteristic is the absence of this primitive beauty of regularity and form.

As soon as we come to a more replete, fuller beauty, however, such as the beauty of a sound as such or of a color, we encounter ugliness as the genuine antithesis of this beauty, an antithesis that stands forth clearly. This applies especially to the higher beauty that appeals to the senses but that is not yet beauty of the second power.

Ugliness resulting from a disturbance of the principle of form

In all those visible things in which a certain inner principle of form holds sway, the disruption or blurring of this principle causes a definite ugliness.[2] This principle of form varies in accordance with the morphic unity of the object.[3] Such a disruption can be distressing even in an ornament; but it is especially distressing when something has a definite "face," when

1. See my *Ethics*, chaps. 34 and 35, and my *Moralia*, chaps. 24 and 27.

2. Cf. chap. 8 of this work.

3. On this and what follows, see *What is Philosophy?* chap. 4, the section entitled, "Unities of a genuine type."

it has a real unity, a harmony of various elements, a composition. Where this is realized, the entity is beautiful. Where this is disrupted, the entity is ugly. If the nose of a human face is too small or too big, tilted upward, or crooked, the facial beauty that appeals to the senses is destroyed. The face is ugly.

As we have mentioned, a human being might have a face like the most beautiful Angora cat or a really beautiful Newfoundland dog; but the very same proportions which are bearers of beauty in these animals would not in the least ground any beauty in a human being. Since different principles of inner form are involved, something that is the realization of the principle of form, or of the "invention" in one particular morphic unity, is a disfigurement in another morphic unity.

This is often foolishly put forward as an argument for the relativity of beauty. It is asserted: "If something is not relative, then it must always and under all circumstances have the same value." This error or false concept of relativity is found not only in connection with aesthetic problems, but also in many treatises on ethics and in many discussions of moral questions. This is to confuse the question whether the value is objective and absolute—for example, whether the value is "morally good" or "beautiful" independently of human evaluations and of historical changes—with the question whether there are bearers of these values to whom or to which the values belong under all circumstances, irrespective of any specific context. There certainly do exist things that are always the bearer of a value or a disvalue, independently of every specific context. Every irreverence in relation to God is always morally bad in every context, as is every hatred of God. Every love for God, every obedience to God's commandments, every genuine *caritas* that derives from love for Christ and is planted in our soul by Him, is morally good.

However, the objectivity and absoluteness of moral value and disvalue is given even in cases where this independence of the bearer from all specific circumstances does not exist. The murder of a human being is the bearer of a terrible moral disvalue. If, however, one kills a criminal in self-defense or in order to defend a third person, this is clearly no murder, and it is at least morally unobjectionable. This does not in any way change the fact that the murder of another person is an absolute moral disvalue and always and eternally remains a moral disvalue, independently of every change of times and customs. Nor does it change the fact that the moral disvalue is something objective, no mere subjective reaction.

This fatal confusion is found when one denies that beauty possesses the character of objectivity and absoluteness, because one and the same thing can be beautiful in one particular context and ugly in another.

In the case of the pure beauty of a human face, the beauty that appeals to the senses, we have to acknowledge as very important the fulfillment that is required by the unity of the face, or the fulfillment of this immanent principle of form. The beauty of expression, which is derived from the metaphysical beauty of the character, the essence, the nature of this individual, is something completely different. Here let me emphasize only that although the face's beauty of form is indeed independent of the expressed metaphysical beauty (since it depends on factors other than those that condition the expression), the two are nevertheless intended to collaborate so closely that the pure beauty of form can become a mask in the absence of the metaphysical beauty expressed in the face.[4]

If someone looks quite stupid and dim-witted, even an extremely refined beauty of form beauty will be gravely disturbed, because it is undermined by the ugliness, by the oppressive wretchedness of the stupidity and dim-wittedness. It is a remarkable fact that the expression of stupidity, dim-wittedness, and mediocrity is even more fatal for beauty than the expression of the much worse ugliness of moral disvalue. Faces that are very beautiful in regard to visible form can have an expression of coldness, heartlessness, or evil passions. But although this disturbs the beauty of the face, the ugliness of this expression is more "juxtaposed to" the beauty of its form than is the expressed ugliness of mediocrity and stupidity. The latter undermines the beauty of form; the ugliness of the moral disvalue contradicts but does not undermine it. We say, "What a pity that this beautiful face has such an evil expression. One cannot take delight in the beauty." One feels an appalling disharmony between the beauty and the evil expression.

4. See chap. 5 in the present work.

We have seen in chapter 5 above that the expressed metaphysical beauty does not play the same role in the body as it does in the face. Through the pure beauty of form, even without metaphysical beauty, the body can attain a high immaterial beauty. We have also seen that the beauty of a human body is conditioned by the principle of form that is contained in the gestalt of the body (proportions, forms of the individual parts, color, material), and is more independent of the expressed metaphysical beauty of the qualitative values of this human person than is the face. Naturally, this does not apply to the expressed ontological value of being a human person. This value is already a decisive factor for the essence of the human body, a factor that is also present in the difference between man and woman. The beauty of the body is also dependent on this difference, that is, on the ontological value of the feminine and the masculine. The proportions that are required for the beauty of the female body would be objectionable in the male body.

The opposite of the beautiful body, its unattractiveness, is conditioned exclusively by many disproportions and infelicitous forms of the individual parts. This can cover a spectrum from an absence of beauty, via unattractiveness, all the way to a definite ugliness. The same exclusive dependence on form and proportion is not found in the human face.

The expressed metaphysical ugliness of certain disvaluable qualities such as impudence or wantonness can indeed limit the overall beauty. But whereas the expressed metaphysical beauty cannot influence the ugliness of the badly built body, the expressed metaphysical beauty of qualitative values can still bestow a high aesthetic value on the face that is ugly in terms of form and proportion.

Up to this point, we have spoken of the ugliness in the realm of the visible, which derives from the disturbance or weakening of the immanent principle of form that belongs to one particular type of essence.

The ugliness of a type (such as a toad or a hippopotamus)

There are, however, living beings whose ugliness is not based on the disruption or debilitation of a formal principle but on their form as such.

Even when everything that belongs to this type is realized to the full, there is a definite ugliness that appeals to the senses, because a formal disproportion belongs to their typical form as such. For example, a toad or a hippopotamus is ugly. We have already seen, in chapter 8 above on the levels of beauty, that this ugliness can be counterbalanced by the aesthetic value of originality and above all of "invention."

There are thus two reasons for ugliness in the realm of the beauty that appeals to the senses. First, there is the disruption of the inherent principle of form, that is, something that contradicts the intention of the invention, the meaningful, individual "face." This kind of ugliness is found when a horse is badly built, as when it has legs that are too short or a sagging back; it is also found when in a human face the nose is excessively large, the mouth is crooked, the eyes squint, the chin droops, etc.

Secondly, the essence [*Sosein*] of a species can itself be ugly. When we say that the species of cat is more beautiful than the species of toad, or that the horse is a more beautiful animal than a gorilla or a hippopotamus, the reason for the ugliness is not a disruption or failure to realize some particular principle of form, nor a contradiction of the special form of these animals, but the aesthetic quality of these forms. Certain forms are as such the bearers of an aesthetic value. They are beautiful. Other forms are as such less beautiful, or even ugly.

Many people deny that such an ugliness exists, because they proceed from the assumption that God could not have created anything ugly. Others, such as Maritain, say that this ugliness is only a subjective aspect which is limited to human beings; for angels, or indeed for God, there is nothing ugly. On the contrary, everything is beautiful. Maritain has in mind here the so-called transcendental beauty that everything that exists possesses as it exists.

For our part, we do not want to take our starting point in theories. Nor do we not want our view of that which is immediately given to be blurred by the difficulty of answering a question or solving a problem—for example, why God has created ugly things. Clearly, there is no doubt that a horse, a Newfoundland dog, a lion, or an Angora cat is beautiful, whereas a hippopotamus, a toad, or a worm is a stark antithesis to the beauty of the aforementioned animals. If we look at them with an open mind, we cannot deny that they are ugly. This does not exclude the possibility that they might make a completely different impression in a larger context, even less does it exclude that their depiction in a work of art might be beautiful. Such a depiction can possess a completely new beauty, specifically artistic beauty. It would, however, be ridiculous to assert that every animal is beautiful in its own way. No: the forms that belong to the invention of an animal and to its essential unity can be more or less beautiful; indeed, they can be definitely ugly. They may possess some other value, but this does not affect the fact that they are negative—that is, less beautiful or even definitely ugly—from the standpoint of the pure beauty that appeals to the senses. We are completely justified in saying that a horse is a more beautiful being than a giraffe, an elephant more beautiful than a camel (although the camel too is beautiful), or a Newfoundland dog or wolfhound is more beautiful than a bulldog. No one can deny this hierarchy. The factors that determine it are not the form principle that is immanent to one particular type, but much more general form principles.

We find a corresponding hierarchy (though never ugliness) in trees and flowers, although many elements in addition to the principles of form come into play here too. In the realm of animals, on the other hand, there exists not only a hierarchy of beauty, but also in fact a definite ugliness.

Triviality: the specific enemy of artistic beauty

We now turn to the second antithesis of beauty, which is the specific antithesis to beauty of the second power in the realm of art, namely, the trivial.

A melody that is kitsch is not ugly in the full and true sense of this word, nor does it possess the qualitative disvalue that characterizes ugliness on all its levels. Triviality does not utter a "no" to beauty. On the contrary, it is a fake beauty, a pseudo-beauty that is the specific antithesis to artistic beauty and plays the role in this context that evil plays in the moral universe. Although it does not "utter" the hostile, public "no" that ugliness utters to beauty, it is the specific enemy of artistic beauty. It is the *negativum*, the *maxime negativum* in the world of art. If we wish to draw a bold comparison in order to indicate the qualitative difference between ugliness and triviality, we could say that ugliness corresponds, as it were, to the negativity of physical pain, but triviality corresponds to the negativity of nausea.

Triviality also occurs in human beings. There are typically trivial people. A trivial atmosphere emanates from them, especially from the way they speak and from their gestures, from the way they express their feelings and thoughts. But the specific home of the trivial is the sphere of art. Works about philosophy can indeed be trivial, but triviality unfolds primarily in art, because beauty is thematic in art and triviality is the antithesis *par excellence* of artistic beauty.

In qualitative terms, it contains many of the disvalues we have already mentioned, such as the flat, the shallow, the cheap, the mediocre, and the philistine, in a certain analogy to the manner in which beauty—which forms a qualitative antithesis to these disvalues—contains their positive counterparts. In its quality, however, the trivial is something wholly specific, and is something new in relation to the flat, the shallow, the inauthentic, and the mediocre.

First of all, we must emphasize that the trivial must not in any way be confused with the outworn, with that which appears too often, with the cliché. This confusion is sometimes made. For example, a celebrated violinist, a man of very good taste, once said to me: "Be careful when you call a piece by Tchaikovsky trivial—for who knows what people in Bach's day would have thought of one of his themes, if every messenger boy had gone around whistling it?" This observation is completely mistaken. A passage in Shakespeare's dramas or in Goethe's *Faust* can never become trivial merely because it has become a well-known saying. Bach's *Air* can never become trivial, even if the radio uses it to fill the space between programs or uses it in commercials. We feel indeed that this is a desecration, and our heart bleeds; but the indestructible nobility of the words or the music remains untouched. Neither the prosaic circumstances nor the frequent inappropriate repetition can ever turn an inherent glorious beauty into something trivial. Let us take the example of the old Austrian national anthem, *Gott erhalte Franz, den Kaiser*, with Haydn's glorious melody, and the indescribable beauty of the variations on this theme in his "Emperor Quartet." This melody possesses a chaste dignity. As a national anthem (especially with the original text), it was characterized by a calm, humble solemnity free of all embarrassing nationalism. The melody as such could never be made trivial by the words of Hoffmann von Fallersleben, *Deutschland, Deutschland über alles*, with their nationalistic, arrogant tone, even when it was bawled out and became an expression of brutal force instead of humble emotion. It was treated trivially and shouted out by trivial people, but the melody as such always remained the opposite of trivial.

The use of a beautiful theme from a symphony as a symbol of something else, even something noble (for example, the beginning of Beethoven's fifth symphony as the symbol of the victory of the Allies over the Axis) leads to a continual repetition of the theme. But although such a repetition in season and out of season, and the uprooting of a theme from its original context, are irritating, this does not make the theme itself trivial. Nor can the deficient presentation of the theme turn something that is truly beautiful into something trivial. Such a desecration is profoundly regrettable, but it cannot affect the beauty of the piece of music as such.

In the "potpourri" which was popular some years ago, a noble piece of music was often juxtaposed to a trivial piece. This too was a desecration, but it did not make the beautiful piece trivial. I once sat in my room and heard a potpourri from the restaurant below, where the glorious theme from Handel's *Judas Maccabaeus* ("Hail the conquering hero!") was immediately followed by the "Weibermarsch" ("Ah, the women, the women!") from Lehár's *Merry Widow*. A tremendous shock! But the contrast only underlined the antithesis between the nobility of Handel's theme and the triviality of the "Weibermarsch."

Triviality is thus mostly a quality of a "work of art" and must certainly not be confused with something worn out or something that has been heard too often. One tires of insignificant works when they are repeated frequently, even though they are not trivial but are just relatively devoid of content. They can no longer unfold their modest charm, and seem hackneyed. This, however, is not a characteristic quality of these pieces of music; and it is very important to note that they do not thereby become trivial, nor do they strike us as trivial. The hackneyed quality is qualitatively completely different from triviality.

On the other hand, triviality is often a presupposition of the popularity of hit songs. They appeal to a shallow popular quality, and the purpose of their existence is to fill the air for a certain time and to play a specific social role. Wilhelm Furtwängler points this out in his fine book *Ton und Wort*,[5] when he says that one meets everyone in a hit song, so to speak, but in a completely peripheral and often ambiguous stratum of experiencing. This popularity is an essential characteristic of hit songs; an unpopular hit song is a stillborn child. But hit songs always have a very short life, here today and gone tomorrow. Usually they are trivial, and their triviality intensifies their success. However, they certainly need not be trivial, and it would be incorrect to equate their character as hit songs with triviality.

After clearing away these misunderstandings from our path, let us return to the analysis of the trivial.

The four different types of triviality

Triviality occurs in qualitatively different types. First of all, it can have a specifically mawkish, sentimental note, like the famous song of farewell in the opera *The Trumpeter of Sackingen*: "The Lord bless you and keep you! It would have been too beautiful—The Lord bless you and keep you! It was not meant to be!" The words by Joseph Victor von Scheffel are just as trivial as the melody by Victor Nessler. This is a "classic" example of maudlin triviality. Another typical example is the Austrian poet, composer, and writer Thomas Koschat.

5. Wilhelm Furtwängler, *Ton und Wort* (Wiesbaden: Brockhaus, 1954), the 1939 lecture "Anton Bruckner," 114.

Unfortunately, there are also pious hymns which possess this mawkish triviality, for example, *Mein Jesus, gute Nacht* ("My Jesus, good night!"), and above all those kitsch devotional pictures which became popular in the nineteenth century, were very widespread in the first half of the twentieth century, but were very different from the beautiful devotional pictures of works from the fourteenth to the seventeenth centuries.

A second variety of the trivial is the vivacious, showy, boisterous triviality. A typical example is the "Weibermarsch" in *The Merry Widow*: "Yes, the study of women is difficult!" This zestful, vibrant triviality possesses a pseudo-power and plays a significant role in operettas, for example, in "Yes, this married life is getting chic, in the Parisian style!" in *The Merry Widow*. This triviality is often accompanied by a certain brilliance. It can bear witness to great talents in the composer; it can hit the nail on the head and be successful. For example, some passages in Bizet's powerful opera *Carmen* are not free of this kind of triviality, and we find it in a cruder manner in Mascagni's *Cavalleria rusticana* and in Leoncavallo's *Bajazzo*. Many naturalistic paintings from the end of the nineteenth century and the beginning of the twentieth possess this triviality and strike an embarrassing, impudent, shameless note.

A third variety is the triviality that is linked to the quality of the mediocre, the bourgeois, the "cute." It is found, for example, in short stories or novels which put forward a conventional bourgeois morality in a tendentious manner or promote a "loyal warmheartedness" [*treuherzige Gemütlichkeit*] in which everything is small-scale and harmless. This is the oppressive triviality of the gnomes or colored glass balls that some people install in their gardens. It is also found in literature, music, and the visual arts.

Finally, there is a fourth form of triviality that characterizes shallow, cheap arguments, for example, in novels where the "space" in which the entire work is set is filled by a shallow spirit, or in short stories where a collection of platitudes determine the atmosphere of the whole, and especially in works that have a tendency to spread false and specifically shallow philosophical ideas. Even when the ideas themselves are not shallow, this triviality can characterize such works through a cheap, tendentious effect. One example of this is Ibsen's drama *The Pillars of Society.* This kind of triviality is also found in music when an effect is achieved through trivial means or when the development of a melody has a specifically cheap, shallow character.

In all these various types of the trivial, we encounter the character of pseudo-beauty. This is why the trivial is never prosaic in the sense that we have set out above as the first possible meaning of "prosaic," namely, that which is completely unartistic. But the trivial pretends to be beautiful. In its pseudo-beauty, it is specifically anti-artistic.

The specifically ugly is not trivial. Not even the monstrous is trivial. As we have already said, monstrous ugliness is the specific antithesis of metaphysical beauty and of the beauty that appeals to the senses, whereas the trivial is the antithesis of artistic beauty, this special type of beauty of the second power.

When we speak of triviality's claim to be beautiful, we do not mean the intention of the author of a trivial work, but rather the pseudo-beauty proper to the trivial work and the claim that the quality of triviality always contains, namely, the claim to be at least a positive aesthetic value as opposed to ugliness. Usually the artist also intends to create a genuine work of art and something that is genuinely beautiful.

The triviality here can be the result of the artist's lack of talent. He ends up producing something trivial, although this was certainly not his intention. Often the artist confuses genuine beauty with triviality and believes that his trivial pieces of music, plays, or pictures are beautiful.

But sometimes triviality is the conscious aim for the sake of the intended effect on the masses, who enjoy the trivial and react to it with particular intensity. This is the case with hit songs and with many operettas. The author is perhaps aware that this music is trivial; he will scarcely believe that it is beautiful in the sense of genuine art. But he possesses a special talent for the trivial, and what counts for him is success with the masses.

This is why we must draw a clear distinction between two types of trivial products. In the first type, the trivial goes hand in hand with a weak talent. The artist aims at a great, noble beauty, and he may be an admirer of the great masters; but his lack of talent means that all he produces is trivial poetry, music, or paintings.

The other type of trivial products is linked to a powerful gift—but a gift for the creation of trivial music, poems, plays, or paintings. In this case, the triviality is intensive, successful, and well constructed, and it hits the nail on the head. On the one hand, therefore, we have the triviality of weak, unsuccessful products; and on the other hand, we have the triviality of successful products in which the trivial effect is achieved with great verve. These are brilliant and give evidence of a particular talent, though only for the trivial. This is the case with brilliant operettas and successful hit songs. In this sphere, where the trivial has been the intention of composers since Lehár (unlike the operettas of Offenbach, or of Johann Strauss and some of his successors), there exists the antithesis between weak and strong, between successful and unsuccessful.

Human ways of relating to triviality

It is important to note the following. Not all trivial people enjoy only trivial things, that is, not all of them lack artistic taste. On the other hand, even sublime persons who are utterly untrivial often admire trivial things, because they lack an artistic sense.

We must distinguish three possible cases. First, there is the trivial person who enjoys only the trivial. He is attracted only by the trivial and has no understanding for true art. Secondly, there is the one who is indeed trivial as a human being, but has a special understanding of art which leads him to react strongly to genuine art and not to take any particular interest in the trivial. I have known very trivial people who had a good taste in music. When I once listened with one of them to a symphony by Bruckner, he made an utterly trivial face at one particularly beautiful passage, in order to draw my attention to the beauty.

Thirdly, there are people who are utterly untrivial as personalities and whose essence irradiates a sublime poetry—yet they do not notice the trivial, nor do they reject it. One example is Saint Thérèse of Lisieux, who was very naïve in the field of art and thus was able to have a very special admiration for the ghastly tombs in the cemetery in Milan.

Here, however, we must draw another important distinction, between those who enjoy triviality and are indeed moved with enthusiasm by it, and other persons who approach the work of art with a non-aesthetic attitude and therefore do not even notice the triviality. It is easy for those whose interest in art is limited to the object depicted—whether they are concerned only with the human significance of the object depicted or with its historical significance—to overlook the triviality of a work of art.

This was the case with Saint Thérèse of Lisieux. She was touched by the cemetery in Milan because the sufferings of the deceased, the operations they had endured, the pains taken by the surgeon, etc., were depicted so drastically and naturalistically. She was impressed by the sufferings of the deceased, by the surgeon's endeavor to save their lives, by the distress of the mourners, and by the religious content of the crucifix or the angel depicted on the tombs. She did not come into contact at all with the tremendous triviality that these graves display from the artistic standpoint, with their tastelessness, brutal naturalism, and lack of every artistic transposition. She overlooked all this. But this is an exception. Generally, we find a great triviality in the personality of those who get enthusiastic about trivial things.

Trivial people of this kind are usually very shallow in their thoughts, and cheap and mediocre in their emotional lives. We encounter in them the different varieties of triviality that we have already mentioned, especially the two principal types, namely, the mawkishly sentimental type and the brash, arrogant, shameless type.

It would be interesting to undertake a study of trivial words and expressions. Doubtless, many people simply adopt them from the milieu in which they live. They employ words such as "super" or "swell" as a matter of habit when they want to express their enthusiasm over great works of art. Often they are the victims of their milieu, and they do not themselves sense the triviality of these expressions; they need not be trivial in their emotional and intellectual life. But there are many people who employ trivial expressions because they enjoy them. In that case, they are trivial in their inner life too.

A trivial person can be described accurately in a work of art. But he is not only called by his right name; he is "translated" into the work of art with the distance that belongs to a genuine work of art, in such a way that it itself does not contain any trace of triviality. We shall speak of this in detail in the second volume of this work when we look at the important theme of artistic transposition.

There is nothing trivial in nature. No animal can ever be trivial, still less a plant or a rock.

Although the trivial in human beings is repulsive and has great disvalue, it is not the antithesis to metaphysical beauty in human beings. This triviality is indeed completely incompatible with metaphysical beauty, but it is metaphysical ugliness that is the primordial antithesis [*Urantithese*] of metaphysical beauty. This is because the primordial antithesis to good in the moral sphere is evil and badness, and these are the bearers of metaphysical ugliness. In art, on the other hand, the trivial is the primordial antithesis of the artistic beauty of the second power.

The boring as the third antithesis to beauty

A third antithesis to beauty is the boring. It is less specifically opposed to beauty than are the ugly and the trivial. It is primarily an opposite of the entertaining, on the one hand, and of that which is rich in content [*das Gehaltvolle*], on the other. Further, it does not contain the "no" of the ugly, the character that is hostile to beauty, nor the specifically contrary character of the trivial that allows us to compare the opposition between the trivial and artistic beauty with the opposition between good and evil in the moral sphere. Instead, the boring, in contrast to all that is rich in content, is also an opposite of the beautiful, and especially of the beauty of the second power. Let me emphasize from the outset that the antithesis of the boring to beauty, as antithesis, has a different character from the antithesis of the ugly or of the trivial to beauty.

The boring is not a simple absence of beauty, like the completely neutral (which is neither beautiful nor ugly). A washing machine is certainly not beautiful, but it need not be ugly; however, it is meaningless to call it boring. The boring is not only a lack of beauty but a qualitative disvalue *sui generis*, and a pronounced disvalue at that.

It is a quality found in various areas in which beauty is not in any way thematic. If one thinks of the phenomenon of the boring, one does not think immediately of the antithesis to beauty. One speaks of boring persons, social get-togethers, or lectures, of boring books about history or philosophy. The positive opposite of the boring is the interesting or the amusing, that which is attractive in some form or other.

The quality of the boring is found in our own experience. Something bores us, whether a piece of work, an activity, a long wait. It also occurs as a pure state of consciousness. If someone says, "I am bored," he is referring to one particular experience that does not include an intentional "aboutness" (like joy or irritation about something), but is meaningful as a pure statement about the state of his soul. Similarly, it does not necessarily include being affected by something. It can be the consequence of having nothing to do, being empty, as it were, and left to one's own devices. There is nothing that occupies, affects, attracts and stimulates, or interests one. This experience of emptiness is something highly negative that belongs to the category of unpleasant experiences, although it is not negative in the sense of that which is painful or causes suffering. It is not the pure, contrary antithesis to joy, to all positive experiences. It is not negative in a "positive" sense. On the other hand, it is not simply the absence of all pleasant or joyful experiences. It has a definite quality of its own. The painful, the profoundly distressing, is just as remote from all that is boring, every bit as much opposed to it, as the joyful and the profoundly delightful. Both of these represent an antithesis to the experience of boredom. The quality of boredom contains an element of the *horror vacui*, the "abhorrence of total emptiness."

This negativity *sui generis* is found both in the concrete state of being bored, in the intellectual boredom from which some people suffer and that darkens their attitude to the world and makes everything seem a matter of indifference, and also in the experience that we express when we say of something, "It bores me." This always involves a personal experience, a mental entity, something consciously lived through, or something that consciously exists. But if we say of a book, a piece of music, or another person that it or he is boring, we clearly have in mind a quality of the book, the piece of music, or the person, rather than something that consciously exists, an experience in our own self. This, at any rate, is our intention when we predicate boring of something. We mean a pure quality when we say that something is beautiful, not an experience that really takes place in our own consciousness.

Naturally, many people will say, "Nothing is ever boring in its own right; it rather generates boredom in us. The affirmation that ascribes boringness to the object as a quality of it is only an inexact manner of expression. In reality, the propositions 'It bores me' and 'It is boring' have the same meaning. Only the first proposition is the correct expression of the real state-of-affairs."

We have examined in chapters 1 and 7 above all the desperate attempts at the subjectivization of beauty, and we have refuted them. We have also seen that it is completely inappropriate, when we speak of the joyfulness of the radiant blue sky or immediately apprehend this joyfulness, to reduce this joyfulness to an effect that is made upon ourselves and to declare that the proposition "The blue sky has a joyful quality about it" is equivalent to saying, "The blue sky makes us feel joyful." We have also seen that the joyfulness of the blue sky is not an "experienced," "felt" joy, and that no one who speaks of the joyful sky intends thereby to affirm the absurd idea that the impersonal blue sky feels joy. What is involved is, instead, an objective quality of joyfulness that is not, as in our own experience of joy, a personal entity, something that consciously exists, but is a pure quality of the blue sky.

Having seen the distinction between the experience of joy and the joyfulness of the blue sky, we must now ask: We have seen the distinction between the experience of joy and the joyfulness of the blue sky. Does the same distinction apply to the experienced boredom, which is something that exists consciously, and the quality of the things that we call boring, such as the boring book or piece of music?

In principle, we certainly find the same distinction. There exists an objective quality of the boring that characterizes something and that is ontologically different from being bored, from the experience of boredom. The qualitative relationship between being bored and the boring book may perhaps not be so strict as in the case of joyfulness; there may perhaps also exist a certain qualitative difference.

At any rate, there is a meaningful, objective predication of boringness that characterizes a thing as such, and is independent of the fact that it bores us. This is not meant as a denial of the fact that the objectively boring usually bores us, nor as an affirmation that there exists no meaningful relationship between the objective boringness and our being bored. When something that is objectively boring bores us, this is the objectively correct and meaningful effect. But it is not boring *only* because it bores us. The objective boringness is definitely distinct from this effect on us. It belongs objectively to a thing, independently of us.

We can see this clearly in cases where it is obvious that we mean the effect on us. If one person says, "Bridge bores me," and another says, "Bridge fascinates me, it is my passion," this is not meant in any way as a description of the game, but refers only to the effect on a person. If someone says in general terms that music means nothing to him, that it bores him, this is only a statement about its effect on him. Even if he formulates this in the assertion "Music is boring," it is clear in this generalization that he is not speaking of a characteristic of music, but saying only that it does not mean anything to him.

If, however, someone who has a deep understanding of music, someone in whose life good music plays a large and important role, says of one particular piece of music, "This is boring, unlike some other particular piece of music," he doubtless intends to state that this piece is objectively weak and that its content is poor. He refers to a characteristic of the piece of music as such, not to an effect on him. Whether his affirmation is correct and does justice to the piece of music, is another question.

In which areas is the objective predication of boringness a possibility? It is meaningless to say that a tree or an animal is boring. In the case of animals, we can say, for example, that they are beautiful, less beautiful, or ugly

—but not that they are objectively boring. Someone can remark that botany or zoology bores him, or that he has no interest in animals; but it would be meaningless to declare that a species of animal is boring. In a remote, analogous sense, however, when we are speaking of a higher animal—of one particular individual horse, and even more of a dog—one can say that it is boring if one uses this word to mean devoid of temperament or sluggish.

It is possible to say meaningfully that a landscape is boring in the broader sense, that is, that it is vacuous from the standpoint of beauty and that its atmosphere lacks all charm. Sometimes the fact that a landscape does not possess either a true, rich "face" or a specific individuality can also give rise to boredom. In some regions we find only anonymous places that constitute a pure, faceless juxtaposition, so that no landscape in the full sense of the word is formed. Here boredom emerges as the clear antithesis of beauty. The comparison between a beautiful landscape, like the view of Lake Geneva from Lausanne or Vevey, and the boringness of the region around Gander in Newfoundland allows us to apprehend the contrast clearly.

As we have mentioned, the quality of boringness is found in typical average persons whose personality is not intellectually interesting and possesses no kind of charm or originality, nor any kind of humor. We find such persons much more frequently among the highly educated than among simple persons of a people, persons whose healthy common sense has not yet been distorted by false, shallow, stupid theories, and whose classic relationship to life has not yet been disturbed. The half-educated person is most at risk of being boring. Above all, the conventional person who lives on the basis of public opinion and who is not a "self" in Kierkegaard's sense, who is an anonymous human being, is boring. Needless to say, by being boring he need not bore himself.

But the boring person need not bore us either. There exist persons who are objectively very boring, persons about whom one must laugh a great deal, because they can be laughable in many respects, though of course they themselves do not know this, nor do they possess any sense of humor. But this is an exception. Usually, the traits in them that make us laugh are accompanied by a certain originality that at least keeps them from being wholly boring.

A person as person is, however, never boring. As soon as we penetrate in genuine love of neighbor through to the awe-inspiring greatness of every immortal soul that is called by God and must give account of itself before God, the entire quality of boringness is left behind. This quality can belong only to the qualitative individual particularity of a human being, to all that he has made out of himself. But as soon as the greatness that adheres to him ontologically as a person breaks through, as soon as we see him as *imago Dei* and in the light of his eternal destiny, the quality of the boring can never characterize him. As soon as a boring person profoundly repents of a fault or converts to God, he ceases to be boring.

Similarly, a villain is not boring. His moral disvalue is incomparably worse, deeper, and more thematic than boringness. In a human being the latter is a secondary disvalue that never characterizes his ultimate stratum. It never touches the nerve of his *raison d'être* and his destiny. The disvalue of moral mediocrity is revolting; it is a mendacious compromise that contains a terrible insult to God, comparable to the compromise entailed by a "grandiose" crime. It is true that this mediocrity can make a person boring when compared to an Iago (in Shakespeare's *Othello*) or a Rakitin (in Dostoevsky's *Brothers Karamazov*), but this is irrelevant in comparison to the moral disvalue and insignificant in comparison to the metaphysical ugliness that belongs to everything that is evil.

It is of course possible for boringness to exist in a person not only to varying degrees, but also in various strata of the person. Someone can be boring because he does everything very slowly, speaks and understands very slowly; but this need not be true of this person as a whole. It is perfectly possible for him not to be boring as a result of his achievements in various fields or of his unconventional awkwardness. A pedant is boring if his pedantry takes hold of him as soon as the appropriate occasion arises; otherwise, however, he may perfectly well be the opposite of boring thanks to the power of his intellect or to his sense of humor.

The specific quality of the boring unfolds most genuinely and thematically in human works. A philosophical book can be definitely boring when it devotes considerable space to the detailed repetition of commonplaces and truisms. It can be boring through its length and the dryness of its presentation, through its verbosity, continual repetitions, etc. This is a very grave disadvantage, a great disvalue. But in comparison to the question whether the work contains true or false assertions, this is merely a secondary disvalue.

Some philosophical books are full of errors and platitudes, and are also very boring. Others, while not asserting anything that is false, are boring because of their verbosity and repetitions, and because of the weakness of the arguments they adduce for propositions that are indeed true, but have actually already been discovered. From the philosophical standpoint, however, these books are a thousand times preferable to brilliant, intellectually stimulating systems which are profoundly false.

As soon as we enter the sphere of art, boringness becomes a central thematic error, a specific antithesis to the artistic beauty of the second power. In literature, painting, sculpture, and music, boringness offends the *raison d'être* of a work of art. It is indeed true that the boring does not have the poisonous character of the trivial; it is not so "positively" negative. But it would be better if the boring novel, drama, picture, or piece of music had never been "born."

This brings us to the important concluding observation that there are two fundamental antitheses to the value of a work of art, namely, triviality—pseudo-beauty, which is the "evil" in art, so to speak—and the weak, the empty, the boring, that which is devoid of substantial content. The ugly, which is the primordial antithesis to metaphysical beauty and to the pure beauty that appeals to the senses, is not a specific antithesis in art, at least as far as the beauty of the second power in art is concerned.

In the second volume of this work, we shall return to the quality of the boring when we discuss the difference between the depth and the perfection of a work of art.

CHAPTER THIRTEEN

Thematic and Unthematic Bearers of Beauty

We have spoken of metaphysical beauty and of its hierarchy, which goes hand in hand with the hierarchy of the other values or with the depth and significance of a truth. This is perfectly natural, since this beauty of the *splendor veri* is the fragrance, the irradiation, of other values.

We have mentioned the cases in which we apprehend this metaphysical beauty: in every intellectual vision, in every kind of intuitive apprehending of the goods that bear these non-aesthetic values. When, for example, we read Plato's *Apologia* or a biography of Saint Francis of Assisi, and the natural moral values of Socrates or the supernatural moral values of Saint Francis stand before our inner eye and perhaps touch our hearts, then we also understand the specific beauty of the figure of Socrates, which is the splendor of his moral values, or the specific beauty of the holiness of Saint Francis.

But metaphysical beauty can also manifest itself in the sphere of the visible, thanks to the significant phenomenon of expression (in the precise sense of this word). And even taking expression in a much wider and looser sense, we find an intuitive givenness of metaphysical beauty in the world of the visible.

Similarly, we have spoken of the beauty of visible and audible data, which, unlike metaphysical beauty, are not the reflection of other values but adhere directly to visible or audible entities: to a color or a sound, to the form of an object, to a melody, etc. Here the relationship between the beauty and its bearer is quite different.

We also make a distinction between the qualitatively more primitive beauty, of which Saint Thomas says, *quod visum placet* ("that which gives pleasure when it is seen") and which, although grounded in its own way, is nevertheless qualitatively inferior both to metaphysical beauty and to the mystery of quasi-sacramental beauty, which we have also called the beauty of the second power, where a sublime immaterial beauty that is qualitatively related to the highest metaphysical beauty appears in visible and audible entities.

The thematic presence of beauty in art, in contrast with its unthematic presence in the philosophical and religious sphere

Now we wish to discuss a completely different important distinction in the realm of beauty, namely, between objects where beauty is thematic and objects where it is not thematic. This distinction relates to the objects, that is, to the bearers of beauty, not to beauty itself or its quality.

In a play, beauty, more exactly specifically artistic beauty, is the theme. Although the moral values of the *dramatis personae* have a significant function for the beauty of the play, and although the moral nobility of Cordelia in Shakespeare's *King Lear* or the moral greatness of Leonora's fidelity in Beethoven's *Fidelio* moves us deeply, the meaning, the *raison d'être*, the theme of these works is artistic beauty.

In Plato's *Phaedo*, on the other hand, the theme is truth. The great metaphysical beauty of this work lies primarily in its truth, in the depth and nobility of its truth. The beauty of the style, the mode of expression, has a purely ancillary function: it is not the theme. Anyone who saw only this beauty, without being in any way interested in the question of the truth, would also be blind to the essential beauty of the *Phaedo*. He could no longer see this, since this beauty cannot be detached from truth: it is indeed a *splendor veri*. All that would remain would be a stylistic beauty that cannot be compared to this sublime beauty of truth. A reader who was interested only in the beauty of the *Phaedo* would utterly fail to do justice to Plato. He would not take him seriously. He would misunderstand the meaning and the *raison d'être* of the *Phaedo* and would bypass the meaning of this work, so to speak, without comprehending it. He would behave like someone who was asked about a lecture on philosophical questions that he had heard, and who answered that the speaker had a pleasant voice. He would also fail to recognize the true beauty of the form and the style of the *Phaedo*, since this cannot be detached from the adequacy that it possesses as the expression of these particular truths. But as soon as one ceases to perceive form and style in their ancillary function, one can no longer do justice to their real beauty.

This applies even more strongly to sacred scripture, the Old and the New Testaments. There can be no doubt that scripture possesses a most sublime beauty. But its theme is not beauty, but truth: the divine, revealed truth. Its beauty is the *splendor divinae sanctae veritatis*, "the splendor of the divine sacred truth." I can apprehend this beauty only if I approach sacred scripture thirsting for divine revelation, in utter reverence and religious devotion. As soon as I prescind from the question of truth and read scripture like a work of art, my eye is blinded to this sacred beauty. Its form is supremely beautiful because of its adequacy as the expression, the narration, the formulation of these sacred facts. If I were to say, "I am not interested in whether the resurrection of Christ actually took place. But the narrative is so beautiful—I regard it purely as a work of art," I would completely misunderstand sacred scripture and fail to recognize its essence and meaning. My behavior would be blasphemous, and I would blind myself completely to the true sacred beauty of scripture. Nor would it any longer be possible to apprehend even the beauty of its form, the unique sacred solemnity of its language and mode of expression, its exact appropriateness to the content, to the divine revelation. As soon as the beauty is detached from the content and from the truth of this content, from the authentic divine revelation, it too is bereft of its soul.

The difference between thematic and unthematic beauty is independent of its quality and its hierarchical rank

We must draw a clear distinction between the question whether or not the beauty of an object is thematic and the question of the rank that its beauty possesses. An object in which beauty is not thematic, for example, the Gospel, can be a bearer of the highest beauty. Even when this bearer is more beautiful than all works of art, its beauty nevertheless remains unthematic. On the other hand, beauty is the theme in a modest work of art—a comedy by Goldoni, or Eichendorff's *Life of a Good-for-Nothing*—although this is a modest beauty, much less sublime than the beauty of the *Phaedo.*

The difference between thematic and unthematic is related neither to the quality of the beauty nor to the place that one particular beauty occupies in the hierarchy of the beautiful, but to the question whether or not the beauty is the meaning, the *raison d'être* of an object. The sublime beauty of the personality of a saint is not the theme, not the *raison d'être* of this person; rather, it is his holiness, his moral and religious value, that are thematic. The beauty is a glorious epiphenomenon, a superabundant extra gift. When we say that it is an epiphenomenon, we do not mean that it is something unessential, still less that it is something accidental. On the contrary, this beauty is highly significant and an essential element in the sense that the link between this most sublime metaphysical beauty and the moral and religious value is an essentially necessary link. This beauty is the fragrance, the irradiation, the *splendor* of holiness. But for this reason, the destiny of the human person is not exactly to be a bearer of this beauty, but to glorify God by becoming holy. The beauty that he thereby displays is a glorious extra gift—but one that is indissolubly linked to holiness. In a work of art, on the other hand, the beauty is the theme, the *raison d'être.*

At first sight, the difference between unthematic and thematic could be confused with that between the metaphysical beauty that is a reflection of other values, and the beauty of the second power that appears immediately in visible and audible things, such as Giorgione's *Pastoral Concert* or Handel's *Largo*. This confusion is caused by the fact that the character of the superabundant in the sense of an "extra gift," which is a mark of metaphysical beauty, is repeated in unthematic beauty. But such a confusion would be a great error. The difference between metaphysical beauty and beauty of the second power is related to the way in which beauty is grounded: in the former case we have a reflection of other values; in the latter case the beauty is mysteriously determined by certain visible or audible elements. In the one case the beauty inheres fully in the bearer, because the moral, "intellectual," and other values are embodied in it, because they elevate the bearer as a real entity and bestow a new preciousness on it; but in the other case, the beauty only "appears" in these ontologically modest visible and audible bearers, which have rather the character of a pedestal and which are not raised up into a higher spiritual sphere by the glory of the beauty.

Only the person who apprehends the artistic beauty in a work of art can also understand the metaphysical beauty of the morality of the figures that make their appearance in this work of art, and of their ethos. As soon as one approaches a work of art in the same way as one approaches a textbook (where the theme is learning), or a philosophical work (where the theme is truth), or the Bible (where the theme is God's revelation), one fails to do justice to the work of art. One must take one's stance before the work of art as a work of art, respect its immanent theme of beauty, and apprehend it with the aesthetic organ. Only then will the moral or religious ethos of the work of art (if indeed it has such an ethos) also be effective as a theme.

This applies only in an analogous manner to works which are entirely at the service of liturgical worship. When a Mass by Mozart is performed during the celebration of the Holy Mass, the theme is naturally only the Eucharist, only the sacrifice of Christ and Holy Communion. The only task of the music is to draw our soul more deeply into this mystery. But the fulfillment of this task presupposes its beauty. If, on the other hand, the same work is performed as a concert, the theme is its beauty, its sacred beauty.

We have seen how many spiritual value qualities are included in the beauty of the second power of a work of art. In the second volume of this work, when we speak of art, we shall return to this matter. We will see that the artistic beauty of the second power contains in itself such a tremendous seriousness that the fullness and depth of its value (albeit in varied gradation) presupposes a special attitude. The one who approaches a work of art with an aestheticist attitude is every bit as unobjective as the one who approaches it from non-aesthetic perspectives.

Beings with unthematic beauty, beings with exclusively thematic beauty, and those with two themes of equal rank (for example, architecture)

There are beings whose beauty is not thematic. There are others whose beauty is indeed a significant theme, but exists alongside another theme that is equally significant. Such a being thus has two themes, which are distinct in principle and are juxtaposed with one another, so to speak, although they can be connected in a very significant manner. And finally, there are entities whose only theme is their beauty.

One example of the first case is a morally good deed. Its exclusive theme is its moral value. Its great metaphysical beauty is superabundant, although it is not thematic in any way.

One example of a being with two themes is an architectural structure. It has an elementary theme of a practical nature, such as serving as a residential dwelling, a palace for great events of state, a temple, a mosque, or a church for liturgical actions. These buildings also have beauty as a significant theme. In the second volume of this work, when we discuss architecture as a genre of art, we shall speak in greater detail of the relationship between the two themes. Here we are interested only in the fact that there are objects where beauty is indeed thematic, but not exclusively so: these objects have two themes equal in rank, and one of these themes is beauty.

Another example of an entity with two themes is the sphere of the applied arts. When we discuss this in the second volume, we will see that the two themes do not always have the same rank. One theme can be much more significant, but not in such a way that it excludes the other. Some things are primarily useful, yet beauty constitutes a genuine specific theme in them; in other things, beauty is the main theme, with another specific, independent theme existing alongside it.

In a work of art—a poem, short story, novel, play, symphony, quartet, opera, or a song, painting, sculpture—only beauty is thematic. But there are also artistic things that, like architecture, have two themes. The first theme of a Requiem or a polyphonic Mass, for example, the Requiem of Verdi or of Mozart, or Beethoven's *Missa solemnis*, is purely religious; at the same time, however, these are works of art whose theme is beauty.

Relations between thematic and unthematic beauty in works of art

We must affirm that the beauty of an object in which this beauty is not thematic can be a beauty of the highest rank. We must also see clearly that something in which beauty is not thematic—for example, a moral deed in a novel or a play—assumes an ancillary function for the total beauty of the work through its unthematic beauty, which contributes to the thematic beauty of the novel or play. This makes the unthematic beauty indirectly thematic. This is one of the most significant relationships between unthematic metaphysical beauty and thematic artistic beauty.

Another such relationship is the beauty, as such unthematic, of the character of a human being or the quality of his grief or joy, which manifests itself through expression in the sphere of the visible and the audible, and then contributes something to the thematic beauty of a work of art, such as a portrait, a bust, or a musical work. Here too the expressed metaphysical beauty is incorporated into a being whose explicit theme is artistic beauty. This significant interweaving of expressed metaphysical beauty (in whose bearer beauty is not the theme) with the artistic beauty of the work of art (whose beauty is thematic) is very important in the visual arts, and even more so in music.

This relationship is completely different from the way in which the non-artistic beauty of visible things in nature (for example, the beauty of a human form or of a horse, mountain, or tree), works in a painting as a bearer of artistic beauty (though certainly not the only bearer or the major bearer). For example, the perfect beauty of the body of Giorgione's *Venus*, which could also occur in nature, is an essential element in the work of art and contributes to the completely new kind of artistic beauty. What is involved here, however, is not so much the transition from unthematic to thematic beauty, but rather the function that a beauty of nature can have for artistic beauty. This problem concerns the relationship of the beauty of that which is portrayed to the beauty of the work of art, or in other words, the significance in the work of art of the beauty of that which is portrayed. We shall return to this topic in detail in the second volume, in the chapter about matter and form in art.

Also different is the relationship between bearers of a more primitive beauty—the beauty of colors, sounds, of the material in sculpture and architecture—to the much more sublime artistic beauty of the whole work. The ancillary function of the more primitive beauty vis-à-vis the lofty beauty of the work of art is in the foreground, and the difference between thematic and unthematic beauty recedes into the background. This involves the general problem of the means which are important for the beauty of the work of art in the individual areas of art, and which are available to the artist for the shaping of one particular work of art. By "means" we refer to all those elements that contribute to the beauty of the work of art. We shall discuss this problem in detail in the second volume, when we speak individually of the various arts. They can be discussed only separately, since each art involves different means.

We mention these last two kinds of relationships only in order to demarcate them from the question of the thematic and unthematic bearers of beauty and of their mutual relationship.

The theme and goal [Zweck] of a work of art.
The error of the thesis "Art for art's sake"

When we emphasize that beauty, or the aesthetic, is the theme in a work of art, this must not be confused with the celebrated principle of *l'art pour l'art* ("art for art's sake"). This principle uproots the work of art from every ancillary function with regard to other goals. It demands that the artist have no motivation in the creation of his work other than to produce something artistic. This goes in a completely different direction from what we mean when we formulate the thesis that artistic beauty is the theme of the work of art.

We must draw a distinction between the theme of an object and its goal. The theme of a philosophical work is the statement of the truth and the objectivization of what one has come to know. Besides this, the motivation of the author is to disclose this truth to other people, and the objective goal of the work is to communicate this truth.

The work of art doubtless has the goal of uplifting people, making them happy, enriching them. But its theme is beauty, and it can truly serve its goal only when this theme is realized. It is not difficult to see the difference between goal and theme. The principle of *l'art pour l'art* contains the assertion that the work of art must not serve any other goal, whereas our thesis (namely, that beauty is the theme in the work of art) does not detach the work of art from serving other goods.

Clearly, when we draw this distinction between theme and goal, we do not have in mind works of art with two main themes that are organically linked, as in architecture. We are not thinking of a second theme, but of another good that the work of art serves in a superabundant manner.

In the thesis of *l'art pour l'art*, on the other hand, the intention is to exclude this superabundant service on the part of the work of art, both in the motivation of the artist and in his work. We are told that a work of art may not have any ancillary goal and that ultimately the artist must create the work of art for its own sake. This is a typical case where attention is drawn to something true, and a justified protest is made against non-artistic and unartistic themes—but the critic overshoots the mark and asserts something false.

The autonomy of the work of art, the wholly specific conditions on which its value and beauty depend, and the fact that beauty is the theme in the work of art, do not in the least prevent a special service of something else from also being present in many works of art; nor do they prevent this goal from playing a significant role in the motivation that prompts the creation of the work of art, or indeed from contributing to the artist's inspiration. This is particularly the case in painting and sculpture, as well as in sacred poetry and music. But it would be wrong to look in every work of art for such a goal that the work of art serves that is over and above serving the human person, making him happy, enriching him, uplifting him, and also over and above the gift that every great work of art is for humanity. We could say that every great work of art is an enrichment that makes the entire spiritual environment more beautiful and more delightful. How much poorer would the world be without Michelangelo's *Dying Slave*, without Raphael's cartoons, without the frescos of Piero della Francesca, without *King Lear* and *Hamlet*, without *Don Quixote*, without many of Goethe's poems, without *Figaro*, *Fidelio*, and *Tristan*!

We thus see clearly that the error of the thesis of *l'art pour l'art* is in no way contained in the extremely important distinction, discussed above, between those works in which beauty is thematic and other works in which the theme is not beauty but either truth or moral or religious values.

CHAPTER FOURTEEN

Beauty in Nature

IT IS DIFFICULT to speak of beauty in nature without mentioning the unique marriage that is possible between architecture and nature. If the architecture is congenial, this marriage can become an outstanding bearer of the most sublime beauty; but architecture that is not congenial, or even more, architecture that is aesthetically disvaluable, can destroy the beauty of nature. This is an important and central question for the beauty of nature, but before we treat it, we must first discuss in detail the essence of architecture in the second volume of this work.

Here we must limit ourselves to the bearers of beauty in nature itself and to the collaboration among expressed metaphysical beauty, beauty that appeals to the senses, and beauty of the second power. Although this theme is comprehensive and significant in itself, we cannot avoid referring briefly at various points to the significance of architecture.

Nature is a primary example of the existence of two themes, one of which is beauty. The entire creation has its own meaning, its own significance. Indeed, when one analyzes the first theme, its *raison d'être*, this inexhaustible theme takes on a great variety of differentiations.

On the other hand, nature is an outstanding bearer of beauty, beauty that is also fully thematic. It is not, as in the case of metaphysical beauty, a highly significant and necessary extra gift; no, nature is an immediate bearer of beauty. In many elements of nature, beauty is a reason why they are as they are. The first theme could be realized without the second, namely, beauty; but in reality, the beauty of nature is an indescribable gift and a full, independent theme. The reasons for this beauty are not identical with the reasons that are decisive for the ecosystem of nature. Its beauty is a completely distinct message from God, an unparalleled gift that is not the only theme, nor the first theme, but is certainly a full and independent theme of its own.

There are many relationships between the two themes. First of all, the bearer of beauty is no mere mirage, but something real that genuinely exists. We shall return in detail at a later point in the present chapter to the role that the reality of the bearer plays for the beauty of nature.

Quite apart from this relationship, the two themes intersect in a significant way. Above all, many elements of the first theme play a significant role for the beauty of nature. For example, agriculture—all the work of human beings on nature, imposing on it an order that makes for a contrast with a primeval forest—has a significant function for its beauty. It is, however, equally possible for this working and shaping, which is carried out for practical motives, to lead to the destruction of beauty; this happens whenever this practical work takes on a technical character, as in the disastrous "technization" of the earth.

We shall return later in this chapter to the relation between the two themes. First, we wish to speak briefly of the first theme in nature and of its diversity. We shall then discuss in detail beauty of nature and beauty in nature. We wish to identify the various types of bearers of beauty in nature, the individual dimensions, their collaboration, and the qualitative hierarchy of beauty. In short, we wish to undertake a philosophical analysis of the great theme of natural beauty, which is also a profound source of joy for human beings.

The first theme of nature

We begin by taking up the first theme of nature. This is in itself such a deep and comprehensive metaphysical theme that our reference to it here cannot meaningfully do more than draw attention to its variegated differentiation, and draw a clear-cut boundary between this and the second theme.

We do not intend to discuss the meaning of creation as a whole. The question why God created the world is a mystery. For the believing Christian creation is an unfathomably superabundant gift of divine love. For Jews and Christians the culmination of creation is clearly the creation of the human person, who alone is an *imago Dei.*

Let me point only to a few elements of this first theme. A mysterious, purposeful tendency permeates the immense structure of nature and makes even the inanimate world serve the sphere of life: the sun for plants, for their growth and their development; the rain that gives them the necessary supply of water and much else besides. Other aspects of this purposefulness are the extraordinary ecosystem represented by the world of plants, their mysterious propagation, their significance for the world of animals; the elimination of dangers through the killing of one animal by another; the mutual dependence which extends from the highest animals via the insects down to the microorganisms.

Material being, mountains, seas, lakes, rivers, all metals and minerals that lie hidden in the earth, have their own meaning as a basic kind of existing object. The *raison d'être* of the great inexhaustible mystery of plant and animal life in its immense diversity is its ontological value, about which we can never be sufficiently amazed. We need say no more here to show that the first theme of nature is its variegated ontological value, its inexhaustible fullness of being and of meaning.

The second theme of nature: its beauty. The five basic types of bearers of beauty

We now turn to the second theme, the beauty of nature. We have already mentioned several times the beauty of the first and the second powers that nature displays in such superabundant fullness. Now we wish to attempt a systematic investigation of the beauty in nature and to examine its individual sources.

First of all, we must distinguish various basic types of bearers of beauty in nature. The first is constituted by basic elements such as light and darkness, clouds, mountains, seas, lakes, rivers, times of the day (morning, midday, evening, night); seasons of the year (spring, summer, fall, winter); above all, the blue sky lit up by the rays of the sun; and much else. Some of these basic elements of nature appear everywhere and always, others only in particular instances, but as one and the same factor in the most varied forms. Each in itself, and all of them taken together, can be bearers of great beauty. Above all, they can be outstanding factors in the total beauty of nature, or a significant background for the natural beauty that influences the beauty of individual landscapes.

The second basic type of bearers of beauty are the individual objects in nature, from a stone to a blade of grass and a flower, from an ear of grain to a fruit, from a leaf to a tree. This type includes the individual species of plants, flora and fauna in their inexhaustible richness, as well as the individual instances in each of these species.

A third principal bearer of beauty in nature is the collaboration of the individual beautiful beings with the fundamental universal elements such as light and shade, the firmament, clouds, and water. In our normal contact with nature, these two basic sources of beauty continuously collaborate. It is seldom that we are entirely absorbed in the contemplation of one individual thing in nature and its beauty—for example, a flower, a fruit, a tree, an animal, etc. And it is relatively seldom that we concentrate exclusively on the beauty of the firmament, the light, or a sunset. Usually, the beauty of nature presents itself as a collaboration between these two factors.

We must draw a distinction between this third principal bearer and a fourth, extremely significant bearer, namely, "nature that is formed" from within, in the sense that something in nature forms an entity *sui generis* and, as such, possesses a very specific aesthetic quality. A special atmosphere characterizes a "region" and bestows a specific aesthetic unity on it.

Although there is no individual composition here, there is an aesthetic unity, a larger piece of nature that possesses a specific atmosphere as landscape and can as a whole be the bearer of great beauty. One such district is the French Riviera, the Côte d'Azur that borders the Italian Riviera and is clearly distinct from Roussillon, the seacoast of Perpignan, Collioure, and Banyuls, the landscape between the Pyrenees and the Mediterranean, north of the Spanish border.

The fifth basic type of bearer of beauty in nature is the "landscape," the composition of many individual elements that forms a unity, a very pure type of unity that is comparable in one sense to a melody. A landscape is a visual, as it were, an "artistic" unity. Its borders are not determined by geographical or geological elements. It is of course true that real objects such as a mountain range, the sea, or a great forest demarcate this unity, but they join with the other elements to form a visual, an aesthetic unity. They construct a new unified form which has a specific "face," a specific atmosphere. One example of this is the Gulf of Spezia.

The first type of bearer of beauty in nature: the basic elements

The firmament. First of all, we must mention the firmament: the sky that arches above us. The all-embracing form of the vault is itself the bearer of a definite beauty. Here we encounter the beauty of breadth, as opposed to the narrow oppressiveness of a prison; here we encounter the beauty of freedom, the majesty of embracing all things. There is also the primordial phenomenon of the "above," of the unlimited "extending above us," in which a primordial category is visibly embodied—a category that permeates in an analogous manner all the spheres of a spiritual kind. In itself the firmament already possesses a great, sublime beauty that is truly a beauty of the second power.

We will grasp the inexhaustible beauty of this primordial element if we go on to think of the elements that can also appear here, such as color, light, the whole "filling" of this firmament—by day its blue color and the splendor of the sun, and by night the stars and the moon. It is not for nothing that Kant defined the two most sublime things as the moral law within us and the starry sky above us. He compares the metaphysical beauty of the moral law—in our vocabulary, the metaphysical beauty of morality, of moral value—to the beauty of the second order that the visible starry sky above us possesses.

The blue sky, lit up by the rays of the sun in the daytime, is doubtless equally sublime. It possesses this inexhaustible primordial beauty just as much as the star-strewn sky at night. The beauty of this blue sky, full of light, is a primary example of the fullness of the spiritual values that lives in the beauty of the second power. We have spoken of this beauty in chapter 10 above, when we showed how this beauty forms the antithesis to all that is prosaic, mediocre, shallow, cheap, and inauthentic.

This blue sky, lit up by the rays of the sun, also has the quality of a primordial joyfulness, a glorious joyfulness, that is in turn the bearer of metaphysical beauty. The sky at night, the firmament strewn with stars or lit up by the moon, has a quality of silent, mysterious greatness, a profound solemnity. With this we encounter the way in which the sublime beauty that belongs to the firmament works together with the elements of light and darkness, with the glory of the day and of the night.

The beauty that this primordial element of the firmament possesses, both in itself and in combination with the primordial beauty of the sun, the moon, and the stars, is of such a kind that a particularly sublime landscape is required, if the "world" of the firmament is to be extended; for otherwise there will be a distinct falling off of the landscape in comparison with this "world." There are landscapes in which there lives and breathes an analogous beauty, and above all a "world" analogous to the "world" of the primordial beauty of the firmament. Then the sublime song and glory that speaks of God through the firmament, its "world" and "atmosphere," is analogously picked up by the landscape. But this is seldom the case. In general, even a beautiful landscape, full of magic and poetry, cannot extend the atmosphere of the sky or the "tone" of the beauty of the firmament. Their "world" is more local and possesses neither universality nor the same sublimity as the firmament. We shall speak again about the "world" of the landscape toward the close of the present chapter. Let us for now put aside the question which landscape can extend the "sound" of this ultimate beauty of the firmament, that is, of the blue sky lit up by the sun, or of the starry sky, and which landscapes cannot do so (architecture too plays a decisive role in answering this question). We can in any case say that every beautiful landscape is intensified through this background. All its potential for beauty is actualized through the beauty of this primordial datum of the sky. Through the sun and the beauty of the blue sky, the landscape receives its "festal garment" as opposed to the "everyday garment" that it wears when a gray-white sky without clouds arches above it (there is something monotonous about a cloud cover).

We have already mentioned that great variations are possible in the primordial beauty of the firmament and of sunlight. These fundamental bearers of beauty display great differences of degree and rank. The blue color of the unclouded sky can take various hues, from a bright blue to an intensive, darker blue, and it can vary greatly from one day and place to another. This applies all the more to light. The beauty of light is much greater on some days than on others. Above all, the light in certain regions has a very particular beauty.

In all these basic elements of nature, we must draw a distinction between the beauty that they possess as species and the beauty of the single individual in which the beauty of the species is expressed in a much more authentic and genuine manner. Besides this, the individual displays special qualities and differentiations which are very significant for their beauty. We must also realize that this involves more than a difference in the degree of beauty; in light, for example, there are differences that represent qualitative variations, although this does not mean that one variation is necessarily superior to another. There exists not only a more beautiful and a less beautiful light: there also exists the difference among the light of morning, of midday, and of evening.

The times of the day. This brings us to another primordial element of great beauty, namely, the times of the day. What beauty the sunrise can possess, what inexhaustible poetry! The whole "world" of the morning—a "world" of hopefulness, youthfulness, freshness, of the sun as it rises higher in the sky—has a unique quality. Here we touch once again on universal qualitative categories that permeate the whole hierarchy of being. These fundamental realities manifest themselves in a particular way in the visible aspect of nature. Like joyfulness, hopefulness naturally exists as a pure quality. It would be utter nonsense to say that nature is full of feelings of hope; to project an experienced, conscious hope into the apersonal world, into the life of apersonal nature, would be a pantheistic absurdity. Nevertheless, the quality that lives in the experienced and consciously lived hope of the human person belongs as a pure quality also to the morning in the literal sense, and to the youth of living beings. This primordial quality of the matutinal is the bearer of a great metaphysical beauty, and since this primordial quality also occurs in the visible, that is, since certain elements of the visible serve to ground it and allow it to appear in an intuitive manner, this metaphysical beauty is experientially given to us in all that belongs to the morning. It is glorious that something like morning exists in nature.

The freshness and the fragrance of the morning air contribute to the great poetry of the morning, as does the "awakening of nature" that is likewise one of the primordial phenomena that permeate many levels of being. The phenomenon of awakening is not something that we project into nature. It is given intuitively in nature and is in fact a process that really occurs in many plants and animals.

Up to this point, we have spoken of the beauty and poetry of the morning as such. But it is clear that this beauty is intensified to an extraordinary degree not only when it is followed by a radiant day as the sun turns the clouds on the horizon gold or pink; another intensifying factor is the specific region or landscape in which this phenomenon takes place. The primordial elements are the great, significant background to all the beauties of the landscape and of nature as a whole; and the reverse holds true too: the beauty of the basic elements can unfold more fully, the more beautiful the landscape is.

In addition to this interplay, there are many special factors that harmonize wonderfully with the entire phenomenon of the morning, for example, the crowing of the cock at sunrise, or the dew that has formed on the plants in the night and now begins to sparkle. Dew has a special quality of the virginal and of freshness. When the phenomenon of morning, especially morning light as it increases, unfolds to the full in its specific beauty together with all the other factors of awakening nature, the temperature, the air, etc., then we have a prime example of the poetic, of which we have spoken in chapter 11 above.

The beauty of the midday is analogous. The peak of brightness, the victorious unfolding of the light, the special beauty that this light possesses when compared with the light of the morning and of the evening, the phenomenon of fullness and repletion, which also includes warmth and a change in the air and its fragrance—this has its own specific beauty.

Evening, with the sinking sun, is once again something uniquely full of content. When we speak of evening we are not thinking of the beginning of the night, but of the sinking sun, of its farewell, of this last part of the day. This light can possess an especially moving sublimity. It begins at different hours of the day, depending on the season of the year. We are thinking of those moments when the full light of the sun, with its unique splendor and power, is followed by a more delicate and spiritualized light that bestows on the phenomenon of evening a wholly special quality that lasts until sunset, a transfigured note that has an element of farewell about it. When the weather permits it to unfold to the full, this light too imparts to nature a sublime splendor that is completely different from the morning light.

It does not have the note of hopefulness, nor the element of awakening, nor the fresh and youthful quality, nor the replete fulfillment of the midday. It has rather a character of farewell. But this farewell is not painful; it has no melancholy note, but it has a special spiritual completion. It contains a reference to eternity, a mood such as lives in the wonderful hymn that Simeon prays after he has been permitted to hold the divine Child in his arms: *Nunc dimittis servum tuum, Domine, in pace* ("Now do you dismiss your servant, O Lord, in peace," Luke 2:29). The departing sun bestows a special character, a spiritual, transfigured note, on the whole of nature. Once again, we find the reciprocal fecundation of nature through this primordial element, and of the beauty of the evening through the beauty of the landscape. The special beauty that the sunset often possesses is an element all its own.

Consider also night. It too has its own specific dignity. We have already spoken of the solemn, mysterious grandeur of the starry sky, and have pointed out the special poetry of the moon and of its splendor. It suffices to think of the beauty that Goethe so uniquely unfolds in his poems to the moon! Doubtless the artistic beauty of the poem makes its own extra contribution here. In a poem like *To the Moon*, beginning with the words "Bush and vale thou fill'st again,"[1] the poetry of the moon in nature, its silent, gentle, contemplative magic, is set before our eyes in a unique way. Greek mythology personifies all these primordial elements of the beauty of nature, thereby emphasizing their specific poetry, their special character. In Artemis, we encounter the chaste beauty that belongs to the night. But the poetical character of Artemis or Diana certainly does not exhaust the full content of the phenomenon of night: it is only one special aspect of its poetry.

Night also possesses a unique solemnity thanks to the silence, the cessation of the stream of activity, the contemplative calm that spreads out over everything. There is a great seriousness surrounding night. Night receives a special note from the silence of human beings and the moving praise of nature that ascends in the night to the Creator alone. The fact that all now unfolds in solitude—the rustling of the brook, the magnificence of the trees—without human beings and without most of the animals, bestows on nature a kind of poetry and majesty that is completely different from what the day bestows on nature.

Various sources collaborate in the beauty of the primordial elements: first, the metaphysical beauty that has become visible; secondly, the beauty that appeals to the senses; and thirdly, the beauty of the second power that we have called in chapter 9 quasi-sacramental beauty. To the metaphysical beauty belong all the significant qualities to which we drew attention—the firmament, light, morning, midday, evening, and night

1. Goethe, *An den Mond* (1789): "Füllest wieder Busch und Tal." English translation by Edgar Alfred Bowring.

—in order to do justice (at least to some small extent) to the fullness of their beauty.

The second realm of beauty: the individual beings in nature

The second realm of beauty in nature contains the individual entities both in the inanimate world and in the world of plants and animals. Here there is an inexhaustible variety of forms and a vast hierarchy. Some of them are definitely ugly, especially in the animal world, such as a toad, a hippopotamus, etc. Nevertheless, these animals represent an interesting, successful "invention." Something would be lacking, even from the aesthetic point of view, if they did not exist. In this charm of the successful invention, which sometimes contains an element of the comical, there lies a quite specific aesthetic value. And the sheer richness of variety is something valuable.

Apart from those cases of a value antithesis in which something ugly (from the point of view of a primitive beauty appealing to the senses) like a hippopotamus has the value of a successful invention, there is clearly a vast hierarchy in the beauty of the individual physical beings. When we speak here of "beauty," we are referring first of all to the beauty of the *species* of something that exists physically, not to the beauty of the single *individual* in this species.

We must recall here the extremely varied gradation that we find in nature with regard to the ontological character of a complete individual.[2] For example, even in the realm of inanimate material things, a stone is a much more "unserious" individual than a hill or a mountain. All that distinguishes one stone from other stones having the same material and the same color, form, and size, is its spatial detachment from them. The various stones that are mere "pieces" of a boulder are entirely random external individuals. In the case of a mountain, on the other hand, its character as an individual is much more defined. Its boundary is the foot of the mountain, which demarcates it either from the flat landscape or from other mountains.

2. Cf. my *Metaphysik der Gemeinschaft*, part I, chap. 1.

A completely new kind of individualization is found in the realm of the living, and in every single organism that possesses an unambiguous unity that is determined from within and makes it an individual.

If, however, we inquire into the beauty of the individual entities in nature, we find that the mountain, which is ontologically less individual, bears a much more definitely individual beauty than a blade of grass, which as an organism is a more serious individual. In terms of its appearance, the mountain is more distinct from its surroundings than the blade of grass. Even a stone can be a more potent bearer of beauty than, for example, an alga.

Clearly, the beauty that a stone may possess thanks to its form cannot be called the beauty of a species. In the case of a stone, the differences in beauty within one species can refer only to the kind of material and to its color. Travertine is more beautiful and noble than the common chalkstone; marble is more noble and beautiful than mica; Greek marble is usually more beautiful than the marble from Carrara.

The situation with hills and mountains is different. There is indeed a species "hill" and a species "mountain," but the beauty of a hill is dependent to such an extent on its individual form—on the kind of forest that grows on it or the kind of grass that covers it—that it is not possible to declare the species "hill" to be more or less beautiful than the species "mountain," or even than the species "plain." The same applies to mountains. The differences in the beauty of mountains, which are determined by their form and color—whether they are naked cliffs or sandy mountains, whether covered by woods or by grass—are so great that one can speak of their beauty only in the sense of the general genus "mountain" or "mountain range" as opposed to the plain. This means that these bearers of beauty belong to the first basic type, the basic elements in nature such as water—seas, lakes, or rivers—or such as the plain and also the steppe.

In inanimate nature, there exists either the very sublime beauty of the primordial elements or the beauty of the form and color of an individual river, lake, rock, mountain, or hill. The primordial elements are one of the greatest and most noble sources of the beauty of nature. Besides this, we have the beauty of an individual mountain such as Monte Pellegrino near Palermo, the mountain near Formia,[3] or the mountain at the Dead Sea. These individual rocks or mountains can also be bearers of the beauty of the second power. Here once again we see that, unlike metaphysical beauty (even when this is expressed), the beauty of the visible is completely independent of the ontological rank of the object.

In the realm of the organic, we likewise find this overwhelming variety of individual types of forms which, as species, are bearers of a particular beauty. As we have already mentioned in chapter 8, flowers occupy a special position here: lilies, roses, carnations, violets, tulips, hyacinths—a whole world of beauty, with each individual blossom a *mirandum*. What beauty fruits have, for example, an apple, an orange, a cherry, a plum! What beauty of form there is in an ear of corn, or indeed in a root! What a wealth of forms comes into play even in the pits of fruit! How perfectly everything is formed, even down to the smallest structures! And what of trees—an oak, a beech, a poplar, a plane tree, and above all a cypress, a pine tree, an olive-tree, an evergreen oak; an orange tree with ripe fruits, an apple or a cherry tree in bloom! What a world of beauty in each individual type! What nobility of form, of color, of the shape of the trunk, the crown, and the leaves!

We find a similar variety of beauty in the realm of animals, beginning with the beauty of sea horses and starfish, of many fishes, and of dolphins, and ascending to the beauty of sheep, goats, horses, donkeys, dogs and cats, lions and tigers, etc.

From the aesthetic point of view, there is one extremely interesting difference between the beauty of plants and the beauty of animals. These are two opposite forms of beauty: the "chaste" form of the fullness of life in the world of plants, their unique kind of aloofness, as opposed to the "hot breath" of the animal world. Nevertheless, the way they work together is a significant element in the total beauty of nature.

The beauty of a tree contributes in two dimensions to the beauty of nature. The first is the beauty that it possesses in itself; we apprehend this

3. A seaside town to the north of Naples.

when we stand before it and contemplate it. The second dimension is its significance for the landscape. When, for example, we think of a pine tree that is like an "antiphon" to the landscape of the Gulf of Naples when seen from one particular vantage point, we recognize the exalted new significance that a tree can take on in the context of a landscape, transcending its own beauty but certainly not independently of this beauty.

The third realm of beauty: the working together of the basic elements and individual beings

A third principal bearer of beauty in nature is the working together of an individual beautiful being with the primordial elements.[4] We normally experience nature by spending time in it, by walking or driving through the region and taking delight in the beauty of the meadow on which sheep are grazing, or taking delight in the brook that meanders through the field, surrounded by poplars and lit up by the rays of the sun. Many basic elements require this totality of nature in order to unfold their beauty to the full, for example, the sun—whether the morning, midday, or evening sun—that shines on trees and meadows and is reflected in the river or the lake. Not only does each of the basic elements bestow a new character on nature; they also reveal themselves in their beauty above all in their collaboration with or in their harmony with individual things. In its totality this piece of nature—to which belong the singing of the birds, the murmuring of the brook or the roar of a mighty river, the fragrance of the fresh air, and an inexhaustible number of other things—is a bearer of beauty.

4. In this third bearer of beauty, the collaboration between the primordial elements and individual entities in nature—whether these entities are found in the inanimate world or in the world of plants or in the world of animals—it must be emphasized that—especially with regard to plants and animals—only a tiny segment of the whole plays a role in the natural beauty that we perceive and enjoy in our life. In numerical terms the great majority either belongs to the microscopic world, or else the individual entities are so small (for example, a fly, a flea, or an individual blade of grass) that they go unnoticed in the "face" of nature which we normally see (as opposed to what we see only through a microscope). This microscopic world can in itself be very beautiful, although it does not belong to the third bearer of the beauty of nature. It is a particular manifestation of the superabundance in nature that its beauty and aesthetic shape reach even into that which is invisible as far as the normal aspect of nature is concerned.

Not only do we find completely different types of nature—for example, a gentle, hilly landscape, a plain, a mountainous landscape, a sandy or rocky sea coast, a desert with its golden sand dunes—but also great differences of degree with regard to beauty. In boring, featureless, monotonous regions, one must take refuge in the primordial elements of nature. Similarly, the light varies greatly in the various regions of the earth; in some places the weather can be primarily bleak and unvarying. Only a foolish prejudice will say, "Nature is always beautiful—this must be the case, for the simple reason that everything is God's creation!" There is a multifarious hierarchy in creation, and it is not an expression of special reverence to place on the same level everything that God has created. On the contrary, this is a form of nihilism! We are not interested here in the question whether anything definitely ugly exists in pure nature, but in the great gradations in the beauty of nature that extend all the way from a boring, barren region to a region of tremendous beauty.

The important point to note is that the collaboration between the primordial elements and individual entities can be a new bearer of beauty in nature. Many non-visible elements also make their contribution: the song of the birds, the bleating of the sheep, the crowing of the roosters, the barking of the dogs, the whinnying of the horses, and the babbling of the brook; the fragrance of the flowers and of the trees in bloom, of the fresh grass, all the herbs that are warmed through and through by the sun in summer; and many, many other things.

Many people relate to nature and take delight in it primarily because of this working together of the primordial elements with the beauty of single individual entities, as well as with non-visible factors. The great, unique value of nature *qua* nature as opposed to all that is artificial and technical, the nobility of its voice and its face, is an inexhaustible stimulus, a source of refreshment and instruction, though the degree of refreshment and instruction varies according to the aesthetic understanding of each person. How many people walk through the woods and meadows on a holiday and enjoy the smell of the conifers or the shade that the trees give, and so on. One who has a deeper understanding apprehends also the poetry that nature possesses in very general terms, thanks simply to the distinctions between day and night, the seasons of the year, the sunshine, the weather.

But for more primitive persons it is largely irrelevant whether the vegetation, the form of the mountains, or the type of rivers and lakes is more beautiful in one region than in another. The fact that they are at home in one region usually conditions them to love this region. Regardless of how much or little natural beauty their homeland has, it is there that they have received their first impressions of nature and experienced the delight of springtime, the frost on the trees, and the beauty of the sunset. They will seldom apprehend the fact that nature in other regions is still more beautiful.

The fifth realm of beauty: the individual, concrete landscape as a structural aesthetic unity

As the fourth bearer of beauty in nature we mentioned nature that is formed from within in the sense of a "region" that has unity as a landscape, for example, the region around Florence as opposed to the region around Siena. We shall deal with it later in this chapter.

The fifth bearer of beauty in nature, which we shall now deal with, is a very concrete, individual "landscape" that reveals itself to us, for example, in the vista of the Gulf of Naples, or of the Gulf of Spezia when one begins to drive down to the sea between Sarzana and Lerici. Various elements of nature come together to form a profound, necessary unity, similar to the way in which individual notes become a glorious, profoundly meaningful melody, for example, in Handel's *Largo* or Bach's *Air.*

We shall now discuss the individual elements of nature that play a role in this unity, that is, build it up. The first significant factor in this unity is composition in the preeminent sense of this word. This completely new unity, which is usually at the same time a visible unity, is a specific bearer of one particular individual quality and often possesses a sublime beauty.

In order to apprehend clearly this unity in its essence, the first thing we must understand is that it represents the uttermost contrast to any random stringing together of various elements in nature. There are areas in nature where trees that are in themselves beautiful, a river, mountains in the background, meadows, etc., do not in the least join together to form such a unity. They merely stand alongside one another like notes with a beautiful sound that do not produce any melody. It is true that beauty can be present even then, namely, as a mere collaboration between the first two sources, the primordial elements and the form of individual entities. But this does not annul the sharp distinction between this completely new unity, this composition, and the mere piece of nature that is inherently "unshaped." The beauty that such an "artistic" unity in nature can possess is in fact of a completely new kind.

When we call this landscape unity a visual unity, this must not be misunderstood. A "visual unity" does not mean something that is established from the outside, through a frame, so to speak; nor is it the unity of a mere vista. In many vistas, all that is offered to us is an unformed piece of nature. A merely accidental, external slice of nature is not at all a "landscape" in our sense. It need not in the least possess any inherent aesthetic unity, nor need it build up any "artistic" unity. The unity of a landscape is also clearly distinct from the mere framing that results from the fact that we look at nature through an arch. There is often a great charm in looking at a slice of nature through a window, or even better through an arch. This framing, which comes wholly from without, can have an aesthetic quality of its own, despite the random character of what is seen.

Here we must draw a distinction between two questions. First, what elements condition the emergence of this new entity that we call "landscape" in the narrower sense of the word? What factors make a completely new entity out of the material of nature, as opposed to a juxtaposition of merely anonymous pieces of nature? And secondly, which factors are responsible for the aesthetic value of this entity? Which factors determine that one landscape is more beautiful than another, for example, that the character of one landscape is only lovely, while the character of another is sublime?

Let us first point to a fundamental distinction. The ascent in the individualization from a piece of matter to an organism, and further, in an incomparable manner, to the human person, is of a quite different kind from the ascent from a mere slice of nature to the unity of a landscape in the narrower sense of the word. This individual unity of the landscape is of a purely aesthetic nature and certainly does not make it an ontological individual. Unlike the ontological individuality, it is not clearly demarcated from that which surrounds it. It is not a substance, and is indeed even further removed from substantial individuality than a work of art. It is true that the work of art is likewise not a real substance; but (like a community) it is an entity that resembles a substance, and both the work of art and the community are entities that scholasticism called moral substances. A landscape is not a moral substance. As a piece of nature it is much more real than a work of art; but as a landscape, it is a purely aesthetic unity, and it is an individual entity from an aesthetic but not from an ontological point of view. It is a "spiritual" [*geistiges*] individual; and naturally "spiritual" here does not in any way mean "personal." In this sense of spiritual we can say that an essay or a melody is a spiritual individual.

Being demarcated from its surroundings is an element of the ontological individuality of an individual; like perseity (that is, the quality of existing on its own), this demarcation is an essential condition for existing fully as a substance. Ontological individuality plays a role when we speak of the beauty of individual beings in nature, but when we speak of a landscape as a fifth bearer of beauty in nature we refer only to a spiritual individual, to a purely aesthetic unity. Thus when we separate the two questions—What makes this landscape a unity? and What determines its beauty? —we remain entirely within the framework of the distinctive aesthetic unity and aesthetic individualization, and prescind completely from the character of a real substance and its metaphysically ontological structure.

The first question has more of a structural character: Which factors determine the emergence of a new entity? The second question has an aesthetic character: Which factors determine the beauty of this new entity, of the landscape? Or which factors determine the difference between the beautiful landscape and the less beautiful, insignificant landscape?

With the structural question of the factors that are capable of building up this new unity, we touch on the general problem of composition, which we have discussed in chapter 8 above. What distinguishes a mere sequence of notes, such as a scale, from a melody? Why is it that one particular combination of notes gives birth to a new entity, a melody, while another combination does not constitute anything of the kind?

This is the mystery of composition, which we encounter in every field. What is the difference between a sentence and the mere stringing together of words, such as "four, green, laughing"? What is the difference between a mere number of persons and a community?

In the constitution of a landscape, composition—the inherent, necessary harmonizing of elements—is the decisive factor for the emergence of this individual entity, the "artistic" unity. The mystery is that one particular dominating building can become the central point that builds up this unity around itself, or that certain trees and meadows, a vista of the sea, and a mountain range can fit together so well that a new entity emerges, an entity that bears an entirely new quality in relation to the individual elements—and indeed, that this combination possesses the potential to constitute a new entity.

We must immediately emphasize here that there is a close link between the structural and the aesthetic questions. The structural question about which factors are responsible for the emergence of this new entity, the landscape in the narrower sense, is linked to the aesthetic question, because the landscape has a much more defined "face" than a mere random piece of nature and is therefore also a much more potent bearer of aesthetic values. There is no such thing as an ugly or trivial landscape. A boring or dull slice of nature remains just that—a slice of nature. It lacks the inner potency that would make it a genuine new entity. In that case, there is always something lacking; a clear and strongly defined "face" does not come into existence. It is precisely this impotence that underlies boringness.

This certainly does not mean that anonymous juxtaposed pieces of nature cannot possess beauty of any kind; we have already mentioned them as one bearer of beauty in nature. But the landscape in our sense of the term, which includes an ascent of a structural kind and is an aesthetic entity, can never have the boring character of a mere juxtaposition of pieces of nature. The greater structural significance is accompanied by a more marked, more eloquent aesthetic quality. Boredom is the exact opposite of an expressive, clearly formed "face." The boringness in nature is linked to the inability to build up a distinct unity of this kind.

Nevertheless, the two questions remain separate: Which factors determine the emergence of the landscape in the narrower sense? Which factors determine the difference with regard to its aesthetic value?

The principal factor that makes a slice of nature into a particular landscape is the composition of elements. The unique manner in which the individual elements fit one another, their harmony, gives birth to this new entity, which has an inner form. But as we shall see in the following section, the composition also plays a decisive role for the beauty of the landscape, of this "artistic" unity.

The individual elements of beauty in a landscape

Let us, however, turn to the question: Which other factors are responsible for the beauty of a landscape?

There is no doubt that the type of vegetation, mountains, light, etc., has a great influence on the special quality of a landscape, of its beauty. In other words, the quality and beauty of the natural elements and entities that build up such a landscape in the narrower sense play a significant role for the quality and beauty of the landscape. The Gulf of Naples would not be what it is without the vegetation with its pines, olive trees and cypresses, without the bare Vesuvius with its especially beautiful form and color, without the southern light, without the blue southern sea, etc. The shape and color of the cypress give the landscape a note all its own; its special beauty, its seriousness and nobility, make a significant contribution to the quality of the landscape in the narrower sense. The same is true of the pine. In addition to the exceptional beauty of this tree, the combination of cypress and pine plays a significant role. The horizontal element of the pine and its broad, velvety splendor unites in a special way with the vertical element of the cypress. The same applies to the silver olive trees with their unique humble poetry, and to the solemn, dark, noble evergreen oak. All these trees possess a definite beauty, an aesthetic quality that is their own and that has a great influence on the quality and atmosphere of the landscape in the narrower sense, in which they function as parts. The palm tree, especially the royal palm, has a definite quality that is completely different; landscapes in which the palm trees are a dominant element have a different quality from those that are built up by cypresses and pines, or by evergreen oaks and olive trees.

We have already mentioned the significance of light for the landscape, as well as of the mountains or hills. Are they naked, rocky mountains, or are they clad in woods—and what kind of woods? Are they covered by grass, or are they only sandy mountains? What color do they have? Does this landscape also include the vivifying element of water? Does it contain brooks, a river, or a lake? Or is it a landscape that includes the sea, like the Gulf of Naples (which we have often mentioned) or the Gulf of Spezia? The question of the natural things out of which a landscape in the narrower sense is built up has a significant influence on the quality of the landscape. The beauty of the things which build it up is of great significance for the beauty of the landscape.

One example is the enchanting landscape of the little town of Damme near Bruges in Belgium. The view of the canal that leads to Sluis and is framed by lofty poplars is a definite landscape in the narrower sense. Its enchanting quality, its beauty, is determined by the quality of the poplars and by the quality of the canal. Its special atmosphere would not come into being if the canal were framed by spruce trees rather than poplars, or if there were a meadow there instead of a canal. The pale, bright blue sky with white, puffy clouds, the special light, the wind, etc., all make their contribution too.

Composition as a decisive factor in a landscape; its "artistic" unity

Although the specific character and beauty of the individual elements are very significant for the quality and beauty of the landscape, composition is a completely new and decisive factor. The special harmonizing of all the factors mentioned above is determinative of the specific character, the unique individual quality of the landscape and its beauty. Here the two questions that we separated above touch one another, the question of the factors that condition such a composition and such a new unity, and the question of the factors involved in the special quality of this unity. The beauty proper to a landscape presupposes not only that this new aesthetic unity, this composition, is realized, but it also presupposes a certain character of the composition. Both the level of its intrinsic necessity and the kind of composition as such play a decisive role for the degree of beauty. Some landscapes are quite simply greater, more significant "inventions"; the harmonizing of elements is more significant in them in other landscapes, and the world they irradiate is more sublime.

The "artistic" unity, the inner composition that makes a slice of nature into a landscape in our sense of the word, is thus not in the least a random selection of elements, but something that is united from within, a new entity that derives from very special causes, a new aesthetic unity. It is visual only in the sense that it is apprehended by our eyes and, like a picture, is a unity that is independent of the ontological juxtaposition of its elements.

Our starting point was the vista of the Gulf of Naples and of the Gulf of Spezia. These two landscapes present views, and they presuppose particular standpoints in order to be able to unfold themselves fully before our eye. This is certainly not true of all landscapes in the narrower sense. Landscapes in this sense are all those pieces of nature that have come together to form an "artistic" unity of this kind. For example, we catch sight of a hill with an alley of cypresses leading upward; halfway up the hill stands a little church, with a row of olive trees alongside it; and all this comes mysteriously together to form such a necessary unity. This unity is a special "invention" which constitutes an atmosphere all its own and an "artistic" unity.

The landscape of the Fonti del Clitunno near Trevi,[5] which was once

5. Northwest of Spoleto in Umbria. Today this landscape is completely spoiled.

distinctly beautiful, was not a vista, nor is the glorious landscape of Cori and Ninfa to the south of Rome, which is still preserved in its entirety today. Such a landscape in the narrower sense can be more or less extensive. The decisive point is that a clear composition, a specific type of unity, comes into being. It is achieved through a particular "face," a particular atmosphere, an aesthetic "invention," so that we can speak of an "artistic" unity.

The following decisive characteristics should be noted. First, from the ontological point of view, the unity is much looser than in individual beings found in nature, for example, in a palm tree, a poplar, or a lion, a horse, or a donkey.[6] In these instances, the "invention" is very closely linked to one particular real being, a plant or an animal. The "invention" is its specific appearance, and is based on an enduring, close conjunction of all the parts to constitute one form. From this ontological standpoint, the "artistic" unity of the landscape is much looser and more difficult to apprehend. From the aesthetic standpoint, it not only just as significant but also has a particularly convincing character. When we see an especially beautiful landscape, the expression forces itself onto our lips: "Yes, this is how it was meant to be!" The fullness of meaning and the depth of this unity give it the character of necessity. Ontologically it remains something "floating," but qualitatively it can even possess the character-

6. We have spoken of this in connection with the type of beauty that belongs to the fulfillment of a principle of form, and in connection with the ugliness that is caused by weakening, infringing, or breaching this principle of form. We also mentioned that something which is especially beautiful in the face of a cat—the relationship of the nose to the mouth and the eyes—would certainly not be beautiful in a human face, because a completely different principle of form is present in the latter. In the case of a landscape in the special sense of the word, however, we are dealing with a unity of things having a variety of forms, for example, a tree, a hill, a street, certain animals, etc. Unlike a tree (such as a chestnut or a pine) or a horse or a dog, this unity is not the constant appearance of a real entity, but a composition of entities with a variety of forms that unite in a unique manner to constitute a completely new type of unity. In their composition here and now, they build up a new unity and present a new type of "invention." To employ a comparison that is weak in many ways: the landscape is like specific notes built up into a melody, or various melodies, harmonies, and sounds built up into a movement in a symphony or in a quartet. What is most important is to apprehend the surprising element in a unity such as that of the Gulf of Naples or of Spezia, this harmonious union of various elements to form an individual aesthetic unity, an "artistic" unity. Equally important is to apprehend the special beauty—a beauty of the second power—that this unity, the landscape in the narrower sense, can possess.

istic of the necessary. However, this necessity must be clearly distinguished from the necessity of an essential law.

Secondly, this landscape in the narrower sense is indeed a visual unity, a composition of visible elements that we can perceive; but unlike a picture, the specific character of this landscape entails that it is a piece of real nature, composed of genuine physical entities, and that the mountain in the background and the trees in the foreground and on the plain are real things. We need not say anything more about this characteristic here, since we shall discuss in detail the significance of reality for the beauty of nature later on in the present chapter.

Thirdly, the composition of various natural entities, which builds up a very specific, concrete new unity, transcends in its identity the "picture" that is seen from one specific standpoint. Something that presents itself to us as very unambiguously formed, for example, the view from Bellosguardo toward the city of Florence with the mountains of Fiesole that lie behind it, the hills of San Miniato that frame the city, the Fortezza, etc., is closely related to the "artistic" unity that presents itself in the view from San Miniato, although this differs purely as a "picture." To put this more precisely, we must distinguish various levels in this "artistic" unity: the "picture" that presents itself only from one particular standpoint, and the composition that remains the same when it is contemplated from various standpoints. The latter is present even when we move around inside this landscape, provided that the composition, which bestows a unique individual character on the landscape, is still somehow visible and asserts itself in its special atmosphere. In both these cases we can speak of a landscape in the narrower sense of the word.

As we shall see, the unity of a landscape, which reveals itself like a picture from one particular standpoint, is not only a picture but is built up of completely real entities. This includes the awareness that this landscape can be apprehended from other points too. Naturally, it often happens that one particular aspect is much more beautiful than another.

This self-contained composition can vary greatly in extension. In the Gulf of Naples or the Gulf of Spezia, it is a very considerable piece of nature that is brought together to form such a unity. In such a piece of nature, there may be numerous self-contained individual situations. On the other hand, the landscape of the Villa Adriana near Tivoli occupies a smaller space.

Distant landscape and landscape near at hand; intimate landscape and extensive landscape

One important distinction in this type of landscape in the narrower sense is that between a distant landscape and a landscape near at hand. Distant vistas, such as the view from the Capitol to the Campagna, with Frascati and Rocca di Papa in the background, can have the character of a composition, of an inner "artistic" unity. There are also typical landscapes near at hand which have come together to form such a composition. This was the conscious aim in the gardens of many Italian villas, for example, in the Villa d'Este in Tivoli.

The difference between an intimate and an extensive landscape is not the same as that between a distant landscape and one near at hand. The demarcation between an intimate and an extensive landscape refers to the spatial extent of this "artistic" unity, whereas the difference between a distant landscape and one near at hand refers to our distance from the landscape, that is, whether we see it from a remote position or stand immediately before it or in it.

Despite these differences, the distant landscape and the extensive landscape often coincide, for example, in the cases of the Gulf of Naples and the Gulf of Spezia. Similarly, the view from Marina di Carrara on the Tuscan Riviera to the mountains where the marble is quarried is both a distant landscape and an extensive landscape. But these need not always coincide. The landscape of the park of the Villa Adriana near Tivoli is more extensive than the landscape of the garden of the Villa Medici in Rome.[7]

The function that the nearby surrounding nature—one or more trees,

7. We make no kind of claim to completeness when we draw these distinctions between a landscape near at hand and a distant landscape, and between an intimate and an extensive landscape. It may be necessary to draw many further distinctions which we have not discussed here.

a meadow, a rock—can have in relation to the distant landscape is particularly significant. These make a significant contribution to the beauty and poetry of the distant landscape. Here it suffices to recall the great pine that we have called an "antiphon" to the Gulf of Naples, or the olive trees above Lerici through which one looks down to the Gulf of Spezia, or the trees and the entire garden of the Villa Rufolo in Ravello south of Naples, with the unique view of the rocks and the sea.

Something analogous occurs when a mountain range or the sea forms the background to an intimate landscape. In such a case, this background is not a factor that is a part of the "artistic" unity or builds this up. The background intensifies the intimate landscape in its beauty, in a manner similar to the contribution of the "antiphon" to the distant landscape. Thus, the intimate small landscape may contain a vista of distant mountains, and in that case, the distant mountains function as the background. This is a very significant factor for the beauty of the intimate landscape, but it has a different function for the landscape near at hand—whether this is a more intimate or a more extensive landscape—than the trees, alleys, paths, meadows, hills, rocks, in short everything that makes this more intimate or more comprehensive landscape an "artistic" unity. There are also glorious intimate landscapes which do not have a background of this kind.

In the extensive landscape, such as the view from Marina di Carrara to the mountains where the marble is quarried, the Apuan Alps, the mountain range is not a background but a factor that helps constitute the "artistic" unity of the landscape.

At this point we must draw attention to an unequivocal destruction of the organic link between the piece of nature in which we are located and the distant landscape that has been brought together to form an "artistic" unity. This takes place when the view is artificially cut out of the immediate surroundings through the creation of a place that serves exclusively for the vista and offers only an opportunity to "enjoy" the panorama. The vista must never take on the character of a mere panorama. It is an essential characteristic of this type of landscape that we are not mere "spectators": the place where the vista is offered to us is rather an organic component of nature. It is true that the beauty of the landscape remains even when we look at it as mere onlookers from an artificial viewing tower; but our experience of the beauty of this landscape that offers itself to our gaze is falsified and perverted. The inorganic quality of an artificial viewing place, like that before San Miniato or on the Piazzale Michelangelo in Florence, turns us into mere spectators.[8] The splendor that is given in our experience when we look from a beautiful building, a villa, or from a hill or mountain at this self-contained "artistic" unity—which is *not* a picture, but a real piece of nature—is impaired as soon as this glorious nature is turned into a panorama. One is no longer integrated into this atmosphere; rather, a false distancing takes place. One looks at the landscape in the same way that one sees a beautiful landscape in the cinema. There is no reason *per se* to object to looking at a beautiful landscape in the cinema. But if one treats the real nature that one sees as if one were seeing only its picture, the entire dimension of the "marriage" with this real nature is lost, and with it, one source of delight. Precisely this glorious vista requires us to remain, as it were, totally *in* nature: we must never become spectators. The more organic and unintended, "unexpected" this vista is, the more the immediate surroundings and indeed the viewing point itself are themselves a beautiful piece of nature and are filled with the same atmosphere, then the more genuine, valid, and truly delightful is the act of seeing the beautiful landscape, the act of apprehending this intimate or extensive "artistic" unity. This is also connected with the great significance that the reality of the landscape has for its delightful beauty. We shall return in detail to this theme later in the present chapter.

Landscape—an "invention" of God

As we have already shown, the section of nature that is accessible to us in one particular place, the section we can apprehend at one glance, certainly

8. Cf. "Aus einem Tagebuch Adolf Hildebrands," *circa* 1875, in *Adolf von Hildebrand und seine Welt. Briefe und Erinnerungen*, ed. Bernhard Sattler (Munich: Callway, 1962), 212ff.

does not constitute the "artistic" unity of the landscape. There are innumerable sections of nature that we can take in at one glance from one particular place, but although they are brought together by the fact that they fill our field of vision, they do not form any kind of landscape in the sense of this new aesthetic unity, no inherently united composition. Although we see them at a single glance and they are externally demarcated from their surroundings, they can remain an "unformed" piece of nature, a mere stringing together, a piece of "anonymous" nature. Even the unity that is brought about by special objective factors, such as a valley that is enclosed by mountains or a lake bordered by woods, is not in the least sufficient to bring about the aesthetic unity of the landscape in the narrower sense. Rather, it is only an inherent organic connection between individual natural entities, a meaningful composition of the whole, that turns a piece of nature into an individual aesthetic unity.

In a significant work of art, this unity is the specific invention of the artist, as in a glorious melody like Handel's *Largo* or the third movement of Beethoven's String Quartet opus 59 no. 1, or in the unity of an opera like Mozart's *Figaro*, of a symphony like Beethoven's "Pastoral Symphony," or a building like the Palace of the Doges or San Marco in Venice. But the landscape in the narrower sense is an "invention," a gift of God. The unifying principle, the composition, is analogous in both cases. This applies both to the distant landscape and to the landscape near at hand, to the glorious vistas and to the intimate landscape.

There is a great gradation in the rank of beauty; one landscape can be much more beautiful than another. There are attractive landscapes in the Po Valley, especially near the river, but they are very modest in comparison with the landscape at the Gulf of Spezia or in Granada with the vista of the Sierra Nevada. The landscape at the river Amper before it flows into the Isar, or in Fürstenfeldbrück near Munich is lovely, but one cannot compare it to the island of Frauenchiemsee with its vista of the Alps, with the landscape around Vienna where we have on the one side the Vienna Woods and on the other side the Danube and the Marchfeld, or with the landscape in the Wachau region near Dürnstein. Again, a landscape such as that between Freiburg im Breisgau and the Rhine—with the Black Forest on the one side and the Vosges Mountains on the other, and the Kaiserstuhl hills to the north—is indeed beautiful, but it cannot be compared to the view from the Parthenon or the landscape of Tivoli.

The fourth realm of beauty: a region and the types of landscape

We must draw a distinction between this landscape in the narrower sense of the word, the "artistic" unity (whether intimate or extensive) that we have presented above as the fifth bearer of beauty in nature, and another type of nature with a unified "shape" that we have called the fourth bearer of beauty in nature, namely, the "region."

This is present when a piece of nature is marked off as a unity by special characteristics and by a shared common quality. In this sense, we can speak of the type of landscape possessed by the Tuscan landscape near Florence, as distinct from the Sienese type of landscape. This is no longer an instance of a composition, a self-contained visual unity: it is a completely different type of unity. Such a part of nature is marked off from its surroundings by a consistent and uniform atmosphere, but it is not a concrete composition that allows us to compare it with a picture. No self-contained situation is built up, in which the individual elements of nature join together to form an individual "artistic" unity as the notes join to form a melody; a qualitative unity is rather built up, a uniform atmosphere that fills a region.

The region of Florence with the grandiose cypress alleys and olive groves, the hills with their pines, and the gardens with evergreen oaks, presents an inexhaustible wealth of glorious individual situations. This region radiates a sublime atmosphere of spiritual joy. As a whole it possesses a consistent aesthetic quality. Despite all the variety of the landscape in the narrower sense around San Casciano, Compiobbi, Pian dei Cerri, and Artimino,[9] this region as a whole is distinguished by a clear, particular quality. It has a festive character, and indeed, for all its sacred sobriety and classical clarity, an exuberant character. It is sharply distinct

9. These are small towns near Florence.

from the entire Sienese landscape that stretches from Siena via Monte Oliveto Maggiore[10] to San Quirico and displays a specifically austere beauty. It has a special contemplative, nay, mystical character. In this sense, we can also speak of an Umbrian landscape, which once again is united by an overall quality and a unique atmosphere. Similarly, the landscape between Ghent and Bruges, and especially from Bruges to the North Sea, presents a uniform whole, a type of landscape that we could call the Flemish landscape.

We must therefore draw a distinction between two types of nature that are shaped from within: first, the concrete composition, in which elements of nature join together to form an "artistic" unity; and secondly, the type of landscape that certain regions display, where a larger area is united by a common qualitative character and is marked off from its surroundings by a particular atmosphere. In this type of landscape, we can also observe that it stops at one particular place, either because a new type of landscape begins or else because it gives way to an anonymous nature. The landscape between Ghent and Brussels is no longer the Flemish landscape mentioned above. It is a much less defined type of landscape.

Some regions contain many landscapes in the narrower sense, while in other regions only a few such landscapes occur. Although these regions may also contain anonymous parts of nature that are juxtaposed, they possess *qua* region a distinctive character. They have a definite quality of their own and a corresponding atmosphere.

Unlike a landscape, a region does not have the character of a self-contained new entity. It is not an "artistic" unity like a movement in a sonata or a symphony. It is more like the general style of a composer, which allows us to recognize the various pieces as works by Chopin, Schubert, or Beethoven.

People often speak not only of the beauty of a region but of the beauty of a country, for example, Italy, Greece, or Morocco. Before we discuss the aesthetic "unity" in a country, we must eliminate one concept of "landscape" that is even more general than the one we have been using;

10. The celebrated abbey of the Olivetan Benedictine monks, south of Siena.

it is a generality that points in a different direction. A landscape is often described as mountainous, hilly, or flat, or as a maritime landscape. In that case, "landscape" is nothing more than a label for one type of nature. The unity is given by means of a general characteristic. The maritime landscape is a piece of nature on the seacoast. It has no doubt a significant character of its own and an atmosphere determined by the sea, the air, and the smell; the same applies to a mountainous landscape as opposed to a plain. But the general atmosphere of the mountainous landscape itself varies. That of the Alps in general is very different from that of the Apennines, and *a fortiori* from that of the Taygetos Mountains in the southern Peloponnesus, from that of Lebanon, or of the mountains by the Dead Sea.

Judgments about the landscape in a country that refer to its beauty are completely different from this more neutral description of a landscape as mountainous or flat, wooded or treeless. Such descriptions do not refer to "artistic" unity; they speak of nature in this country, of the beauty of the mountains, the vegetation, etc., and of the many beautiful landscapes in the narrower sense.

The difference between the type of landscape of a general kind, on the one hand, and the beauty of the landscape in a country, on the other hand, is that in the first case we are looking at general neutral characteristics, while in the second case we are speaking of beauty, and hence are going far beyond the general characteristics. In the second case, the observation that a place is "wooded" does not mean a great deal, as long as we do not know what kind of trees are present. If all that is noted is "a mountainous landscape," we do not yet know anything about the kind and form of the mountains. But the affirmation that the landscape in Kashmir or Nepal is very beautiful—even if "landscape" here means only nature, not the concrete situation, and still less the composition—already presupposes many detailed elements that play a more decisive role for the bearers of beauty in this country than the information about the mere type of nature. Naturally, among the many elements that condition the beauty of nature in a region, the presence of beautiful landscapes in the narrower sense plays a significant role. The richer a country is in such self-contained, beautiful "artistic" unities, the more beautiful is the country as a whole.

The overall atmosphere of some countries

We wish now to turn to what we have in mind when we say that Morocco is more beautiful than Finland. We are now predicating beauty no longer of one region, but of a whole country. The obvious question is: What bestows on this country the unity which justifies our calling it beautiful as a whole?

Some countries are united by a definite character despite all the variety not only of individual landscapes in the sense of a self-contained picture-like composition, but also of different types of landscape.

This is true to an unusual degree of Italy. Despite all the difference of types of landscape, there is a total Italian quality that runs from Trent to Syracuse and from Aosta to Lecce. Naturally, many other factors are at work. The type of architecture is one decisive factor; without including this, it is surely impossible to speak either of this uniform total atmosphere of the landscape of a country or of its special overall beauty. We shall discuss this in detail in the second volume of this work when we speak of architecture. It plays a decisive role in the total atmosphere of Italy, as does the unique marriage between architecture and nature that is a specific characteristic of Italy.

But when we speak of the total atmosphere of another country, it is not the architecture or the type of landscape, but above all the whole national character, the *cachet* of a country, that determines the unity, as for example in France. In terms of landscape and architecture, Brittany and Normandy are completely different from Provence and the Côte d'Azur, or from the atmosphere of the landscape in the province of Biarritz or the Atlantic coast. Here it is above all the language, national traits of the entire population, customs, clothes, and cuisine that allow us to experience a uniform French atmosphere, despite the great differentiations from one region to another.

We shall return to all these factors in the present chapter, when we discuss how the atmosphere of a country is constituted. It goes without saying that the state borders do not necessarily coincide with this national atmosphere, and still less with the total atmosphere of the landscape. Gossensaß, Brixen, and Merano have a definitely Austrian atmosphere, even if they now belong politically to Italy. Italy begins as a type of landscape only in Trent,[11] where one frequently sees cypresses and the architecture takes on a completely different character.

We must be content to point to the existence of the overall atmosphere of a landscape that can pervade a whole country despite all the differences in individual details. This atmosphere is determined by the vegetation, the type of trees, the forms of the mountains, the light, and to a large extent also by the type of architecture. It forms a new concept of landscape.

Let us sum up: we must note that in our aesthetic context we can disregard the concept of "landscape" that refers only to certain general characteristics of nature (the mountainous landscape, the flat landscape, etc.). It is, however, important for us to distinguish the following types:

First, a uniform type of landscape that is united by a specific aesthetic quality. This is what we have in mind when we speak of the specific beauty of the landscape in Greece, Italy, Spain, or Morocco.

Secondly, a more specific type of landscape, a region with a very specific aesthetic quality, an individual atmosphere, for example, the Sienese landscape as opposed to the Florentine.

Thirdly, landscape in the sense of a composition, of a self-contained visual unity, of a landscape in the narrower sense. This was our starting point; we have designated this the fifth principal bearer of beauty in nature.

With reference to landscape in the narrower sense, we must also draw the distinction, mentioned above, between an intimate and an extensive landscape, between a landscape near at hand and a distant landscape, as well as the landscape in which we ourselves dwell.

11. The linguistic boundary was Salurn (Salorno in Italian).

The contribution of human beings to the beauty of the landscape

We mentioned at the beginning of the present chapter the great significance of architecture, that is, of the marriage between architecture and nature, for the beauty of nature. We must therefore draw attention to a fatal preconception. It is an error to believe that the more untouched by human beings nature is, the more beautiful it is. The contrary is true! From the standpoint of beauty, nature is dependent, so to speak, on the cooperation of human beings. Through this cooperation on the part of human beings, nature can become more beautiful in many respects and can display its specific beauty even more effectively. It suffices here to think of the introduction of a new kind of tree, the planting of alleys, etc.

But wherever the human being can intervene and change the world which surrounds him, there exists equally the possibility of destruction. Through congenial cooperation he can increase the beauty of nature; but he can also destroy it. Unfortunately, this destruction has completely occupied the foreground since the industrialization of the earth, since the triumph of technology and the machine. This destruction, or at least disturbance, of the natural beauty occurs as soon as architecture has a tasteless, inartistic character, although nature is damaged to an incomparably greater extent through industrialization and commercialization.

But just as the fact of sin should not lead us to take a negative attitude to the freedom of the will, and we must always be aware that this freedom is the indispensable presupposition for all high morality and indeed for holiness, so too this destruction of the beauty of nature by human hands must not blind us to the beauty that nature can achieve precisely through the cooperation of the human person. It is an illusion to see the primeval forest as an ideal of undestroyed nature. On the contrary, the primeval forest has a chaotic character in which the beauty of individual entities such as trees cannot come into its own, and the primordial elements cannot burgeon in their immaterial beauty. Still less is it a landscape in the sense of a formed, self-contained, individualized landscape. It is doubtless true that even the nature that is untouched by human beings can attain a great beauty thanks to the primordial elements —for example, the golden sand dunes of the desert, a lofty mountain peak covered in snow, the sea on which no ship is to be seen, or storms and tempests. But human cooperation plays a significant role already in the type of vegetation. For example, many kinds of trees that have a prominent role in Italy's landscape today, such as the cypress, were imported from the Orient in the Roman period.

Another noble human element is contributed by agriculture, which is a significant factor in the beauty of nature and the poetry of life. Naturally, we are not thinking here of the modern agriculture that is controlled by machines, but of the agriculture that predominated from the earliest times until the nineteenth century.

We must distinguish the following factors here. First, agriculture introduces a certain form into nature by planting fruit trees and making vegetable gardens, wheat fields, vineyards in countries where the grapes ripen, and paths that cross the whole territory. Often, this imparting of a form is seen as impairing the untouched free nature, but this is a grave error.

Secondly, the congenial treatment of nature through agriculture not only does not destroy its beauty; on the contrary, it bestows on nature an additional beauty. Who could deny the beauty of a field of rapeseed in bloom, or of corn fields, especially when the ears are ripe? Who could fail to see the charm of vegetable fields, the wealth of forms and colors of various kinds of vegetables, whether beans or tomatoes or different sorts of cabbage? Systematically arranged plantings of olive trees have a very special beauty. The form of their trunks and the silvery color of their leaves are bearers of a specific, refined beauty; they have a mild and humble quality. What splendor distinguishes the fig tree through its form, the gray color of its trunk, the size and beauty of its leaves! One very significant factor in the shaping of a piece of nature is the planting of vines. Sometimes they climb up certain trees, for example, on the so-called *chioppi*, as was often the case in Italy in former times, and sometimes they are supported by a wooden frame; but they are always bearers of beauty. This is especially true of vineyards, which possess a poetry all of their own and bestow a special charm on a landscape. And naturally, this charm reaches its peak when the grapes are ripe. The *balzi*, terraced ledges that are usually cut for the sake of the wine, structure a hill in a very meaningful manner. Even the earth that is loosened up by the plow has its own beauty.

Another factor that enriches the beauty of nature is the animals that have a function in agriculture: oxen, cows, horses. Their beauty and their organic link to nature certainly make a great contribution to the natural beauty and poetry.

This brings us to something that no longer belongs to nature as such, but already belongs to the poetry that life can possess; we shall speak of this poetry in the next chapter. What poetry, what classical beauty lies in the activity of the farmer as he plows, waters the vegetable patches, irrigates the fields, and brings in the harvest—a poetry that is linked to the seasons of the year! Haydn's *Seasons* reproduces this poetry in a wonderful way. Sadly, this poetry of life is completely destroyed when instruments such as the plow and the animals are replaced by machines.

The poetry of life also includes the primordial natural sounds that the farmer employed when speaking to his horses and oxen, and the songs that were sung during work. Goats and sheep at pasture with their shepherd and sheepdog constitute a whole world of poetry.

Not only those trees that are planted because of their beauty, but also those trees that are significant for the practical life of the human person contribute to the beauty of nature. When we speak of significance for the practical life, we mean not only what is significant for naked existence, that which is indispensable in order to sustain life, but also everything that is desirable in view of a cultivated human existence. This, however, brings us already to the decisive factor that increases the beauty of nature in the most significant way, that is to say, to architecture in all its branches, including the lordly estates and parks of which we shall speak in detail in the second volume of this book.

The significance of reality in nature. Illusion [Schein], objectively valid aspect, existentially autonomous visual unity and its real bearers

It is particularly interesting to note that the reality of an object in nature has a significant function for its beauty, or perhaps one should rather say, for the serious existence of the beauty and its delightful quality.

We may be impressed and delighted by the beauty of the clouds that tower up on the horizon, taking the form of snow-covered mountains; but if we finally realize that these are not mountains, but only clouds that look like mountains, we will be disappointed, or at least we will register that this beautiful mountainous landscape was only an illusion. It is true that the appropriate appearance suffices to ground beauty—the forms of the supposed mountains, the light, and the colors build up a visual unity—and it would be false to deny that this view is beautiful. When the landscape in a painting is very beautiful, we know *a priori* that this is not a real landscape. It is completely irrelevant to the beauty of the painting, whether or not the landscape portrayed in it exists. But things are different in nature; here the visual unity does not suffice. This unity must be composed of genuine objects.

The visual unity becomes "valid," so to speak, only when its bearers are in reality what they purport to be.

The clouds, especially the cumuli, are a significant factor in the beauty of nature. They belong to the basic elements of the beauty of nature that were mentioned at the beginning of this chapter. As long as clouds appear as clouds, they are completely real. Although they constantly change in their form and color, their specific function for the beauty of the landscape is very significant. The sun can gild the clouds; or else, when it stands behind them, it can transform their edges into a shining gold contour. At sunset, the clouds can take on the most glorious colors. If, however, they look like mountains, this is clearly nothing more than a beautiful illusion. The necessary reality is lacking—the reality that bestows on this beauty the specific validity without which it cannot fully delight us.

Artificial flowers are a glaring instance of an illusion which not only robs the beauty of its delightful reality, but is in fact the bearer of an aesthetic disvalue. Not only do they lack the fragrance that belongs in many flowers to their full "face," to their poetry: they are a fake, and the quality that adheres to them has a negative value from an aesthetic standpoint. One who adorns a private room, a ballroom, or (worse still) the altar with artificial flowers shows poor taste.

The illusion in nature remains beautiful, and only the dimension of validity and delightfulness is lacking; but the imitation of nature by artificial flowers—which are of course not a *depiction* of flowers but are meant to simulate real flowers—has the aesthetic disvalue of the spurious and the tasteless. This can be seen very clearly in the example of the fake wooden log that burns in a fireplace. This is not a log of wood, nor does it really burn. Such an artificial fireplace is definitely kitsch.

Sometimes, however, reality plays a different role in nature, namely, when what is involved is not an aesthetic disvalue but only an invalidity, which however limits in a special way the delightfulness of beauty. The role played by reality in such an instance is even more vital to our present theme. But the unreality of the beautiful view exists only when what we see simulates another dimension of reality than what it actually possesses. A light that falls on a mountain only for a short time, or the glowing of the Alps in some places (for example, in St. Moritz), is certainly a fully valid beauty. It is a full reality and no illusion. A large percentage of the bearers of sublime beauty in nature are not stable elements like a mountain range, but are in constant change: the light, the clouds, the colors of certain things according to the light that falls on them, and much else. Indeed, the change makes a significant contribution to the beauty and is itself a significant bearer of beauty.

Let us take one example: the fact that the mountains in the far distance look blue, and are green when seen close at hand, does not in any way limit the validity of the beauty. It does not undermine the full reality of this beauty. Their blue color is not an illusion: from a distance, they really look blue, and this appearance is the bearer of a completely valid reality of beauty. It is a great gift that contains a significant message from God. The distant mountains are meant to look like that. How much beauty would be lost, if it were not so! Goethe marvelously expresses this beauty of the blue mountains: "And when by day the distance of blue mountains draws me longingly . . ."[12]

The beauty of the external aspect is a completely valid and real beauty, even when it is determined by spatial distance or lasts only for a short

12. "Vermischte Gedichte," in *Goethes sämtliche Werke*, vol. 2 (Stuttgart and Tübingen: Cotta'scher Verlag, 1840), 89. English translation by BM.

time. We must draw a clear distinction between the external aspect and what we have called an illusion in nature. In an illusion an object pretends to be something other than it is in reality. This is not the case with the external aspect. In an illusion, we are led astray; but as soon as we have recognized that a structure of clouds is not a mountain, all that we see in it is a beautiful combination of clouds. The tower of clouds is not a mountain range and cannot do for the landscape what the mountain range can do. This is why we will say, "What a pity that it is not a mountain range! How glorious that would be!" The clouds are just clouds, and as such they are a significant factor in the beauty of nature. But if we take them to be mountains, the beauty that the landscape would have possessed, thanks to the supposed mountain range, loses its reality.

The difference between an external aspect and an illusion also emerges clearly when we consider that the uniquely self-contained glorious combination of nature and architecture that we find, for example, in the city of Florence with its surroundings offers various external aspects, depending on the place from which we look at them. The view from Fiesole offers a completely different "picture" than that from Bellosguardo, from San Miniato, or from the Fortezza. These are different external aspects of one and the same thing, and each is a completely valid reality. None of them is more real in itself than any other, although one may be more beautiful than the others. Each is a completely valid bearer of beauty, not in the least an illusion. The city and its surroundings have a different appearance, although they remain completely the same, objectively speaking, and they do not change (as is the case, for example, when significant buildings are destroyed). This changing external aspect of the city, this varying appearance in accordance with one's position, is a completely serious reality *sui generis*, not any kind of illusion or deception.[13]

Similarly, if the landscape or palaces are reflected in the water, this is not a mere illusion, but a valid, real, external aspect. And the blue color of the sea and the lakes is a reflection of the blue sky. But this reflection

13. Unless one wished to interpret the shifts in perspective as an illusion or deception; but obviously, this is something completely different from the situation where we take the clouds to be mountains.

does not in any way rob the blue of the sea or the lakes of the fully valid reality that alone can truly delight us. The reflection of the *palazzi* in the Grand Canal in Venice has a special charm and contributes to the beauty of the total situation of the city. It would be ridiculous—and stupid—to say that this reflection was a mere illusion. The fact that water has this ability to reflect is a great gift, and a real factor that makes a significant contribution to the beauty of the external world that surrounds us. Indeed, it possesses a beauty of its own. Let us once again quote Goethe, who is of course the poet *par excellence* of the beauty of nature: "And the ripen'd fruit brightly mirrors itself in the lake."[14]

All these external aspects, these visual impressions, "are meant" to be so. They belong to the extraordinary fullness of the "artistic" composition of nature and are thus clearly distinct from the supposed mountain range about which we are deluded because something is a false external aspect. It is only in this instance of the illusion that deceives us, where an object pretends to be something else, that the beauty of the view is bereft of the reality that brings us delight.

This is why it is extremely important not to confuse the reality that is required for the beauty of nature with the scientific stratum of reality. That would be a gross and foolish misunderstanding. We have already drawn attention, both in the present book (especially in chapters 1 and 2) and in *What is Philosophy?*, to the completely valid reality of the human aspect as a whole, showing that the question whether this aspect exists independently of the human spirit or of any kind of personal spirit is not in any way decisive for the objective validity of this aspect and of the content and value that are constituted in this aspect. The existence and validity that is independent of every person—which is indispensable for the metaphysical essences and laws governing existence, as well as for the reality of other persons—is not given here; but this is not necessary for the kind of reality and validity that belongs to the content and value that are constituted in this aspect.

It would be completely erroneous to hold that colors and sounds are

14. *Auf dem See* ("On the Lake"). English translation by Edgar Alfred Bowring.

less real than waves because they are not apprehended by certain persons, or not apprehended by other persons in the same way, or even because they presuppose a conscious personal being if they are to be constituted. If we understand reality as an image of God, the question, "What is more significant and richer in content in its qualitative content and meaning, what has a higher value?," is a decisive factor for the rank that an existing object occupies in reality. The value and content are completely objective. They stand on their own feet and do not depend in any way on human consciousness. Although the constituting of the reality of colors and sounds presupposes a human spirit, the quality of what we come to know through them—their beauty and the message from God that is contained in them—is completely objective and independent of our attitude to this quality.

This is comparable to the situation in which a truth is communicated to me in a language that I know. I must understand the language in order to learn the truth; the communication of this truth presupposes that I hear the words (and hence, that I am not deaf) and that I understand the sentences. But none of this makes the truth of the sentences that is communicated to me relative to my spirit. This truth possesses its validity independently of myself and of all human beings.

There are many layers in this human aspect. A dog doubtless hears notes, but it cannot apprehend any melody. The melody is an external aspect that presupposes more than notes. Similarly, the visual unity of a landscape is a different external aspect from that which a geographer describes: what interests him is the presence of a specific number of trees, of rocks, the location of brooks, hills, etc. The visual unity of the landscape acquires its objective validity and reality thanks to the fact that its bearers bring forth a meaningful unity, a harmony which resembles the melody. This inherently necessary connection—as opposed to the mere addition, for example, of trees, meadows, hills, or of a sequence of notes that is not a melody—bestows objectivity and autonomy of being on the visual unity. It is the opposite, not only of a mere addition, but also of every arbitrary, insubstantial drawing of boundaries, of every "artificial" unity.

The visual unity is, however, a layer in the framework of the human aspect other than the colors and tones; and apparently, it is even less objective. In truth, it is filled with an even higher substantial message from above, and is therefore not in any way less objective. On the contrary, it is even more valid. But it presupposes the reality of the bearers: it must not be a mere mirage, a dream, or a hallucination. The trees, the river, the mountains, the meadow, the hills must be completely real and possess all the qualities that belong to the layer of the first degree of what we might call the human aspect which is "owed." The analogous visual unity of a picture is in its own way completely realized in a completely new way that belongs to the work of art, if it possesses the inherent necessity and fullness of meaning. In nature, on the other hand, full reality and the validity that is an element of the delightfulness of this reality require the bearers of this unity to be real components of the external world. The term "external world" here means the real existence of the space, of the light, water, trees, animals, human beings, etc., an existence that is completely independent of our consciousness; it does not mean merely an artificial section to which physics and chemistry limit themselves.[15] This reality is presupposed. It grounds the level of the first degree of the human aspect, the colors and sounds, contents that are an objective reality for the natural sciences too.

The new level within the human aspect consists of visual unities such as landscapes. These too demand the full concrete and individual reality of their bearers. In their case too, the difference remains between a landscape that is dreamed, or is constructed on a mere delusion, and a genuine landscape.

The borders of a landscape are determined by real factors. The landscape of the Gulf of Naples is defined in its unity by the extent of the Gulf, or by what one can survey from one single standpoint, as well as by the objective distance of the individual factors from one another and from the point from which this vista, this prospect presents itself. But whether or not the prospect that manifests itself to the eye at this place is a true

15. As Henri Bergson has shown in the first part of his *Creative Evolution*, this limitation is made for pragmatic reasons.

visual unity, a landscape, depends on the inherent necessary content of the visual unity. Full delightfulness also means that the bearers of this visual unity really exist, and are not a mirage or a dream.

We have selected the visual unity of a landscape, as this is given in the vista, in order to investigate the role of reality in the beauty of nature. But what we have said here is not in the least restricted to this special case, as is clear from our earlier discussion of the source of the beauty of the landscape in general.

The constituting of the atmosphere of a landscape, a region, a country

We would now like to point briefly to completely different dimensions of reality that are significant for the beauty of a landscape.

Paradoxical as it may sound, the nature behind a hill that is at the end of a landscape influences the character of the landscape that lies before us.

First of all, we must point out an important distinction. When we think of the beauty of nature, we are confronted by two dimensions of aesthetic values: first, the beauty that we apprehend with our physical eye and with the eye of our spirit; and secondly, the beauty of the atmosphere, the poetry, the "beautiful world" that embraces us and delights us. Both these dimensions find their highest realization in the beautiful landscape in the narrower sense. But it is clear that the bearers that play a role for the constituting of the "beautiful world" are different from those that play a role for the pure beauty of the landscape.

Neither the song of the birds, nor the fragrance of the flowers and fields, nor the sea air contributes to the beauty of the visual unity; but they make an eminent contribution to the constituting of the "beautiful world."

Even a mere piece of knowledge, that is to say, something that is not apprehended by means of our senses, can be a significant factor for the constituting of the "beautiful world."

When we see a glorious landscape, the knowledge of how it looks behind the mountain or the hill that is at the end of this landscape also plays a role. We do not refer here to the precise acquaintance with the landscape behind the hill, but rather to the knowledge of whether the general atmosphere of the region continues there.

There is a mysterious link between the reality of the landscape in the narrower sense and the region mentioned above. It makes a great difference to the reality of the atmosphere, of the "beautiful world" of this landscape, whether or not it is embedded in a congenial region. If this region possessed a completely different quality, a totally opposite atmosphere, the atmosphere of the beautiful landscape in the narrower sense would be less real. Its visual beauty would not be affected by this, but the total delightful, poetic, or transfigured atmosphere that it emanates and with which it embraces us would not be so real; it would be influenced by this.

Not only the knowledge of the region in which the landscape is located, but even the entire country in which it lies plays an important role here.

In order to understand this, we must realize that there are not only individual visual unities in nature. It is not only these that can be beautiful; it is not only these that possess a particular atmosphere, an individual style. Rather, there is also a beauty of whole regions, and even of whole countries. Despite the great variety of its individual parts and regions, Italy as a whole, from Trent to Sicily or Apulia, nevertheless possesses a uniform style, a consistent quality, that distinguishes this country from other countries such as Spain, France, or Austria. This specific quality of the landscape of entire countries is realized to varying degrees. The uniformity of the atmosphere of this type of landscape is more or less well defined in the various countries; indeed, it may be entirely lacking, especially when the concept of "country" is oriented to the national, or even merely the political unity.

Architecture is a central factor in the constitution of the total atmosphere of a country, although this does not mean that the architecture of every country is consistently characterized by particular features, nor that it always differs in a typical manner from one country to another.

A second significant factor is the kind of vegetation. What kinds of trees shape the character of a country? In Italy, this is the work of the cypresses, pines, olive trees, holm oaks, and fig trees that are found more or less everywhere in the country, naturally with varieties of emphasis. These trees are not found in Germany or Austria, in Switzerland (with the exception of Ticino), or in any of the Scandinavian countries. This plays a great role for the total atmosphere of a country and its landscape in general. In France, these trees are found on the Côte d'Azur and in Provence; they also occur sparsely in southwestern France, for example, in the region around Toulouse.

Another significant factor is of course the question whether a country is predominantly flat, or has many hills and mountains. The lack of mountains is characteristic of Hungary and of many parts of Russia, as well as of the Pampas in Argentina; in Austria and Switzerland, high mountain ranges and hills predominate. In many countries, of course, we find both flat regions and numerous hills and mountains, as in Germany. Apart from the broad Po Valley, Italy as a whole is a country traversed by mountain ranges and hills.

Finally, the inhabitants of a country play a decisive role with regard to its atmosphere, its *cachet*. What language do they speak? What customs are prevalent? Such factors range from the literature and music, the visual arts, and the history of a country to the clothing, cuisine, and even many institutions of the state. The temperament of the inhabitants plays a special role.

Up to this point, we have spoken only of those factors that determine the total atmosphere of a country. At first glance, many of these are very far removed from the landscape as a visual unity, and one could perhaps say that they are mere associations that one connects to the landscape. But although this view is widespread, it is completely unobjective and false. Naturally, everyone will admit that the type of vegetation, the predominance of plains, hills, or mountain ranges, and the architecture are significant for the character of a country, even from a purely visual standpoint. But one will classify the special national quality of the inhabitants as something that does not belong to the visual, immediately given character of a country. One will judge that this special quality is unessential, as far as the "beautiful world" of a landscape is concerned, no matter how significant it may be (thanks to associative links) for our subjective joy in the country.

The influence of the inhabitants on the atmosphere of a landscape

Nevertheless, an objective atmosphere exists. It can be prosaic, poetic, or filled with spirit. As we shall shortly see in greater detail, a "beautiful world" or a "sad world" can embrace us. There exists a qualitative congruence, independently of all associations, between a people and the landscape in which they dwell. This need not exist; but it often does exist, and then has a decisive significance for the total atmosphere. It also plays a vital role in allowing the beauty of a landscape or a country to make a spiritual impact. Here we need only think of the unique congruence that existed between the ancient Greek people and the landscape of Greece, washed around by the sea and completely formed by the spirit. The period of the Turkish occupation of Greece is a typical example of incongruence.

Accordingly, when we say that there also exists a congruence among the inhabitants and the "world" and the atmosphere of a country, we are indicating a very significant factor.

The specific kind of people is manifested in various directions, first of all in the general external type of face and figure. Although there are great varieties within one and the same people, Scandinavians nevertheless look different from Italians or Spaniards, and it is meaningful to say, "This person looks like a Swede or an Italian." We leave aside the more pronounced differences in skin color and facial structure that distinguish people of European descent from those of Japanese, Chinese, or African origin, and limit ourselves here to the less pronounced differences in external appearance among Europeans and their descendants in North and South America (though, again, prescinding from black and Native Americans in America).

The specific character of the people is manifested not only in their external appearance, but equally in their temperament and their movements and gestures. It is typical of some peoples that they accompany speech with particular gestures. When they speak, the Italians gesticulate much more than the Germans, and *a fortiori* more than the English.

Another significant factor is language, for example, the musicality of Italian, the elegance of French, or the frequently humorous character of German. The characteristic elements in a language include not only the vowels, or the diphthongs (as in English), or the consonants (as in many Slavonic languages), but also the widely divergent modes of expression. One and the same content is formulated differently in the individual languages—and how much more poetic one language can be than another! It suffices to compare a popular Mexican love song with a North American love song! Some peoples are very reserved. They are embarrassed about showing their feelings, whereas others are highly expansive. Compare an Englishman's declaration of love with that of a Frenchman or an Italian!

The specific character of the people can also vary in keeping with the regions of a country. This finds a very drastic expression in the dialect. The awareness of life and the normal attitude that are reflected in the Berlin dialect are very different from the very attractive, humorous, graceful attitude reflected in the Viennese dialect. Even the intonation and the accentuation express the spirit and the rhythm of life of a people.

The diversity of the inhabitants naturally also leaves its mark on customs, the way they greet one another, good manners in society, the celebration of feasts, and many other things. This should suffice to show the influence that the specific type of population has on the atmosphere of a country and of a region, and the significance of the congruence (which usually occurs automatically) among the people and the nature and the architecture in a country. Rome would no longer be Rome if it were inhabited by Germans or Frenchmen. The atmosphere of the glorious landscape that surrounds the city, and of the unique architecture of the classical, medieval, and Baroque Rome, would no longer be the same. Paris would no longer be Paris if the inhabitants were Englishmen; London would no longer be London if the inhabitants were Spaniards; and Vienna would no longer be Vienna if the inhabitants came from Saxony. This is true not only of cities but also of regions, and indeed of the total atmosphere of a country.

As we have seen, the specific character of the inhabitants, where this relates to their external appearance and gestures, is reflected even in the visible beauty of a country. Above all, it is decisive for the atmosphere and the "world" of a city, a region, and an entire country.

We must draw a further distinction between two things: first, the congeniality, the manner in which the particular quality of the inhabitants fits the landscape and architectural atmosphere of a country; and secondly, the fact that there is a varied gradation in the beauty, the poetry, the charm, and the nobility of various populations. Sometimes, indeed, there is an embarrassing atmosphere that is expressed in the dialect, especially in the case of the inhabitants of certain regions. Where the atmosphere of the inhabitants does not fit the atmosphere of a country, this is a grave deficiency for the "beautiful world" of a region. This discrepancy is almost always the result of the lack of any great tradition, as in North America where, for example, a gulf yawns between the landscape of Arizona (one of the most beautiful in the world) and the atmosphere of the inhabitants. Wherever there exists a genuine tradition with roots back into the world before industrialization, the automatic result is a congeniality between the atmosphere of the inhabitants and the nature.

The variety of the atmosphere of the inhabitants, even where congeniality exists, contributes to the beauty of the "world," of the atmosphere of a country. This atmosphere includes elements that do not belong to the world of the visible, but are likewise significant bearers of the beauty of the "total world" of a country and of the delightful reality of its beauty.

Tourists often impose considerable limitations on the "beautiful world," firstly, because the atmosphere that derives from the specific character of their own people is not congruent with the atmosphere of the country in which they are spending time as tourists; and secondly, because their presence diffuses an attitude of "onlookers" that corresponds to the panorama.

How a landscape is embedded in the atmosphere of a region or of a country

At the moment, however, our theme is the dimension of reality that the total country represents for the beauty of the individual landscape—the dimension of reality that grows out of the atmosphere of one particular landscape, in the sense of a self-contained unity, and that continues in the surroundings. This is a significant factor for the reality of the atmosphere.

We may say of a landscape in Germany that it looks as if it were in Italy; but things are very different if this landscape is in fact in Italy. Someone may say of the rocky landscape on the west coast of Ireland, "It looks almost like a Greek landscape"; but the simple fact that it is not in Greece gives this individual landscape a different character. What element does a landscape receive from being embedded in a total environment that is congenial to it? Why is a landscape much more valid and delightful when it not only looks as if it were in Italy or in Greece, but is in fact located there? It is only very seldom that a landscape, as a pure visual beauty, wholly resembles a landscape in Greece or in Italy, but even then it would possess a different character from a landscape that is genuinely located there. This is a particularly interesting dimension of reality. It is completely different from the dimension mentioned above; but there can be no doubt that it plays a role both objectively and legitimately for the validity and reality of the atmosphere of this landscape.

This factor is related to the delightful reality of a completely specific "beautiful world," whether the sublime sweetness and the incomparable nobility of the "world" of Florence and its surroundings, or the unique greatness and grandeur of the "world" of the Campagna around Rome, or the "mystical world" of Siena and its surroundings. If the "world" that a landscape emanates is to achieve its full, delightful realization, it must be embedded in an entire region that continues this "world" in its basic traits and its loftiness, though with a great qualitative modification. The larger this region is, the more it extends to encompass the unity of an entire country that despite all its variations is filled in a uniform manner by this "beautiful world," the richer is the "world" of the landscape that is limited to a visual unity.

The significance of history for the atmosphere of a landscape

History too is one of the factors that can have an influence on the atmosphere of a landscape, a region, or an entire country. Its influence is very significant. Doubtless, it primarily affects architecture, since this speaks to us of the historical epochs of time. But it also makes a significant contribution to the beauty of the atmosphere, to the "world" that particular landscapes embody.

This is surprising, since history is something purely "known." We must learn it from books, and we must have learned it, since we cannot apprehend it. This brings us to a very interesting general problem, namely, the legitimate function of that which is purely known in the constituting of the atmosphere of the "beautiful world" in nature and art. We shall discuss this question in detail when we speak of art in the second volume of this book.

Let us first point out that there is an illegitimate role of knowledge, for example, in those persons for whom the title of a painting is the primary source of their interest in the painting. People who have no genuine sensitivity to art often attempt to compensate for this deficiency by knowing something about the history of a work of art, whether about the biography of the artist or about other historical facts connected with the work of art.

However, there is also a legitimate and extremely significant function of knowledge for the understanding and experiencing of the artistic content which is immediately given to us, especially in architecture and literature.

What interests us is the legitimate role of knowledge about history for understanding and apprehending the atmosphere, the poetry, the "beautiful world" of landscapes in both the narrower and the wider senses.

First of all, we must note that a piece of nature must be a genuine "artistic" unity, a landscape in the narrower sense, in order for its history to form an organic unity with it. The mere fact that a significant historical event occurred in a place is not enough to contribute to the constituting of the atmosphere, except in the case of those places on which sacred history has left its mark, or places of pilgrimage. The Catalaunian Fields near Châlons-sur-Marne in Champagne, the Rubicon to the west of Rimini, or Jerez de la Frontera in southern Spain do not form a landscape unity, although they were the arena of great historical events.

Waterloo south of Brussels is indeed marked by a monument, but the surrounding region is somewhat anonymous and is truly not a landscape in the narrower sense, not a self-contained "artistic" unity like the Gulf of Spezia. The individualization of a place through history has a completely different character from the individualization that comes about through the aesthetic "artistic" unity. However, when it is added to the "artistic" unity, it can intensify the character of that which is individualized and bestow on it a new note of significance.

One who travels through Greece without the relevant knowledge of ancient Greek history is no doubt able to apprehend the incomparable beauty of Greek landscapes, such as the view from the Parthenon, the landscape and the view from Delphi, or the landscape of Nauplia or Corfu. But he will miss the special total atmosphere, its unique character, its specific poetry. The knowledge of the glorious history of Greece—the birthplace of all the branches of culture, the place in which a unique awakening of the human person took place, the primordial cell of the world of the spirit—is essential, if one is to understand the "world," the atmosphere of this landscape.

Another example is Rome and the landscape around Rome. We can indeed apprehend the pure beauty without any historical knowledge. But we cannot apprehend the unique atmosphere of the central point of the world, the historical greatness and majesty that are expressed especially in the architecture, but also in the nature of the Campagna and the Alban and Sabine Hills, without knowledge of the history of Rome. Only a primitive misunderstanding regards this function of knowledge as a mere association.

Apart from this exceedingly significant role of history for the atmosphere of a landscape in the narrower sense and of a region, an event can also bestow a special atmosphere on one particular place in nature. Indeed, it can bestow on it a consecration that is the bearer of an eminently religious atmosphere. In Palestine, the unique (in the full sense of the word), unparalleled significance of the history of salvation coincides with a wonderful landscape. The birth of Christ, the time spent by Jesus, and his life in these places—all the unique miracles of Jesus that cannot be compared to any other historical event, the proclamation of the divine revelation, and above all the event of events, the death of Christ on the cross, his resurrection and ascension—bestow objectively on these places a significance, a sacred consecration that far surpasses all that can be expressed in the word "atmosphere." It is a special gift that the ultimate, highest consecration is united here to a wonderful, transfigured natural beauty.

The miracles that take place in places of pilgrimage bestow on them too a consecration, albeit one that is incomparably smaller. They too create an atmosphere, a "beautiful world." Lourdes possesses a unique religious atmosphere which takes hold of us—despite the unbeautiful architecture. But this sacral atmosphere, which the miracle of the apparition of the Mother of God and the innumerable miraculous healings, the pilgrimages and processions of the faithful have bestowed on this place, is united to an especially fresh and pure landscape.

Naturally, these contributions by "history" (which is more than history) are something completely new in relation to the general role that history can play for a landscape. History is an eminent bearer of atmosphere. Its link with the place in nature where an event occurred is something objective, something completely independent of our imagination. In order for an event to imprint its atmosphere on a landscape, the landscape as such must possess a certain quality; there must also be a certain (even if only slight) congruence between the atmosphere of the landscape and the atmosphere of the event that took place there. Above all, we must know about the event. The vista of the landscape as such cannot inform us about the event. The atmosphere of the event, which we apprehend thanks to our knowledge, then unites organically to the atmosphere of the landscape and intensifies its beauty. Indeed, it is through the atmosphere of the event that we often understand the landscape better and apprehend it more deeply.

The beauty of nature—a natural revelation of God

In conclusion, we must emphasize a fact that is also of decisive significance for the role played by the total dimension of reality for the beauty of nature, namely, the fact that nature has two fundamental themes, to which we referred at the beginning of the present discussion. In themselves, these are clearly different. In its real existence, the inanimate and the living nature—quite apart from the human person, who forms a completely new theme—is the first theme, with the inexhaustible wealth of its ontological types and values and the qualitative character of its entities. Its beauty is the second theme. For its reality, it presupposes the first theme, but not in the sense that it would be the metaphysical beauty of the first theme.

When we bear in mind the happy fact that the world is God's creation, that it presupposes the existence of God in its contingency and bears the stamp of the created—not of an emanation from God—then we see in the beauty of nature not only something that contains in itself a theme of its own, its *raison d'être*, but also a profound and significant message from God. The beauty of nature contains a natural revelation of God; it is a word addressed to the human person, and at the same time a song in praise of God.

CHAPTER FIFTEEN

Beauty in Human Life

WE HAVE seen how deeply beauty—the beauty that appeals to the senses, and above all the beauty of the second power—is at home in nature. We have inquired into all the bearers of beauty in nature. When we now turn to beauty in human life, we do not exclude the beauty of nature in our life, any more than we exclude art (which we shall discuss in detail in the second volume of this work).

"Lived life" [das gelebte Leben] as a distinct bearer of beauty

Nevertheless, "lived life" is a distinct bearer of beauty. The distinction lies in the theme. In the one case, the beauty of nature and art is as such the theme; in the other case, the theme is our lived life, which is penetrated by the beauty of nature and art. Accordingly, we shall now speak of the beauty or the aesthetically positive character of things that belong to life and whose theme is not exclusively nor even primarily beauty. On the contrary, beauty or poetry is here a superabundant gift. We must distinguish three things.

First, many situations and events in our life are new bearers of beauty, in addition to nature and art. These include especially great, profound experiences, above all love, as well as all *joie de vivre* and all charming atmospheres.

Secondly, the beauty of nature and of architecture plays a great role in our daily life. This includes the beauty of the city in which we live: where it is situated, the nature that surrounds it, the architecture, and above all its whole atmosphere. Some cities possess an incomparably attractive, enchanting atmosphere, such as Salzburg, Vienna, or Paris.

If we live in such a city, all of our daily life is filled with this beauty and with the charm of its atmosphere. If someone travels to a city in order to look at it and to contemplate its beauty, the theme will be its location, the beauty of nature and of architecture. But this beauty has still another role in the city in which we live, namely, the role of the setting within which our daily life takes place. If we live there, we can indeed address this beauty thematically; but in this chapter about the beauty in our lived life, we are thinking only of the beauty of the city as the setting for our daily life.

Something similar applies to our house or apartment. A beautiful house, even if it is quite simple, certainly gives form to our daily life! It is also the setting for significant encounters with other persons, for the unfolding of life with the beloved person with whom we are married, and for being together with our children.

When we look at some beautiful house or apartment with noble furniture and fabrics and take delight in it, the theme is the beauty of the architecture, of the interior design, and of the surrounding nature. But now let us think of the house in which we ourselves dwell, of the beauty and the atmosphere that fills it, as the setting for our daily life and for all the great and significant things, as well as the small and everyday things, that happen here. The beauty of the interior design, the furniture, the curtains, perhaps also the view from the house, but certainly above all, the atmosphere—all this belongs to the beauty of the lived life. All those things in life that are bearers of beauty—the awakening of love for another person, all good conversations, and for many people their intellectual work—are invested in a special way in the atmosphere of the house or apartment.

Thirdly, we have in mind the function of art in opening our eyes to the beauty of the poetry of our lived life and in revealing to us in greater depth the beauty of love in all its categories, the beauty of nature—and especially as the setting for our daily life—the beauty of every celebration, and of all the poetic situations in life. Apart from its own value as a bearer of beauty, art (as has been pointed out above all by Konrad Fiedler) has this function of awakening the human spirit.[1] We shall return briefly to this third point in the course of the present chapter, but we reserve its detailed treatment for the second volume of this work, where our theme is the beauty of the arts. Here we wish to concentrate primarily on the first two points.

The beauty of life to which we draw attention first of all is the beauty of many situations in life, the metaphysical beauty of the persons with whom a deeper fellowship unites us, and the beauty of the joy that is granted to us. In lived life there are many sources of genuine beauty, and not merely of qualities that can be described as "beautiful" only by way of analogy. If we say to a friend, "How beautiful that you have come!", it is clear that this term is no longer being employed to designate an aesthetic value, but in a much more general, analogous sense. Now, however, we wish to speak of the beauty in the lived life that is a genuine aesthetic value and that adheres to many situations and to entities of various kinds, for example, to an occasion of celebration, to the rhythm of events in public life, or to conversations with other people.

Metaphysical beauty plays a significant role in this beauty of life, but not only metaphysical beauty; the beauty that appeals to the senses also has its part. The question that interests us is: Which bearers of beauty do we find in lived life, apart from nature and art? Which entities in our life are bearers of beauty?

There still exist today poetic situations—and there were many more of them in the past—such as the bustling life in a marketplace, for exam-

1. Cf. *Konrad Fiedlers Schriften über Kunst*, ed. Hermann Konnerth (Munich: Piper Verlag, 1913), 98.

ple, on the Piazza delle Erbe in Verona or in front of the cathedral in Freiburg im Breisgau, in the morning freshness with the shining colors of the fruit, vegetables, and flowers, with the lively hustle and bustle of sellers and buyers. An oriental bazaar like the souk in Tunis is particularly poetic—naturally, it is at its best without tourists, who usually bring along an oppressive prosaic spirit.

What poetry there was in situations like watering the animals, or drawing water and bringing the full jars home! Even today one can witness this in Greece. Such situations, which belong entirely to everyday life and are not in any way festal, can possess a great poetry. At one particular time of day, one sees the women coming from all sides. They draw water and bear full jars home on their heads. The entire situation—the drawing of the water, the confident steps the women take, balancing as they walk home with the jars on their heads—has a definite poetry, to which of course the type of well and the surrounding landscape make their contribution.

Another example: when the women wash their clothes in the beautiful pool in San Gimignano with the glorious view, this has a great poetry. Naturally, the beauty of nature and of the architecture of the pool play a decisive role here. But this primordial human situation, where the women do their washing together and have the opportunity to talk about many things and to gossip, is filled with a specific poetry of life.

Similarly, the stage-coachman in the countryside with his coach and his horn was a source of definite poetry. I can still recall his white-blue costume with the red waistcoat and the yellow postal coaches. They were beautiful, and the coachman's costume was charming. And he blew with his horn pleasant melodies as he drove across the landscape to bring people the letters with news that was eagerly awaited or feared, news that was joyful or sad. This activity, so human and classically woven into the fabric of life, was in itself charming and poetic. The fact that the beauty of visible and audible elements plays a significant role here does not in any way alter the fact that the bearer of aesthetic qualities—of a poetry and sometimes of a definite beauty—is a situation in life that is linked to a classic human activity.

Or let us think of a ball that is organized with great splendor: a festive, beautiful room, elegant evening dress, beautiful dances, good dancers, and above all the festive mood. Not every ball is a bearer of beauty; today, it is more difficult than in the past to find this aesthetic quality at a ball, because of the widespread degeneration of the dances and the general de-poeticization and austerity of life. But in earlier times, when people's clothing was not just elegant but definitely beautiful, the special, aesthetically positive quality of the festal celebration, of an activity dedicated to joy, could be clearly seen in the elegant parties that were held in many cities, in public or in private, before the First World War.

What interests us here is this type of bearer of aesthetic qualities. Like all potential bearers of aesthetic values, these can also be bearers of disvalues. Just as the moral disvalues, the shallow and mediocre thoughts of human beings, are the bearers of a specific ugliness, so too these human situations and festivities, and the activities on certain occasions, can be the bearers of disvalues. There are festivities and balls that are unbridled orgies. Their aesthetic character is negative; they are nasty, repulsive, and oppressive. Besides this, there are festivities that are boring, unsuccessful, and lackluster—but festivities can also possess a great charm. They can be splendid and truly festive, with the magic of the extraordinary, that which stands out from the prose of everyday life. It goes without saying that they can therefore be delightful and attractive. Now, however, we wish to point to the aesthetic value that they can possess. Many visible factors contribute to this: the beauty of the ballroom, the beauty or at least the elegance of the clothes, the cultivated good manners, the gracefulness of the dancers, and not least the excitement of the persons present and the intensity of the festal atmosphere, which is so difficult to describe.

Aesthetic values belong also to the experience and enjoyment of the whole event. This emerges clearly when someone is present as an onlooker, and it is only the aesthetic quality of the festivity that delights him. But the aesthetic charm of the entire celebration plays a role even in one who is completely drawn into the festivity, one who is dancing with a person with whom he is in love. It is true that the presence of a person with whom he is in love, and the act of dancing with this person, occupy the foreground to such an extent that even a celebration that as a whole is unsuccessful and boring remains very delightful for *him*. On the other hand, his love also makes him more capable of feeling the aesthetic value of the entire event, if it is completely successful and truly festive.

These are only a few examples of the varied types of situations in life that can be bearers of aesthetic values, and above all of a definite poetry. In a festivity, the prominent point is not so much the poetic quality but rather the beauty of the festive dimension, the splendor of the entire atmosphere. It is the activity in a market, or the activity of the stage-coachman, that is the bearer of a certain poetry. The poetic element was even more pronounced in olden days, for example, when all the upper classes drove in beautiful carriages drawn by noble horses along the Corso in Rome at one particular hour of the day. No doubt, the beauty of the buildings, the light, the coaches, and the horses stood in the foreground, but the situation itself was the bearer of a value, the value of the life that took place there.

In the same way, tournaments were bearers of a specific beauty. Naturally, the beauty of the armor and the horses played a great role, but the deployment of courage and the tension of combat also possessed a definitely aesthetic quality of a positive kind. A tournament was something quite different from the act of looking at beautiful armor in a museum or beautiful horses in the circus ring. It was an event embedded in life—not only a representation of the event but a genuine event, to which there belonged a festive, splendid atmosphere. In short, it was the bearer of a definite aesthetic value, although it can scarcely be permissible, morally speaking, to expose human beings to such a risk.

Similarly, bullfights have a definitely aesthetic quality of a positive kind. Despite all the cruelty to the bull and the danger to the bullfighter, the whole event has its own beauty and poetry in its style, in the beauty of the garments, the horses, the bull, the gracefulness of the bullfighter, and his courage.

It is interesting to compare these events with others such as baseball or football games, or even boxing matches. Many people find these attractive because of the tension—"Who will win?"—and because of the bets they place. Nevertheless, these possess no kind of poetry, nor any aesthetic value. The contribution (mentioned above) made by beautiful garments and animals is missing, as are the unity of style, the cultivated form, and the genuinely festive character. Such events are indeed exciting, but they are not in any way festive. Indeed, boxing matches have a definitely ugly and brutal character. They are the opposite of the splendid.

In an analogous manner, hunting had a definite poetry in the past. The beauty of the horses and the hounds, the blowing of the hunting horns, the beauty of the surrounding nature and of the quarry (for example, a deer) contributed to this poetry, as did the poetic atmosphere of the event, the whole meet, the animated activity.

The poetic element emerges even more specifically when we observe the activity of fishermen on a seacoast as they cast their nets from their boats, catch fish, and bring them ashore.

Similarly, the activity of the farmer who plows, as he walks alongside the plow that is drawn by an ox or a horse and occasionally encourages the animal, is the bearer of a definite aesthetic value, of a very particular poetry.

In general, one underestimates the great significance of aesthetic values, and especially of beauty, for the true happiness of the human person. People fail to recognize the heavenly gift of the elevation of the soul through the beauty and poetry of the situations that surround us. They need not be conscious of this function of beauty, nor need they know the benefit that beauty is for their soul and for the health of mind and soul—nevertheless, this effect exists objectively. Naturally, they also come consciously into contact with this beauty, but above all they breathe it in as something taken for granted, while other themes form the central focus of their experience.

The metaphysical beauty of the values of personality in "lived life"

We often say, "How beautiful it was to be together with that person!" It is indeed true that in such instances we usually do not employ the word "beautiful" in its proper sense; we mean that the time spent together was harmonious, delightful, without friction, deep, rich in content. But all these qualities are also bearers of a certain beauty, and precisely when the depth and the rich content of the time spent together are emphasized, this time can be said also to be beautiful in the proper sense of the word. It was full of light, it raised us up into a world that is mysteriously connected to beauty.

The mystery of sexuality is likewise the bearer of poetry and beauty.[2] Naturally, we are speaking only of the magic which goes hand in hand with nuptial love, with being in love, the magic that the feminine has for the man and the masculine for the woman—not an isolated sensuality that can indeed be seductively attractive but is not in any way a bearer of beauty. It rather bears in itself the ugliness of the desecration of a high good and the ugliness of a great sin, namely, impurity. It may disguise itself with an apparent poetry, with a magic like that of the flower maidens in *Parsifal.* But in reality behind the beautiful mask there grins the hideous face of viciousness and baseness, and with it the metaphysical ugliness of these two moral disvalues.

We are also speaking of the entire splendor possessed by the mystery of sexuality taken in a broad sense of the word: the hope, full of promise, of a young person who looks to the life that lies ahead of him or her; the alertness of the senses to so many elements in nature; the divinely-willed role that is played by this state of being in love and by the existence of this mystery. How much richer is the world because this exists!

It is significant that this aspect of the world and of life is so significant in poetry. Goethe speaks like this of the expectant beauty with which life and the world present themselves to the one who loves: "How fair doth nature appear again! / How bright the sunbeams! How smiles the plain!"[3] Here the poet is indeed speaking of the beauty of nature, but we think not of this beauty as such, but of the beauty of the "light" that falls on everything thanks to the state of being in love; or, to put it more precisely,

2. Obviously, when we speak of the beauty of sexuality we do not mean the beauty of the human body.

3. *Mailied.* English translation by Edgar Alfred Bowring.

the beauty of nature that we apprehend more deeply and radiantly when we are in love.

The role of metaphysical beauty in our lived life now emerges clearly. For it is the metaphysical beauty of all the values of the personalities whom we encounter, and especially of those with whom we share a deeper fellowship, that primarily makes our life rich and a source of joy. Goethe rightly says: "In personal being lies / A human being's chief happiness."[4] But is it not likewise possible for the metaphysical ugliness of base and vicious persons, or the triviality of certain people, to play an extremely negative role in our lived life?

Like all metaphysical beauty, the beauty of a personality full of charm and gracefulness, and the poetry of his or her entire being, are grounded in personal values, and the friendship with such a personality—or *a fortiori* the spousal love one has for him or her, and being loved by such a one—belongs to the intimate sphere of the lived life. In the *Phaedrus* (255 ff.), Plato describes in glorious words the metaphysical beauty of love, and especially of the state of being in love (in the highest sense of the term); but it receives its most sublime expression in the Song of Songs, which is known in German as the *Hohelied*, the "high song" of love.

It is here above all that the metaphysical beauty of all values speaks to us—even more than when we explicitly contemplate moral and other values, or turn thematically to truth.[5]

The beautiful atmosphere of particular situations

When we speak of beauty in our lived life, we are also referring above all to the "lovely world [*schöne Welt*]," the beautiful atmosphere that leaves its mark on a situation, or we are referring to significant conversations in which complementary truths unfold in dialogue. These conversations can possess a beauty that resembles a Platonic dialogue such as the *Sympo-*

4. *West-Eastern Divan*, "Book of Zuleika." English translation by Edward Dowden, but amended by JFC.

5. It goes without saying that we are not referring here to religious contemplation.

sium. We have already mentioned in chapter 13 above, with reference to thematic and unthematic bearers of beauty, that books that have truth as their theme can have great beauty, whether it is the metaphysical beauty of the truth that is expressed in them, or the beauty of the form of their construction, their style, and the atmosphere of the book as a whole. In principle, this can apply to conversations as well. Apart from the fact that the various entities that possess an unthematic beauty demand a thorough analysis and must be kept distinct from the beauty of nature and of art, our interest here concerns those conversations in which we ourselves can take part, since they are genuine events in our life. In this sense they once again form a situation in life that is a bearer of aesthetic values.

Travels, too, apart from the beauty of nature and of architecture that one sees while traveling, not only can be interesting, but can have a positive aesthetic value because of everything that we encounter, for example, the customs and way of life of other nations and peoples. There is certainly positive value in the fullness of life that unfolds thanks to the variety of the continuously changing poetical situations, each with its own character, and thanks to the encounter with many persons. This value is likewise an aesthetic value, though of a particular kind. Traveling as such has a charm all its own.

Naturally, this beauty in life is, in itself, partly a metaphysical beauty and partly a beauty that appeals to the senses; even the beauty of the second power penetrates into our life and belongs to particular entities. Although the quality of the beauty is not different, the bearers are partly of a different kind. For example, the beauty of nature is not thematic in the same way as when we contemplate a landscape and immerse ourselves deeply in its beauty. But a natural beauty such as glorious weather has a special effect upon our life. It creates what we might call a setting for everything that we undertake on a given day.

Here we must draw attention to another significant aesthetic value that must be clearly distinguished from beauty, although it also plays a great role in art as a bearer of beauty, namely, the comic. We shall discuss the significant role of this particular value in art in the second volume of this work. It ranges from light farce to noble comedy in which the comic is united to the most sublime poetry and beauty, as in Shakespeare's comedies and even in certain passages in his tragedies (for example, the porter in *Macbeth*). In *Don Quixote*, the comic is woven into all the splendor of the novel; in union with other elements of the highest artistic beauty, it is a bearer of the greatest artistic values.

The phenomenon of the comic is in itself so fundamental that we shall devote chapter 19 specifically to it. Here we mention it only as a spice of life, as an element that invests many occasions with a positive value and therefore belongs to the aesthetic values of life, or in other words an element that is a bearer of the aesthetic values of lived life.

We need not discuss again the second source of beauty in the lived life that we distinguished at the beginning of this chapter, namely, the beauty of nature and of architecture, and all that is great and beautiful in our life. We wish only to point out the special atmosphere that a city can have. The atmosphere is a completely singular entity, and we must distinguish clearly between a beautiful atmosphere and one that is oppressive and depressive. This atmosphere can be the bearer of an aesthetic value or a disvalue. Great varieties are possible within the qualities that have a positive value. The atmosphere can be exhilarating, stimulating, full of charm; it can be noble or sublime. Many Italian cities—Venice, Florence, Rome—have a sublime, beautiful atmosphere, while Vienna and Paris have an exhilarating, charming, delightful atmosphere.

The people who live in a city play a decisive role for the genesis of an atmosphere. Their lifestyle, their national *cachet*, and everything that goes on in a city—the intellectual life, theater, music, work of every kind—has an influence on this. Another very significant factor is the history of a city. Great personalities who have worked there have left a special mark on this atmosphere. The unique atmosphere of Vienna is marked by Haydn and Schubert; nor should we forget personalities such as Johann Strauss, who cannot match a Haydn or a Schubert in depth but are nevertheless full of charm.

The beauty, the charm of an atmosphere is in very general terms a rich source of happiness, and its value is a significant bearer of the aesthetic dimension in the life that we live.

The significance of art for apprehending the beauty of love

As for the third source distinguished above, the role of art in opening our eyes to the beauty in our lived life, let us say just a word about this function in relation to love: the significance of art for apprehending the beauty of love in all its categories, especially for the love for Christ and for human nuptial love. Goethe's words in his *May Song* well illuminate various aspects of this human spousal love and of what it means to be deeply in love:

Oh love! Oh loved one!
As golden bright
As clouds of morning
On yonder height![6]

And how the mystery of the deepest spousal love is disclosed to us in Wagner's *Tristan*! And think of what the poems of Saint John of the Cross reveal to us about the love for Jesus in its highest dimension, and about His love for us! We shall return to this function of art in the second volume of this work.

The meaning of particular periods in our life *"Regions of time"*

We wish now to discuss a phenomenon that belongs in a specific manner to the bearers of beauty in our life. It is not indeed given to everyone to be acquainted with this phenomenon, but for all who do know it, it is a typical bearer of beauty in lived life. We refer to the remarkable fact that certain shorter or longer stretches of time can form a unit. Such a stretch is lifted as an individuality out of the uniform stream of life and exists as an interpersonal reality. The reasons for this can be various, but there is always one special theme that dominates this stretch of time and bestows on it a particular character, a special atmosphere. The theme can be very profound, for example, the preparation for conversion to the Church by

6. *Mailied.* English translation by Edgar Alfred Bowring.

receiving instruction, or the beginning of a deep love for someone which pervades and colors a stretch of time, or the preparation for a journey that one hopes will make a deep impression on someone, and so on. But the remarkable thing is that such a "region of time" [*Zeitwelt*] is not only an experience in the soul of one human being, but is also an interpersonal reality. A number of persons who are close to one another have the consciousness that a special time has begun and a particular atmosphere fills the air. We are enfolded by this region of time, a specific qualitative rhythm fills this time, so to speak, and supports us. Suddenly it comes to an end. Usually this cessation is accompanied by a change in the external situation. When the same situation is restored later on (although this is of course not always possible)—with the same persons, the same place, the same activity—this region of time need not continue. The occurrence of such a region of time is completely outside our own power. We cannot cause it to happen by our own will. It is a pure gift.

This remarkable phenomenon has the following characteristics. First of all, it is an experience of an objective reality that exists outside our own selves. Secondly, the days of this stretch of time are completely permeated by a specific atmosphere that supports us and makes us happy.

Thirdly, it is as if one awakes and sees everything more brightly and deeply. One awakes out of a certain automatism of daily life that is imposed upon us by practical necessities of every kind—sleeping, eating and drinking, our normal professional activities. One emerges out of the state of being driven by these various tasks and encounters a new, intensive life that is lifted out above this stream of everyday life. Naturally, this does not mean that the daily things cease: but everything is pervaded by the melody of this region of time.

Fourthly, the present moment is experienced then in a more real manner. For the air is mysteriously filled with the beauty of the world, with the light of the world of values. One is transposed into an importance, into a more intensive and fuller life. One feels oneself borne and enfolded by this region of time.

In a certain manner, it is a miniature version of a cultural epoch, of an interpersonal entity such as the *Quattrocento* in Florence or the

Baroque or Rococo eras, which were formed by a particular sense of life [*Lebensgefühl*] and by certain ideals that were in the air. In this comparison, however, we are thinking only of epochs that deserve the name of cultural epochs because of the genuine culture that flourished in them. We are not thinking of the mere fashions of a time that is marked by the historical-sociological reality of certain idols, nor of periods characterized by the absence of true culture, as in the epochs that loom in the twentieth century.

It is of course true that this comparison limps in many ways. Naturally, the reasons for the genesis of an epoch, and the factors that constitute its inherent unity and lift it out of the flow of history as a period that is a uniform entity, are completely different from those involved in the "regions of time." Their extent in temporal and spatial terms is incomparably greater and the interpersonal character is much more defined, so that one could justifiably say that the differences between them are much more striking than what they have in common. Nevertheless, it makes sense to point to this distant analogy, since it draws our attention to one particular element: it brings out the fact that one period is lifted out of the continuous stream of time and possesses a particular atmosphere that bears us and enfolds us. We feel that we move in this atmosphere and that it is an interpersonal reality, even if only for a few persons.

One could say much more about this theme, but it will suffice to note that such regions of time are bearers of beauty; the world that is actualized in a special way in this time can be pervaded by beauty; a "lovely world" enfolds us. It may be that not everyone experiences such regions of time, but many do so without being aware of the specific character of such a phenomenon—they simply note that it is a happy period of their life. But for all who consciously experience such regions of time, they are definite bearers of beauty and a typical example of the appearing of aesthetic values in the phenomena of human life.

The shared expectation of an imminent event with great appeal, such as a significant journey from which one hopes to receive much, can sometimes construct one particular region of time out of a few preceding days. Everything suddenly becomes more significant; indeed, every event speaks more intensively to us and leaves a deeper mark on us. As in all regions of time, certain pieces of music that one frequently hears in this time can link together with this region of time; later on nothing has a greater ability to transpose us back into it than hearing such a piece of music.

The remarkable thing is that these curious stretches of time come into existence only with some positive value. There are indeed especially heavy and sad phases in life, such as the anxiety about a beloved person or the time after his or her death, a tragic public event, or a grave illness that one experiences. These sad times do not have the character of a self-contained unit, of being enfolded by such a potent atmosphere of time in which one has an experience of awakening and feels as if all the gates to the world of values were opened. Such heavy periods—for example, when we suffer extremely severe pain, or events plunge us into the deepest grief—oppress us. We are completely absorbed in the pain and are less awake than beforehand; and this means that no definite region of time can come into existence. A night settles upon our mind and our heart, making it impossible for this interpersonal unit of time with a definite atmosphere to come into existence for us.

Love as a bearer of beauty in our life

It is easy to see that the poetry of many situations in life is an aesthetic value. But if we mention love as a bearer of beauty in our life, a clarification is necessary, for one could object, "Beauty is always something that we apprehend as standing over against us in the object. Did you not assert in chapter 1 that beauty can never be something that exists consciously, a lateral experience, but is always the quality of an object which it is apprehended in a 'consciousness of'? In what sense, then, can we call the act of love that we experience in ourselves a bearer of beauty in our lived life?" The apprehending of the metaphysical beauty of the person whom one loves, and of his or her beauty that appeals to the senses, does not constitute a problem. In these cases there is a clear "consciousness of," to which we respond with our love. I have written about this in detail in chapter 1 above, and in my book *The Nature of Love* (especially chapters 1 and 10).

The same applies to the metaphysical beauty of love that we apprehend in other persons, that is to say, the beauty of their value. This is uniquely intensified in the experience of being loved, in which the metaphysical beauty of love unfolds before the eye of our spirit in a special way. This self-disclosure of metaphysical beauty in fact reaches its zenith in being loved, that is, in the love that reciprocates our own love.

As for the act of loving itself, it does indeed make one uniquely happy —but how can one speak of "beauty" in this instance? If one says of one's own act of loving, "How beautiful it is to love!", is this not to equate "beautiful" with "making happy"? But as we have seen, even one's own act of loving has a relationship to the "consciousness of" beauty, since through the act of loving we are awakened in a unique way to all the bearers of beauty, and above all to the beauty of life, nature, and the "lovely world" into which we are transposed.

This is why the affirmation that our lived life becomes more beautiful through love does not contradict the fundamental fact that was emphasized in chapter 1, namely, that beauty can never be something consciously lived through, like joy or grief. This will become even clearer in the following chapter, in which we offer a detailed analysis of the aesthetic experience, of the *frui* of beauty.

The contemplative element in the tasting of beauty

Before we conclude the present chapter, we must emphasize as vigorously as possible that the true thematic enjoyment of beauty, especially of the beauty of the second power, possesses an extraordinary significance for the spiritual development of a human being. Up to this point we have not spoken of the role played for the human person by the thematic beauty in nature and art.

The specifically contemplative element in the *frui* of genuine beauty in nature and art has an eminent significance for the entire personality. Few things depersonalize a human being as much as the complete absorption in practical tasks. The mountain of things to be done—whether the tasks that belong to our life as a matter of course, whether normal professional requirements, or extraordinary demands made on us, or the struggle of life in general—can result in a rhythm of daily living in which one is always on the go, hastening to tackle the next practical task. In this case there is no full personal presence; one becomes a total *homo faber* (man the maker). This means the loss of the complete "self" (as Kierkegaard understands this term). One remains on the periphery, without ever entering into one's own depths. It is only when contemplation and contemplative acts receive their due in our life that we can truly be persons. It is only then that we come to our own true self.

Once one has apprehended the decisive role of contemplation and the contemplative experiences for the human person, their liberating effect, the unique thematic role of the object in contemplation, which at the same time leads to the true self, then one can appreciate in full the significance for the human person of beauty in nature and art.

Naturally, the aesthetic experience is not the only contemplative behavior. The highest contemplative act is the loving, adoring immersion in God, it is religious contemplation in all its forms. Besides this, every genuine, deep human love is as such a contemplative act, although so much very noble activity is generated by it. And there is a contemplative element in every value-response to moral values, as well as in knowledge (especially philosophical knowledge), as I have shown in chapter 6 of my book *What is Philosophy?*, where we discuss the two fundamental themes in knowledge, the notional theme and the contemplative theme.

The important point to be grasped here is that the true aesthetic experience is likewise a classical form of contemplation. Accordingly, it frees the human person from his pragmatic enslavement. In the aesthetic experience, in the aesthetic *frui*, we find both a full *propter se ipsum* ("for its own sake") and the elimination of the instrumental means-end relation. This too is very significant for the development and deepening of the personality. Naturally, the formal value of paying attention to something *propter se ipsum* acquires its true value only when the object in question is the bearer of genuine values, as is the case with beautiful things.

But the broadening, liberating, personalizing effect of beauty goes much further still. We have already mentioned its unique objectivity. Besides this, the soul is given wings by beauty in a special way. When it is seized and irradiated by beauty, it itself becomes more beautiful, just as the one who loves becomes himself more lovable and more beautiful in the act of loving.

We shall return to this central fact in the following chapter on the aesthetic experience; but we shall discuss it fully only in the second volume of this work, where our theme is beauty in art.

CHAPTER SIXTEEN

The Aesthetic Experience

We have already spoken of beauty as a genuine value and of the special character of its aesthetic value as compared with other value families. We have discussed the difference between metaphysical beauty and the beauty that appeals to the senses, and we have seen above all that the visible and the audible can be bearers not only of a beauty that appeals to the senses, but also of a special sublime spiritual beauty, a beauty of the second power. We have spoken in detail of the specific natural mystery that is here entrusted to the visible and the audible.

In the present chapter, we wish to investigate the essence of the aesthetic experience, and of true and false aesthetic enjoyment. Obviously, this is a completely new theme in relation to those we have discussed above.

Being pleased [das Gefallen] in the narrow and in the broad sense

The aesthetic experience, which is the principal stance taken to the beautiful, is often traced back to "pleasing me." Even Saint Thomas speaks of the beauty which appeals to the senses as *quod visum placet*, "that which pleases when seen." Kant too calls the joy at beauty "being pleased."[1]

Accordingly, we begin by examining "being pleased," investigating its essence and its role in the experience of the beautiful. This will clear the path, so to speak, for the analysis of the essence of the true aesthetic experience, of the *frui* of the beautiful.

What is the essence of being pleased? Is it only an effect that something has on us, in this case the kindling of a pleasure? It is clear that one can employ the expression *gefallen* ("to be pleased") in a broad and imprecise sense, or in a strict sense that is especially relevant in relation to aesthetic values.

In the broader sense, the German verb *gefallen* means the same as the English verb *to like* (*mögen* in German colloquial usage). When we say, "I like this," or "I do not like this," we are expressing a definitely subjective judgment. But is even this subjective *liking* truly the equivalent of "It causes a pleasant sensation in me?" Obviously, it is meaningless to say, "I do not like the heat when it burns my finger," or to say, "I do not like the knife when I cut myself with it." If an object provokes general physical displeasure, physical pain, there is obviously no point in saying that I do not like it, for that would be so obvious as to be distinctly comical.

If we say of an object that it pleases or displeases us, we are certainly expressing a relationship that it has to us. The "giving pleasure" requires a "to me." It is not a judgment such as "It is beautiful," where a "to me" and a "for me" are meaningless. But the giving of pleasure or displeasure, even in this improper use of the word, is related not only to the ability of the object to cause pleasure or displeasure in me. In this general, loose sense, it includes a subjective element. I am not stating something about the thing that describes it as such, independently of my own self; rather, I am stating something about my subjective attitude to it. On the other hand, a judgment is made about this object that goes beyond the simple affirmation that it awakens pleasure in me.

In our present context, being pleased in the narrower senses is much more important for us. When Saint Thomas says of beauty, *quod visum*

1. Immanuel Kant, *Critique of Judgment*, part 1, division 1, book 1, paragraph 5.

placet, or when Kant speaks of a pleasure in which no pragmatic interest or use of any kind makes its voice heard,[2] being pleased means something more, something much more special. The use of this word draws attention to an aesthetic quality of an object; it is not merely a general observation that it is agreeable to me, as in the use of the verbs *mögen* or *to like.* What interests us is the being pleased that we express in the proposition, "This person pleases me," or in the question, "Does this garment, this piece of music, or this poem please you?"

Here it is clear that an aesthetic "effect" of the object is involved. The affirmation, "It pleases me," includes a relationship to my own self, on the one hand, and a judgment about the object, ascribing a positive significance to it, on the other. As long as something merely kindles a pleasant physical sensation in me, being pleased in the narrower sense is not present. If all I mean is, "I find it pleasant," or "It is satisfying in some way," the specific thing of being pleased is not yet present. If we wish to state that we find warm baths very agreeable, and we say, "Warm baths please me," this formulation is inexact in terms of the narrower sense of "being pleased." If someone feels a great satisfaction at the death of an enemy, he cannot say, "The death of this man pleases me." The typical being pleased is related to a positive value of the object, but—unlike a value judgment—it refers to the significance that it has for me because of its value. Sometimes one person utters a negative judgment about a thing or a person, and someone else then says, "This thing or this person pleases *me* greatly." Often such a statement virtually amounts to a positive value judgment about that thing or person. If, however, we say, "He may have many faults, but he nevertheless pleases me," it is clear that the emphasis lies on the relationship to myself, on his endearing character, on the element of the "for me."

Unlike a judgment about the object, being pleased is always related to the immediate impression that it makes on me. It is this that stands in the foreground, not the purely intellectual affirmation about the positive character of the object. But being pleased is also distinct from the immediate apprehension of value, which is entirely directed to the object. It does indeed include the relationship to myself, but it is not identical

2. Ibid., part 1, division 1, book 1, paragraphs 2 and 5.

with being affected by the bearer of the value. No genuine state of being-affected is necessary in order to affirm, "It pleases me."

For lofty values such as a noble act of forgiveness or heroic moral conduct, the affirmation, "It pleases me," is inexact. One is aware that this value appeals to a completely different response from us—profound emotion, enthusiasm, or an objective praise of the other person, a judgment about his conduct. The expression, "It pleases me," would be inappropriate. It strikes the wrong note. If, however, our judgment as a whole, after getting our first impression of a person, is expressed in the words, "He pleases me," this is not a misuse of the concept of being pleased, for all that we are doing is speaking of a positive total impression, an impression that has won us over to him and that promises many positive qualities. Clearly, however, this being pleased by him is sharply distinct from a profound impression that someone makes on me already at our first meeting where he reveals himself to me as an extraordinary personality in his kindness or his brilliance. "Being pleased" would be inexact in that case too. Plato would never have said of Socrates, "He pleases me," or "I like him," not even on the occasion of their first meeting.

Being pleased is thus first of all a special, immediate contact with a positive value of an object. It is clearly distinct from the mere act of apprehending value, and from the typical forms of being affected by value, such as being moved, stirred, lifted up, or edified, as well as from all value-responses, such as enthusiasm. *A fortiori*, it is distinct from affirmations such as that this object is beautiful, possesses a value, etc.

Secondly, it is clear that one is referring to certain values of the object when one states, "It pleases me." And these are aesthetic values. It is inexact to say of moral or "intellectual" values, and still less of the value that the truth bears, "It pleases me."[3] We can declare that a garment or a jewel

3. It is certainly meaningful to say, "It gives me great pleasure that this person has found the strength to stop smoking." This is indeed a valuable trait in a person, but here it is not being considered in the specifically moral sense: what we are acknowledging is not the moral value that such conduct may possess, but the energy. This use of "give pleasure" emerges with particular clarity when someone says of a completely extra-moral conduct, "It gives me pleasure." If I say, for example, "This man talks too much," someone may reply, "No, that gives me pleasure, because it is the expression of a great vitality."

pleases me, or someone's voice, the way he laughs, eats, walks, etc. In these cases, we are referring to specifically aesthetic values.

However—and this is the third characteristic of pleasing—not everything that is aesthetically valuable pleases in the specific sense. The highest aesthetic values appeal to the person and affect him or her in a manner that is clearly different from being pleased. If someone says that Beethoven's ninth symphony, Michelangelo's *Dying Slave*, or Shakespeare's *King Lear* pleases him, he demonstrates that he has not understood the true value of these works. In order to speak exactly of being pleased, one must relate this to a more modest aesthetic value or to a secondary element, for example, the way in which a drama, an opera, or a symphony is performed.

Fourthly, there is an emphasis in "being pleased" on the impression that something aesthetically valuable makes on us, as opposed to the value judgment about the objective fact that something is the bearer of an aesthetic value. Being pleased indicates explicitly the position of the object in relation to myself. This is its theme. Unfortunately, there are innumerable people who are pleased precisely by trivial, sentimental, and tasteless things. Doubtless, they also believe that these are beautiful; in their case, however, it is the relation of the object to themselves that stands in the foreground.

Every attempt to derive beauty or any kind of aesthetic value from being pleased is absolutely erroneous. Being pleased is a separate phenomenon. The fact that something pleases someone says nothing about the aesthetic value it possesses. Even when something pleases many people, this does not mean that what pleases them must possess a genuine aesthetic value, or indeed that it must be beautiful in the full sense of the word. For the fact that many people hold something to be true does not mean that it must therefore *be* true.

This brief analysis of being pleased suffices to show, on the one hand, that Saint Thomas and Kant rightly point to being pleased in relation to aesthetic values, since this does play a role in these values. On the other hand, we can see clearly that the beauty of the object certainly cannot be derived from a mere being pleased, and that the aesthetic value does not consist in my being pleased. Rather the being pleased presupposes an aesthetic value in the object, either a genuinely existing aesthetic value or an apparent one.

If an object is pleasing to someone, this does not prove that it truly possesses an aesthetic value. The precise meaning of being pleased does indeed presuppose that the object appears aesthetically valuable to me, but not that it genuinely possesses this value.

As for a mere *liking*, which we discussed above, it has no value of any kind for aesthetics.

The apprehension of value as a presupposition for the frui of a genuine beauty

Now we wish to begin by investigating only the overall aesthetic enjoyment, the *frui* of a genuine, true beauty. This *frui* comes into being when the object objectively bears true beauty, such as the Gulf of Naples or Dürnstein in the Wachau region of Austria; Giorgione's *Pastoral Concert* or the *Resurrection* by Piero della Francesca in San Sepolcro, north of Arezzo; the Pantheon in Rome or the Town Hall in Perugia; the chorus at the close of the first Part of J. S. Bach's *Saint Matthew Passion* ("*O Mensch, bewein dein Sünde groß*," "O man, bewail your great sin") or Beethoven's "Harp Quartet"; a poem by Goethe such as *Fetter grüne, du Laub*,[4] or the third canto of the "Inferno" in Dante's *Divine Comedy*.

We need not discuss the basis of the *frui* of beauty, that is, the act of apprehending in each specific case the bearer of beauty. For apprehending beauty in nature and the visual arts, this is of course the act of perceiving with the eyes. If I were blind, I could not apprehend the bearer of beauty, and thus I would be unable to enjoy its beauty. I must see the bearer. In music, this basis is an apprehending with the ear. If I had been born deaf, I could not apprehend the bearer of beauty; accordingly, I would not attain to the *frui* of the beauty of a piece of music. In literature,

4. "Flourish greener as ye clamber, / Oh ye leaves, to seek my chamber," from Goethe, *Herbstgefühl* ("Autumn Feelings"). English translation by Edgar Alfred Bowring.

this link with the bearer of beauty is much more complicated. The apprehending with eye and ear is only a first and relatively insignificant presupposition for understanding what is written or read aloud. It is only this understanding that establishes the contact with the bearer of beauty that corresponds to the apprehending in the other arts. We will discuss all this in greater detail when we speak of the individual arts in the second volume of this work.

Although this first basis is an indispensable presupposition for the genuine *frui* of beauty, it can exist without being followed up by any kind of *frui*. For the one who sees, hears, or reads the things we have mentioned may be incapable of apprehending their beauty. He may be devoid of artistic sensitivity, have poor taste, be completely unmusical, etc. This first basis varies, depending on whether we are dealing with visible or audible things or literature. Although it is indispensable, we need say no more about it here, since it is not a genuine part of that presupposition for the *frui* of beauty that we will now discuss.

We begin with the apprehending of beauty, the perception [*Wahrnehmung*] of it. This differs both from perception by the senses (apprehending in the narrower sense of the term) and from the intellectual [*geistig*] perception of other persons and states-of-affairs, since it is not only an intellectual perception but also a perception of value. We employ the term "perception" here consciously and explicitly, since the essence of perception, as we have written elsewhere,[5] consists not in the apprehending of data accessible to the senses but in the presence of the object, the immediate contact with it, and the fact that the object discloses itself to me, that it informs me about its essence and its existence, and that this contact is an intuitive contact. We can see all this clearly when we compare perception with mere imagination and also with the drawing of inferences.

As we have said, values too can be perceived. The apprehending of values possesses all the essential characteristics of genuine perception. For this perception of values, just as for the perception of other persons and

5. In my book *What is Philosophy?* chap. 6.

of states-of-affairs, much more is required than for the seeing of colors and the hearing of sounds. This, however, does not alter the fact that not only the receptive character which all the forms of apprehending and knowing possess, but also all the characteristics of immediacy and of the self-presence of the apprehended object (which are typical of the perception of a color), are present to the same degree in values. Every apprehending of a value is a personal act that presupposes more in the one who apprehends than is presupposed by the seeing of colors and the hearing of sounds. This is likewise true of the apprehending of the moral values of conduct.

However, the perception of beauty presupposes a different sense in the human person than does the apprehending of moral values. This is why the ability to apprehend beauty is, as we have already mentioned, much rarer than the ability to grasp moral values; or, to put it better, while every human being has received in principle the gift of understanding moral values, it is given only to certain persons to apprehend beauty fully. This means that every blindness to moral values is more or less a person's own fault, but blindness to beauty is culpable only in very special cases. Blindness to moral values is the disturbance of an ability to see that is in principle present; it is comparable to a cataract. But the blindness of the person who is wholly insensitive to art is comparable to the blindness of one born blind, that is, to the total lack of the ability to see.

As we have already seen, however, the fact that one needs a particular sense that not every human being necessarily possesses, does not mean that absolute certainty is impossible in apprehending the beautiful.

Nor can one infer from this presupposition that beauty plays a role only for a small circle of particularly cultivated persons, but is not a great objective good either for the masses or for the human being as such. We have already pointed out in the Introduction that beauty is one of the greatest sources of happiness for human beings, and is a high objective good for their spiritual [*geistig*] health.

There are many gradations in the apprehending of beauty. Even one who is totally insensitive to art, an utter philistine, can see the beauty of a flower, a sunny day, a lofty mountain covered in snow, and especially the beauty of a lovely face. Nevertheless, it must be emphasized that the philistine is definitely a misshapen human being, since the normal, simple, uneducated, uncorrupted person certainly possesses a sensitivity to beauty. Naturally, the depth and *a fortiori* the differentiation of this sensitivity vary from person to person; but one who is by nature absolutely insensitive to art is an exception.

This, however, does not in any way alter the fact that a special sense is presupposed in order to apprehend beauty. There are innumerable gradations with regard to the range of areas in which someone can apprehend beauty. There is even more a varied scale with regard to the depth at which a person apprehends beauty and recognizes the hierarchy within beautiful things, and especially the degree to which someone sees through pseudo-beauty; and this is to say nothing of the various gradations of the role that beauty plays in the life of a person. Within this gradation, there exists a clear break between those who have and those who lack a specifically artistic sensitivity; there are also differences according to how subtle and deep this sensitivity is for the world of art in general, and for one specific artistic genre in particular.

After these observations, we return to our affirmation that there is a genuine perceiving of beauty and that this is the first and the decisive presupposition for the aesthetic experience, the *frui* of the beautiful.

Being fully open

A significant new element makes its appearance here. To what extent does someone open his soul when he sees a beautiful landscape? To what extent is he willing and able to receive this beauty? One who is preoccupied with other things, such as cares or plans, may indeed perceive that the landscape is beautiful, but he will not be capable of enjoying it and letting himself be affected by it. This factor plays a role in every act of experiencing things having value. To what extent do I receive something with full consciousness, to what extent am I distracted? To what extent am I absent in some way, to what extent am I fully present in an experience? Naturally, the distraction can go so far that one does not notice the beauty: one simply overlooks it. A certain degree of attention is necessary for every perception, and all the more so, the more meaningful [*geistig*] the object is. This is especially true of every act of apprehending values. What we have in mind at the moment is not this minimum of attention, but rather the situation in which we do indeed notice the beauty but are distracted or preoccupied, and hence do not concentrate upon it in any way. We do not open our spirit for it. Within ourselves, we are neither empty nor free to drink it in. This inner state, this opening oneself fully, or better, this state of being fully opened, is a new and significant element of the phenomenon of aesthetic enjoyment as a whole.

The first point, already discussed, is the perceiving of beauty, which presupposes an organ for beauty. There is a multileveled hierarchy both with regard to the range of one's aesthetic sense and also with regard to the objects in which one is capable of apprehending beauty. At present we are speaking of those elements of aesthetic enjoyment (especially the element of being opened) that are always present whenever a genuine aesthetic *frui* occurs. We assume that the basis for the act of apprehending beauty, namely, the sensitivity to beauty in nature and art, is fully realized.

So the second point, after the perception of beauty, is the inner *vacare*, being free, being opened, the absence of everything that disturbs being completely receptive in this moment. Here, of course, there are many different degrees. In the case of certain works of art, a great role is played by an explicit devotion of one's self to the work, an act of accompanying the work, and a reverent reception of it.

Being-affected in general

The third decisive factor is being-affected. We have already written in several other books about this form of experiencing, which has a general significance and occurs in many areas of our life. We have drawn a clear distinction, especially in *The Heart* (especially in part I, chapter 2),[6] between being-affected and giving a response; we limit ourselves here to

6. I draw this distinction most fully in my *Ethics*, chap. 17.

repeating its three basic characteristics. Being-affected is first of all a receptive way of relating to the world, as opposed to the "spontaneity" of the value-response (although "spontaneity" must be understood in a special sense of this word).[7] Secondly, it is not a mere apprehension in the broadest sense of the word, but the effect in my soul of something I have come to know—an affective effect. Thirdly, it is a markedly intentional experience. The "effect" is not of a simply causal nature like the pain in my finger when I burn myself or cut myself, but a relationship that is every bit as intentional and meaningfully motivated as a response such as joy, enthusiasm, grief, etc. Just as in the case of knowing, the direction of the intentional relationship runs from the motivating object to my mind—not (as in the response) from my mind to the object. This is the meaning of the term "receptive" that we employ as a description of being-affected. For there are two basic directions in the realm of the intentional experiences, namely, the direction from the object to my mind and the direction from my mind to the object.[8]

It is obvious that there are completely different types of being-affected. One significant type with a character all its own is being-affected in connection with being loved, whether this is the experience of being made happy when the true love of neighbor penetrates into our soul with its breath of holy goodness, or whether this is the completely different experience of being touched by the ray of a profound natural love, especially of a spousal love.

Naturally, we must draw the important distinction here that I have discussed in detail in my books *Metaphysik der Gemeinschaft* (chapters 2 and 4) and *The Nature of Love*[9] (chapters 6 and 10). Does the kind of being-affected correspond or not to the content of the love that someone shows me? Am I affected by the holy goodness of the love of neighbor? Does it raise me up, move me, and make me happy—or does a perverted arrogance prevent me from doing justice to the content of this ray of love?

7. See my *Ethics*, chap. 22, and my *The Nature of Love*, chap. 4, pp. 88–89, 93–94, 98–100.

8. I set out this distinction already in my first book, *Die Idee der sittlichen Handlung* [and it is elaborated in *Ethics*, chap. 17].

9. *The Nature of Love*, chap. 6, pp. 129–30; chap. 10, pp. 229–321.

Does it fail to affect me? Or does it affect me in a false way? Does nuptial love make me happy, or do I see this love as an encroachment upon my own private domain? Here it suffices to mention one special type of being-affected, namely, through acts of another person that are addressed to me. The specific character of this type of being-affected consists in the way it is directed to me and intends to affect me in some special way. Whether or not the intended state of being-affected actually occurs is another question altogether; and it is also possible that the act may affect me in a completely different manner.

Being-affected has still another character when it is not based on someone addressing me but on my encounter with beings having value or disvalue. We need not speak of the eminent role that being-affected plays in love, as when we are affected, indeed enchanted, by the beauty of a personality, as preliminary to giving the value-response of love. It is perhaps in the case of being in love that this being-affected emerges with the greatest clarity.

Being-affected does not necessarily play any special role in the apprehending of morally relevant goods. The experience of the call that is addressed to us (especially after we have apprehended the moral significance of the good), being moved by the call, the experience of obligation that touches our conscience—all this is very different from the typical being-affected. It possesses a different, indeed a unique, kind of affectivity.

But we are back to a typical being-affected when we are profoundly impressed by the conduct and the virtues of another person, or when the moral greatness of a personality moves us and edifies us. In its metaphysical beauty moral value—which we apprehend only in other persons—makes possible a *frui* in the broadest sense of the term. It also appeals in a special way to our heart. It would thus be false to assert that being-affected plays no great role in the moral realm. On the contrary, it is highly significant, precisely as a typical being-affected, if what we encounter in another person is moral value; but as soon as it is a question of morally relevant goods, and especially when an obligatory call goes forth from these goods, the typical being-affected moves into the background or assumes another form.

When it is a question of the *frui* of beauty, we come to a very specific classical type of being-affected, namely, being affected by beauty in nature and art, which is where beauty is fully thematic and no other values (not even truth) are thematic.

In that case, it is a question of being affected by the mere beauty that appeals to the senses or by the beauty of the second power, the spiritual beauty in nature and art that adheres to visible and audible things or to a work of literature.

Clearly there are once again great qualitative hierarchies within the framework of this being-affected, depending on whether it involves only a beauty that appeals to the senses, or a beauty of the second power, and also depending on the rank and loftiness of the beauty of the second power.

A more precise analysis of being affected by the beauty that appeals to the senses

We shall first concentrate on being affected by the beauty that appeals to the senses. We begin with the more substantial, more intensive beauty that appeals to the senses.

We hear the sound of a wonderful tenor or soprano voice. Let us suppose that what is sung is neither beautiful nor ugly: it is an insignificant, indifferent piece of music, but one that gives the voice the opportunity to unfold itself and to do full justice to the beauty of its timbre. We apprehend the beauty of the voice; it affects us and enchants us. We experience clearly how the beauty of this sound penetrates our soul, making us happy and refreshing us.

Obviously, this enjoyment of beauty, this *frui* with which we drink in the beauty, as it were, is no mere experience of a bodily pleasure. We do indeed often say that something is a "delight to the ear." But although this expression refers to a genuine phenomenon—to something that is clearly different from the deep enjoyment of a beauty of the second power—the "delight to the ear" is not a bodily feeling. This expression is never employed to refer to a genuine bodily pleasure.

There is a bodily sensation of displeasure that can be caused by a shrill sound, for example, the sound of scraping a glass surface with a sharp knife, or a noise so loud that it becomes unbearable for our ears and we feel that our eardrum is about to burst. And clearly there also exists a bodily sensation that is pleasant, as when a sound is smooth and treats our ears "gently." This is especially the case after a din has "hurt" our ears with its high volume.

It is clear that this has nothing to do with the "delight to the ear" when we listen to music. It is no mere din that gives us this delight, but a dulcet tone or the harmonious sound of various instruments. This is definitely a purely mental [*psychisch*] pleasure, although it is of course clearly an enjoyment of that which is apprehended with the ear. We must draw a sharp distinction between this "delight to the ear" and the real *frui* of a beauty that appeals to our senses, which in this case is the beauty of a wonderful voice. It is the experience of the bliss of the harmony and of certain melodies. It always remains relatively secondary when compared with real being-affected by beauty. It is an accompanying phenomenon that is found in only a few special instances. It is not in any way a presupposition for the *frui* of beauty; or, to put this differently, there is certainly no necessary link between the quality of the "delight to the ear" that an object gives and its beauty. Indeed, in the case of the beauty of the second power, this quality is completely superseded (even if it were present). Or better: the *frui* of the beauty of the second power excludes the enjoyment of the "delight to the ear."

Accordingly, bodily feelings of pleasure (to say nothing of localized feelings of pleasure) have nothing to do with the *frui* of beauty. The so-called delight to the ear is not a bodily feeling of pleasure, although it has a special relationship to "hearing." It is a delight for the sensation of hearing. This is not the same thing as the delectability of the beauty that appears in the object, nor the same as the spiritual *frui* of this beauty.

By contrast, real being-affected by the beauty of a voice or a glorious red velvet is primarily of a purely mental [*psychisch*] kind. The beauty which we clearly apprehend delights and enchants us; it does not generate any state of pleasure in us. We are entirely oriented to the object. We look in its direction. Its beauty gives something to our spirit, it says something to us. This meaningful relationship characterizes being-affected. But this word is addressed, not to our intellect, but to our affective sphere. The beautiful thing delights us and enchants us. This is a very special form of being delighted: this beauty is delectable in a special way.

The delectability [*Delektabilität*] of other values, such as great virtues, or the lofty intelligence of a rich, deep mind, values that play a large role in love, are profoundly tied up with metaphysical beauty, even though these values are themselves thematic in a way in which their beauty is not thematic. Humility moves us and edifies us as a moral value, even though the element of delectability is not thematic. But the special beauty of humility, the *splendor* of this moral virtue, is specifically delectable.

The profound link between delectability and beauty emerges all the more strongly when we think of the beauty of the visible and the audible, which (unlike metaphysical beauty) is not the fragrance and the irradiation of other values, but adheres directly to the object. The beautiful voice, the glorious red velvet, the beauty of an orange tree laden with fruit —all these are specifically delectable. However, their beauty and their value do not in the least consist in this delectability. The opposite is true! When we apprehend beauty, we understand precisely the importance that rests in itself. We understand its nobility and its dignity. But the fact that it is delectable, enchants us, and appeals to a *frui*, is a special quality of beauty. The delectability is grounded in the value of the beauty, in its special essence; the beauty is not grounded in the delectability.

Kant's "disinterestedness" in the beautiful

Now we wish to attempt to investigate this special kind of being-affected by the beauty which appeals to the senses. Being enchanted and delighted by beautiful objects is qualitatively different from the quality of being affected by other things. Kant[10] had something correct in mind when he spoke of "disinterestedness" in our relationship to the beautiful. Certainly it is easy to misunderstand the expression "disinterested." If one interprets it to mean "indifferent," it would of course be completely inappropriate to

10. Kant, *Critique of Judgment*, part 1, division 1, book 1, paragraphs 2 and 5.

describe as "disinterested" our relationship to the beauty that appeals to the senses (and it is only of this beauty that Kant speaks; in other words, he identifies beauty with the beauty that appeals to the senses). If, on the other hand, "disinterestedness" means that we do not approach the beautiful object as a means to obtain something that provides a merely subjective satisfaction, something that brings us an advantage, it is of course correct.

We must distinguish two elements. First of all, in the experience of the beauty of an object, this object never has the function of a means, not even of the means to attain some other valuable good. We approach it *propter se ipsum* ("for its own sake"). Secondly, no interest in the sense of personal advantage is involved.

These two traits characterize our relationship not only to the beautiful, however; they are to be found in every value-response (apart from a value-response to something that is a mere means for the realization of a value). These traits characterize the appropriate conduct that is required of us in relation to all those "direct" goods that are, as such, bearers of a value. The transcendence of "for its own sake" is just as present in the moral realm as in the aesthetic realm. Of course, the means to attain a valuable good are likewise bearers of a value; they participate in the value of the good that they serve. As means, however, they are only indirectly valuable, whereas the good that is the goal is directly valuable.[11]

The Kantian "disinterestedness" also contains an element of the con-

11. The question arises how far the "borrowed" value of the means is qualitatively similar to that of the valuable goal. An effective medicine is valuable as a means for restoring the health of the patient, because of its effect on his health. Obviously, the quality of this value resembles in principle the value of health. The morally relevant good represented by the health of a human being gives this medicine an indirectly moral significance.

It is interesting that although the means for the establishing or the maintenance of a beautiful entity are certainly indirectly valuable rather than merely "neutral," they are not indirectly beautiful. The mortar that joins together the stones in a building is not beautiful, nor is the invisible substructure, nor are all those things that are necessary in order to lay the foundation for the building. Similarly, the artist's brush and the chisel are not beautiful. Nor does the simple fact that the piano is an indispensable instrument for the playing of a beautiful sonata make it beautiful, unless it is beautiful as a piece of furniture. As a visible entity, the bearer can be beautiful, but its indirect value for the sound of the beautiful sonata on the piano is not beautiful. (Naturally, in the case of musical instruments such as the piano or violin, the sound of its tone can be more or less beautiful. The judgment whereby we call one instrument better than another is based on this difference. In that case, the instrument itself has a genuine aesthetic value that is both a direct value and an indirect value.)

templative,[12] of that which is opposed to all activity. Though the transcendence and the *propter se ipsum* are also to be found in the attitude of moral value-response, which also involves no interest in the sense of a personal advantage, as we saw, the value-response to morally relevant goods, appealing as it does in a special manner to the will, is not contemplative.

Kant and Schopenhauer on the contemplative element in relation to beauty

Here we see the common element in the aesthetics of Kant and of Schopenhauer, namely, the emphasis on the contemplative character in our attitude toward the beautiful. The antithesis between will and imagination, between active and contemplative, plays a central role here.[13]

Naturally, there exist contemplative value-responses to the moral values of other persons, responses such as veneration or joy, and above all, religious meditation and contemplation.

As we have seen, however, one cannot define beauty as the object of the contemplation. In order to apprehend the essence of aesthetic delight, one must already have apprehended and understood the essence of beauty, and specifically of thematic beauty. Important as it is to underline the contemplative and completely unpragmatic essence of aesthetic delight, this is not enough to do justice to the essence of aesthetic delight. We must know [*Kennen*] both beauty as a primordial phenomenon and thematic beauty: only this knowing allows us to distinguish the type of contemplative element in aesthetic delight from the contemplation found in the moral sphere and above all in the religious sphere.

This attempt to identify the experience of beauty with the contemplative attitude as such is found especially in Schopenhauer's aesthetics.[14] It clearly leads to unfortunate intellectual constructions.

12. Kant, *Critique of Judgment*, part 1, division 1, book 1, paragraph 5.

13. It goes without saying that the term "will" does not have the same meaning in Kant and in Schopenhauer. For the latter, all striving and all yearning, even the apersonal, instinctive being-driven, is "will" (*The World as Will and Idea*, I, book 2; book 3, §38). For Kant, on the other hand, "will" is restricted to the personal act that is the king of actions (see his *Foundations of the Metaphysics of Morals*, sections 2 and 3).

14. Schopenhauer, *The World as Will and Idea*, I, book 3; see also §§34, 41–42, and 45, which is also important for the issues that we are about to discuss in this study.

Schopenhauer commits the grave error of not acknowledging beauty as a quality of the object and as an objective value. In this connection, he asserts that everything can be found to be beautiful, provided only that one has the genius required in order to transpose the beauty onto the object. The decisive subjectivism emerges clearly in this act of transposition: it is an act not of discovering, but of importing. The comparison with love does not make matters any better, for in love too there lies initially a value-response—independently of whether the value truly or only supposedly belongs to the person who is loved. But when love goes beyond this and discloses the values of the beloved more deeply to us, and even uncovers new values in him, this too is an act of discovery, not of transposition onto him or projection into him.

Moreover, the comparison with love is flawed. For although it is true that an artistic genius apprehends beauty more deeply and sees it even in places where it is hidden from the average person, the thesis that all things are beautiful and that there are no ugly things remains questionable even in the sphere of the visible and the audible in nature; in art, it is clearly false. The same applies *a fortiori* to human attitudes such as envy, malicious pleasure, impurity, shallowness, stupidity, mendacity, or spuriousness, that is to say, to the entire realm of the metaphysically ugly.

Despite the incorrectness of his thesis, Schopenhauer's assertion that all things are beautiful for the perfect genius points to something significant. It is assuredly true that in the imitative arts, the artist of genius penetrates into a hidden beauty of beautiful things and reveals these to us in the work of art.[15] We have already spoken in the third point of the previous chapter about this function of art, which Konrad Fiedler rightly emphasized. Nature discloses to us entirely new strata of beauty and poetry after we have seen Giorgione, Titian, Rubens, and Rembrandt, after we have come to know and to understand Shakespeare, Goethe, Keats, Hölderlin, and Leopardi. This enrichment in the apprehending of the beauty and the poetry of the visible and the audible, of nature and life, that we receive from the artist, is certainly very significant.

15. Schopenhauer, *The World as Will and Idea*, I, §36–37, and II, chap. 30.

It is also true that the ugliness of that which is portrayed in the work of art can be beautiful thanks to the artistic transposition. We shall discuss this problem in detail in the second volume of this work.

Despite all this, however, it is false to assert that everything is beautiful, provided only that the one who sees it possesses the ability to discovery its beauty. There are ugly things in nature; and above all, there are trivial, boring works of art. Besides this, of course, many things are bearers of metaphysical ugliness, such as the morally base, the mean-spirited, and the wicked, or stupidity, shallowness, arrogance, or mediocrity.

Similarly, Schopenhauer's assertion that all that emerges in the concrete beautiful object of aesthetic delight is the species of the object, and that we are set free from our individuality, is a pure construction that is determined by his system as a whole.[16]

Where Schopenhauer is right and where he is wrong in saying that one must be free from abstract thinking when one experiences the beautiful

However, Schopenhauer is correct when he says that, in order to experience the true aesthetic enjoyment, we must be free from desiring [*Begehren*] and from abstract thinking.[17] Being free from desiring is another form of the Kantian "disinterestedness," but being set free from abstract thinking is a new and important contribution by Schopenhauer. In order to detach what he has seen correctly from all the encumbrances of his system, we must say, first of all, that in aesthetic delight we approach the object *propter se ipsum*; it is never a means to attain something else. Our attitude is contemplative. Secondly, our relationship to the object is completely different from that of an intellectual investigation. It is radically different from every pragmatic attitude, from every appeal to our will and our action, and from any kind of research.

There are some people—especially philosophers—who can never escape from an attitude that is focused on knowledge. If they see a beautiful landscape, they begin to reflect on the essence of the landscape or of

16. Ibid., I, §38 and 45.
17. Ibid., II, chap. 30, and I, 1, §34.

beauty, instead of enjoying this beauty and immersing themselves contemplatively in it. They adopt this attitude even more strongly vis-à-vis architecture and other works of art. The beautiful object immediately becomes an object of analysis, questioning, and seeking. This reaction need not always be of a philosophical nature. In a church, for example, the reaction may be to reflect, expound, or interpret—one may ask how many forms of church building reflect monotheism or the Christian faith. Instead of enjoying its beauty, or letting oneself be drawn contemplatively by this beauty into the world of God, one enters the mode of intellectual research. This reflection on the beautiful object may be vitally interesting and valuable, but it is not the attitude that is appropriate to the bearers of the beauty. This attitude is purely contemplative, whereas all investigating, seeking, and questioning is no longer purely contemplative, for now the theme is truth and coming to know the truth. In the *frui* of beauty in nature and art, beauty is the theme. In the loftiest works of art and in the sublime beauties of nature, the world above us discloses itself and we are drawn *in conspectu Dei* ("before the face of God"). Naturally, this is the primary theme in every sacred work of art and in all churches. But it is precisely through beauty that this happens, not through speculation and investigation.

Indeed, all philosophical and artistic reflection and investigation presupposes the immediate, purely contemplative *frui* as a pre-philosophical contact, if the reflection is to be fruitful. But this must never take the place of aesthetic enjoyment; it must never prevent the full *frui.*

However, this full contemplative *frui*, which Schopenhauer rightly identifies as a characteristic of aesthetic enjoyment,[18] is found not only in aesthetic enjoyment, but in many other spheres as well. The immersion of two souls in each other in a deep love—especially in spousal love—has this contemplative character, this total dwelling in the presence of the beloved, and this pure *propter se ipsum.* The contemplative *propter se ipsum* attains its climax in the most significant realm of contemplative life, namely, in the immersion of the self in God.

18. Ibid., I, §38.

The thematicity of beauty in being affected by it, as opposed to excitement, amusement, comedy, and entertainment

This brings us to a second characteristic of the experience of beauty: the thematicity of beauty. In the loving way of looking at another, the theme is the beloved person, the *unio* with his or her soul, the mutual love. In contemplative prayer, the theme is God and the loving adoration of God.

But when beauty is the theme—naturally, what we have in mind here is not metaphysical beauty but the beauty of the visible and the audible in all its gradations—the *frui* too takes on a different character. We shall return to this shortly.

Up until now we have spoken only of that part of the aesthetic experience that has the character of being-affected, and thus of a specifically receptive intentional experience. But in no way are we saying that the value-response to the beautiful object, such as the value-response of enthusiasm, joy, or admiration (as responses these are not of a merely receptive nature, though they are indeed contemplative) does not equally belong to the total aesthetic experience.

Naturally, the way in which one is affected by the beauty of the visible and the audible varies in keeping with the degree and kind of beauty of the object. And it goes without saying that it also varies in keeping with the capacity of the subject to understand the beauty. This is first of all a question of the fundamental capacity, of the subject's sense of beauty, of his aesthetic organ, and of the degree to which he possesses it. In addition, his general depth and his total relationship to the world of values play a role. Being-affected also varies in one and the same person in keeping with his momentary receptivity, which in turn can be influenced by various factors.

Before we discuss those variations of being affected by beauty that are conditioned by the kind of object or its kind of beauty, or by the subject, we must speak of this radical difference: the difference between being-affected in aesthetic enjoyment, in which beauty is the theme, and other kinds of being-affected such as being amused and excited.

There are many things that amuse us: parties, formal dances, games in which we ourselves take part, or those at which we are present only as spectators (such as soccer games, the circus, or bullfights). In the latter instances, the amusement is linked to excitement about the outcome. We are completely captivated by the course of the game, by the tension as we wait to see who will win, and so on. This experience is pleasurable and forms a typical antithesis to being bored. Naturally, there are innumerable differentiations both in amusement and in excitement. Excitement can take on a perverted character; it can have a dangerous, sensational character, or it can have a harmless character. Amusing oneself can be serene and relaxed; it can also be linked to excitement. Countless other elements can play a role, such as the satisfaction of winning or the ambition to win when one is a player.

We are interested in those forms of being amused and being excited that come nearest to aesthetic enjoyment. Sometimes, indeed, they can be drawn into aesthetic enjoyment as a secondary element; in that case, of course, they modify it considerably.

Let us turn first to being amused, and let us think of a hilarious farce that possesses no artistic value, or of an excellent comedian. Both of these can make us laugh, and we can enjoy this very much. What kind of enjoyment is this? It is an exhilaration, a delight of a special kind, to laugh at this comedy. As we shall see in chapter 19 below, it is a being-affected *sui generis*, a likable, cheerful being-affected that takes place in a legitimate periphery of our being. It has nothing in common with being gripped, with the passionate note of the specific experience of being excited. The enjoyment of a humorous story or the accomplished imitation of another person is a typical experience of being amused. In the case of jokes, of the quality of the witty, being affected by a spirited element (*esprit*), plays a role. And this brings us closer to aesthetic enjoyment.

In a good detective novel we find a form of being-affected that is completely different from being amused. This is the typical case of finding satisfaction through excitement. This enjoyment is much less likable and less cheerful; it does not in the least remain in a harmless periphery. The novel grips us, and we are held captive by the story. The excitement does not at all lead us into our depths. It has a much more dynamic character than the experience of being amused that we have discussed above. This enjoyment gives us a completely different kind of satisfaction.

Although these distinctions are very interesting in themselves, we cannot examine them in the present context. All we wish to do is to draw a clear line between these two types of being-affected and the specific experience of being affected by the beauty of the visible and the audible, and to investigate the extent to which being amused and being excited can be drawn into aesthetic enjoyment, and the way in which they thereby modify it.

In the aesthetic enjoyment of beauty, a consciousness of the value, of the intrinsic significance of beauty and of the beautiful object, is always present. No matter how much I enjoy the beauty of a flower, no matter how much its contemplation is an objective good for me, the main emphasis always lies on the being of the flower that is noble in itself, on the nobility that it possesses independently of myself and of every act of enjoyment. The theme is the beauty of its color and shape, and in many cases also its fragrance. Being affected by beauty varies greatly in accordance with the kind and rank of the beauty in question, but—in a manner analogous to the attitudes that respond to the object, such as enthusiasm and joy—it does not affect the thematicity of the valuable object.

One essential characteristic of this "value experience," of being affected by beauty, is the fact that although this objective good is given to *me*, my being-affected never becomes the main theme, nor does it abolish the thematicity of the value.

In every true enjoyment of the beauty of visible and audible things there lies an attitude vis-à-vis the beautiful object that is analogous to reverence. When confronted with sublime, transfigured beauty in nature, it is not only a reaction analogous to reverence. A landscape like the Grand Canyon or the Alban Hills as seen from the Capitol in Rome grips us in a way that also fills us with reverence for this beauty. Wherever it is a question of the beauty of the second power, this reverent act of looking upward is clearly given, irrespective of whether it involves a beauty in nature or in art. In every aesthetic enjoyment, even the enjoyment of a more modest beauty, there lies at least an element analogous to reverence. This element goes hand in hand with the primacy of the value of the object, with the fact that this value (and not my enjoyment) is the main theme. Herein lies the decisive difference between being amused or excited, on the one hand, and being affected by beauty, on the other.

There is certainly no doubt that the quality of being exciting plays a legitimate role in literature. What we have in mind here is not the interest that every good novel and every powerful drama must kindle in us, nor the curiosity about how the story will develop, which the unfolding of the story in the novel or drama must arouse in us. If this element were completely absent, the novel or drama would be boring. This kind of interest is one type of being-affected: it is indispensable for the novel and the drama, and unfolds entirely within the framework of the genuine artistic being-affected. Rather, what we have in mind is an excitingness that one novel possesses and another does not possess, although both are of the same artistic rank—indeed, the novel that is less exciting in this sense may even be artistically superior. The short stories by Heinrich von Kleist, such as *Michael Kohlhaas*, *The Earthquake in Chile*, or *The Duel*, are very exciting. The short stories by Adalbert Stifter do not have this specifically exciting character. The novels of Dostoevsky are extremely exciting, whereas the king of all novels, Cervantes' *Don Quixote*, does not have this character. It is impossible to put an exciting book down—it impels us to find out what happens next. We are drawn into the course of the narrative in such a way that it does not relax its grip on us.

The important point here is to show how this experience of being gripped by a genuine work of art differs from the non-artistic being-affected (for example, by the exciting quality of a detective novel) that we described above. The difference is not only that a "naked" excitement is present in the latter, whereas in the former the excitingness is linked to the beauty and all its elements of greatness and depth. No, the quality of the excitement is also different. In great literary works of art, the excitingness is ancillary: it is at the service of the unfolding of the beauty, the depth, and the greatness of the work of art. But it is the excitingness that gives the detective novel its life. The excitingness of a significant novel that sheds light into the depths of the human soul, such as a novel by Dostoevsky, is full of content; it is an instrument at the service of the artistic greatness of the whole, just as a crescendo is a glorious device in music, as well as a bearer of beauty. This excitingness is itself something deep, whereas it has a thin and peripheral quality in the detective novel. In the great literary work, it does not appeal to us as sensational, not even sensational in a harmless or legitimate way.

This applies by analogy also to the amusing. The comic element in a novel and a drama that is a genuine work of art not only amuses us, but affects us in a completely different way. The great classical comedy that we find in Cervantes' *Don Quixote* touches us in a completely different stratum. It enchants us deeply and is an ancillary factor in the overall beauty of the work. Genuine wisdom is linked to the comic aspects of Sancho Panza, while the comic aspects of Don Quixote are tragically interwoven with the nobility of his greatness and depth, with his noble lunacy. In all this, there lies a great truth that touches us deeply.

There is a vast difference between the delight that this high artistic world grants us and the amusement that the comedian gives us. Of course, in both cases one must laugh; but there are many kinds of laughter. Laughing can have various qualities, almost in the same way as weeping can. In *Don Quixote*, the amusing is not woven into the work of art, but only the comic elements. The comic displays a great wealth of various qualities, values, and differences of depth. In the case of a comedian or a farce, there is a peripheral comedy all its own that amuses us. But the experience of being amused has nothing whatever to do with the greatest, deepest comedy in *Don Quixote*. The effect on us, the quality of being-affected, is completely different.

There are also comedies which are genuine works of art, such as Molière's *Le médecin malgré lui* or *Monsieur de Pourceaugnac* or Goldoni's *Locandiera*, in which an element of the amusing is woven into the work of art. What we have here is not only one particular type of lighter comedy; there is also (especially in Goldoni) a graceful tone that entertains us. A certain entertainment is one of the intended effects, and is also the expression of a noble modesty.[19]

The artistic content that is presented in such comedies—the graceful charm, the artistic value—is much less deep than in many other, greater works of art, for example, in Shakespeare's comedies *Twelfth Night* or *As You Like It.* The light, entertaining form in which this charming artistic content is presented has an analogy to the amusing in non-artistic contexts. In a manner analogous to the exciting, however, this amusing element can be integrated into certain works of art which are not meant to move us, not to enchant our soul through a profound poetry, not to stir us by its greatness or touch us and elevate us through a sublime beauty, but simply to present its charming beauty, its lovely spirit to us in "light vessels" and to entertain us. However, this entertainment is of a completely different nature from the mere farce. The work of art, its grace and charm, remain the principal theme—not our being entertained. The light and delightful form, the appeal which a work like Goldoni's *Locandiera* or *La bottega del caffè* addresses to us, is the given form for this special kind of artistic content.

In conclusion let us return to the decisive points. We have seen in chapter 1 the falsity of the thesis of G. E. Moore, who sees aesthetic value only in the totality of adequately apprehending and enjoying the beautiful. The decisive aesthetic value adheres to the object independently of us and of our enjoyment. This is true both of metaphysical beauty and of the beauty of the visible and the audible, though in very different ways. This beauty is a value in the full sense of the term, something that is important-in-itself, something whose importance is independent of the passing of time or of any kind of relation to the person.

19. I remember the words of an Italian stonemason who did unskilled jobs in my father's studio for many years. He once went to the theater in Munich, probably to an opera. Afterward, he made the following characteristic remark to my mother: "In Italy, people go to the theater to be entertained. In Germany, they go to be instructed" (*In Italia vanno al teatro per divertirsi, in Germania per istruirsi*). These are not the classical attitudes to art (in this case, to the theater). Nevertheless, he was pointing out something very significant.

Both the act of apprehending this value and being affected by it, as well as the adequate value-response to it, are bearers of a value, but of a completely different value, namely, a personal value which must be sharply distinguished from beauty. Finally, the fact that an adequate response is made to something beautiful also possesses a value, that of the fulfillment of the due relationship. The opposite of this value is the disvalue that lies in failing to understand something beautiful, and in giving the wrong response to it.

We have also seen the role that the genuine being-affected plays for the special essence of aesthetic enjoyment; it is a special kind of being-affected. In the case of metaphysical beauty, the beauty itself is not thematic. Being affected by it always remains intimately linked with being affected by the value that is the bearer of this beauty, whereas the enjoying, the *frui* of beauty in the realm of the visible and the audible, always has a special character. Being affected by this beauty is not linked to being touched by other goods and their values; rather, the beauty of the visible and the audible as such speaks directly to us. We have pointed out the specific delectability of beauty, which naturally also displays itself in the kind of being-affected.

The beauty of the second power in art, which we shall study in the second volume of this work, has various effects on us. It seizes us, enchants us, moves us, elevates us, and makes us happy. It broadens our spirit and enriches it; it draws us into the depths of our being. It relaxes us, although it also generates in us a tension in the highest sense of the term.

However, there is an additional special element in art that goes beyond enjoyment; true artists disclose to us the beauty of nature and life in a deep way. Without their help, this would not be accessible to us in such depth.

No doubt, there are particularly alert persons who apprehend life and nature in their profound beauty even though they themselves are not artists. In general, however, it is certainly correct (as was emphasized especially by Konrad Fiedler) to say that art has the significant pedagogical mission of opening our eyes to the treasures of beauty which life and nature possess. Hugo von Hofmannsthal speaks of this in beautiful words:[20]

> For that, I believe, is what artists are for: so that all those things that pass through their inner life receive a meaning and a soul. 'Nature wanted to know what she looked like, and so she created Goethe for herself.' And Goethe's soul reflected thousands of things and redeemed them into life. And then there are artists who were much smaller mirrors, like narrow, still wells in which only one single star twinkles: they poured the enamel of their soul around one single thing and immersed one single feeling in beauty. Such a one was Eichendorff, who revealed the longing searching and the enigmatic resting of the breathing night when the fountains burble. And Lenau heard the reed speaking and gave a name to the beauty of the heath. And many clouds, heavy golden clusters, receive their soul from Poussin, while many rosy-round clouds receive their soul from Rubens . . . And there are emotions of our soul that Schumann created; and there are thoughts that would never have come to us without Hamlet; and many of our wishes have the colors from a forgotten painting and the fragrance of a song that has passed away.

20. Hugo von Hofmannsthal, *Gesammelte Werke*, I, "Eleonora Duse. Die Legende einer Wiener Woche" (Frankfurt am Main, 1979), 478. English translation by BM.

CHAPTER SEVENTEEN

The Variety of Aesthetic Values

Beauty in the narrow and in the broad sense

WE MUST now say something about beauty in the narrow and in the broad sense of the word. In the realm of moral values, we draw a distinction between the general "moral good" which encompasses all of morality, and the "goodness" or kindness [*Güte*] with which we designate one particular moral value. Similarly, we also have the concept of "beautiful" which is equivalent to the general quality of the aesthetically valuable, and beauty in a narrower sense which is characterized by a special element of loveliness [*Holdheit*], of delightful splendor.

We encounter this beauty in the narrower sense of the word, for example, in the chorus *Torna, o bella, al tuo consorte* at the close of the second act of Gluck's *Orfeo ed Euridice*, in Mozart's *Laudate Dominum*, or in the quintet *Einer Weise mild und hehr* in the third act of Wagner's *Die Meistersinger*, whereas J. S. Bach's mighty Toccata and Fugue in D minor, or Beethoven's Great Fugue in his string quartet in B flat major, opus 133, do not possess the heart-melting quality of this beauty. It would be completely wrong to regard the beauty in the narrower sense as a mere beauty that appeals to the senses. This beauty too—for example, the beauty of

Raphael's *Miraculous Catch of Fish* or Michelangelo's *Dying Slave*—is a highest beauty of the second power. It possesses the same spiritual quality as the beauty possessed by power, by that which is mighty.

Today many people are at risk of confusing the specific beauty, even in the most sublime sense, with a mere beauty of the more primitive kind that appeals to the senses. This leads them to include it among the other, non-specific forms of beauty in the general sense. Such people are filled with a hatred of harmony, even in the highest sense of the word. Indeed, they go so far as to idolize appalling disharmony. They play the art of the Mayas in Mexico off against Greek art.

Our primary aim here is to draw the boundary between the two meanings of "beautiful": first, beauty as more or less equivalent to aesthetically positive; and secondly, beauty as a special (though still very comprehensive) aesthetic value. Clearly, this distinction does not involve differences in rank. It is thus completely different from the difference between beauty which appeals specifically to the senses and sublime spiritual beauty (beauty of the second power).

Nothing that we have said here contradicts our earlier observation that the relationship between the fundamental value of "beautiful"—that is, "beautiful" in the broader sense of the word—and all the aesthetic values is not the same as the relationship between "morally good" and all the moral values. There exist aesthetic values such as elegant, witty, and entertaining which cannot be regarded even as subspecies of beauty in the broader sense. On the other hand, one cannot deny that they are aesthetic values, although they lie on the edge of the aesthetic.[1]

The variety of aesthetic value qualities

We must also point out the wealth of aesthetic values, the variety of aesthetic qualities of differing kinds. In this regard, the sphere of the aesthetic

1. [Perhaps the best way to harmonize this paragraph with the first paragraph of this chapter is to say that some aesthetic values fall outside of the beautiful, and then to say that within the beautiful we can distinguish the aesthetic values that represent the broad sense of beauty from those that represent the narrow sense of beauty, as explained in the first paragraph. This way of putting it deviates slightly from the letter of Hildebrand's text but captures what he means to hold. JFC]

is even richer and more variegated than the sphere of the moral. Not only are there qualitative differences in the realm of metaphysical beauty; this beauty also has a qualitatively different character depending on the type of value of which this beauty is the splendor and fragrance. The beauty of holiness is not only greater and higher than all other metaphysical beauties—it also has a completely new aesthetic quality. In terms of its quality, it is completely different from the beauty of moral values. In turn, the metaphysical beauty of moral values is qualitatively different from that of the various families of values which we have grouped together in earlier books, in an inexact manner, as the "intellectual" values.

The qualitatively new character of the respective metaphysical beauty extends likewise to the various value qualities within a family of values. The beauty of humility or purity is not only a higher beauty, because of the loftiness of these values; it also possesses a different note in qualitative terms from the beauty of honesty or reliability. What interests us here is not so much the qualitative wealth within metaphysical beauty, as the fact of the completely different aesthetic value qualities which we also find in the realm of the visible and the audible, and especially within the beauty of the second power.

We have spoken in detail about the wealth of the spiritual qualities which this beauty contains. Now we shall demonstrate from another perspective the diversity of aesthetic values in general. A distinction has often been drawn between the lovely and the grandiose, between the charming and the sublime; but we wish to show that the differentiation of aesthetic values goes much further than this.

Genius [Genialität], depth, potency, and necessity as aesthetic values

When we call a work of art a thing of genius, we have in mind one very definite aesthetic value. Certainly, this value too is a subspecies of the beautiful taken in the broader sense; but it is something new in relation to beauty in the narrower sense. The difference can be seen in the mere fact that this quality within the aesthetic relates only to works of art, and not to nature. Doubtless, we can also predicate this value of a philosophical work, a discovery, a military campaign, and so on. One could therefore ask: Is not "expressing genius" a much more general type of value, which (like all genuine values) also possesses a metaphysical beauty? Does not the fact that a philosophical work, a scientific discovery, a strategic plan for a battle, and a "masterstroke" of a statesman can all be works of genius, and that persons too can be called "geniuses" because of their great gifts, indicate that genius is not an aesthetic type of value, but an independent, special type of value which (like all the other values) also possesses a specific metaphysical beauty?

But even if this were the case, we still have in mind a special aesthetic value whenever we call a work of art a thing of genius, for in the various other fields such genius has more of an analogous character. We could say that what is involved in a work of art is an aesthetic genius, a genuine value which is different from beauty in the narrower sense but is an element of beauty in the broader sense. Thus there can be no objection to the affirmation that the term "work of genius," when applied to a work of art, represents one specific aesthetic value.

Another predication which we can apply not only to works of art, but also to nature and of course to many other areas, is depth. This is a very elementary, universal value, a primordial phenomenon. It plays a very special role in the aesthetic sphere. When we judge Mozart's *Marriage of Figaro* to be much deeper than Rossini's *Barber of Seville*, for example, we have in mind something that plays a decisive role for the artistic aesthetic value. When we call the beauty of a material (such as a beautiful velvet) less deep than the beauty of a glorious landscape, or the beauty of a landscape like that of Lake Geneva less deep than that of the Gulf of Spezia, we are likewise referring to something that is decisively important from the aesthetic perspective. Obviously, this is a question not of the metaphysical beauty of depth in general, but of a direct characteristic of beauty. We are thinking not of a metaphysical beauty which collaborates with the beauty of the second power of the visible and the audible, but of a characteristic of beauty itself.

Two things are present, as it were, when we say, for example, that one work of art or one landscape is deeper than others. First of all, there is the value quality of depth, which as such is extremely important. We say of Shakespeare's *King Lear* or of Beethoven's ninth symphony that they have an ultimate depth. Secondly, we can speak of a deeper and a more peripheral beauty. In that case, we are not describing the entity in question as the bearer of the depth, which constitutes a value of its own; rather, the depth is a characteristic of the beauty itself.

Another aesthetic value quality is potency [*Potenz*]. This belongs primarily to works of art; we can scarcely predicate it of landscapes. When it is predicated of beauty, it is a specifically aesthetic value, but its relationship to beauty is not the same as the relationship of depth to beauty.

A completely different aesthetic value lies in the necessity [*Notwendigkeit*] which can characterize a work of art and also a landscape. Here we mean first of all the inner necessity which is the opposite of all that is arbitrary, random, or meaninglessly strung together. As we have seen, there are landscapes of which one can say, "They could have been otherwise." But one says of other landscapes, "This is how they must be!" This inherent necessity plays an incomparably greater role in art. It is so significant that we can say: the greater the inner necessity, the higher the work of art.

This necessity possesses an analogy to the necessity of an essential law [*Wesensgesetz*], as opposed to a mere fact, but the necessity is not the same. We shall discuss this in the second volume of the present work; here we want only to underline the significance of the aesthetic value of inner necessity. This value has a decisive influence on the beauty—in the broader sense—of a landscape or a work of art.

Another kind of inner necessity both in works of art and in philosophical and religious books relates not so much to the composition of the work as to the fact that it contains a "word" that had to be "said," a word that was to be "uttered." This other dimension of necessity is likewise very significant for the rank of a work of art. The more a work possesses this dimension of necessity, the more significant and aesthetically valuable it is. We shall return to this phenomenon of necessity in the second volume of this work, where we shall discuss it in greater detail.

The aesthetic value qualities listed here, which are distinct from beauty in the narrower sense, should be sufficient evidence of the vast variety of aesthetic values. We have spoken of beauty in the narrower sense and in the broader sense (which includes the powerful, the mighty, the magnificent). Above all, we have pointed out the significance of other aesthetic values such as depth, genius, and potency. In the next chapter, we shall examine the aesthetic value which in one sense lies on the border of the realm of beauty, that is, the value of elegance.

CHAPTER EIGHTEEN

Elegance

Its this-worldliness; its relationship to gracefulness [Grazie] and to the fashionable [Mondänen]

ELEGANCE is an aesthetic value quality which lies on the border of beauty in the broader sense of the word; but it is indubitably a genuine aesthetic value. Unlike the amusing, it is not a quality which derives its importance from the effect it has on a person. It is something important-in-itself, something which belongs objectively to an object.

Like the other qualitative values, the elegant has a definite opposite, the inelegant, which is not only a pure absence of elegance but also a genuine antithesis. If we say that someone dresses inelegantly, messily, scruffily, in colors that do not match, or if we say that his figure is ungainly and that he lets himself go in his behavior, then what we are referring to is a genuine antithesis to elegance. If, however, we observe that someone is properly dressed, and that his clothes are not ugly but are nevertheless boring, then what we are referring to is only the absence of elegance.

Unlike most of the typical aesthetic values, and especially the beauty of the second power, elegance is entirely this-worldly. It has no place in eternity. Nor is it to be found *per eminentiam* in God and in eternity, as are all the typically aesthetic values, such as lovely, graceful, or poetic. It is not a message from God. Often it has a fashionable flair, and is therefore on the margin of the world of values. Elegance can appear conjoined to a certain beauty; but the beauty of the second power cannot join with elegance.

Among the other aesthetic values, it is closest to gracefulness [*Grazie*], but there are great and decisive differences between the two. In elegance there is often an element of the fashionable which is completely lacking in gracefulness. But that which is definitely ungraceful is also not elegant. The graceful has no trace of the fashionable, and it often appears in a form in which elegance is completely superseded. Their only point of contact is the fact that the ungraceful and ungainly likewise form an antithesis to elegance.

Bearers of elegance: clothes, dance, ballet, music

We shall understand more clearly the character of this aesthetic quality which we call "elegance" if we begin by reflecting on the spheres in which we speak of elegant and inelegant, or by thinking of the objects that can be elegant.

We shall speak first of elegant clothes, and especially of the modern clothing for men and women. In modern men's clothing elegance replaces beauty; in other words, there is no question of beauty in these clothes.[1] In

1. Men's clothing was often beautiful even as late as the Biedermeier period; it was definitely beautiful above all in the Middle Ages, in the Renaissance, and in the Baroque and Rococo periods. But the prosaic long trousers which are customary today, and have been worn for the last 150 years, cannot be bearers of beauty; unlike riding breeches, the connection between long trousers and the form of the legs is more or less eliminated. The jacket too has this kind of prosaic quality, which is incompatible with beauty. Even the material and colors are plainer than in former times. Above all, men's clothing today has a different function. The depoeticizing of the space we inhabit, which is profoundly linked to industrialization, goes hand in hand with a lack of interest in adequate external expression, and with a loss of the meaning and value of the "forming" of our life. This is the victory of comfort and usefulness over beauty. The adequate forming of clothing, which varied in earlier times in accordance with one's social class and professional work, is regarded as superfluous. The fact that different social classes and professions are expressed in different clothing is felt to be undemocratic. The necktie is the last remaining part of men's clothing which can be not only elegant, but even beautiful.

It is only in the uniforms of officers, especially of the Navy, that we still find the principle of the exact external form of a profession.

Today one can often observe a desire for men's clothing that is less plain and prosaic. This sometimes finds expression in the clothes of "hippies," where the decisive thing is not only letting oneself go, that is, the protest of the bohemian against order and cleanliness, but also a meaningful longing to escape from the plainness of clothing and appearance. Their colorful clothes and long hair can be definitely beautiful.

women's clothing elegance and beauty can appear conjoined. Naturally, one element in this elegance is the figure of the clothed person. A human figure can not only be beautiful, as may be the case especially with the naked figure; it can also be elegant, as we see above all in the clothed figure. Similarly, the way one carries oneself, and especially the way one moves, can be elegant. Of course, this overlaps with the sphere of the graceful [*das Graziöse*]. The way a person moves can be graceful, ungainly, or stiff. But the nobler sister of elegance, the graceful, remains a quality that is clearly distinct from elegance, even when both appear simultaneously in one and the same object. Something need not be graceful just because it is elegant; even less is something elegant just because it is graceful.

We also encounter elegance in the sphere of dance, where we find one of the most important antitheses between elegance and inelegance. In the dances of earlier days, such as the minuet, beauty and gracefulness played the principal role. But in the waltz, the polka, the mazurka, and all the more in dances such as the foxtrot or the tango, the specific aesthetic value quality which is involved is elegance. In these dances, the good dancers are the elegant ones as opposed to the inelegant ones who dance clumsily, awkwardly, uncertainly, or without verve and *élan*. Good dancing also entails a special sensitivity to rhythm, which plays a central role in the realm of the dance. The more the dancer is imbued with rhythm, the more elegant is his dance.

It goes without saying that barn dances, country dances, etc., are not elegant. Rather, they involve a certain heaviness and roughness. Neither elegance nor gracefulness is at home in these dances. Their rhythm is indeed important, and one must develop it to the full and enter in to it, in order to bring out the rustic charm; but these dances will never be elegant. We have already pointed out the fashionable character of the elegant, and the world of country folk is not fashionable.

While we lay stress on rhythm and insist that, within the world of dance, elegance demands that one resonates with the specific rhythm (which itself is already elegant), we do not mean to exclude other factors which are required for elegant dancing. Naturally, the figure of the dancer, the feeling he has for his own body, along with other factors play a role. Not only the one who dances against the rhythm is inelegant; the ponderous, stiff, or stout person is likewise inelegant. A Falstaff cannot be an elegant dancer.

Ballet is another sphere in which elegance is an essential aesthetic value. A splendid, successful ballet is almost always specifically elegant, unlike the contemporary kinds of dance which often have a pantomimic character. No doubt the typical ballet is also graceful when it is fully successful; but elegance stands even more in the foreground. But not only the dance itself is a typical bearer of elegance or inelegance; in the dance music too (for example, the waltz, the tango, or the polka), elegance is the decisive aesthetic value quality. The music for minuets can be beautiful, lovely, or gracious; elegance is not a typical value quality for minuets. Compare the minuet of minuets, the one that occurs in Mozart's *Don Giovanni*, with the waltzes *The Blue Danube* or *Voices of Spring* by Johann Strauss! A minuet is poetical, beautiful—but not fashionable. These waltzes are not exactly beautiful, but they are enchanting in their elegance.

Elegance is a quality which not only can occur in a certain piece of music, but also plays an essential role in it. Indeed, elegance is the specific value of some music. For example, many pieces by Chopin are specifically elegant. In the waltzes and the operettas of Johann Strauss elegance is *the* aesthetic value. In Chopin, by contrast, it is one value among others. Beauty and genuine gracefulness are also to be found in Chopin's works—it suffices to recall his two noble piano concertos. Nevertheless, many of his pieces belong in the salon and contain a special appeal to an elegant society. Schubert is often specifically graceful in his piano music, for example, in his *Impromptus*, but he never has the fashionable aspect which often belongs to elegance.

The combination of elegance with other aesthetic values, and the disvalue of triviality

Elegance can appear conjoined to other genuine aesthetic values. But the great musical works can no longer be elegant: in them the sphere of elegance is left behind. The depth, the poetry, and the specifically non-fashionable world of great music exclude elegance.

Although something beautiful and poetic can also be elegant—for example, the movement which portrays the ball in Berlioz' *Symphonie fantastique*, and above all many of Chopin's works—an artistically negative, trivial music can also be elegant. Léhar's *Gold and Silver* waltz is certainly not free of triviality, but it is indubitably elegant.

Accordingly, the following possibilities exist. First of all, music in which no elegance can be found, since this aesthetic value quality has been left behind; this is true of almost all great music. Secondly, beautiful music in which elegance is conjoined to other aesthetic value qualities. Thirdly, a type of beautiful music in which elegance plays an essential role. Fourthly, pieces of music which are only elegant, but are otherwise neutral, without other aesthetic values and disvalues. Fifthly, music which is trivial but elegant; the only positive aesthetic value it possesses is elegance.

This last case is particularly instructive with regard to the essence of elegance. It can characterize not only pieces of music which otherwise have no aesthetic value, and *a fortiori* no artistic value, but also trivial pieces of music that have artistic disvalue. This fact is very surprising, and manifests the gulf between elegance and all other full aesthetic values. At the same time, it must be emphasized that in these cases the quality of elegance itself possesses a different coloring. The link to artistic values has a great influence on the type of elegance. The fashionable character can retreat wholly into the background, as in the movement of Berlioz' *Symphonie fantastique* mentioned above. The elegance which even trivial pieces possess has a different quality. But despite their variety, these are subspecies of elegance, and it is correct to designate them all by means of the same term; they are all distinct from "graceful" and form a contrast with "beautiful" and "poetic."

Elegance is scarcely to be found in nature. This quality finds expression only in some animals. Some dogs are definitely elegant, such as greyhounds and Pomeranians. Some birds can likewise be elegant, whereas deer are specifically graceful, not elegant. On the whole, elegance in the proper sense is restricted to the human sphere and to man-made things.[2]

In the second volume of this work, in the chapter on applied art, we

2. We must also draw a distintion between the quality of the elegant and the fashionable and smart. The fashionable is that form of the elegant in which the sophisticated unfolds in a special manner. The fashionable is limited to clothing.

shall also speak of the elegance of certain machines. The examples that we have given of things that can be elegant or inelegant suffice to illustrate the special quality of elegance.

It possesses a certain analogy to what the French call *esprit*, and is in part expressed by the English word *wit*. Its relationship to beauty resembles the relationship between *esprit* and the depth, power, and nobility of spirit. In the realm of the aesthetic values, elegance occupies a place similar to that of *esprit* in the realm of the "intellectual" values. This analogy goes so far that we can even speak of the elegance of a witty remark or a particular kind of joke.

CHAPTER NINETEEN

The Comical

The comical, a primordial datum in human life

THE COMICAL has the same earthbound character as the elegant. Like the latter, it has no place in eternity; it is no message from God, neither a dew that falls from above nor an incense that rises up. It does not praise God. But whereas the elegant has something fashionable about it, the comical has something non-fashionable and natural about it.

The comical is a primordial datum in human life. Its role is incomparably greater than that of the elegant, which is a relatively minor value quality. We shall speak in the second volume of this work about the great significance of the comical in art.

The elegant is clearly an aesthetic value. Now we must ask: Is the comical really a value in human life? Is it something important-in-itself, or only something subjectively satisfying, only something agreeable in virtue of its effect on us?

In order to be better able to answer this question, we must briefly draw the line between the comical and other qualities which are related to it in some way.

The comical and the witty

In some ways, the witty resembles the comical; at the same time, however, the two are clearly distinct. It is obvious that the witty is much closer to the comical than are qualities such as beautiful, delightful, or sublime. If we call the comical and the witty aesthetic qualities, we are thereby thinking of them both as forming a subspecies of the aesthetic, one that differs from the typical form of the aesthetical, that is, from the beautiful, the lovely, the sublime, etc., which form the center of aesthetic values.

The witty always presupposes human beings. It adheres only to things made by human beings. Only a human being can tell a joke, just as only a human being can formulate a declarative sentence (no subhuman, apersonal being can speak). The quality of wittiness which we ascribe to a witty remark always belongs to an entity deriving from a person and made by a person. Similarly, the quality of wittiness which we ascribe to a person as a permanent characteristic is related to the ability to make witty utterances. But the comical belongs not only to utterances by a human being, not only to his conduct, but also to events, situations, and movements, and to certain higher animals.

Although a joke can be comical, and wit and the comical can make us laugh, the witty is at home in the sphere of the "intellectual" values. On the one hand, it is the quality of *esprit*, intellectual cleverness, a special sharpness of mind. Naturally, this applies primarily to the quality of the wittiness of a human person, but it also applies to the quality that makes a remark witty. On the other hand, however, the witty is at home in the sphere of aesthetic values. Its quality has a specifically aesthetic note. It is genuinely related to the elegant, and it engenders an aesthetic delight.

It is otherwise with the comical. It does not belong in the sphere of the "intellectual" values. Indeed, whereas the witty is indubitably a value, this is not so clear in the case of the comical. This is why it is not possible without further qualification to call it an aesthetic value quality. If we say of someone that he or she, taken as a whole, is comical, it is highly questionable whether this must really be something valuable.

In order to apprehend more clearly the difference between the witty and the comical, let us compare the comical quality belonging to certain sentences with witty sentences. In these two cases there is no difference as to the bearer of the quality. And they have in common that they can both make us laugh.

When someone makes a slip of the tongue and the sentence which he in fact utters completely diverges from the sentence he wanted to utter, this can be highly comical. This is often the case, for example, when one who does not know a language well tries to speak in it by naïvely translating from the language that is known to him—and the meaning of the sentence comes out as something entirely different. An elderly English spinster once asked the driver of a passing cab, "*Êtes-vous fiancé?*" ("Are you engaged?"). When he replied, "*Non!*" she said, "*O prenez-moi!*" ("Oh, take me!"). This was comical. Since the English word *engaged* is used in the two senses of "booked" and "engaged to be married," she assumed that the French word *fiancé* carried the same meanings. In such a case, one says something one does not want to say and moreover something which the other person must understand in a sense that is very comical. Clearly, however, this mistake in the linguistic expression is not in any way witty.

Wit is always something devised in a voluntary and conscious manner. The comical sentence and the comical situation derive from a "mistake," an involuntary malfunction. This distinguishes the joke clearly from the comical quality that can characterize utterances of the most various kinds. This, however, does not prevent a joke from also being comical over and above the special quality of the "brilliant," of *esprit.*

When we laugh at a joke, is this caused by the comical or by the specifically witty? Doubtless, there are many jokes that amuse us but do not really make us laugh. At most, we will put on a facial expression similar to the expression when we laugh, showing our satisfaction at the wittiness. We respond cheerfully to the witty, sometimes with a smile; but we do not really laugh. But many jokes are not only witty, but also comical—very frequently, because of the subject on which the joke touches—and then we have to laugh in the full and genuine sense of the word.

When we laugh at jokes in this way, the laughter appears to be the tribute paid to the comical which is linked to the joke, rather than to the witty as such.

Although the comical qualities that arise when someone says something other than what he intends to say is based on the involuntary character of the mistake, this does not exclude the possibility that what is said may also be said intentionally. While comical situations can obviously occur by themselves in our lives, as when someone who behaves comically is involuntarily comical, there is surely also a voluntary comedy. Let us just think of a clown or a person who is a brilliant impersonator, or someone who is deliberately playing around [*Unsinn macht*]. All these persons are in a sense putting on a show. They are portraying something that is comical. They are playing the part of a person in whom the comical occurs involuntarily. Although one cannot include this comedy among the comical situations which we encounter in our daily life, the comical quality nevertheless attaches here to something that is involuntary, because the person who is "portraying" this comical person, this comical situation, intends to create the illusion that what we see is an involuntary comical behavior.

The witty, on the other hand, is a typical expression of the *esprit* of a person. It adheres to a product of the human mind. Its charm and its value are inseparable from the fact that it is an intended, conscious product of the human mind—and of one particular kind of human mind to which we give the name *esprit*. As we have said, this is certainly not the case with the comical.

Despite this clear difference between wittiness and the comical, they are related in important ways. The witty and the comical share the note of the amusing [*des Erheiternden*]. When we draw a comparison with the quality of a profound truth—the quality which belongs to a proposition that formulates a great and solemn truth that summons us to take it seriously in an attitude of reverence—we see that both the comical and the witty appeal to a completely different stratum and a different capacity in us. Both are amusing, although in very different ways. This is why it was necessary to say something about the difference between the witty and the comical, whereas the difference between the serious and the comical is obvious.

Satire and caricature

Like the joke, satire and caricature are typical products of the human mind. They differ from the joke through their polemical character, through the tendency to poke fun at something that in itself is meant seriously. This is one way to rob a thesis, a work of art, a specific behavior, or a human being of its or his seriousness, shedding on something meant seriously a light that makes it comical, or that elicits laughter in us.

Many things objectively call for satire, which is an excellent instrument to unmask them in their hollowness, untruthfulness, etc. If, however, the satire is directed at something that in itself is noble, beautiful, true, or precious, it becomes specifically disvaluable, impertinent, and even stupid.

The important point for us here is that the quality of the satirical includes the taking of a position toward something, a hostile poking fun at something that is meant seriously; this is not at all the case with the comical as such. The satirical is one particular way to treat something. It is a product of the human mind like the joke, but it differs from the joke in that the joke as such need not have any polemical character. Naturally, there are also "satirical" jokes, but it is certainly not the case that all jokes are satirical. The specifically witty, a quality of *esprit*, is not the same thing as satire.

Caricature is much closer to satire. In caricature, a certain comical effect is achieved through a gross exaggeration of traits which belong to a face, a figure, or a movement. We can say that the caricature is a subspecies of satire. It can be comical but need not be so. It seldom elicits true and genuine laughter in us.

All these cases involve something consciously intended, a quality which is the expression of an attitude.

We shall return to these matters in the second volume, when we discuss a completely new situation: the role that the comical and other qualities such as the witty, the satirical, and caricature play in the work of art.[1]

Culpable and non-culpable ridiculousness, in contrast to the comical

The ridiculous is much closer in many respects to the comical, since it too elicits in us laughter in the full sense of the word. We must, however, distinguish the comical equally sharply from the ridiculous, which is in fact clearly a disvalue.

The term "ridiculous" can be used in two meanings. First, it can designate conduct that is in some sense culpable. Someone behaves presumptuously. He wants to make an impression whether by means of affected feelings or professorial self-importance or by pretending to understand something in a field about which he is completely ignorant. This is the typically ridiculous. The person in question makes himself ridiculous. The Italians say, *far brutta figura* ("to cut an ugly figure"); the French, *le ridicule tue* ("ridiculousness kills"); the Germans speak of *sich blamieren* ("making a fool of oneself"). The attitude of the one who makes himself ridiculous contains a definite disvalue. But although the impression which such a person makes has disvalue, it also contains a comical note that makes us laugh. If, on the other hand, someone makes a fool of himself by his narrow-mindedness, by his false and shallow assertions, he certainly does not in the first place move us to laughter; he disgusts us, he irritates us, he depresses us. However, making oneself ridiculous always includes an element of the comical. We might say that such a person is a satire on his own self. There is nothing comical in him that gives us pleasure; his behavior elicits a different kind of laughter than our response to the typically comical. The ridiculous as such possesses a negative value. Whereas the witty contains an element of success, there lies a typical failure in the ridiculous.

1. The ironical is an especially interesting quality, which belongs in the entire realm that has the comical as its center, so to speak. Cf. also Theodor Haecker, "Über Humor und Satire" and "Dialog über die Satire," in *Opuscula* (Munich: Kösel Verlag, 1949); cf. also his *Satire und Polemik* (Munich: Kösel Verlag, 1961).

The second kind of the ridiculous, the non-culpable, is based on the contrast between a situation and a person's behavior in it. At the solemn moment when someone is about to begin a speech, he suffers a sneezing fit so severe that he cannot speak. Or someone who wants to make a declaration of love begins to stutter. Someone who holds a high office wishes to take his place with solemnity on his chair, but he slips and lands on the floor. No personal disvalue is contained in this ridiculousness. The discrepancy between the demand of the objective situation and the conduct of a person is the bearer of a specific comical quality. Since the person is not at fault, and this discrepancy is caused not by any personal disvalue but only by an "accident" that befalls him, one cannot speak of any personal disvalue in him. And yet he appears ridiculous; the contrast between what the situation objectively demands and the "failure" (even though inculpable) is something ridiculous, not only something comical.

Humor as a value of its own

We must also draw a distinction between the comical and another important, indeed central, phenomenon, namely, humor. Humor is an attitude of the person, not an objective entity like the comical, and it must not be equated with an appreciation of the comical. Naturally, the works of humorists also contain comical elements, but the humorous, the irradiation of humor, is something other than the comical. There can be no doubt that humor, as the expression of a capacity of the human person, has a positive value. It is a deficiency when someone does not possess this aptitude. If we say that a person is definitely humorless, we are pointing to something that has a clearly negative value, not merely to the absence of something positive.

At this point, we do not yet wish to discuss the essence of humor. We merely mention its difference from the comical in order to show that humor is something unambiguously valuable. This could, however, also be said of having a feel for the comical, which is undoubtedly something valuable.

The comical lacks a negative counterpart

But is the quality of the comical a value in the same sense as moral, "intellectual," and aesthetic values?

The first point to be noted is that if the comical is a genuine value, it can be only a qualitative value, not an ontological value. But if it is a qualitative value, what then is its negative counterpart? As we have seen, one of the characteristics of the qualitative values that distinguishes them from ontological values is that their opposite is not just an absence of value, but a qualitative disvalue.[2] "Ugly" is a fully existing contrary opposite of "beautiful," in a manner analogous to "bad" which is the opposite of "good": this is not simply the absence of a value, as in the case of an ontological value such as the value of the person. An animal is not a person—it lacks the ontological value of the person—but this does not make it the bearer of a disvalue. On the contrary, it is the bearer of a specific ontological value; doubtless, this is much lower than the value of the person, but it is not a disvalue.

When we look for the qualitative counterpart of the comical, the quality which is opposed as a disvalue to the value of the comical in the same way as the ugly is opposed to the beautiful or the morally bad to the morally good, it appears that no such antithetical opposite exists. We can only note the absence of the comical. This by itself indicates that the comical, if it is permissible to call it a value in the genuine sense, would occupy a unique position in the realm of the qualitative values.

The earthly quality of the comical that draws us into the periphery of our being

A second element which illustrates the special position of the comical is the fact that it has a place exclusively in our earthly situation. In other words, the comical has no place in eternity. Unlike many other values, it is not contained *per eminentiam* in God, nor does it continue to exist in

2. [Hildebrand is referring here to chapter 10 of his *Ethics*, where the distinction between qualitative and ontological values is developed more fully than anywhere else in his corpus. JFC]

eternity. Rather, it would be meaningless to say that the comical continued to exist in eternity. The comical is bound to the earth in a completely different sense from all other genuine values.

A third element is connected with this. All the high values proclaim God in a special manner, whereas the comical certainly does not proclaim Him. No doubt, it does not contain anything that is hostile to God, and it is certainly a gift of God. But it does not lead us *in conspectu Dei* ("before the face of God") nor into a deep place. It is of course true that this proclamation of God, the character of being a message from God, is present in high values to various degrees, in accordance with their hierarchy; there are genuine values which do not proclaim God in a specific manner. But the situation of the comical is unique. Apart from its function in art, it does not lead us into a deep place, nor does it appeal to the depth in our being. Not even the most modest beauty which appeals to the senses—a beautiful sound, a beautiful material such as marble, velvet, or silk—has the relationship to the periphery of our being which the comical possesses. Every beauty appeals to our reverence and to a typical value-response. This means that beauty—naturally, in various ways, depending on the type of beauty—draws us into a deep place. The comical, which takes hold of us in such a way that we have to laugh, and shake with laughter, draws us rather into the periphery of our being.

Legitimate and illegitimate periphery

We must emphasize as forcefully as possible that there are two radically distinct kinds of periphery. There is a legitimate, healthy periphery, a stratum of human life which does not cut us off in any way from our depth and does not contain any kind of "hostility" vis-à-vis depth. On the other hand, there is an illegitimate periphery, where one lets oneself go. This is not only a contrast to depth, but is hostile to depth. If we allow ourselves to sink into this periphery, we flee from our depth, we escape from it. This periphery is a refusal of the *sursum corda* ("Lift up your hearts!"), a stratum in which we devote ourselves to superficial things which are hostile to the *logos* of values. It is only when we have drawn a distinction between these two kinds of periphery that we can see the sense in which the comical addresses the periphery, or can see which of the two peripheries it appeals to.

It lies in the nature of earthly life that we cannot always abide in a deep place. We cannot always dwell in the stratum of contemplation, of deep value-responses, of a state of strong emotion. We must direct our attention to many things that appeal to the peripheral stratum in us because of their relative lack of content.

Some things are such that they draw us into the legitimate periphery. Many activities belong to this category. When we add up a bill, cook a meal, put on our clothes, or do some practical chore, we must direct our attention to these activities, which—thanks to the poverty of their inner content—neither lead us to a deeper place nor affect us deeply. Such activities, which demand that we concentrate rather intensely on their own inner logic, naturally compel us to move away from depth and into the periphery of our being. This is a part of our existence on earth and is unavoidable. As we have said, this way of dwelling in a peripheral stratum does not necessarily mean that we are cut off from depth and still less that we are antagonistic to it.

It has often been emphasized that one can offer up even these activities to God and that one can see them as obligations laid upon us by God. During many of these activities one can lift one's eyes again and again to God; we have written about this in detail in our essay, "Holiness and Efficiency," in our collection *The New Tower of Babel*. It is only when we go beyond the indispensable concentration needed for these activities and allow ourselves to be completely absorbed by them that they can cut us off from deeper things. One inevitably wonders whether religion is not the only thing that makes it possible to maintain this inner link with the depth in ourselves. Naturally, the distinction between actual and superactual attitudes plays a decisive role here. We have discussed this thoroughly in a number of books;[3] here it suffices to point out that some superactual stances, such as the spousal love for another person, resound

3. As in my *Ethics*, chaps. 17, 26, and 27.

throughout the entire day like a delightful melody and continue to live in us and shape the entire situation of our lives, even when in our actual consciousness we are completely occupied with our work. This is true *a fortiori* of the love for Christ and of the love for God, when these are truly alive in a person.[4]

It is not this obligatory periphery that we have in mind here, but rather a peripheral stratum in the human person to which the charm of many things appeals. Everything that is amusing, whether games, social get-togethers, dances or balls, exciting things such as detective novels, or funny things such as making jokes and having fun—all this appeals to "antennae" in us which, in themselves legitimate, are all located in the periphery of our being. Sport, too, largely belongs there. It is indeed often linked to the enjoyment of many aspects of nature, such as the beautiful landscape through which we are riding, or the beauty of the coast or the sea which we see when swimming, or the poetry of a lake or river in which we are swimming, or the beauty of the mountainous landscape and the surface of the snow when we are skiing. But even though this natural beauty appeals to us at a deeper level, the delight taken in sport as such appeals to "organs" located in the periphery of our being.

This is not changed by the fact that the principal interest of many persons is some kind of sport, as when games such as tennis and golf are the greatest passion of their lives. The difference between the periphery and the depth corresponds to the content and the value of the things that attract us and to the strata in us in which these things can affect us; it does not depend on the role that these things play in our life. The fact that someone sets his heart above all on peripheral things, and that these indeed become his passion, does not supply any additional depth either to these things or to the organs to which they appeal. Such a person gets lost in the periphery and sinks down into it.

It is important to see that these peripheral things do not necessarily separate us from the depth in ourselves, and that the presence of this kind of periphery in the human person need not be a thing of disvalue. It is

4. See my *The Nature of Love*, chap. 2.

true that the amusing, that which is merely entertaining, the exciting, and the funny contain more dangers for the human person than the obligatory activities which practical life and many professions impose upon us. And yet these too may pose a great danger, as when people are wholly absorbed by the autonomous laws of their profession and are dominated, or even consumed, by them. At any rate, the amusing things which appeal to a kind of enjoyment pose a different risk of slipping into the periphery. They can become a special temptation to flee from depth into what Kierkegaard in *Either/Or* calls the "aesthetic life."[5]

But it would be wrong to fail to see that even this periphery is in itself legitimate. Normally, it plays a great and entirely justified role in the lives of children. In the adult it need not necessarily lead to a separation from depth, provided that one is aware of the danger that it contains. The adult can remain superactually united to God and to the entire world of high and noble things, especially when he is always grateful to God in times of "recreation," even for things that are merely amusing and relaxing.

We could say that three conditions must be met in order for this sphere to remain legitimate and not separate us from our depth. First of all, it is important to maintain superactually the link with God and the world of great goods; to keep alive, even in things that are entertaining, gratitude for the goodness of God, and to see games, sport, and funny and amusing things against the background of the world of the truly important and serious things, and of the splendor of their values. Secondly, these things must never occupy a large part of our life; they must not lay claim to too much of our time. Thirdly, we must never be so attached to them that we would be unwilling to renounce them if there were some reason to do so. We must never be attached to them in a way that makes us dependent on them. This "enslavement" must never arise, either through custom or through the pleasure that they give us.

There can undoubtedly exist special vocations to renounce all these things completely, to shut down this periphery, so to speak. Normally,

5. However, he does not use the word "aesthetic" in the same sense as I do in this work, but in a completely different sense, in which the aesthetic life is a mere life of enjoyment.

however, it is legitimate for it to occupy a specific place in the human person, provided that the three conditions mentioned above are met.

The gladdening [erheiterende] element in the comical

The comical addresses this kind of periphery in human life. It is this periphery, in itself legitimate, that we have in mind in saying that the comical in life appeals to the periphery and, within this stratum, to the noblest and deepest part of it. The organ for the comical, the enjoyment of the comical, the joy and the laughter it elicits, also pose the least danger to all that is deepest in ourselves. Indeed, we must say more than this: there lies in hearty laughter an element of good-naturedness, a friendly relaxation, which is incompatible with the malicious attitudes such as hatred, vengeance, jealousy, envy, or rage. This does not mean that the wicked person would be incapable of laughing; but it does mean that in the moment when he laughs heartily at something comical, he steps out of his wickedness—not in the sense that he disavows it, but in the sense that he momentarily leaves behind the tension of the wicked passions. His wickedness continues to exist at a deeper level in him, but he can step out of it for a moment precisely because this laughter occurs in the peripheral stratum. This is connected with the disinterestedness and the objectivity that lie in this hearty laughter. It is true that one cannot usually find this hearty laughter in wicked persons; many wicked persons are incapable of it and are instead capable only of scornful laughter, the laughter of Mephistopheles. Of course, the good-naturedness of laughter is an antithesis only to explicit wickedness, not to every sin. The thief can laugh, as can the lecherous person; and the thief can also be good-natured, and the lecher even more so.

The comical has also an inherent relationship to the joyous, more precisely to that which is a source of fun [*das Lustige*]. Considered in itself, the joyful, the delightful is anything but comical; usually, it excludes the comical. But in the experience of the comical and in the specific response to it in laughter, there lies an element of the joyful or of having fun. The comical amuses us. This relationship of the quality of the comical to the joyful or the gladdening, and its antithesis to the sad, is an important characteristic of the comical.

When we say that the comical forms an antithesis to the sad, this does not in any way mean that the sad is the specific antithesis to the comical; it is rather the serious that forms this antithesis. Both the seriously joyful and the seriously sad are opposed to the comical. If something is serious, the comical is out of place; as soon as we find something comical and have to laugh at it, we no longer take it seriously and we cease giving the response demanded by all that is serious.

This element of the gladdening and entertaining belongs essentially to the comical. It is a particular kind of joyousness which goes hand in hand with the comical.

In many ways, the seriously joyful and the seriously sad have more in common than the seriously joyful and the joyful element of the comical; they have in common the element of seriousness. Everything in the comical that is positive and amusing and a source of fun is qualitatively of a very special kind and is different from all the other kinds of the joyful. When we say that the comical has the joyousness of fun, we do not mean thereby that everything that is fun is comical; far from it! There are many things which we call fun—for example, a ball or an exciting, amusing game—but which are certainly not comical and which assuredly do not move us to laughter.

Laughter

We may perhaps come closer to the quality of the comical as a characteristic of a situation, of an occurrence, or of behavior, when we begin with the specific response to the comical, that is, laughter. Laughter is in itself just as remarkable and curious in the sphere of our responses as is the comical in the sphere of the aesthetic qualities. It was not for nothing that Henri Bergson gave his important little treatise about the comical the title *Le Rire*.[6] It is in truth impossible to investigate the essence of the comical without at the same time looking into the essence of laughter.

6. Henri Bergson, *Laughter. An Essay on the Meaning of the Comic* (New York: The Macmillan Co., 1911).

This is a unique type of response, since the physical occurrence which we experience is so closely united to the meaningful psychical and indeed personal response to the comical that one cannot detach the psychic response. Laughter does not at all involve a personal or mental act which is first complete and then finds its expression in the bodily sphere. Even when such an expression is unambiguously and consciously experienced —for example, the clenching of one's fists in anger, shouting in rage, or leaping and dancing for joy—the experienced bodily occurrence is clearly distinct from the personal act and does not form a part of it. Even in weeping, which has many analogies to laughing, the physical occurrence is clearly distinct from the personal experience which finds its expression in weeping.[7]

There are tears of grief, of deep emotion, tears of repentance, of anger, of hurt, tears of joy. Doubtless, weeping has a qualitatively different character, even just as a bodily experience, in all these instances. The interesting point for us here is that when we grasp these various responses, attitudes, and feelings which can express themselves in weeping, we need not take account of the weeping. In an analysis of the essence of grief, joy, deep emotion, anger, and so on, we do not need to discuss weeping. Their essence can be clearly apprehended without the tears that can be their expression. In an analysis of weeping, on the other hand, we must point out the different qualities of the tears of pain, joy, deep emotion, repentance, etc., because the affective experience on which these tears are based determines the quality of the weeping. In the comical, however, we cannot analyze the essence of the experience in detachment from the physical laughter. Finding something comical and laughing at it are much more closely interwoven.

Is laughter based on a response to the comical, an attitude that one takes to it, or is it rather a typical being-affected by the comical? When we see something comical and laugh at it, what is it that we are experiencing?

Obviously, it is completely different from the laughter that is caused by tickling. One bodily experience, that of being tickled, elicits another

7. Cf. Balduin Schwarz, *Untersuchungen zur Psychologie des Weinens* (Munich, 1928).

bodily experience. There is no meaningful link between the two, any more than there is a meaningful link in the case of the weeping that is caused by cutting onions. In the case of being tickled, there is no quality on the side of objects that we must understand and apprehend in its distinct character in order to be able to laugh at it.

But in the case of the laughter that occurs when we see something comical, there is a very meaningful link between the content of the comical and the reaction of laughter; this is by no means a mere causal connection. We apprehend something that is of a purely immaterial nature, that is, the quality of the comical. We understand it in its distinct character, and our behavior, our laughing at it, has a meaningful inner relation to the comical object. Of course, this relation concerns primarily the conscious experience which lies at the basis of the laughter, that is, the unique experience of finding something funny, an experience which is closely linked to the physical occurrence. We expect that someone will laugh in a situation that is full of the comical. We regret it when he does not laugh, because he fails to give the correct response. We assume either that he has no sense of the comical, or that he overlooked the comical because he was absent-minded or distracted.

Does this meaningful reaction to the comical, this "reaction" which is appropriate to it, exist as a response, that is, a taking of a stance like joy, grief, enthusiasm, and indignation? Or is it more a being-affected, like being touched? We have pointed out in chapter 16 above the difference between being-affected and affective responses.

In being-affected, the object speaks to me and has an effect on me. For example, the beauty of a piece of music or the kindness of a person moves me. But in enthusiasm, reverence, joy, grief, etc., we respond to the significance of the object. We speak to it the word that is appropriate to it. We grieve at something objectively sad, at the sin of a human being; we rejoice at his conversion. In both cases, there exists the meaningful intentional relationship between the object and our experience. In being-affected, the meaningful relationship runs from the object to us; in the response, it runs from us to the object. Being-affected and responding are usually closely connected.

Is laughter, or the conscious attitude on which the laughter is based and which is completely embedded in laughter, a being-affected, or is it a stance that we take? It seems that this attitude has more the character of being-affected. The comical "brings" us to laughter. In many cases, it overwhelms us, we are convulsed with laughter, we feel that we cannot resist it. The more we try (for whatever reason) not to laugh, the more are we "provoked" to do so. Typically, we say that our laughter makes us "weak." The comical "has us in its grip." All this goes much more in the direction of being-affected than in the direction of taking a position. Finding something funny is more a receptive than a spontaneous experience (note that we employ the term "spontaneous" here in the sense that we have given it in other books[8]). On the other hand, laughter at the comical is also the response that is meaningfully due to the comical.

It is very difficult to detach this conscious experience of finding something funny from the physical occurrence of laughing. This experience is neither a typical form of being-affected (like being moved, edified, or stirred) nor a taking of a stance (like joy, enthusiasm, grief, or indignation). This experience has traits both of being-affected and of taking a stance. In this regard, as also in regard to the unique link to a bodily occurrence (laughing), it occupies a special position.

We will understand this even more clearly once we have drawn a distinction between the response to the comical in laughter and the mocking laughter at someone. If we laugh at someone, this is clearly completely different from laughing at the comical. When we laugh at someone, we explicitly take a position in his regard, and a definitely unfriendly position. Of course, laughing at someone can be very different in character, ranging from a derisive mockery to a harmless failure to take seriously what the other person says or does. It is always the taking of a negative position; it is always the opposite of a respectful, reverent, or loving attitude.

The comical plays no role when we laugh at someone, nor is this mocking laughter a genuine laughter. Another difference from genuine laughter is that this laughter does not come over us on its own. It does

8. See my *Ethics*, chap. 22, and *The Nature of Love*, chap. 4, pp. 88–89, 93–94, 98–100.

not overwhelm us, it does not have us in its power; rather, it is an artificial laughter, it is explicitly "willed." It is a weapon which we employ in order to degrade and humiliate the other person.

When we laugh at someone, there is no mysterious, unique link between the physical occurrence and the conscious experience, as in the act of laughing at the comical. The contemptuous laughter is an intended expression of the position we take, that is, mockery. The mockery, the jeering, the poking fun at someone is clearly different from the laughter that is a mere expression of this position. For we can mock or deride someone, or poke fun at him, without necessarily laughing at him.

We mention this inauthentic laughter, this laughing at someone, which *per se* belongs much more to the analysis of the ridiculous, in order to show that in this case, unlike laughter at the comical, a clear stance is being taken, which is not in any way a being-affected.

The elements of "seeing from the outside" and detachment in apprehending the comical

Unlike the experience of art, the experience of the comical in reality always involves an act of "seeing from the outside." If someone slips and falls flat on his face, this can appear comical. But we will see it as comical only when the person who falls is not a beloved person, for in that case we cannot see this misfortune from the outside. Our concern that he may have hurt himself, our sympathy if he feels pain, prevents us from apprehending the movement of slipping and falling as comical. If we do apprehend it as comical, we are in the specific attitude of a spectator, and we are not involved with our heart. This "being uninvolved" is not at all what Kant means when he speaks of the "disinterestedness" that he regards as the foundation of the act of apprehending beauty.[9] Nor is it the disinterestedness which Schopenhauer sees as the presupposition for the apprehending of beauty,[10] that is, the deactivation of the "will" (in the

9. See the references to Kant given in chap. 16 above.
10. See the references to Schopenhauer given in chap. 16 above.

sense in which he uses this term) and the purely contemplative attitude. No, a lack of involvement of a completely different kind is presupposed in the act of apprehending the comical. We repeat that we are not speaking here of the comical quality found in comedy or in art, but exclusively of what is found in reality. In the apprehension of this comical quality, being uninvolved signifies an antithesis to every kind of profound sympathy; it means concentrating on an external aspect.

This applies also to the comical aspect which is provoked by a malfunction, for example, when someone stutters while giving a speech, or has a facial tic (a nervous muscular twitch) and makes faces while delivering a solemn oration. Here too we will not laugh if the person in question is one whom we love, one to whom we are bound by a deep solidarity. We will not see the comical: we will suffer with him. Instead of laughing, compassion will fill our heart. This most certainly does not mean that the act of apprehending the comical and laughing at it always entails an uncharitable attitude. By no means! But it does entail seeing from the outside.

But does the apprehension of the comical involve this seeing from the outside in every case where something is comical? Naturally, this does not apply to what Bergson calls the comical use of words—to the comical turn of speech or to a slip of the tongue as such, that is, to every instance that involves not a real person but a joke, a comical fictitious happening. The comical excludes involvement; but in this case, the simple fact of the unreality of such a happening makes this involvement impossible.

No one likes becoming involuntarily a cause of laughter in others. If someone makes a slip of the tongue in a serious speech, or stutters at a solemn moment, he is embarrassed when the comical aspect which really exists provokes laughter. Naturally, this need not always be found embarrassing; for some people possess such a freedom of spirit and objectivity that they themselves apprehend the comical aspect and have to laugh at themselves. This, however, occurs seldom.

In this context, we must draw a clear distinction between the following three cases. First of all, there is the comical situation of a gaffe which makes other people laugh, as when someone makes a slip of the tongue in a lecture and what he says is comical. He wants to say something utterly serious, but his slip of the tongue opens the door to some indecent idea. Both the content or the wording of the slip of the tongue and the gaffe which it contains are comical. If the audience bursts out laughing, the one who has caused this reaction feels humiliated; he senses it as a disgrace and sees himself as a *brutta figura.* He believes that he has made himself ridiculous. Although this inculpable ridiculousness is objectively quite different from culpable ridiculousness, he himself can feel it as mortifying. Doubtless, the ridiculousness which occurs when someone involuntarily causes laughter through comical behavior is completely different in qualitative terms from objective, culpable ridiculousness. The audience which laughs at him does not find *him* ridiculous. But he himself feels this inculpable, involuntary comical behavior to be humiliating: it is as if he has in fact made himself ridiculous.

This feeling of being humiliated can take various forms. As a reaction on the part of a proud person who feels himself wounded in his arrogance, it is regrettable because of the underlying arrogance. He ought not to feel humiliated in this way. But it is also possible for someone to feel humiliated and to be ashamed because he is a timid, helpless person who perhaps has a very poor opinion of himself. In that case his reaction is very understandable and not a mistake, even though he ought not to feel humiliated, since there is no objective reason for this. He himself is not ridiculous; it is only the situation that is objectively comical. Persons who possess a great freedom of spirit and objectivity apprehend the comical aspect of themselves and do not feel humiliated.

Secondly, the situation may involve a theme which is objectively so serious that the comical situation of the gaffe generates a definite disharmony. For example, during a liturgical service in which the sacred is the theme and our response ought to be recollection and adoration, a situation suddenly arises for some reason with a comical aspect that makes us laugh. This does not indeed mean that the priest is humiliated who causes this comical aspect through a slip of the tongue, stuttering, or something similar. But it is an occasion for regret. His person ought not to play any role in worship; it is only the theme of the liturgy that counts. The fact that he has been the cause (albeit inculpably) of a comical situation which is incompatible with the sacred seriousness of the liturgy ought to be only an object of regret, of sadness. He ought not to get annoyed at having made himself ridiculous.

In a third case, the seeing from the outside in the act of apprehending the comical, and all the more in laughing at it, emerges most clearly. We are thinking here of situations in which such a gaffe occurs in a conversation with a person to whom we are communicating something very deep, something that moves us profoundly. If we find his laughter painful, this is not because we are afraid of having made ourselves ridiculous, but because he is so little responsive to the theme that moves us that he laughs at the gaffe. If someone makes a declaration of love and has a fit of sneezing in the middle of a sentence, or if he gets stuck because of his stammering, or if he expresses himself comically because of his poor command of the language, and the person he is addressing laughs out loud, this is deeply painful—because it shows how little she is affected by the declaration of love. The laughter shows that she is not truly moved and does not experience the situation from within, but rather sees the entire situation from the outside and so apprehends the comical aspect which is genuinely and objectively caused by the gaffe. This example shows clearly the significance that being detached and uninvolved has in the act of apprehending the comical and in being gripped by it.

This, however, applies only to involuntary comical behavior. If someone "plays the fool," he intends something comical. If he impersonates someone else, the act of apprehending the comical does not contain any kind of non-involvement. The same is true of the narration of a comical event which did not truly take place, or of the narration of real events which belong to the past.

It is at any rate a characteristic of the comical as found in real life that it is always an external aspect. This is also connected with our earlier observation that the comical (except in a work of art) always appeals to a legitimate periphery in us, not to the specific depth in us, as do the serious things, whether sad or joyful.

On Bergson's interpretation of laughter and the comical

In his above-mentioned work, *Le Rire*, Bergson interpreted laughter as a "censure" on the part of society. It seems to us that this is correct only in the case of "laughing at," which concerns the ridiculous in the authentic, negative sense. "Laughing at" does indeed contain an explicit rejection. But there is no censure in the case of things that are only comical and that elicit genuine laughter.

Perhaps he confuses the non-involvement of which we have spoken, the seeing from the outside, with a censure. But the seeing from the outside is itself limited only to particular cases of the comical. It contains no unkindness and of course no rejection. As soon as someone intends to make other people laugh—either by playing the fool, by impersonating someone, or even by telling a funny story—the laughter contains neither a censure nor the moment of non-involvement.

Let us think of the many comical situations which arise through a misunderstanding: here too there is no kind of censure or seeing from the outside. We recall the story of the French officer in 1859, after the victory over the Austrians, who noticed big Brazil nuts in the window of a fruit store in Como. He asked the shop-girl, "*Comment cela s'appelle?*" ("What is that called?"). She replied in the fine dialect of Como, "*Ça ne se pèle pas, ça se peste*" ("You don't peel that, you break it open.") The officer did not understand and replied, "*Comment?*" ("How?"). The woman retorted, "*Con le man o col pié—comme la veu*" ("With the hand or with the foot—as one wishes"). The officer, who by now understood even less, replied, "*Je ne comprends pas*" ("I do not understand"), and the woman said, "*Se no la vol comprar, lo lasci star*" ("If you don't want to buy them, leave them there"). When the officer went away, she said, "At least you can talk with the Frenchmen. With the Austrians, you don't understand a single word." This conversation, which is based on nothing but misunderstandings, is definitely comical. Neither of the two persons commits a gaffe, neither displays any weakness; the comical situation is a pure joy. Such misunderstandings are rich sources of the comical.

It is understandable that Bergson views laughter as a censure, when one bears in mind that there exists the general danger in philosophy, as soon as one has discovered something, to attempt to interpret everything in the light of this discovery. One no longer listens to the voice of reality, but begins to construct artificially. Despite all the reverence that is due to Bergson as a great thinker, it must be firmly underlined that it is wrong to interpret the authentic, typical laughter as a censure.

Bergson lists many sources of the comical, but he does not draw the sharp distinction between the comical in real life and in art, a distinction which seems to us absolutely necessary. Although of course much in the quality of the comical is common to the two spheres, the comical takes on a completely new value in art, since it is at the service of the total artistic beauty of the specific work of art. This is why it seems to us necessary to separate the comical in real life and in art.

For Bergson the primordial source of the comical is the application of the mechanical to living beings, that is, to treat living beings like machines, to make puppets out of human beings. It is doubtless correct that this is one source of the comical, but it is only one source among many others. One cannot regard it (as Bergson does) as the main root of the comical as such.

The indecent [das Unanständige] as a source of the comical

We must point to a further element that is a source of the comical: the indecent. Let us first consider the comical effect of the contrast of something suddenly breaking into the normal space of society even though it is completely out of place there. This comical situation can occur when something indecent is not involved. A lady who always carried a wound-up alarm clock with her, so that she would arrive on time for all her appointments, once attended the funeral of one of the children of her cook. The child had died in an accident in the park—it was a particularly tragic case. At precisely the most serious moment, when the coffin was lowered into the grave, the alarm clock suddenly went off. The contrast between the neutral, technical, everyday atmosphere of the alarm clock and the tragic moment of the burial doubtless had a comical effect.

Now a contrasting effect of this kind is often found with the indecent. First of all, the irruption of certain things into a social situation which is not indeed serious, but where the social atmosphere is shaped by good manners, has a comical effect because of the contrast. Secondly, the special comical effect is determined not only by the contrast as such, but also by the special character of the things forming the contrast.

We must draw a distinction between two completely different types of the indecent. The first type concerns an unaesthetic bodily sphere, such as digestion, vomiting, and other things which are a tribute that the human being pays to his earthly frailty. In themselves these are neutral things, but one is justifiably ashamed to do them in public. As I have shown in my book *Purity*,[11] this kind of shame is related to things that are unaesthetic and in some way negative. Shameless behavior of whatever kind—both that of the coarse person and that of the cynic who wants to bear witness to his independence of what other people think of him—is as such not in the least comical; it is repulsive and disgusting. The comical effect occurs only when something deriving from this sphere breaks into the public realm not only unintentionally, but even against the will of the person concerned.

The other type of the indecent is the sphere of the sexual, which as such is something deep and intimate. It is a mystery which is meant to be the expression and fulfillment of spousal love in marriage. This area possesses a special power of attraction, an incomparable charm. In itself it is anything but comical.

If someone laughs bashfully in some way as soon as this area is mentioned, that is not in the least a genuine laughter at something comical. It can also be the laughter of embarrassment. If, however, something emerges from this eminently intimate sphere into the public realm, this can be very comical, but only if the behavior is not intentional, and only if it is not shameless. Rather, the allusion to this sphere must occur involuntarily, through an oversight, as when someone makes a slip of the tongue and uses against his will an indecent word in a sentence, or as when something in his clothing is not correct, so that intimate parts of

11. Dietrich von Hildebrand, *Purity*, part 1, chap. 1, footnote 1.

his body are on public display. The exhibitionist is not in the least comical; he is disgusting and repulsive. But if a respectable and honorable man is absent-minded and appears in public in his underwear, this provokes laughter and is definitely comical.

The comical aspect of the indecent plays a great role not only in many jokes, but also in many comical "off-color" stories. It is surprising that the mention of such an intimate sphere, which is in itself so serious and has such a lofty destiny, can appear comical. God has destined it to fulfill a solemn function in marriage, and in this context it is anything but comical; rather, it is specifically serious. Similarly, the misuse and desecration of this sphere is anything but comical. Like every sin, such conduct is dreadful and profoundly regrettable.

We can understand the comical aspect which this sphere can possess only if we are clear about three things. First, as we mentioned above when speaking about seeing from the outside, the comical represents a merely external aspect. Secondly, because of the strongly intimate character of this sphere, its unintentional irruption into the normal social sphere is comical, especially in the case of a more formal social setting or of people who are not linked by any close relationship; it provokes laughter. Finally, thanks to its general charm, the sexual sphere has an enlivening [*erheiternd*] effect, when one is discreetly reminded of its existence—not by arousing sexual instincts in someone, but by means of an allusion. This sphere is not comical as such. Rather, the enlivening effect, together with the contrasting effect mentioned above, prepares the ground for laughter of a specific kind.

Naturally, there is a great gradation of differences in the realm of the comical, depending on the kind of irruption—whether it is an utterance that evokes this association [with the sexual sphere] against the will of the one who speaks, or a story in which the words explicitly create some suggestive meaning.

We are fully aware of the incompleteness of this analysis of the comical effect of the indecent, but in the present context this must suffice. Let us only mention once again the profound difference between the two mentioned types of the indecent. They possess the same character only because of the factor of concealment (though for completely different reasons) from the public sphere.

The bearers of the comical

The bearers of the comical are very varied. We find the comical in the sphere of the spoken word, of conduct, of certain events, situations, sights, confusions, etc. We do not intend to make a list of all the possible bearers of the comical; let us only emphasize explicitly that everything that is comical is connected in some way with the human person. Plants and inanimate nature cannot be comical. Even in the realm of the animals, one can speak of the comical only in the case of certain higher animals and only when their behavior possesses in some way or other an element analogous to the human. Dogs and cats can be comical in their facial expression when this contains something that recalls, as it were, the comical in the human person. I once saw how two tomcats that were both courting the same cat looked at each other in a way that made exactly the same impression as when two human rivals look at each other with smugness, contempt, and irritation. Some movements by animals, such as apes, for example, can also be definitely comical. Here the analogy and the comparison to the human person play some kind of role. But a fish cannot be comical; nor can a snake or a rhinoceros, to say nothing of a spider, an ant, or a bee.

When we ask which entities can be comical and which cannot, we must of course also remember that there are many qualities which are closely related to the comical. Although one can laugh at them, they lack the ability of the specifically comical to make us shake with laughter and to shed tears of laughter. When Wilhelm Busch speaks of the *Possierlichkeit* [a certain way of being funny] of the ape,[12] he is alluding to one such quality, which is very close to the comical, but is distinct from the authentically comical.

12. In his celebrated and very witty *Naturgeschichlichtes Alphabet*, in Wilhelm Busch, *Gesammelte Werke* (Munich: Braun und Schneider, 1959), 120.

The this-worldliness [Diesseitigkeit] of the comical

It is indubitable that the comical is a great gift of God and a significant factor in the course of human life, something that bestows joy. The ability to apprehend the comical and to laugh at it is a primordial human trait. Saint Thomas rightly says that laughing is specifically human. Animals cannot laugh. The idea that an angel laughs is an impossible fiction. This means that it would be false to say that laughter is an essential trait of the person. No, it is limited to the human person; superhuman persons cannot laugh. Indeed, we must say more than this. Laughter is a specifically human trait which is limited to the earthly existence of the human person, to the specific this-worldly situation. The idea that a human being would laugh in eternity is incompatible with the *status termini* ("the final state"). What is true of laughter is also true of the comical. It is a specifically earthly phenomenon which presupposes the entire this-worldly situation and has no place in eternity.

This does not prevent the comical and laughter from being great gifts of God. The positive role of the comical is of a very specific kind. It is not a consolation in the *vallis lacrimarum* ("vale of tears") like hope, like the immanent promise that is contained in all moral values and especially in beauty. It is not a message from on high, like a glorious sunset, a great work of art, or the purity of a human being. Nor is it something that leads us *in conspectu Dei* ("before the face of God"). The comical is neither a dew descending from on high nor an incense that ascends; in these respects it is unlike other values. But it is a great gift of God and a consolation of a very specific kind in the course of human life.

The liberating function of the comical

The comical is something that relaxes and enlivens, something that again and again gives us new vital energies in our cares and trials. It is true that it can neither assuage deep pains nor relieve the night of suffering. But in unpleasant, oppressive situations, it can be a light that raises us up above the situation in many ways and liberates us. It suffices here to think of the role that jokes and comical observations have played in times of oppression, for example, in the Third Reich.

It is especially when we are depressed because we have not succeeded in accomplishing some task, or when we cannot stop our thoughts from circling around some harmless failure, that is, when nothing objectively sad is present but our pride finds it difficult to swallow something, or also when we are intimidated and despondent because of a mistake that is in fact harmless—it is especially at such moments that laughing at something comical has a liberating effect. If we apprehend the comical side of the situation, and especially the comical aspect of our own conduct, we experience a liberating distance from our selves. This liberating function of the comical comes into its own in a particular way when it shatters false seriousness, for example, when two persons are wrangling about something that is basically unimportant, or when someone feels insulted without any cause, or when pure conventions are being taken much too seriously. Whenever a third person succeeds through something comical in making those involved laugh, they acquire a distance to their "much ado about nothing." Sometimes, indeed, they then see the comical aspect of their dispute, their taking offense, or their conventional seriousness.

The great significance and the liberating effect of the comical appear with special clarity when we apprehend that the comical is the antithesis to false seriousness. It is ill suited to that which is *genuinely* serious; everything that is truly serious and valuable deserves a response which is the antithesis of the "seeing from the outside" which is characteristic of the comical. Nevertheless, the correct response to everything that contains a *false* seriousness is to see its comical aspect and to employ this aspect to shatter the false seriousness.

The element of kindness [Güte] in the comical

At this point, we must also mention the element of kindness that can be present in the comical, or rather in seeing the comical and laughing at it. If one sees in a comical light mistakes such as false seriousness, and weaknesses such as a certain narrowness or oversensitivity, and laughs at them instead of only being disgusted by them, one experiences an element of kindness, a conciliatory way of looking at a person's mistakes and weaknesses against the background of the universal human frailty. Naturally, it would be completely wrong to see moral disvalues, such as a base and vicious behavior, in a comical light and to substitute laughter for the response of rejection and indignation.

To see the comical in a situation and to laugh at it imply a specific distance and objectivity which are the opposite of being entangled in purely personal interests. To be able to laugh at a humiliation or an affront, if this also possesses a comical element, is the antithesis to the irritable state of being hurt and brooding about how one can get revenge. Naturally, this laughter is not the true moral antithesis to revenge, for that is forgiveness. It is, rather, an objective attitude, a state of being superior to the situation; but it is not at all the bearer of the sublime moral value of forgiveness. This seeing of the comical aspect, the facetious element which we have in mind here, is the complete opposite of laughing at someone. All the more is it the opposite of scornful laughing at someone, for this is not only devoid of every breath of kindness, but is a distinctly unkind attitude.

The natural home of the comical in the interpersonal sphere

We now draw attention to a very significant characteristic of laughter and the comical, that is, the relationship of both of these to the interpersonal sphere. The comical emerges in a particular way when one is not alone. It is relatively seldom that one bursts out laughing or laughs from the bottom of one's heart when one is completely alone. We do not wish to deny that this is certainly possible. If we prescind from the comical as found in a literary work of art and think of the comical in life, it is indubitable that the presence of other people plays an important role in bursting out laughing. In general, one weeps in solitude. One feels the need to withdraw when one bursts into tears. But laughter is the exact opposite of this: it is a definitely social phenomenon. We have no need of solitude when someone involuntarily makes us laugh, unless our laughter contradicts the seriousness of the situation, or we wish for particular reasons that the person in question should not notice our laughter. Indeed, laughter is intensified by the presence of other people. When the comical occurs in the interpersonal sphere, it makes us laugh even more. The great difference between being completely alone and being together with other persons with whom we are in some kind of contact makes itself particularly felt in the effect of the comical, that is, in laughter.

The role of the interpersonal situation also emerges clearly in the fact that one likes to tell other people a funny story, and indeed, one would like to tell it in a social gathering. The comical is destined for the interpersonal sphere. The same is true for two phenomena which are related to the comical, namely, practical jokes and playfulness.

Practical jokes [Scherze] and nonsensical play [Unsinnmachen]

Normally, human beings enjoy practical jokes. Not only do they find delight in them, they like to play them on other people. With children practical jokes feature prominently.

The practical joke can take various forms. There are endearing jokes, witty jokes, and jokes that specifically make us laugh, jokes that are comical in the narrower sense of the word; but there are tactless jokes and even malicious jokes. By means of practical jokes one can make fun of another person in a way that offends him; then the joke borders on mockery. In general, however, jokes are endearing. It would be sad if no one in the world made practical jokes.

One typical endearing practical joke was made by Goethe in Sesenheim when he put on George's clothes and went disguised to Friederike.[13] In many countries, it has long been the custom on April 1 to pull the wool over the eyes of one's acquaintances. The practical joke consists of telling them lies in jest, hoping that they will fall for it. This is a typical form of practical joke. Disguises which do not serve some particular purpose are a common kind of practical joke. Certain people indeed

13. Goethe, *Dichtung und Wahrheit*, part 2, book 10.

provoke us to play practical jokes on them through their credulity or through certain weaknesses, such as excessive timidity or vanity.

As long as this does not offend against love of neighbor, the practical joke is certainly legitimate; it has a legitimate place in the world. It is explicitly unserious, but it is definitely not incompatible with the serious, when it stands alongside the serious and is not confused with it. Serious situations such as very solemn moments, and above all the presence of the sacred, exclude practical jokes. In the former case, practical jokes sound the wrong note; in the case of the sacred, they are a desecration. The principle here is that there is a time for practical jokes and a time for seriousness. In some Catholic countries the Carnival is a time of practical jokes and peripheral fun; on Ash Wednesday begins the full seriousness of Lent, which puts an end to all the practical jokes and foolery of the Carnival and excludes them. Thus, there are situations which prompt practical jokes, and other situations with a theme such that practical jokes are wholly out of place.

The essence of the practical joke consists precisely in the fact that what is said and done in it is not meant seriously. But in many kinds of practical joke, the partner must initially take it seriously. The disguise which is worn by the joker must deceive the other person for a moment. Above all, the practical joke with which one pulls the wool over the other person's eyes must be believed. For if the "lies" of April 1 are to succeed, and if they are genuine practical jokes, they must initially be believed—at least for a few moments.

As we have said, there are charming, warm-hearted, witty practical jokes, all of them unobjectionable. But there are also irreverent, tactless, cruel, loveless, and malicious practical jokes. The practical joke as such is, however, something positive, and the world would be poorer if the human race were to lose its appreciation of practical jokes.

The result of a practical joke (apart from the bad kind of practical joke) is funny, amusing, and above all comical in some way. It certainly need not be comical in the most central sense of the word; we need not be convulsed with laughter. But an element of the comical must be present, otherwise the practical joke has failed. It often also has a witty character.

One typical, unobjectionable practical joke is played by the lord on Christopher Sly in Shakespeare's *The Taming of the Shrew.* The lord arranges for the drunkard who is sleeping on the ground to be clothed in splendid garments. He has him brought to a wonderful bed. When he awakens, he does not know where he is. He is told that he is a lord who has been asleep for many years, and he believes this. If this had involved a man like Goethe or Beethoven, such a practical joke would have been a cruel and tactless act, an irreverent, stupid prank. It would not have been in any sense comical or witty. We need the very rough, brutish drunkard which Sly is to legitimate this practical joke.

On the other hand, truly delightful was the practical joke which Saint John Bosco played on the two priests who regarded him as a madman because of the work he had founded.[14] A group of priests had commissioned these two to have him locked up in a madhouse. They visited the saint and proposed that he should accompany them on an excursion in their carriage, on the grounds that this would be good for his health. In reality, they hoped that he would enter the carriage alone and that the coachman, who had already received his instructions, would drive him immediately to the madhouse, where the keepers were already waiting. Don Bosco, however, immediately saw through their ruse and insisted that the two priests should get into the carriage first. He declared that it would be a grave impoliteness if he as a simple priest were to get in before them. Without any suspicion, they got in, convinced that Don Bosco would follow them. He, however, slammed the carriage door shut as soon as they had taken their seats, and called to the coachman: "Quick! Drive to the madhouse! The two gentlemen are expected there." On the basis of the information he had been given, the coachman drove as quickly as possible, without paying heed to the protests of the priests, who were obliged to spend several hours in the madhouse before the misunderstanding was cleared up. This practical joke, the correct response to the attempt to pull the wool over his eyes, and to do so not in jest but in all seriousness, was a kind and well-deserved lesson, which is expressed in the proverb, "One

14. Cf. J. B. Lemoyne, *Der heilige Johannes Bosco*, I (Munich: Salesianer-Verlag, 1927), I, 370f.

who digs a pit for others, falls into it himself." This does not contradict the holiness of Don Bosco; on the contrary, it makes him particularly lovable and is an expression of his great freedom of spirit and his humor.

There is a kind of nonsensical play [*Unsinnmachen*] that is related to the practical joke but is different from it. The human person sometimes needs to leave the sphere of the serious for a short time by doing something that is neither useful nor obligatory nor deep—something that has no "meaning." Naturally, this negative description is inadequate. The meaningless [*das Sinnlose*] can be barren, oppressive, and boring. The "non-sense" of which we are speaking here must be funny, enlivening, and somehow comical. Leaving behind the normal course of the day—which extends from doing indispensable things such as getting dressed, eating, drinking, etc., to doing work of every kind, including even the great and exhilarating phases of beautiful, creative work or of deep human encounters, as well as of prayer and contemplation—leaving all of this behind for an act of nonsensical play is the expression of a superabundant vitality. This has a "meaning" of its own, which is nothing other than the meaning of nonsensical play. It must be something comical and joyous, where the person involved himself laughs. Naturally, there are great gradations in the quality of nonsensical play. There is a silly and childish kind of such play, a funny and witty kind, and a comical kind.

Nonsensical play is as such legitimate and positive. It is an enrichment for a person when he plays like this from time to time and can laugh at other people's nonsense. It is an enrichment for life here on earth that people play nonsensically. Nonsensical play is a specific antithesis to taking oneself too seriously, as well as to every kind of bureaucratic mentality, as well as to every kind of conventional mentality. It contains a special freedom of a certain kind. It was deeply meaningful when jesters were kept at royal courts in olden days.

The comical as a qualitative value all its own

We see then how the comical, or the realm which has the comical as its heart and center, plays a role in human life in many different forms.

We must indeed distinguish the primordial phenomenon of the specifically comical from the qualities which are related to it, such as the ridiculous and the witty, the practical joke and nonsensical play, irony, satire, and caricature. All these, however, when compared to all the other aesthetic qualities, form a realm of their own, with the comical as its center. The comical plays a role, in different specific forms, in all these related phenomena.

This comical is a thoroughly immaterial quality. It does indeed presuppose the senses in one way or another, but it is not a sense quality, and it is much further removed from a sense impression than the beauty of a sound and of a color.

Once again, we must ask: Is the comical a value, something important-in-itself? Or is it only an objective good for the person? If it is an objective good for the person—as it undoubtedly is—we must then ask: What kind of objective good is it? It is obvious that it is not an elementary objective good which derives its significance from its relationship to the needs of our life (such as health, necessary nutrition, etc.). Accordingly, the question is: Is it an objective good because it is something that is legitimately subjectively satisfying? And does it then belong to the realm of the agreeable? Or is it an objective good for the person because of its value? Is the comical the same kind of gift for us as a cooling breeze in warm weather or the entertaining quality of a game? Or is it a gift like a beautiful landscape or a glorious melody, that is, something that makes us superabundantly happy because of its objective value?[15]

We have already seen that the quality of the comical does not possess all of the traits which characterize the other qualitative values. It does not have a specific negative counterpart, nor does it praise God like all the other values. And yet we are reluctant to declare it to be something merely agreeable. The comical is too rich in content; as we have seen, the comical can be deep. Finally, the comical in a work of art is indubitably

15. [In this paragraph Hildebrand is presupposing the different kinds of objective good for the person that he distinguished in his earlier ethical writings. See his *Ethics*, chaps. 7 and 9, for his account of four main kinds of objective good for the person. JFC]

a definite value. Indeed, it is a whole broad dimension of reality and makes itself felt almost every day in human life.

We must rather say that the comical is a qualitative value all its own, which stands apart from all other values and lacks many of the essential traits of the other values. It surely belongs to the realm of the aesthetic values, but it is not a subspecies of the beautiful. In its quality, the comical possesses a special relationship to the human person. Whereas the beautiful, the significant, the poetic rests in itself and bestows gifts on our spirit out of its fullness, the comical as such addresses the human spirit. Its relationship to us cannot be detached from its quality, and this is why it has a unique relationship to laughter and why it appeals to laughter.

But the greatest significance, depth, and authentic value of the comical will be revealed to us only when we study the role of the comical in art in the second volume of this work. In art it attains a completely new meaning and is an essential factor in many works of art; it makes a decisive contribution to their beauty and to their artistic value.

CHAPTER TWENTY

Beauty and Truth

WE HAVE repeatedly spoken of truth as a bearer of metaphysical beauty. At the end of chapter 10, we mentioned a mysterious connection between the beauty of the second power and truth. Now we wish to discuss briefly the relationship between truth and beauty.

The levels of truth and the beauty which corresponds to these

First of all, truth is the bearer of a metaphysical beauty which has been called the *splendor veri* ("splendor of that which is true"). Like all values, truth too has a specific beauty which is the splendor, the fragrance of truth.

When we speak of truth we can have various things in mind. First, there is the truth of propositions; it aims at an existing state-of-affairs. The proposition which affirms the existence of something which does not exist is false, as opposed to a proposition which affirms an existing state-of-affairs. This is truth in the narrowest sense. Its scholastic formulation is *adaequatio intellectus ad rem* ("the agreement of the intellect with reality").

In my book *The Trojan Horse in the City of God* (chapter 20) I have drawn attention to the numerous other meanings of truth. Here let us only recall that the nature of the state-of-affairs determines the kind of truth that is possessed by the proposition that agrees with the state-of-affairs. The significance and depth of the state-of-affairs also has an effect on the significance and depth of the truth of the proposition. The truth of the principle of contradiction has a different ring and a different weight from the proposition, "The weather is beautiful today."

Similarly, truth takes on a new quality when it refers to an essentially necessary state-of-affairs. The proposition, "Moral values can inhere only in persons," has a different depth and a more solemn character than the truth of the proposition, "Heat expands bodies." The formal levels of being which are found in each specific state-of-affairs also have an influence on the truth of the propositions which deal with them.[1] States-of-affairs in which a high value is discerned confer a completely new splendor on the truth of the proposition which affirms them.

We mention these distinctions only in order to identify the kind of truth in which the deep relationship to beauty becomes evident. We have already mentioned the first relationship between beauty and truth: truth is a bearer of metaphysical beauty, of that beauty which is a *splendor veri.* It is the same relationship that all values have to their metaphysical beauty. As we saw, the higher the value, the greater the beauty which is its splendor, its fragrance. Now the same applies to truth: the more significant, the more fundamental the truth—and here we include all the levels just mentioned of the states-of-affairs which are being affirmed—the greater the beauty.

We shall speak in the second volume of this work about the second relationship between beauty and truth, which concerns the role of truth in art.

Validity [Gültigkeit], uninventibility [Unerfindbarkeit], necessity, and the classical

We wish now to investigate a very profound and mysterious relationship between truth and beauty. The beauty of the second power possesses its

1. Josef Seifert, "Die verschiedenen Bedeutungen von 'Sein,'" in *Wahrheit, Wert und Sein: Festgabe für Dietrich von Hildebrand* (Regensburg: Josef Habbel Verlag, 1970), 301–32.

own kind of truth. The "word" which is uttered in it is true. This beauty lifts us into the realm of truth. It possesses the element of the validity of truth. In order to understand this better, we must first examine some elements of truth.

There are things whose existence we cannot establish by means of perception. One of these is history. Our knowledge about past events is constructed on the basis of reports and archaeological data. In the case of reports, the principal source of our knowledge in this field, confidence in their credibility plays a decisive role. If the majority of the sources which derive from various contemporary authors more or less agree, this undoubtedly provides an important support for our conviction that what they relate did in fact occur. The credibility of the content of the narrative and of the facts which it describes also plays a role, both with regard to the credibility of the narrator and with regard to our acceptance of the truth of the account. Naturally, underlying philosophical problems play a decisive role in the question of the credibility of the content; for example, whoever is attached to the philosophical error that miracles are impossible will regard the narrative of a miracle as being *a priori* unworthy of belief.

In the present context, what interests us is the relationship between truth and uninventibility. If the figure of a person is uninventible, the narrative about this person is thereby shown to be true. This, however, is a unique case, and applies only to Jesus. As Kierkegaard so often emphasized, the figure of Jesus—unlike all the heroes of mythology—is uninventible.[2] His figure guarantees its objective existence by means of its uninventibility. The completely new element which reveals itself to us, transcending all human ideals, places the person of Jesus beyond all possible inventions. His person can be known to us only if it truly exists and has revealed itself to the apostles as an absolute "surprise." This case is unique. Here uninventibility demonstrates to us absolutely the concrete, real existence of Christ.

In the realm of essences, too, the realm of the laws governing essences, there is a deep general relationship between autonomy of being, ideal

2. Cf. Søren Kierkegaard, *The Sickness unto Death* (Princeton: Princeton University Press, 1983), 125–31.

mode of being, and uninventibility. Unlike fictions of every kind, all genuine essences—time, space, number, the color red, or justice, love, and forgiveness—are uninventible. Here the uninventibility goes in the direction of their inner necessity and the ontological autonomy of their necessary essential structure. The question of concrete real existence does not arise here.

These essences, along with the states-of-affairs grounded in them, are given with evidence to our minds and impose themselves on our understanding in such a way as to form a radical antithesis to that which is inventible. This kind of uninventibility differs from the uninventibility mentioned above in the case of Christ.

But the entire wealth of the external world—whether it be a pine tree or a lion—is completely different from that which is uninventible in either the sense of the person of Christ or in the sense of a necessary essence. As I have said in chapter four of my book *What is Philosophy?*, these morphic unities are "inventions" by God, as distinct from the necessary essences which are grounded in God.

This uninventibility is closely linked to truth, reaching up to the truth of essentially necessary propositions.

Another quality of truth, especially of the truth of fundamental, metaphysical entities, is its classical character [*die Klassizität*]. Obviously, the expression "classical" must be understood in a particular sense, namely, the sense which I have explained in our discussion of the classical character of the Tridentine liturgy in the final chapter of my book *Liturgy and Personality*. This sense of "classical character" envisages a central, profound phenomenon which is clearly distinct from the historical meaning of this word—whether one calls the art of Greek antiquity "classical" or applies the term "classical" to the music of the eighteenth century in order to distinguish it from the "romantic" music of the nineteenth, or whether one uses the term "classical" as a simple word of praise, or equates it more or less with "typical," as when one says, "This is a classic case of tragedy, or of loyalty."

What we are here calling "classic" is completely different from all these meanings. It is the phenomenon of validity which is profoundly related to what the scholastic philosophy called "ontological truth." It is fulfillment; it is standing in the correct metaphysical place. The classical is filled and permeated by the breath of the truth.

We must be content with this short analysis of the uninventible and the classical, and of their relationship to truth, although we are fully aware that it is inadequate and merely touches on some points. But a thorough investigation of these phenomena belongs in a work about metaphysics and epistemology; here the brief reference to these phenomena is meant to help uncover a profound relationship between beauty and truth.

The mysterious kinship of truth and the beauty of the second power

We find in the beauty of the second power in nature and art the same elements of the uninventible and the classical that we find in truth. Before we discuss this, we must clear away various obvious misunderstandings.

First of all, it will be rightly objected: How can one speak of the uninventibility of the beauty of a work of art, when in fact the work of art is a prototype of that which is "invented"? For the artist does not discover something that previously existed. He creates a completely new entity. He invents a story or a melody, he creates a symphony, a picture, a sculpture.

It is true that the work of art, as an ontological entity, is not uninventible; on the contrary, it is always something invented. Nevertheless, as we shall see in the second volume of this work, every true work of art also contains in its making an element of discovering. Above all, however, we do not have in mind the work of art as such, but its beauty, which appears mysteriously in an entity created by the artist. We refer to the value quality of the beauty as such, which we find equally in nature. In a manner analogous to truth, this beauty possesses a sovereignty and uninventibility. Even when it appears in a typically invented entity, it is in itself uninventible.

Secondly, it will be rightly said that the beauty of something does not in the least guarantee the concrete real existence of its bearer. If someone says, "Certainly, it would be much more beautiful if there were an immortality of the soul, and the human person did not cease to exist at death," is the fact that this would be more beautiful a guarantee that the soul does continue to live on after death? How can one say that beauty somehow guarantees a real existence and therefore possesses an analogy to truth?

To this we must reply that this objection employs the term "beauty" in an analogous sense. "More beautiful" here means above all "more meaningful, more conducive to happiness." In this analogous sense, paradise would be more beautiful than the *vallis lacrimarum* ("vale of tears") in which we live. Clearly, the beauty of the second power is not the real theme here: "more beautiful" means primarily "more conducive to happiness."

Apart from the analogous character of this beauty, it is completely correct to say that beauty in a real sense is not a guarantee of the real existence of a beautiful being. We can after all dream of glorious landscapes and architecture; but despite all their beauty they do not exist. It would indeed be a fatal error to adduce the beauty of a being as evidence of its real existence. First of all, as we have mentioned, the uninventibility of the figure of Jesus is a completely different, radical uninventibility. Secondly, this uninventibility concerns not beauty but holiness, the epiphany of the absolute. Thirdly, this is the wholly unique instance in which the quality guarantees real existence and excludes the possibility of any mere idealizing fiction.

And yet, as we have said, we find in the beauty of the second power a different uninventibility, one which is related not to the sphere of real existence but to the autonomous being of beauty, to the truth of the "word" that is contained in beauty. For the beauty of the dreamed-of landscape is, *qua* beauty, something that is not invented: it is something that only "discloses" itself, a true word. The landscape of which we dream does not indeed exist, but it is really beautiful. Although in general everything is less clear in a dream, this beauty too remains as such an uninventible, valid word.

This profound inherent relationship between beauty and truth becomes even clearer when we think of the phenomenon of the classical to which we have drawn attention earlier. The beauty of the second power possesses the classical quality in full measure. It is utterly valid and is the opposite of all that is arbitrary. The Gospel of John says, "The truth will make you free" (John 8:32); so too, one can speak by analogy of the liberating effect of the beauty of the second power. The classical quality is deeply linked to this liberating effect.

We begin to see the kind of deep link which exists between beauty and truth. In both, we encounter the autonomous being of that which is uninventible, we encounter classical character and validity; in both, a valid word is uttered. The beauty of the second power transposes us into the realm of the true, into the world of truth. In a manner analogous to truth, this beauty forms an antithesis to all falseness and to the "father of lies."[3]

3. We want this profound inner link between beauty and truth to be clearly distinguished from the inner link between metaphysical beauty and truth. In the former case, the link lies in a similarity between high metaphysical truth and beauty of the second power in general, especially because of the uninventibility, the classical character, and the element of validity. In the metaphysical beauty of truth, on the other hand, truth is the bearer of beauty. Beauty is the splendor, the fragrance of the true, *splendor veri*. In our present context, however, we are concerned not with the beauty of truth, but with that which is shared by both beauty and truth.

CHAPTER TWENTY-ONE

The Bond of Beauty with Morality and with Love

The deep relationship between beauty and the morally good

In the Introduction we have already pointed out the profound intrinsic connection between beauty, especially beauty of the second power, and the morally good in general. In the chapters of the second volume of this work we will discuss in detail the relationships between the morally good and the beauty in literature, painting, and sculpture. At the close of this first volume we want to point out anew the deep intrinsic bond existing between beauty and the primordial value of the moral sphere, which is the morally good.

In the previous chapter, on the relationship between beauty and truth, we did not have in mind the metaphysical beauty of truth, and in the same way we do not here have in mind the metaphysical beauty of moral values, but rather another relatedness, that is, the "word" which is uttered both in beauty and in the primordial moral value.

Nor are we thinking of that which is held in common by all genuine values, but of something much more intimate and profound: their common ground in the radiant glory of God. God, the infinitely Holy One, is the embodiment of all goodness, of all moral values; He is also the infinitely Beautiful One. It is of course true that only moral values presuppose a person; they alone give glory to God in the narrower sense of this term, and it is their counterpart, sin, that gives offense to God. All this does not apply in the same way to beauty; nevertheless, despite the profound difference between beauty and moral value, there exists at the deepest level a qualitative inner kinship between the highest and most sublime beauty and the morally good in its highest form. It is scarcely possible to find an exact conceptual expression that will do justice to this common bond.

The beauty of love. That which is qualitatively common to beauty and love

Let us draw attention very briefly to one other deep qualitative kinship, namely, that between beauty and love. To begin with, as I have shown in the first chapter of my book *The Nature of Love*, love is a specific response to the beauty of the beloved. Naturally, beauty is meant here in the broader sense, and above all the metaphysical beauty of this unique individual personality. Tristan's words in his vision in the third act of Wagner's *Tristan und Isolde* express the truth of this affirmation: "Isolde, how beautiful you are!"

It may be that metaphysical beauty in its breathtaking greatness shines out nowhere so strongly as in love, which Siegfried Johannes Hamburger calls the "most primordial of all primordial phenomena."[1] There is nothing more beautiful than the love of Christ. And what beauty is possessed by holy love, this stream of holy goodness which can come into being only in the love for Christ, and then lets God's light blaze out in the world in the form of *caritas* to one's neighbor! But the beauty of love shines out also in all true natural love, the love of parents or children, or the love of friends. This unique beauty reaches its high point, at least within natural love, with spousal love, which is unfathomably beautiful in its boldness, fervor, and fidelity.

1. Siegfried Hamburger, "Kühnheit der Liebe," in *Wahrheit, Wert und Sein*, 100.

It is characteristic of the relationship between love and beauty that spousal love should be such an inexhaustible inspiration for the various arts. Pope Pius XII referred to this inspiration in glorious words: "This enchantment of human love has been for centuries the theme inspiring admirable creations of the human spirit in literature, music, and the visual arts. It is an ever ancient and ever new theme on which successive generations have played their variations in the most sublime and poetic ways, without ever exhausting it."[2]

But we have in mind yet another link between beauty and love. This is not the link of a deep relationship between value and a meaningful response to it; nor do we have in mind the metaphysical beauty of love. Rather, we refer to the quality that the splendor, the light, the transfigured quality shining forth in love has in common with all great and lofty beauty. It is as if this beauty possessed a quality which in love exists as a conscious, personal reality, just as the blue sky irradiates a quality of joyfulness which in the experienced act of joy is lived by a person.

As we have seen, beauty can never exist as something consciously enacted by a person, although it is true that many acts are bearers of beauty thanks to their value. Nevertheless, one can go so far as to say that the inner gesture of beauty is a "love"—not indeed a personally performed act nor something that exists consciously, but a gesture carried out in love, a gesture which is present here as a purely qualitative analogy to the dawning radiance, to the shining and sparkling of all love as it awakens. It is as if, when something of great beauty stands before us, we were tempted to say, "It loves."

We close this first volume with this reference to the deep qualitative inner connection of three primordial phenomena: beauty, the value of the morally good, and love—a connection which reaches into metaphysics.

2. Pius XII, discourse to newly married couples, October 23, 1940.

Acknowledgements

In 2006, a friend encouraged me to meet Dana Gioia, then chairman of the National Endowment for the Arts in Washington, DC, to tell him about the nascent Hildebrand Project. For our second meeting, I conspired to bring with me the formidable Alice von Hildebrand, widow and leading exponent of Dietrich von Hildebrand. After she quizzed the chairman ("What is the greatest work of literature?"), we came to the heart of our encounter as she lamented the lack of contemporary art that aims to be *beautiful* (as opposed, say, to being titillating or shocking). Moments later, the otherworldly tones of Morten Lauridsen's 1994 *O magnum mysterium* were soaring through the Old Post Office building. I will never forget her response: "Why, this is a revelation to me. It means we are once again capable of creating a masterpiece."

Dana Gioia gave us two tremendous gifts. At that meeting with Alice von Hildebrand, he pledged a Chairman's Extraordinary Action Award, which not only provided the crucial leadership funding for the translation of this volume, but also the credibility and visibility of NEA support. But of much more lasting consequence, he brought me into his great friendship and partnership with the writer, speaker, and philanthropist Roberta Green Ahmanson.

My first meeting with Roberta Ahmanson took place at Gioia's offices in Washington. What was meant to last an hour spilled into many, many hours, as our conversation spanned history, theology, politics, and, of course, art. By mid 2007, Roberta and her husband, Howard, had pledged the major, multiyear support to complete the translation of both volumes of the *Aesthetics*. In Dietrich von Hildebrand they had found a contemporary spokesman, not just for the importance of the *arts*, but for the reality and spiritual potency of *beauty*. All whose work in cultural renewal is aided by Hildebrand's vision of beauty will forever be in the debt of Dana Gioia and of Howard and Roberta Ahmanson.

This volume is our first translation to appear in our very own Hildebrand Press, which would not exist without an initial investment from James N. Perry, whose support allowed us to build the infrastructure to deliver on our ambitious plans to present Hildebrand's works across an integrated print, ebook, and online platform.

A crucial second wave of support for production and dissemination came from the Cushman Foundation as well as from the Budnik Family Foundation, where Theodora Budnik and her sons Peter and John Budnik carry on the philanthropic and cultural vision of her father, the late, great Chauncey Stillman.

A very special debt of gratitude is due to Steven Ferguson, who leads philanthropy for the Ahmansons, for embracing this project from the start and for his deep grasp of the contribution that a philosophical aesthetics can make in arenas far beyond academia.

Fr. Brian McNeil worked with great dedication on the translation, which was then revised by John F. Crosby, general editor of the Hildebrand Press and one of Dietrich von Hildebrand's final American students.

Our first managing editor was Kathleen McCann, who brought exceptional devotion to her work. She was succeeded by Christopher T. Haley, who as our Director of Publications has not only contributed immensely to the quality of the final text but has also poured his gifts in design and communications into every aspect of the creation of Hildebrand Press.

Elizabeth Shaw expertly copyedited the text, which was carefully proofread by Sarah Blanchard; Mark McGarry helped realize our own aesthetic ideals in creating the page layout; and Marylouise McGraw developed our distinctive cover design.

I would not have the privilege of thanking so many wonderful people were it not for Alice von Hildebrand's undying support for the Hildebrand Project, of which she is not just a co-founder but also a loyal friend and generous benefactor.

John Henry Crosby
Founder & President, Hildebrand Project
December 8, 2015

Index

Index of Names

Made in the USA
Middletown, DE
11 January 2025